A PILGRIMAGE TO NEJD

Born in 1837, Lady Anne Blunt was a daughter of the first
Earl of Lovelace, and a granddaughter of Byron. She married Wilfrid Scawen Blunt, who had been travelling since he
was six years old, in 1869—though they went their separate
ways in 1896.

First published in two volumes in 1881, this book is Lady
Anne's own account of their two thousand mile trek to the
home of the Bedouins in remotest Central Arabia. The
Blunts embarked on this journey together in 1878 and it
remains an arduous undertaking even today. The nature
of their getting there was as romantic as the idea itself: both
wore Bedouin cloaks and coiled turbans, and at one time
were set upon by galloping horsemen.

Instead of taking the standard retinue of servants, the
Blunts looked after their needs themselves and sometimes
their traveller's fare might have a truly non-European
flavour—such as when they sustained themselves on grilled
locusts.

As a result of this escapade, Lady Anne Blunt was only the
second woman to penetrate the interior of Arabia. She
died in 1917 and Wilfrid did so three years later. They
had one daughter.

Dervla Murphy, who introduces this new edition of *A Pilgrimage to Nejd*, is herself a well-known inveterate traveller
of inviolable routes. Her books of her wanderings include:
Full Tilt, In Ethiopia with a Mule, Where the Indus is Young
and *Eight Feet in the Andes*.

Also available in the Century Travellers series:

A PILGRIMAGE TO NEJD

THE CRADLE OF THE ARAB RACE

A VISIT TO THE COURT OF THE ARAB EMIR, AND
"OUR PERSIAN CAMPAIGN"

LADY ANNE BLUNT

Introduction by Dervla Murphy

CENTURY PUBLISHING
LONDON

LESTER & ORPEN DENNYS DENEAU
MARKETING SERVICES LTD TORONTO

Introduction copyright © Dervla Murphy 1985

All rights reserved

First published by John Murray (Publishers) Ltd in 1881

This edition published in 1985 by
Century Publishing Co. Ltd,
Portland House, 12–13 Greek Street,
London W1V 5LE

Published in Canada by
Lester & Orpen Dennys Deneau Marketing Services Ltd
78 Sullivan Street, Ontario, Canada

ISBN 0 7126 0989 X

*The cover painting is from the collection at the
Mathaf Gallery, 24 Motcomb Street, London SW1
The drawings in the text are by the author*

Reprinted in Great Britain by
Richard Clay (The Chaucer Press) Ltd,
Bungay, Suffolk

𝔗𝔥𝔢𝔰𝔢 𝔙𝔬𝔩𝔲𝔪𝔢𝔰 𝔞𝔯𝔢 𝔇𝔢𝔡𝔦𝔠𝔞𝔱𝔢𝔡

TO

SIR HENRY CRESWICKE RAWLINSON

K.C.B., F.R.S.

BY

THE AUTHORESS.

INTRODUCTION

Whenever a Bedouin requested some explanation of the Blunts' identity, Lady Anne described herself and her husband as "persons of distinction from England". Fair enough. Lady Annabella King-Noel—she became plain Anne only after her marriage—was a granddaughter of Lord Byron and daughter of the first Earl of Lovelace. Wilfrid Scawen Blunt's family-tree was less title-spangled but he had been, in his own words, "born under circumstances peculiarly fortunate as I think for happiness. Those of an English country gentleman of the XIXth Century—my father a Sussex squire of fair estate, owning some four thousand acres . . . my mother of the same social rank, respectable both and locally respected". Also, he was closely connected with the powerful Wyndhams of Petworth House, a valuable connection in that age of bland but effective nepotism.

The couple first met in Italy in 1866. Anne was then a rich, chaste, robust twenty-nine-year-old spinster wandering alone around Europe; Wilfred was a poor, lecherous, tubercular twenty-six-year-old bachelor struggling to escape without too much dishonour from his latest entanglements. (He was rarely entangled with only one woman at a time.) A mutual friend decided that it would make a lot of sense if these two talented, unconventional drifters married. Wilfred agreed. Much later, he wrote of Anne at that time—"She thought herself plainer than she was, and had none of the ways of a pretty woman, though in truth she had that sort of prettiness that a bird has . . . agreeable to the eye if not aggressively attractive. Her colouring, indeed, I used to think was like a robin's with its bright black eyes, its russet plumage and its tinge of crimson red. She had beautiful white teeth and complexion rather brown than fair . . . In stature less than tall, well poised and active, with a trim light figure set on a pair of small high-instepped feet. It is thus I see her in recollection, an unobtrusive quiet figure, rather behind the fashion of the day but dignified and bright ". Had Anne been less financially well-endowed, Wilfred might have been less observant of her good points. At that time, however, his own younger son's capital had dwindled to £700, whereas Anne had inherited an annual income of £3,000 from her grandmother, Lady Byron. (A sum equivalent to at least £30,000 today.) But alas! The course of prudent love did not, in 1866, run smoothly.

Lady Annabella King-Noel had problems. She was aged fifteen when her mother Ada—Lord Byron's only legitimate child—died, and soon after she went to live with her emotionally scarred maternal grandmother. Lady Byron obsessively discouraged her interest in poetry but provided her with two *Stradivarius* violins, and Joachim as her music-master, and John Ruskin as her drawing-master. A few years later her exceedingly disagreeable father, Lord Lovelace, began to take her with him on his continental holidays and she quickly perfected her German, French, Italian and Spanish. (This linguistic training no doubt helped her when she came to study Arabic, in which she was even more fluent than her husband.) By 1865 both Lady Byron and Anne's elder brother, Byron, had died and in that year her father remarried. He then made determined efforts to dissuade his daughter from ever doing likewise, because he coveted the fortune left to her by Lady Byron for his son by his second marriage. Anne's younger brother, Ralph, was so unstable that she could never hope to make a home with him and thus it was that she embarked on those solitary European wanderings during which she first met Wilfred. Around the time of their meeting she wrote to a friend—"My visit to England and speaking with my father has, in spite of myself, discouraged me so much—he is so strongly persuaded, I have so difficult a disposition that I should not be able to contribute to anyone's happiness". In a letter to Wilfred dated July 1867, Anne mentioned her "doubting and hesitating character" as one reason why she could not accept his proposal of marriage. She explained that she had already broken off an unofficial engagement to Count Trivulzio "in a kind of terror". At that stage Lord Lovelace's undermining of his daughter's self-confidence was going well. But Wilfred rightly interpreted this communication as "an adjournment, perhaps of victory, not an absolute defeat . . ." He accepted a posting to Buenos Aires as a sinecure diplomat and on his return to Europe resumed his courtship, this time successfully. To Lord Lovelace's fury, the Blunts were married in June 1869 at St. George's, Hanover Square.

Nowadays many women think of marriage as inevitably entailing a diminution of their "autonomy". A century ago it often seemed otherwise, though on a personal level the partnership might be—as in the Blunts' case—tense and troubled. When Lady Annabella King-Noel became Lady Anne Blunt her real character, long suppressed and distorted by cruelly confusing family pressures, emerged strongly and enabled her to survive a long lifetime of disappointment and sorrow. Not least of her griefs were many miscarriages; only one child lived—a daughter, Judith, born on 6 February 1873. Less than a year earlier she had given birth to premature twins, who soon died. Wilfred was away from home at the time but wrote to his wife—"Of course there is a dismal satisfaction that the children were not boys". They had already lost their only son—aged four days—in November 1870. This infant's death had devastated Wilfred, who soon after inherited the family home, Crabbet Park, on the death of his only brother, Francis; he was very conscious of belonging to one of the sixty-eight families still existing in England who had accompanied the Conqueror from Normandy. As time passed, Anne was no less devastated by her repeated failures to satisfy her beloved "Master's" deepest desire.

The Blunts had been nine years married when they set off on their "pilgrimage to Nejd", the last of several long and arduous Middle Eastern journeys undertaken together. Knowing what disillusionment and loneliness lay immediately ahead for Anne, there is a particular poignancy about this account of what was evidently one of the happiest phases of their relationship. The desert offered no temptations to the compulsively promiscuous Wilfred—even he forbore to pursue the wives or daughters of Bedouins and the consequent atmosphere of emotional tranquillity allowed the travellers to share all they had in common and forget what divided them. Both were interested in Arabic literature and history, in Arab horses (already they had established the famous Crabbet Arabian Stud) and in the Bedouins' social structure and the influence of the Ottoman Empire on Arabian town life. Both enjoyed the unique brutal beauty of Central Arabia—rarely seen before by European eyes—and both were capable of meeting the varied and frequently perilous challenges of desert travel with remarkable fortitude. Had they spent the rest of their days wandering to and fro across the Nefud they might have lived happily ever after.

In *A Pilgrimage To Nejd* the author reveals herself as nobody's idea of a gently-nurtured mid-Victorian female. She was physically resilient, level-headed in crises, immensely brave, self-assured, resourceful, adaptable, unsentimental and scholarly. Many years later her grandson Anthony (fourth Earl of Lytton) was to describe her as " tiny and shy, with something of the wistful disposition of a mouse or jerboa ". This however is not the impression given in her travel books. And Wilfred insisted towards the end of his life, when the Blunts had been many years estranged—" There was never anybody so courageous as she was. The only thing she was afraid of was the sea ".

By this stage some restive readers must be longing to ask— *"Where is Nejd?"* This is a reasonable question and it would be tiresome to reply that it is now known as "Najd". In the

Blunts' day, the exact location of Nejd/Najd was a controversial matter. Everyone knew that it was in a remote part of Central Arabia—but then almost every part of Central Arabia was (and is) remote. When Wilfred read a paper to the Royal Geographical Society entitled "Visit to Nejd", the experts present afterwards argued that the Blunts had not been to Nejd, this being a term applicable only to the district bounded by the Jebel Toweykh and the lesser Nefuds, and including neither Jebel Shammar nor Kasim. Their objection greatly annoyed Wilfred, who believed that "Hail is not only an integral part of Nejd, but Nejd *par excellence*". In his *Preface by the Editor*, at the beginning of *A Pilgrimage To Nejd*, he went into great detail about this controversy, quoting from the Jesuit traveller and emissary of Napoleon III, Gifford Palgrave, who also explored Central Arabia—in disguise—eighteen years before the Blunts' "pilgrimage". He did not however bring Charles Doughty into the argument. The Doughty achievement was something of an irritant to the Blunts—or at least to Wilfred, who liked to claim that "No European or Christian of any sort had penetrated *as such* before us to Jebel Shammar". In fact Doughty had been to Jebel Shammar just before them, travelling undisguised as a lone European and with only a few phrases of Arabic in contrast to the Blunts' fluency in that language. But his massive two-volume best-seller, *Travels In Arabia Deserta*, did not appear until 1888, seven years after *A Pilgrimage To Nejd* was brought out by Byron's publisher, John Murray.

A comparison of Wilfred's map of the Blunts' journey with the *Times Atlas* map of modern Saudi Arabia suggests that the RGS pedants may have been correct and that the Blunts did not travel through what map-makers describe as Nejd/Najd—though they certainly travelled through territory described by the Bedouins as "Nejd". However, this geographical inexactitude detracts nothing from our enjoyment of the expedition so readably recorded in Anne's journal—an astounding trek of 2,000 miles from the Mediterranean to the Persian Gulf through regions which even in the 1980s remain for the most part roadless. Over the last 500 of those miles the Blunts were driving their camels unaided across areas reputed to be impassable even to non-local Arabs. Anne cultivates understatement in her published account of this experience. But she did relax her upper lip when writing to her brother Ralph about their "Persian Campaign"—undertaken against her better judgement at the end of the Nejd pilgrimage and described in the last quarter of this book. That journey, she declared, "was fit only to be damned with six Ds—not only disagreeable, difficult, dangerous and all but disastrous, but disappointing and disheartening . . . Wilfred will *never* want to go *any* hard journey again, I will swear to that!"

Anne's forecast was correct: she knew her Wilfred only too well. Having persisted in trekking from Baghdad to Bushire without adequate preparations, against Anne's advice, he almost died of dysentery on the way. As he lay delirious, Anne concocted potions of homeopathic bryonia and laudanum and they continued the following night—to avoid the heat—using the Scorpion constellation as compass. When they camped at daybreak they were tormented by spiked grass— "like fish-hooks"—which got into every crevice of their bedding. By this stage—" we care little, now, how or where it is we lie, the ground is always soft as a feather-bed". Tormented by worry about Wilfred's health, Anne had slept little for over a week and often dozed off in the saddle as she rode through the night. They still had three more deep rivers to cross before reaching Bushire, including the Kurdistan. " This was the deepest of any we had forded . . . the water was up to our saddle bows, and running almost like a mill-race . . . Unfitted though the country has been in many ways for camels, we may nevertheless congratulate ourselves with the thought that with no other beasts of burden could we have got our luggage across the rivers at all. Loaded mules must have been swept away.'

As Elizabeth Longford has pointed out in her superb biography of Wilfred Scawen Blunt (*A Pilgrimage Of Passion*: Weidenfeld & Nicolson), the Blunts were DIY travellers, who did not dress according to their station, or travel with an escort of fifty men and the standard retinue of twenty-five servants. For months they had only one helper and they loaded and unloaded camels, swam them and their horses across rivers, man-handled their baggage onto goat-skin rafts, carried their own anti-bandit guns, pitched their own tent and shot their own suppers—or, if there was nothing to shoot, caught and grilled their own locusts. When at last they reached Bushire, the immaculately-uniformed, musket-armed sepoys on guard at the British Residency assumed them to be Bedouin intruders and turned them away from the entrance.

The Blunts' predilection for travelling rough, and sharing in the everyday life of the local peoples, sets them apart from those Victorians who—like the rich tourists of our own day— used their wealth to insulate them from the realities of non-European life. The majority of 19th-century explorers of the Middle East (however intrepid) were not much interested in the details of ordinary life as it was then lived in Persia and throughout the Ottoman Empire. They tended to be specialists of one sort or another: merchants, linguists, archaeologists, painters, geographers, diplomats, soldiers, engineers or self-absorbed eccentrics. The Blunts were exceptional in the range of their interests and the liveliness of their curiosity about the contemporary political and social scene. James Elroy Flecker might have been thinking of Anne and Wilfred when he wrote:

> We travel not for trafficking alone:
> By hotter winds our fiery hearts are fanned:
> For lust of knowing what should not be known
> We make the Golden Journey to Samarkand.

DERVLA MURPHY

PREFACE BY THE EDITOR.

—+—

READERS of our last year's adventures on the
Euphrates will hardly need it to be explained to
them why the present journey was undertaken, nor
why it stands described upon our title page as a
" Pilgrimage." The journey to Nejd forms the
natural complement of the journey through Mesopotamia and the Syrian Desert; while Nejd itself,
with the romantic interest attached to its name,
seems no unworthy object of a religious feeling, such
as might prompt the visit to a shrine. Nejd, in the
imagination of the Bedouins of the North, is a
region of romance, the cradle of their race, and of
those ideas of chivalry by which they still live
There Antar performed his labours of Hercules,
and Hatim Taï the more historical hero entertained
his guests. To the Ánazeh and Shammar, especially, whose northward migrations date only from
a few generations back, the tradition of their birthplace is still almost a recollection; and even to

the Arabs of the earlier invasions, the townsmen
of such places as Bozra, Palmyra, and Deyr, and
to the Taï Bedouins, once lords of Jebel Shammar,
it appeals with a fascination more than equal to
that of the Hejaz itself. Nejd is to all of them
what Palestine is to the Jews, England to the
American and Australian colonists; but with this
difference, that they are cut off from the object of
their filial reverence more absolutely in practice
than these by an intervening gulf of desert less
hospitable than any sea. It is rare to meet anywhere in the North an Arab who has crossed the
Great Nefûd.

To us too, imbued as we were with the fancies
of the Desert, Nejd had long assumed the romantic
colouring of a holy land; and when it was decided
that we were to visit Jebel Shammar, the metropolis
of Bedouin life, our expedition presented itself as
an almost pious undertaking; so that it is hardly an
exaggeration, even now that it is over, and we are
once more in Europe, to speak of it as a pilgrimage.
Our pilgrimage then it is, though the religion in
whose name we travelled was only one of romance.

Its circumstances, in spite of certain disappointments which the narrative will reveal, were little
less romantic than the idea. Readers who followed
our former travels to their close, may remember a

certain Mohammed Abdallah, son of the Sheykh of Palmyra, a young man who, after travelling with us by order of the Pasha from Deyr to his native town, had at some risk of official displeasure assisted us in evading the Turkish authorities, and accomplishing our visit to the Ánazeh. It may further be remembered that, in requital of this service and because we had conceived an affection for him (for he appeared a really high-minded young fellow), Mohammed had been given his choice between a round sum of money, and the honour of becoming "the Beg's" brother, a choice which he had chivalrously decided in favour of the brotherhood. We had then promised him that, if all went well with us, we would return to Damascus the following winter, and go in his company to Nejd, where he believed he had relations, and that we would help him there to a wife from among his own people.

The idea and the promise were in strict accordance with Bedouin notions, and greatly delighted both him and his father Abdallah, to whom they were in due course communicated. Arab custom is very little changed on the point of marriage from what it was in the days of Abraham; and it was natural that both father and son should wish for a wife for him of their own blood, and that he should be ready to go far to fetch one. Moreover, the sort of help we proposed giving (for he could hardly have travelled to Nejd alone) was just such as beseemed our new relationship. Assistance in the choice of a wife ranks in Bedouin eyes with the gift of a mare, or personal aid in war, both brotherly acts conferring high honour on those concerned. Mohammed too had a special reason in the circumstances of his family history to make the proposal doubly welcome. He found himself in an embarrassing position at home with regard to marriage, and was in a manner forced to look elsewhere for a wife. The history of the Ibn Arûks of Tudmur, the family to which he belonged, will explain this, and is so curious, and so typical of Arabia, that it deserves a passing notice here.

It would appear that seven or eight generations ago (probably about the date of the foundation of the Wahhabi empire) three brothers of the noble family of Arûk, Sheykhs of the Beni Khaled of south-eastern Nejd, quarrelled with their people and left the tribe. The Ibn Arûks were then a very well-known family, exercising suzerain rights over the important towns of Hasa and Katif, and having independent, even sovereign, power in their own district. This lay between the Persian Gulf and Harik, an oasis on the edge of the great southern

desert, and they retained it until they and the
rest of their fellow Sheykhs in Arabia were reduced
to insignificance by Mohammed Ibn Saoud, the
first Wahhabi Sultan of Nejd.* At the beginning of last century, all Arabia was
independent of central authority, each tribe, and
to a certain extent each town, maintaining its
separate existence as a State. Religion, except in
its primitive Bedouin form, had disappeared from
the inland districts, and only the Hejaz and Yemen
were more than nominally Mahometan. The
Bedouin element was then supreme. Each town
and village in Arabia was considered the property
of one or other of the nomade Sheykhs in its
neighbourhood, and paid him tribute in return for
his protection. The Sheykh too not unfrequently
possessed a house or castle within the city walls, as
a summer residence, besides his tent outside. He
in such cases became more than a mere suzerain,
and exercised active authority over the townspeople, administering justice at the gate daily, and
enrolling young men as his body-guard, even on
occasion levying taxes. He then received the title
of Emir or Prince. It was in no other way

---

* Such at least is the family tradition of the Ibn Arûks.
Niebuhr writing in 1765 gives Arär as the name of the Beni
Khaled Sheykhs.

perhaps that the "Shepherd Kings" of Egypt acquired their position and exercised their power; and vestiges of the old system may still be found in many parts of Arabia.

In the middle of the eighteenth century, however, Ibn Abd-el-Wahhab, the Luther of Mahometanism, preached his religious reform in Nejd, and converted Ibn Saoud, the Ánazeh Sheykh of Deriyeh, to his doctrines. By Ibn Abd-el-Wahhab's help Ibn Saoud, from the mere chief of a tribe, and sovereign of one city, became Sultan of all Arabia, and reduced one after another every rival Sheykh to submission. He even ultimately destroyed the system of tribute and protection, the original basis of his power, and having raised a regular army from among the townsmen, made these quite independent of Bedouin rule. Arabia then, for the first time since Mahomet's death, became a united empire with a centralised and regular government. It must have been about the year 1760 that the three Ibn Arûks, disgusted with the new state of things in Nejd, went out to seek their fortunes elsewhere. According to the tradition, partly embodied in an old ballad which is still current in Arabia, they were mounted all three upon a single camel, and had nothing with them but their swords and their high birth to gain them credit among strangers. They travelled northwards and at first halted in Jôf, the northernmost oasis of Central Arabia, where one of them remained.   The other two, quarrelling, separated ; the younger going, tradition knew not whither, while the elder held on his way still further north, and settled finally at Tudmur (Palmyra), where he married a woman of the place, and where he ultimately became Sheykh.   At that time Tudmur consisted but of a few houses.   His name was Ali, and from him our friend Mohammed and his father Abdallah, and his uncle Faris, the real head of the family in Tudmur, are descended.

Mohammed then had some reason, as far as his male ancestry were concerned, to boast of his birth, and look high in making a " matrimonial alliance ; " but *par les femmes* he was of less distinguished blood ; and, as purity of descent on both sides is considered a *sine quâ non* among the Arabs, the Ibn Arûks of Tudmur had not been recognized for several generations as *asil*, or noble. They had married where they could among the townspeople of no birth at all, or as in the case of Mohammed's father, among the Moáli, a tribe of mixed origin.   The Ánazeh, in spite of the name of Arûk, would not give their daughters to them to wife.   This was Mohammed's secret grief, as it had been his father's, and it was as much as anything else to wipe out the stain in their pedigree, that the son so readily agreed to our proposal.

The plan of our journey was necessarily vague, as it included the search after two families of relations of whom nothing had been heard for nearly a hundred years. The last sign of life shewn by the Ibn Arûks of Jôf had been on the occasion of Abdallah's father's death by violence, when suddenly a member of the Jôf family had appeared at Tudmur as avenger in the blood feud. This relation had not, however, stayed longer there than duty required of him, and having slain his man had as suddenly disappeared. Of the second family nothing at all was known ; and, indeed, to the Ibn Arûks as to the other inhabitants of Tudmur, Nejd itself was now little more than a name, a country known by ancient tradition to exist, but unvisited by any one then living connected with the town.

These singular circumstances were, as I have said, the key-note of our expedition, and will, I hope, lend an interest beyond that of our own personal adventures to the present volumes. To Mohammed and the Arabs with whom we travelled, as well as to most of those we met upon our journey, his family history formed a perpetual romance, and the *kasid* or ballad of Ibn Arûk came in on every occasion, seasonable and unseasonable, as a chorus to all that happened. But for it, I doubt whether the journey could ever have been accomplished; and on more than one occasion we found ourselves borne easily on by the strength of it over difficulties which, under ordinary conditions, might have sufficed to stop us. By extreme good luck, as will be seen in the sequel, we lit upon both branches of the family we set out in search of, the one citizens of the Jôf oasis, the other Bedouins in Nejd, while the further we got the better was the Arûk name known, and relations poured in on us on all sides, eager to shew us hospitality and assistance. We were thus passed on from kinsman to kinsman, and were everywhere received as friends; nor is it too much to say that while in Arabia we enjoyed the singular advantage of being accepted as members of an Arabian family. This gave us an unique occasion of seeing, and of understanding what we saw; and we have only ourselves to blame if we did not turn it to very important profit.

So much then for the romance. The profit of our expedition may be briefly summarised.

First as to geography. Though not the only Europeans who have visited Jebel Shammar, we are the only ones who have done so openly and at our leisure, provided with compass and barometer and free to take note of all we saw. Our predecessors,

three in number, Wallin, Guarmani, and Palgrave,
travelled in disguise, and under circumstances unfavourable for geographical observation. The first,
a Finnish professor, proceeded in 1848, as a
Mussulman divine, from the coast of the Red Sea to
Haïl and thence to the Euphrates. The account of
his journey, given in the Proceedings of the Royal
Geographical Society, is unfortunately meagre, and
I understand that, though one more detailed was
published in his own language, he did not live long
enough to record the whole body of his information.
The second, Guarmani, a Levantine of Italian origin,
penetrated in disguise to Jebel Shammar, commissioned by the French Government to procure
them horses from Nejd ; and he communicated a
lively and most interesting account of his adventures
to the "Société de Géographie" in 1865. He too
went as a Turkish mussulman, and, being rather
an Oriental than a European, collected a mass of
valuable information relating chiefly to the Desert
Tribes through which he passed. It is difficult,
however, to understand the route maps with which
his account is illustrated, and, though he crossed the
Nefûd at more than one point, he is silent as to its
singular physical features. Guarmani started from
Jerusalem in 1863 and visited Teyma, Kheybar,
Áneyzeh, Bereydah, and Haïl, returning thence to

Syria by Jôf and the Wady Sirhán. Mr. Palgrave's journey is better known. A Jesuit missionary and an accomplished Arabic scholar, he was entrusted with a secret political mission by Napoleon III. and executed it with the permission of his superiors. He entered Nejd, disguised as a Syrian merchant, from Maan, and passing through Haïl in 1864 reached Riad, the capital of the Wahhabi kingdom, and eventually the Persian Gulf at Katif. His account of Central Arabia is by far the most complete and life-like that has been published, and in all matters of town life and manners may be depended upon as accurate. But his faculty of observation seems chiefly adapted to a study of society, and the nature he describes is human nature only. He is too little in sympathy with the desert to take accurate note of its details, and the circumstances of his journey precluded him from observing it geographically. He travelled in the heat of summer and mostly by night, and was besides in no position, owing to his assumed character and the doubtful company in which he was often compelled to travel, to examine at leisure what he saw. Mr. Palgrave's account of the physical features of the Nefûd, and of Jebel Shammar, the only one hitherto published, bears very little resemblance to the reality ; and our own observations, taken quietly in the clear atmosphere of an Arabian winter, are therefore the first of the kind which have reached Europe. By taking continuous note of the variations of the barometer while we travelled, we have been able to prove that the plateau of Haïl is nearly twice the height supposed for it above the sea, while the granite range of Jebel Shammar exceeds this plateau by about 2000 feet. Again, the great pilgrim-road from the Euphrates, though well-known by report to geographers, had never before been travelled by an European, and on this, as on other parts of our route, we have corrected previous maps. The map of Northern Arabia appended to the first volume of our work may be now depended upon as within its limits substantially accurate.

In geology, though possessing a superficial knowledge only of our subject, we have, I believe, been able to correct a few mistakes, and to clear up a doubt, much argued by Professor Wetzstein, as to the rock formation of Jebel Aja ; while a short memoir I have appended, on the physical conformation of the great sand desert, will contain original— possibly valuable—matter. The sketches, above all, which illustrate these volumes, may be relied on as conscientious representations of the chief physical features of Central Arabia.

Botanists and zoologists will be disappointed in the meagre accounts of plants and animals I am able to give. But the existence now proved of the white antelope (*Oryx Beatrix*) in Nejd is, I believe, a fact new to science, as may be that of the *Webber*, a small climbing quadruped allied to the marmots.

A more important contribution to knowledge will, I hope, be recognised in a description of the political system to which I have just alluded under the name of Shepherd rule, and which is now once more found in Central Arabia. I do not know that it has ever previously been noticed by writers on Arabia. Neither Niebuhr nor Burckhardt seem to have come across it in its pure form, and Mr. Palgrave misunderstood it altogether in his contempt of Bedouin as contrasted with town life. Yet it is probably the oldest form of government existing in Arabia, and the one best suited for the country's needs. In connection with this matter too, the recent history of Nejd, with an account of the downfall of the Ibn Saouds, for which I am mainly indebted to Colonel Ross, British Resident at Bushire, and the decay of Wahhabism in Arabia, will prove of interest, as may in a lesser degree the imperfect picture given in the second volume of the extreme results produced in Persia by despotic rule, and the iniquitous annexation of Hasa by the Turks. The value, however, of these "discoveries" I leave to our readers to determine, premising only that they are here pointed out less on account of their own importance, than as an excuse in matter for the manner of the narrative.

With regard to the sequel of our Arabian journey, the further journey from Bagdad to Bushire, I should not intrude it on the notice of the public, but that it serves as an additional proof, if such be wanting, of the folly of those schemes which, under the name of " Euphrates Valley " and " Indo-Mediterranean " railway companies, have from time to time been dangled before the eyes of speculators. A country more absolutely unsuited for railway enterprise than that between the Mediterranean and the Persian Gulf, has probably never been selected for such operations ; and, if the recital of our passage through the uninhabited tracts, which form nine tenths of the whole region, shall deter my countrymen from embarking their capital in an enterprise financially absurd, I feel that its publication will not have been in vain.

One word before I end my Preface. It was objected to me at the Royal Geographical Society's meeting, where I read a paper on this "Visit to Nejd," that though we had crossed the Great Sand

Desert, and visited Jebel Shammar, we had after all not been to Nejd. Nejd, I was told on the "best authority," was a term applicable only to that district of Central Arabia which is bounded by the Jebel Toweykh and the lesser Nefûds, neither Jebel Shammar nor Kasim being included in it. Strange as this statement sounded to ears fresh from the country itself, I was unable at the time to fortify my refusal to believe by any more special argument than that the inhabitants of the districts in question had always called them so,—an argument "quod semper et ab omnibus" which to some seemed insufficient. I have therefore taken pains to examine the grounds of the objection raised, and to give a reason for the belief which is still strong within me that Haïl is not only an integral part of Nejd, but Nejd *par excellence.*

First then, to repeat the argument "quod ab omnibus," I state emphatically that according to the Arabs themselves of every tribe and town I have visited, Nejd is held to include the lands which lie within the Nefûds. It is a geographical expression including three principal sub-districts, Jebel Shammar and Kasim in the North, and Aared in the South. The only doubt I have ever heard expressed was as to the Nefûds themselves, whether they were included or not in the term. The

Bedouins certainly so consider them, for they are
the only part of Nejd which they habitually inhabit, the stony plateaux of the centre being unfit
for pastoral life. Jôf is considered outside the
limit northwards, as are Kheybar and Teyma to the
north-west, while Jobba and Harik are doubtful,
being towns of the Nefûd.

Secondly, I plead written authority :—1. Abulfeda and Edrisi, quoted by Colonel Ross in his
memorandum, include in the term Nejd all those
lands lying between Yemen, Hejaz, and Irak.
2. Yakut, an Arabian geographer of the thirteenth
century, quoted by Wetzstein, expressly mentions
Aja as being in Nejd. 3. Merasid confirms Yakut
in his geographical lexicon. 4. Sheykh Hamid of
Kasim, also quoted by Wetzstein, says, "Nejd in its
widest sense is the whole of Central Arabia ;—in its
narrowest and according to modern usage, only the
Shammar Mountains and the Land of Kasim, with
the Great Desert bordering it to the South."
5. Niebuhr, the oldest and most respectable of
European writers, enumerating the towns of Nejd,
says, "Le mont Schamer n'est qu'à dix journées de
Bagdad ; il comprend Haïl, Monkek, Kafar, et
Bokà. L'on place *aussi* dans le Nejdsjed une
contrée montagneuse nommée Djof-al-Sirhan entre
le mont Schâmer et Shâm (la Syrie)," &c. ; thus

showing that all, and more than all I claim, were in Niebuhr's day accounted Nejd. 6. Chesney, in his map of Arabia, published in 1838, includes Kasim and Jebel Shammar within the boundary of Nejd, and gives a second boundary besides, still further north, including districts "sometimes counted to Nejd." 7. Wallin defines Nejd as the whole district where the *ghada* grows, a definition taken doubtless from the Bedouins with whom he travelled, and which would include not only Jebel Shammar, but the Nefûds and even the Southern half of the Wady Sirhán. 8. In Kazimirski's dictionary, 1860, I find, "*Ahlu'lghada*, surnom donné aux habitants de la frontière de Nejd où la plante *ghada* croit en abondance." Finally, Guarmani gives the following as the result of his inquiries in the country itself: "Le Gebel est la province la plus septentrionale du Neged. C'est, comme disent les Arabes, un des sept Negged;" and on the authority of Zamil, Sheykh of Aneyzeh, explains these seven to be Aared, Hasa, and Harik, in the south, Woshem in the centre, and Jebel Shammar, Kasim, and Sudeyr, in the north.

Opposed to this mass of testimony, we find among travellers a single competent authority, Mr. Palgrave; and even his opinion is much qualified. After explaining that the name Nejed signifies

"highland," in contradistinction to the coast and the
outlying provinces of lesser elevation, he sums up
his opinion thus : "The denomination 'Nejed' is
commonly enough applied to the whole space
included between Djebel Shomer on the north, and
the great desert to the south, from the extreme
range of Jebel Toweyk on the east to the neighbourhood of the Turkish pilgrim-road or Derb-el-
Hajj on the west. However, this central district,
forming a huge parallelogram, placed almost diago-
nally across the midmost of Arabia from north-east-
by-east to south-west-by-west, as a glance at the
map may show, is again subdivided by the natives
of the country into the Nejed-el-aala or Upper
Nejed, and the Nejed-el-owta or Lower Nejed, a
distinction of which more hereafter, while Djebel
Shomer is generally considered as a sort of appendage to Nejed, rather than as belonging to that
district itself. But the Djowf is always excluded
by the Arabs from the catalogue of upland provinces,
though strangers sometimes admit it also to the
title of Nejed, by an error on their part, since
it is a solitary oasis, and a door to highland
or inner Arabia, not in any strict sense a portion
of it."

The exact truth of the matter I take, then, to be
this. Nejd, in its original and popular sense of

"Highlands," was a term of physical geography, and necessarily embraced Jebel Shammar, the most elevated district of all, as well as Kasim, which lay between it and Aared; and so it was doubtless considered in Niebuhr's time, and is still considered by the Bedouins of the North, whose recollections date from an age previous to Niebuhr's. With the foundation, however, of the Wahhabi Empire of Nejd, the term from a geographical became a political one, and has since followed the fluctuating fortunes of the Wahhabi State. In this way it once embraced not only the upland plateaux, but Jôf and Hasa ; the latter, though a low-lying district on the coast, retaining in Turkish official nomenclature its political name of Nejd to the present day. At the time of Mr. Palgrave's visit, the Wahhabis, from whom doubtless his information was acquired, considered Jebel Shammar no longer an integral part of their State, but, as he expresses it, an appendage. It was already politically independent, and had ceased in their eyes to be Nejd. But since his day the Nejd State has seen a still further disruption. Kasim has regained its independence, and Hasa has been annexed to the Turkish Empire. Nejd has therefore become once more what it was before the Empire of Nejd arose, a term of physical geography only, and one pretty nearly co-extensive with our term Central Arabia.

I hold, then, to the correctness of our title, though in this matter, as in the rest, craving indulgence of the learned.

WILFRID SCAWEN BLUNT.

CRABBET PARK,
August 1, 1880.

PILGRIM BANNER.

CONTENTS

CHAPTER I.

CHAPTER II.

CHAPTER III.

CHAPTER IV.

CHAPTER V.

CHAPTER VI.

CHAPTER VII.

CHAPTER VIII.

CHAPTER IX.

CHAPTER XV.

CHAPTER XVI.

OUR PERSIAN CAMPAIGN.

—◆—

CHAPTER I.

CHAPTER II.

CHAPTER III.

CHAPTER IV.

CHAPTER V.

CHAPTER VI.

APPENDICES.

LIST OF ILLUSTRATIONS

A

PILGRIMAGE TO NEJD.

CHAPTER I.

" You have been a great traveller, Mercury ? "
" I have seen the world."
" Ah, a wondrous spectacle. I long to travel."
" The same thing over again. Little novelty and much change.
I am wearied with exertion, and if I could get a pension would retire."
" And yet travel brings wisdom."
" It cures us of care. Seeing much we feel little, and learn how
very petty are all those great affairs which cost us such anxiety."
IXION IN HEAVEN.

The charm of Asia—A return to old friends—Desert news—The
Palmyrene colony at Damascus—New horses and camels—
Mrs. Digby and her husband Mijuel the Mizrab—A blood feud
—Abd el-Kader's life—Midhat Pasha discourses on canals and
tramways—He fails to raise a loan.

DAMASCUS, *Dec.* 6, 1878.—It is strange how
gloomy thoughts vanish as one sets foot in Asia.
Only yesterday we were still tossing on the sea of
European thought, with its political anxieties, its
social miseries and its restless aspirations, the
heritage of the unquiet race of Japhet—and now
we seem to have ridden into still water, where we
can rest and forget and be thankful. The charm of
the East is the absence of intellectual life there, the
freedom one's mind gets from anxiety in looking
forward or pain in looking back. Nobody here
thinks of the past or the future, only of the

present ; and till the day of one's death comes, I suppose the present will always be endurable. Then it has done us good to meet old friends, friends all demonstratively pleased to see us. At the coach office when we got down, we found a little band of dependants waiting our arrival—first of all Mohammed ibn Arûk, the companion of our last year's adventures, who has come from Palmyra to meet and travel with us again, and who has been waiting here for us, it would seem, a month. Then Hanna, the most courageous of cowards and of cooks, with his ever ready tears in his eyes and his double row of excellent white teeth, agrin with welcome. Each of them has brought with him a friend, a relation he insists on calling him, who is to share the advantage of being in our service, and to stand by his patron in case of need, for servants like to travel here in pairs. Mohammed's *cousin* is a quiet, respectable looking man of about five and thirty, rather thick set and very broad shouldered. He is to act as head camel man, and he looks just the man for the place. Hanna's *brother* bears no likeness at all to Hanna. He is a young giant, with a rather feckless face, and great splay hands which seem to embarrass him terribly. He is dressed picturesquely in a tunic shaped like the ecclesiastical vestment called the " dalmatic," and very probably its origin, with a coloured turban on his head. He too may be useful, but he is a Christian, and we rather doubt the prudence of taking Christian servants to Nejd. Only

Ferhan, our Agheyl camel-driver, is missing, and this is a great disappointment, for he was the best tempered and the most trustworthy of all our followers last year. I fancy we may search Damascus with a candle before we find his like again. The evening we spent in giving and receiving news. Mohammed in his quality of Wilfrid's "brother," was invited to dine with us, and a very pleasant hour or two we had, hearing all that has happened in the desert during the summer. First of all, the sensation that has been caused there by our purchase of Beteyen's mare, which after all we have secured, and the heart-burnings and jealousies raised thereby. Then there have been high doings among our friends in the Hamád. Faris and Jedaan have (wonderful to relate) made peace,* and between them have it all their own way now on the Euphrates, where the caravan road has become quite unsafe in consequence. Ferhan ibn Sfuk, it seems, marched against his brother with some Turkish troops to help him, and Faris retreated across the river ; but most of the Shammar have, as we anticipated last year, come over to him. The Roala war is not yet finished. Ibn Shaalan, rejecting the proposals made him through us by Jedaan, persisted in reoccupying the Hama pastures last spring, and Jedaan attacked and routed him ; so that he has retreated southwards to his own country. Mohammed Dukhi and Jedaan have parted company,

---

* A truce only, I fear.

the Sebaa having cleared off scores with the Roala, and being satisfied with the summer's campaign ; while the Welled Ali are still a long way on the creditor side in their blood feud. Mohammed Dukhi is a long-headed old rogue, but it is difficult to see how he is to hold his own with Sotamm in spite of a new alliance with Faris el Meziad, Sheykh of the Mesenneh, who still has some hundred horsemen to help him with, and of another with Mohammed Aga of Jerúd. The Welled Ali are at the present moment encamped close to Jerúd, so we shall probably go there, as the first step on our road to Nejd.

Mohammed of course knows nothing about the roads to Nejd or Jôf, except that they are somewhere away to the south, and that he has relations there, and I doubt if anybody in Damascus can give us more information. The Welled Ali, however, would know where the Roala are, and the Roala could send us on, as they go further south than any of the Ánazeh. The difficulty, we fear, this winter will be the accident of no rain having fallen since last spring, so that the Hamád is quite burnt up and without water. If it were not for this, our best course would undoubtedly be outside the Hauran, which is always dangerous, and is said to be especially so this year. The desert has often been compared to the sea, and is like it in more ways than one, amongst others in this, that once well away from shore it is comparatively safe, while there is always a risk of accidents along the coast.

But we shall see. In the meantime we talk to
Mohammed of the Jôf only, for fear of scaring him.
Nejd, in the imagination of the northern Arabs, is
an immense way off, and no one has ever been
known to go there from Damascus. Mohammed
professes unbounded devotion to Wilfrid, and he
really seems to be sincere ; but six hundred miles
of desert as the crow flies will be a severe test of
affection. We notice that Mohammed has grown
in dignity and importance since we saw him last,
and has adopted the style and title of Sheykh, at
least for the benefit of the hotel servants ; he has
indeed good enough manners to pass very well for a
true Bedouin.

There is a small colony of Palmyra people at
Damascus, or rather in the suburb of the town
called the Maïdan, and with them Mohammed has
been staying. We went there with him this
morning to see some camels he has been buying
for us, and which are standing, or rather sitting, in
his friends' yard. The colony consists of two or
three families, who live together in a very poor little
house. They left Tudmur about six years ago " in
a huff," they say, and have been waiting on here
from day to day ever since to go back. The men
of the house were away from home when we called,
for they make their living like most Tudmuri as
carriers ; but the women received us hospitably,
asked us to sit down and drink coffee, excellent
coffee, such as we had not tasted for long, and sent

a little girl to bring the camels out of the yard for us to look at. The child managed these camels just as well as any man could have done. Mohammed seems to have made a good selection. There are four deluls for riding, and four big baggage camels ; these last have remarkably ugly heads, but they look strong enough to carry away the gates of Gaza, or anything else we choose to put upon their backs. In choosing camels, the principal points to look at are breadth of chest, depth of barrel, shortness of leg, and for condition roundness of flank. I have seen the strength of the hocks tested by a man standing on them while the camel is kneeling. If it can rise, notwithstanding the weight, there can be no doubt as to soundness. One only of the camels did not quite please us, as there was a suspicion of recent mange ; but Abdallah (Mohammed's cousin) puts it " on his head " that all is right with this camel, as with the rest. They are not an expensive purchase at any rate, as they average less than £10 a piece. One cannot help pitying them, poor beasts, when one thinks of the immense journey before them, and the little probability there is that they will all live to see the end of it. Fortunately they do not know their fate any more than we know ours. How wretched we should be for them if we knew exactly in what wady or at what steep place they would lie down and be left to die ; for such is the fate of camels. But if we did, we should never have the heart to set out at all.

Next in importance to the camels are the horses we are to ride. Mohammed has got his little Jilfeh mokhra of last year which is barely three years old, but he declares she is up to his weight, thirteen stone, and I suppose he knows best. Mr. S. has sent us two mares from Aleppo by Hanna, one, a Ras el Fedawi, very handsome and powerful, the other, a bay three year old Abeyeh Sherrak, without pretension to good looks, but which ought to be fast and able to carry a light weight. We rode to the Maidan, and the chestnut's good looks attracted general attention. Everybody turned round to look at her; she is perhaps too handsome for a journey.

December 7.—We have been spending the day with Mrs. Digby and her husband, Mijuel of the Mizrab, a very well bred and agreeable man, who has given us a great deal of valuable advice about our journey. They possess a charming house outside the town, surrounded by trees and gardens, and standing in its own garden with narrow streams of running water and paths with borders full of old fashioned English flowers—wall-flowers especially. There are birds and beasts too; pigeons and turtle doves flutter about among the trees, and a pelican sits by the fountain in the middle of the courtyard guarded by a fierce watch-dog. A handsome mare stands in the stable, but only one, for more are not required in town.

The main body of the house is quite simple in its

bare Arab furnishing, but a separate building in the
garden is fitted up like an English drawing-room
with chairs, sofas, books, and pictures. Among
many interesting and beautiful sketches kept in a
portfolio, I saw some really fine water-colour views
of Palmyra done by Mrs. Digby many years ago
when that town was less known than it is at
present.

The Sheykh, as he is commonly called, though incorrectly, for his elder brother Mohammed is reigning Sheykh of the Mizrab, came in while we were
talking, and our conversation then turned naturally
upon desert matters, which evidently occupy most
of his thoughts, and are of course to us of all-
important interest at this moment. He gave us
among other pieces of information an account of his
own tribe, the Mizrab, to which in our published
enumeration of tribes we scarcely did justice.

But before repeating some of the particulars we
learned from him, I cannot forbear saying a few
words about Mijuel himself, which will justify the
value we attach to information received from him as
from a person entitled by birth and position to
speak with authority. In appearance he shews all
the characteristics of good Bedouin blood. He is
short and slight in stature, with exceedingly small
hands and feet, a dark olive complexion, beard
originally black, but now turning grey, and dark
eyes and eyebrows. It is a mistake to suppose that
true Arabs are ever fair or red-haired. Men may

occasionally be seen in the desert of comparatively
fair complexion, but these *always* (as far as my
experience goes) have features of a correspondingly
foreign type, showing a mixture of race. No
Bedouin of true blood was ever seen with hair or
eyes not black, nor perhaps with a nose not aquiline.

Mijuel's father, a rare exception among the Ánazeh,
could both read and write, and gave his sons, when
they were boys, a learned man to teach them their
letters. But out of nine brothers, Mijuel alone took
any pains to learn. The strange accident of his
marriage with an English lady has withdrawn him for
months at a time, but not estranged him, from the
desert; and he has adopted little of the townsman
in his dress, and nothing of the European. He
goes, it is true, to the neighbouring mosque, and
recites the Mussulman prayers daily; but with this
exception, he is undistinguishable from the Ibn
Shaalans and Ibn Mershids of the Hamád. It is
also easy to see that his heart remains in the
desert, his love for which is fully shared by the
lady he has married; so that when he succeeds to
the Sheykhat, as he probably will, for his brother
appears to be considerably his senior, I think they
will hardly care to spend much of their time at
Damascus. They will, however, no doubt, be in-
fluenced by the course of tribal politics, with which
I understand Mijuel is so much disgusted, that he
might resign in favour of his son Afet; in that
case, they might continue, as now, living partly at

Damascus, partly at Homs, partly in tents, and
always a providence to their tribe, whom they supply
with all the necessaries of Bedouin life, and guns,
revolvers, and ammunition besides. The Mizrab,
therefore, although numbering barely a hundred
tents, are always well mounted and better armed
than any of their fellows, and can hold their own
in all the warlike adventures of the Sebaa.

According to Mijuel, the Mizrab, instead of being,
as we had been told, a mere section of the Resallin,
are in fact the original stock, from which not only
the Resallin but the Moáhib and the Gomussa themselves have branched off. In regard to the last-
mentioned tribe he related the following curious
story :—

An Arab of the Mizrab married a young girl
of the Suellmat tribe and soon afterwards died.
In a few weeks his widow married again, taking
her new husband from among her own kinsmen.
Before the birth of her first child a dispute arose
as to its parentage, she affirming her Mizrab husband
to be the father while the Suellmat claimed the
child. The matter, as all such matters are in the
desert, was referred to arbitration, and the mother's
assertion was put to the test by a live coal being
placed upon her tongue. In spite of this ordeal
she persisted in her statement, and got a judgment
in her favour. Her son, however, is supposed to
have been dissatisfied with the decision, for as soon
as born he turned angrily on his mother, from

which circumstance he received the name of Gomussa or the "scratcher." From him the Gomussa tribe are descended. They first came into notice about seventy years ago when they attacked and plundered the Bagdad caravan which happened to be conveying a large sum of money. With these sudden riches they acquired such importance that they have since become the leading section of the tribe, and they are now undoubtedly the possessors of the best mares among the Ánazeh. The Mizrab Sheykhs nevertheless still assert superiority in point of birth, and a vestige of their old claims still exists in their titular right to the tribute of Palmyra.

Mijuel's son, Afet, or Japhet, whom we met at Beteyen's camp last spring, has taken, it would appear, an active part in the late fighting. During the battle where Sotamm was defeated by the Sebaa and their allies, the head of the Ibn Jendal * family, pursued by some Welled Ali horsemen, yielded himself up a prisoner to Afet whose father-in-law he was, and who sought to give him protection by covering him with his cloak. But the Ibn Smeyr were at blood feud with the Ibn Jendals, and in such cases no asylum is sacred. One of Mohammed Dukhi's sons dragged Ibn Jendal out of his hiding-place and slew him before Afet's eyes. On that day the Sebaa took most of the mares and camels they had lost in the previous

* One of the noblest of the Roala families.

fighting, and our friend Ferhan Ibn Hedeb is now in tolerable comfort again with tents and tent furniture, and coffee-pots to his heart's content. I hope he will bear his good fortune as well as he bore the bad.

Mijuel can of course give us better advice than anybody else in Damascus, and he says that we cannot do better in the interests of our journey than go first to Jerúd and consult Mohammed Dukhi. The Welled Ali after the Roala are the tribe which knows the western side of the desert best, and we should be sure of getting correct information from them, if nothing more. The Sebaa never go anywhere near the Wady Sirhán, as they keep almost entirely to the eastern half of the Hamád; and even their ghazús hardly ever meddle with that inhospitable region. Mijuel has once been as far south as to the edge of the Nefúd, which he describes as being covered with grass in the spring. The Wady Sirhán, he believes, has wells, but no pasturage.

Another interesting visit which we paid while at Damascus was to Abd el-Kader, the hero of the French war in Algiers. This charming old man, whose character would do honour to any nation and any creed, is ending his days as he began them, in learned retirement and the exercises of his religion. The Arabs of the west, "Maghrabi" (Mogrebins), are distinguished from those of the Peninsula, and indeed from all others, by a natural taste for piety and a religious tone of thought. Arabia proper, except in the first age of Islam and latterly during the hundred years of Wahhabi rule, has never been a religious country. Perhaps out of antagonism to Persia, its nearest neighbour, it neglects ceremonial observance, and pays little respect to saints, miracles, and the supernatural world in general. But with the Moors and the Algerian Arabs this is different. Their religion is the reason of their social life and a prime mover in their politics. It is the fashion there, even at the present day, for a rich man to spend his money on a mosque, as elsewhere he would spend it on his stud and the entertainment of guests, and nothing gives such social distinction as regular attendance at prayer. There is too, besides the lay nobility, a class of spiritual nobles held equally high in public estimation. These are the marabous or descendants of certain saints, who by virtue of their birth partake in the sanctity of their ancestors and have hereditary gifts of divination and miraculous cure. They hold indeed much the same position with the vulgar as did the sons of the prophets in the days of Saul.

Abd el-Kader was the representative of such a family, and not, as I think most people suppose, a Bedouin Sheykh. In point of fact he was a townsman and a priest, not by birth a soldier, and though trained, as nobles of either class were, to arms, it was only the accident of a religious war that made him a man of action. He gained his first victories by his sermons, not by his sword ; and, now that the fight is over, he has returned naturally to his first profession, that of saint and man of letters. As such, quite as much as for his military renown, he is revered in Damascus.

To us, however, it is the extreme simplicity of his character and the breadth of his good sense, amounting to real wisdom, which form his principal charm. " Saint " though he be " by profession," as one may say, for such he is in his own eyes as well as those of his followers, he is uninjured by his high position. It is to him an obligation. His charity is unbounded, and he extends it to all alike ; to be poor or suffering is a sufficient claim on him. During the Damascus massacres he opened his doors to every fugitive ; his house was crowded with Christians, and he was ready to defend his guests by force if need were. To us he was most amiable, and talked long on the subject of Arab genealogy and tradition. He gave me a book which has been lately written by one of his sons on the pedigree of the Arabian horse, and took an evident interest in our own researches in that direction. He made the pilgrimage to Mecca many years ago, travelling the whole way from Algeria by land and returning through Nejd to Meshhed Ali and Bagdad. This was before the French war.

Abd el-Kader returned our visit most politely next day, and it was strange to see this old warrior humbly mounted on his little Syrian donkey, led

by a single servant, riding into the garden where
we were. He dresses like a mollah in a cloth gown,
and with a white turban set far back from his forehead after the Algerian fashion. He never, I
believe, wore the Bedouin kefiyeh. His face is now
very pale as becomes a student, and his smile is that
of an old man, but his eye is still bright and piercing
like a falcon's. It is easy to see, however, that it
will never flash again with anything like anger.
Abd el-Kader has long possessed that highest
philosophy of noble minds according to Arab
doctrine, patience.

A man of a very different sort, but one whom we
were also interested to see, was Midhat Pasha, just
arrived at Damascus as Governor-General of Syria.
He had come with a considerable flourish of
trumpets, for he was supposed to represent the
doctrine of administrative reform, which was at
that time seriously believed in by Europeans for the
Turkish Empire. Midhat was the protégé of our own
Foreign Office, and great things were expected of
him. For ourselves, though quite sceptical on these
matters and knowing the history of Midhat's doings
at Bagdad too well to have any faith in him as a
serious reformer, we called to pay our respects, partly
as a matter of duty, and partly it must be owned out
of curiosity. It seemed impossible that a man who
had devised anything so fanciful as parliamentary
government for Turkey should be otherwise than
strange and original. But in this we were grievously

disappointed, for a more essentially commonplace,
even silly talker, or one more naïvely pleased with
himself, we had never met out of Europe. It is
possible that he may have adopted this tone with
us as the sort of thing which would suit English
people, but I don't think so. We kept our own
counsel of course about our plans, mentioning
only that we hoped to see Bagdad and Bussora and
to go on thence to India, for such was to be
ultimately our route. On the mention of these two
towns he at once began a panegyric of his own
administration there, of the steamers he had
established on the rivers, the walls he had pulled
down and tramways built. " Ah, that tramway,"
he exclaimed affectionately. " It was I that devised
it, and it is running still. Tramways are the first
steps in civilisation. I shall make a tramway round
Damascus. Everybody will ride in the trucks. It
will pay five per cent. You will go to Bussora.
You will see my steamers there. Bussora, through
me, has become an important place. Steamers and
tramways are what we want for these poor countries.
The rivers of Damascus are too small for steamers,
or I should soon have some afloat. But I will
make a tramway. If we could have steamers and
tramways everywhere Turkey would become rich."
" And canals," we suggested, maliciously remem-
bering how he had flooded Bagdad with his experiments in this way. " Yes, and canals too. Canals,
steamers, and tramways, are what we want." " And

railways." " Yes, railways. I hope to have a railway soon running alongside of the carriage road
from Beyrout. Railways are important for the
guaranteeing of order in the country. If there was
a railway across the desert we should have no
more trouble with the Bedouins. Ah, those poor
Bedouins, how I trounced them at Bagdad. I war-
rant my name is not forgotten there." We assured
him it was not.

He then went on to talk of the Circassians, "*ces
pauvres Circassiens,*" for he was speaking in French,
"*il faut que je fasse quelque chose pour eux.*" I-
wish I could give some idea of the tone of tender-
ness and almost tearful pity in Midhat's voice as he
pronounced this sentence ; the Circassians seemed
to be dearer to him than even his steamers and
tramways. These unfortunate refugees are, in truth,
a problem not easy of solution : they have been a
terrible trouble to Turkey, and, since they were
originally deported from Russia after the Crimean
war, they have been passed on from province to
province until they can be passed no further. They
are a scourge to the inhabitants wherever they go,
because they are hungry and armed, and insist on
robbing to get a livelihood. To the Syrian Arabs
they are especially obnoxious, because they shed
blood as well as rob, which is altogether contrary
to Arab ideas. The Circassians are like the foxes
which sportsmen turn out in their covers. It is a
public-spirited act to have done so, but they cannot

be made to live in peace with the hares and rabbits.
Midhat, however, had a notable scheme for setting
things to rights. He would draft all these men
into the corps of zaptiehs, and then, if they did rob,
it would be in the interests of Government. Some
score of them were waiting in the courtyard at the
time of our visit, to be experimented on ; and a
more evil-visaged set it would have been difficult
to select.

On the whole, we went away much impressed
with Midhat, though not as we had hoped. He
had astonished us, but not as a wise man. To
speak seriously, one such reforming pasha as this
does more to ruin Turkey than twenty of the old
dishonest sort. Midhat, though he fails to line
his own purse, may be counted on to empty the
public one at Damascus, as he did at Bagdad, where
he spent a million sterling on unproductive works
within a single year. As we wished him good-bye,
we were amused to notice that he retained Mr.
Siouffi, the manager of the Ottoman Bank, who
had come with us, with him for a private conference, the upshot of which was his first public act
as Governor of Syria, the raising of a loan.*

---

* Midhat's reign at Damascus lasted for twenty months, and is
remarkable only for the intrigues in which it was spent. It
began with an *action d'éclat*, the subjugation of the independent
Druses of the Hauran, a prosperous and unoffending community
whom Midhat with the help of the Welled Ali reduced to ruin.
The rest of his time and resources were spent in an attempt to gain
for himself the rank and title of khedive, a scheme which ended in

his recall. Of improvements, material or administrative, nothing at all has been heard, but it is worth recording that a series of fires during his term of office burnt down great part of the bazaars at Damascus, causing much loss of property, and that their place has been taken by a boulevard. Midhat has been now removed to Smyrna, where it is amusing to read the following account of him:—

"MIDHAT PASHA.—September 28 :—' A private correspondent of the *Journal de Genève*, writing ten days ago from Smyrna, says that Midhat Pasha, being convinced that he possessed the sympathy of the inhabitants and could count on their active co-operation, conceived a short time since vast schemes of improvement and reform for the benefit of the province which he has been called upon to administer. The first works he proposed to take in hand were the drainage of the great marshes of Halka-Bournar (the Baths of Diana of the ancients), the cleansing of the sewers of Smyrna, and the removal of the filth which cumbers the streets, pollutes the air, and, as an eminent physician has told him, impairs the health of the city and threatens at no distant date to breed a pestilence. He next proposed, at the instance of a clever engineer Effendi, to repress the ravages of the river Hermus, which in winter overflows its banks and does immense damage in the plain of Menemen. Orders were given for the execution of engineering works on a great scale which, it was thought, would correct this evil and restore to agriculture a vast extent of fertile, albeit at present unproductive, land. Administrative reform was to be also seriously undertaken. The police were to be re-organized, and order and honesty enforced in the courts of justice. The scandal of gendarmes being constrained, owing to the insufficiency of their pay, to enter into an alliance, offensive and defensive, with all the thieves and cut-throats of the city—the disgrace of judges receiving bribes from rogues and other evil-doers—were to be promptly put down. It was ordered that every caïmacan, mudir, chief of police, and president of tribunal, guilty either of malfeasance or robbery, should be arrested and imprisoned. The municipalities were to cease being the mere mouthpieces of the valis, and consider solely the interests of their constituencies. The accounts of functionaries who, with nominal salaries of 800 francs a year, spend 10,000, were to be strictly investigated and their malversations severely punished ; and many other measures, equally praiseworthy and desirable, were either projected or begun. But energy and good-will in a reformer—whether he be a Midhat or a Hamid—are, unfortunately, not alone sufficient to accomplish reforms. To drain marshes, embank rivers, cleanse sewers, remove filth, pay magistrates and policemen, procure honest collectors of revenue, much money is necessary. How was it to be obtained? Not from the revenues of the port or the province; these are sent regularly, to the last centime, to Constantinople, for the needs of the Government are urgent and admit of no delay. Midhat Pasha, not knowing which way to turn, called a *medjeless* (council), but the members were able neither to suggest a solution of the difficulty nor to find any money. In this emergency it occurred to the Governor that there existed at Smyrna a branch of the Ottoman Bank, at the door of which are always stationed two superb nizams in gorgeous uniforms, who give it the appearance of a Government establishment. Why should not the bank provide the needful? The idea commended itself to the Pasha, and the manager was requested to call forthwith at the Konak on urgent public business. When he arrived there Midhat unfolded to him his plans of reform, and proved, with the eloquence of a new convert, that the public works he had in view could not fail to be an unspeakable benefit to the province and restore its waning prosperity. Never, he assured the wondering manager, could the bank have a finer opportunity of making a splendid investment than this of lending the Government a few million francs, to be strictly devoted to the purposes he had explained. The projected schemes, moreover, were to be so immediately profitable that the bank might reckon with the most implicit confidence on receiving back, in the course of a few years, both interest and principal. Unfortunately, however, all these arguments were lost on M. Heintze, the manager; and he had to explain to the Pasha that, although he, personally, would have been delighted to advance him the millions he required, his instructions allowed him no discretion. He was there to do ordinary banking business, and collect certain revenues which had been assigned to the bank by way of security; but he had been strictly enjoined to make no loans whatever, however promising and profitable they might appear. And this was the end of Midhat Pasha's great schemes of public improvement and administrative reform. In these circumstances it would be the height of injustice to accuse him of not having kept the promises which he made on entering office; for nobody, not even a Turkish Governor-General, can be expected to achieve impossibilities.'"

CHAPTER II.

" This shadowy desert, unfrequented woods,
I better brook than flourishing peopled towns. '

SHAKESPEARE.

Brotherly offices—We prepare for a campaign—Mohammed Dukhi
comes to court—A night robber—We start for Nejd—Tale of a
penitent—The duty of revenge—We are entertained by poor
relations—The fair at Mezarib.

WE spent a week at Damascus, a week not altogether of pleasure, although it was to be our last
of civilised life. We had an immense number of
things to buy and arrange and think over, before
starting on so serious a journey as this, which we
knew must be very unlike the pleasure trip of last
year. We could not afford to leave anything to
chance with the prospect of a three months' wandering, and a thousand miles of desert, where it was
impossible to count upon fresh supplies even of the
commonest necessaries of life. Jôf, the first station
on our road, was four hundred miles off, and then
we must cross the Nefúd, with its two hundred
miles of sand, before we could get to Nejd. The
return journey, too, to the Persian Gulf, would
have to be made without coming to anything so
European as a Turkish town. Nobody could tell
us what supplies were to be had in Nejd, beyond
dates and corn. Mr. Palgrave's account of Jebel

Shammar was, in fact, the only guide we had to go on, and its accuracy had been so much doubted that we felt obliged to take into consideration the possibility of finding the Nejd towns mere oases, and their cultivation only that of the date. Mohammed, less "insouciant" than most of his countrymen are on such matters, now made himself most useful, spending many hours in the bazaars with Wilfrid, as I did with the cook and the camel-man ; and being a town Arab and a trader born, he saved us an infinity of trouble and time, and no few mejidies.

They began by choosing a complete suit of Bedouin clothes for Wilfrid, not exactly as a dis-guise, for we did not wish, even if we could have done so, not to pass for Europeans, but in order to avoid attracting more notice than was necessary on our way. The costume consisted of a striped silk jibbeh or dressing-gown worn over a long shirt, a blue and white abba of the kind made at Karieteyn, and for the head a black kefiyeh embroidered with gold which was fastened on with the Bedouin aghal, a black lamb's-wool rope. Mohammed had brought with him a sword which had belonged to his grand-father, a fine old Persian blade curved like a sickle. He gave it to Wilfrid and received in return a hand-some weapon somewhat similar but silver-mounted, which they found in the bazaar. Thus rigged out, for Mohammed too had been reclothed from head to foot (and he much required it), they used to sally

out in the town as two Bedouin gentlemen.
Wilfrid by holding his peace was able to pass with
the unwary as an unconcerned friend, while Mohammed did the bargaining for cloaks, kefiyehs, and
other articles suitable as presents to the Sheykhs
whose acquaintance we might make. Mohammed
was an expert in driving a hard bargain and knew
the exact fashion in vogue in each Bedouin tribe, so
that although his taste did not always quite agree
with ours, we let him have his way. The only
mistake he made, as it turned out, was in under-
estimating the value of gifts necessary in Haïl.
Not one of us had the least idea of the luxury
existing in Nejd, and Mohammed, like most of the
northern Arabs, had heard of Ibn Rashid only as a
Bedouin Sheykh, and fancied that a red cloth jibbeh
would be the *ne plus ultra* of magnificence for him,
as indeed it would have been for an Ibn Shaalan or
an Ibn Mershid. We had, however, some more
serious presents than these to produce, if necessary,
in the rifles and revolvers we carried with us, so that
we felt there was no real danger of arriving empty-
handed.

The purchases which it fell to my share to make,
with the assistance of Abdallah and the cook,
were entirely of a useful sort, and do not require a
detailed description here. As to dress, it was unnecessary for me to make any change, save that of
substituting a kefiyeh for a hat and wearing a
Bedouin cloak over my ordinary travelling ulster.

Hanna and Abdallah were both of them masters in the art of haggling, and vied with each other in beating down the prices of provisions. Dates, flour, burghul (a kind of crushed wheat, which in Syria takes the place of rice), carrots, onions, coffee, and some dried fruit were to be the mainstay of our cooking, and of these we bought a supply sufficient to last us as far as Jôf. We had brought from England some beef tea, vegetable soup squares, and a small quantity of tea in case of need. We had agreed to do without bulky preserved provisions, which add greatly to the weight of baggage, and that as to meat, we would take our chance of an occasional hare or gazelle, or perhaps now and then a sheep.

All began well. Our servants seemed likely to turn out treasures, and we had no difficulty in getting a couple of Agheyls to start with us as camel drivers. We thought it prudent to keep our own counsel as to the direction we intended to take, and it was generally supposed that Bagdad was to be our first object. Only Mohammed and Hanna were informed of the real design, and them we could trust. Not but what Hanna had occasional fits of despondency about the risk he ran. He did not pretend to be a hero, he had a wife and children to whom he was sincerely attached, and he felt, not quite wrongly, that Central Arabia was hardly the place for one of his nation and creed. He came to us, indeed, one morning, to announce

his intention of returning home to Aleppo, and he
required a good deal of humouring before he
recovered his spirits ; but I do not think that he ever
seriously intended to desert us. He had come all
the way from Aleppo to join us, and, besides, the
companionship of the young giant he called his
" brother," who was to share his tent, reassured
him. Once started, we knew that he would bear
patiently all that fortune might inflict.

By the 11th the necessary preparations had been
made, and we were ready to start. As a preliminary, we moved into a garden outside the town
with our camels and our mares, so as to be at
liberty to go off any morning without attracting
notice and in the direction we might choose. It
was generally believed in Damascus that we intended going to Bagdad, and we had made up our
minds to start in that direction, partly to avoid
questions, and partly because at Jerúd, the first
village on the road to Palmyra, we should find
Mohammed Dukhi with the Welled Ali. He seemed
the most likely person to put us on our way, and
in expeditions of this sort the first few marches are
generally the most difficult, if not the most dangerous.
The edges of the desert are always unsafe, whereas,
once clear of the shore, so to speak, there is comparatively little risk of meeting anybody, friend or
foe. We thought then that we should be able to get
a man from Mohammed Dukhi to take us in a straight
line from Jerúd to some point in the Wady Sirhán,

keeping well outside the Hauran, a district of the worst reputation, and following perhaps a line of pools or wells which the Bedouins might know. But just as we had settled this, Mohammed Dukhi himself appeared unexpectedly at Damascus, and our plan was changed.

Mohammed Dukhi ibn Smeyr is the greatest personage in the north-western desert next to Ibn Shaalan, and as I have said before was at that time hotly engaged in a war with the Roala chief. His object in visiting Damascus was as follows : in the course of the autumn a detachment of fifteen Turkish soldiers attacked his camp without provocation and, firing into it, killed a woman and a child. This camp numbered only a few tents, the tribe being at the time scattered on account of pasturage, and the Sheykh himself was absent with most of the men. Those, however, who had remained at home managed to cut off and surround the soldiers, one of whom was killed in the fray. The Welled Ali would have killed the rest but for Mohammed Dukhi's wife, Herba,* who rushed in among the combatants, and remonstrated with her people on the folly of involving themselves in a quarrel with the Government. Her pluck saved the soldiers' lives. She took them under her protection, and the next morning sent them under escort to a place of safety.

Now Mohammed Dukhi, having the Roala war

---

* Daughter of Faris-el-Meziad, Sheykh of the Mesenneh.

on his hands and being obliged to shelter himself
from Ibn Shaalan under the walls of Jerúd, was
naturally anxious to clear up this matter of the
soldier's death ; and, directly he heard of Midhat's
arrival at Damascus, he shrewdly determined to
make his count with the new Pasha by an early call
at the Serai. Ibn Shaalan was out of the way, and
the first comer would doubtless be the one most
readily listened to. Ibn Smeyr had besides a little
intrigue on foot respecting the escort of the Damascus pilgrims, which he in part provided or hoped to
provide. Abd el-Kader was his friend, and it
was at the Emir's house that he alighted and that
we found him. Mohammed Dukhi, noble though
he is in point of blood, is not a fine specimen of a
great Bedouin Sheykh. His politeness is over-
strained and unnatural, reminding one rather of
city than of desert manners ; there are also ugly
stories of his want of faith, which one finds no
difficulty in believing when one sees him. He
affected, however, great pleasure at seeing us again,
and professed an entire devotion to our welfare
and our plans. He would himself accompany us
on the first stages of our road, or at least send his
sons or some of his men ; offers which dwindled,
till at last they resulted in his merely writing some
letters of recommendation for us, and giving us a
large amount of good advice. As regards the latter,
he informed us that a journey such as we proposed
outside the Hauran would not at the present

moment be practicable. No rain had fallen during
the autumn, and the Hamád was without water;
indeed, except in the Wady Sirhán, where the wells
were never dry, there was no watering place southwards at any distance from the hills. He advised
us, therefore, to leave Damascus by the pilgrim
road, which keeps inside the Hauran, and follow it
till we came across the Beni Sokkhr, whom we
should find encamped not far to the east of it.
There was besides a capital opportunity for us of
doing this in company with the *Jerdeh*, now on
the point of starting for Mezárib, a station on the
Haj road. The Jerdeh, he explained, for the name
was new to us, are a kind of relief party sent every
year from Damascus, to meet the pilgrims on their
homeward route, carrying with them supplies of
all the necessaries of life, provisions, and extra
camels to replace those broken down. The party is
escorted by Mohammed Dukhi, or rather by his
men, and the idea of joining them seemed exactly
suited to our purpose; though when we came to
put it in practice, it turned out to be of as little
value as the rest of the smooth-spoken Sheykh's
offers. It was something, however, to have a plan,
good or bad, and letters from so great a man as Ibn
Smeyr were of value, even though addressed to the
wrong people.

Accordingly, on the 12th we bade good-bye to
our Damascus friends, wrote our last letters to our
friends in England, and said a long farewell to

the pleasures and pains of European life. On the
13th we started.

December 13.—We have started at last, and on
a Friday, the 13th of the month. I have no
personal objection to any particular day of the
week, or of the month. But, as a matter of fact,
the only seriously unfortunate journey we ever
made was begun on a Friday, and Wilfrid professes himself to be superstitious and full of dark
forebodings. He, however, insisted on starting this
Friday, and with some inconsistency argues that
forebodings are lucky, or that at any rate the
absence of them is unlucky, and that it would not
be safe to begin a journey in a cheerful frame of
mind.

We were roused in the middle of the night by a
cry of thieves in the garden, and running out of
our tent found a scuffle going on, which, when
lights were brought, proved to have been caused by
two men, one the keeper of the garden and the
other a soldier, whom he was taking prisoner. Our
servants were standing round them, and Hanna,
seeing the man to be securely bound, was belabour-
ing him with a stick, ejaculating at intervals, " O
robber, O dog, O pig! O pig, O dog, O robber ! "
The story told us was that the gardener had found
this man prowling about, and had, after a terrible
engagement, succeeded in his capture. There were,
however, no blood or wounds to show ; and, the
evidence of the prisoner's wicked designs not being

very overwhelming, Wilfrid gave orders that he should be let go as soon as it should be daylight. In the first place, any handing over of the man to justice would have delayed our start, and secondly, it was more than probable that the whole thing had been got up by the gardener with the accused person for the sake of the present the two would receive. Such little comedies are quite common in the East; and when we declined to take it seriously, the two men very good-humouredly let the matter drop.

At the first streak of dawn we struck our tents, loaded our camels, and a little after sunrise were on our mares and well away from the town in marching order for Nejd! At first we skirted the city, passing the gate where St. Paul is said to have entered, and the place where he got over the wall, and then along the suburb of Maïdan, which is the quarter occupied by Bedouins when they come to town, and where we had found the Tudmuri and our camels. Here we were to have met the Jerdeh, and we waited some time outside the Bawâbat Allah, or "Gates of God," while Mohammed went in to make inquiries, and take leave of his Tudmuri friends. It is in front of this gate that the pilgrims assemble on the day of their start for Mecca, and from it the Haj road leads away in a nearly straight line southwards. The Haj road is to be our route as far as Mezárib, and is a broad, well worn track, though of course not a road at all according to English ideas. It has, nevertheless,

a sort of romantic interest, one cannot help feeling,
going as it does so far and through such desolate
lands, a track so many thousand travellers have
followed never to return. I suppose in its long
history a grave may have been dug for every yard
of its course from Damascus to Medina, for, especially on the return journey, there are constantly
deaths among the pilgrims from weariness and
insufficient food.

Our caravan, waiting at the gate, presented a
very picturesque appearance. Each of the delúls
carries a gay pair of saddle-bags in carpet-work,
with long worsted tassels hanging down on each
side half way to the ground; and they have ornamented *reshmehs* or headstalls to match. The
camels, too, though less decorated, have a gay
look; and Wilfrid on the chestnut mare ridden in a
halter wants nothing but a long lance to make him
a complete Bedouin. The rest of our party consists,
besides Mohammed and Hanna, who have each of
them a delul to ride, of Mohammed's "cousin"
Abdallah, whom we call Sheykh of the camels, with
his two Agheyl assistants, Awwad, a negro, and a
nice-looking boy named Abd er-Rahman. These,
with Mohammed, occupy one of the servants' tents,
while Hanna and his "brother" Ibrahim have
another, for even in the desert distinctions of religious caste will have to be preserved. It is a great
advantage in travelling that the servants should be
as much as possible strangers to each other, and of

different race or creed, as this prevents any combination among them for mutiny or disobedience. The Agheyls will be one clique, the Tudmuri another, and the Christians a third, so that though they may quarrel with one another, they are never likely to unite against us. Not that there is any prospect of difficulty from such a cause ; but three months is a long period for a journey, and everything must be thought of beforehand.

Mohammed was not long in the Maïdan, and came back with the news that the Jerdeh has not been seen there, but might be at a khan some miles on the road called Khan Denún. It was useless to wait for them there, and so, wishing our friend, Mr. Siouffi, good-bye (for he had accompanied us thus far) we rode on. Nothing remarkable has marked our first day's journey ; a gazelle crossing the track, and a rather curious squabble between a kite, a buzzard, and a raven, in which the raven got all the profit, being the only events. From the crest of a low ridge we looked back and saw our last of Damascus, with its minarets and houses imbedded in green. We shall see no more buildings, I suppose, for many a day. Mount Hermon to the left of it rose, an imposing mass, hazy in the hot sun, for, December though it is, the summer is far from over. Indeed, we have suffered from the heat today more than we did during the whole of our last journey.

At Denún no sign or knowledge of the Jerdeh, so we have decided to do without them. On a road like this we cannot want an escort. There are plenty of people passing all day long, most of them, like ourselves, going to Mezárib for the annual fair which takes place there on the occasion of the Jerdeh visit. Among them, too, are zaptiehs and even soldiers; and there are to be several villages on the way. We filled our goat-skins at Denún and camped for this our first night on some rising ground looking towards Hermon. It is a still, delightful evening, but there is no moon. The sun is setting at five o'clock.

December 14.—Still on the Haj road and through cultivated land, very rich for wheat or barley, Mohammed says, though it has a fine covering of stones. These are black and volcanic, very shiny and smooth, just as they were shot up from the Hauran when the Hauran was a volcano. The soil looks as if it ought to grow splendid grapes, and some say the bunches the spies brought to Joshua came from near here. The villages, of which we have passed through several, are black and shiny too, dreary looking places even in the sunshine, without trees or anything pleasant to look at round them. The fields at this time of year are of course bare of crops, and it is so long since there was any rain that even the weeds are gone. This is part of what is called the Leja, a district entirely of black boulders, and interesting to archæologists as being

the land of Og, king of Basan, whose cities some
have supposed to exist in ruins to the present day.
In the middle of the day we passed a small ruin,
about which Mohammed, who has been this road
before, as his father was at one time camel-con-
tractor for the Haj, told us a curious story. Once
upon a time there were two children, left orphans
at a very early age. The elder, a boy, went out into
the world to seek his fortune, while the other, a
girl, was brought up by a charitable family in Damascus. In course of time the brother and
sister came together by accident, and, without
knowing their relationship, married, for according
to eastern usage the marriage had been arranged
for them by others. Then, on comparing notes,
they discovered the mistake which had been made ;
and the young man, anxious to atone for the guilt
they had inadvertently incurred, consulted a wise
man as to what he should do in penance. He was
told to make the pilgrimage to Mecca seven times,
and then to live seven years more in some desert
place on the Haj road offering water to the pilgrims.
This he did, and chose the place we passed for the
latter part of his penance. When the seven years
were over, however, he returned to Damascus, and
the little house he had built and the fig-trees he had
planted remain as a record of his story. Mohammed could not tell me what became of the girl, and
seemed to think it did not matter.

He has been talking a great deal to us on the duties

of brotherhood, which seemed a little like a suggestion. The rich brother, it would seem, should make
the poor one presents, not only of fine clothes, but of
a fine mare, a fine delúl, or a score of sheep,—while
the poor brother should be very careful to protect the
life of his sworn ally, or, if need be, to avenge his
death. Wilfrid asked him how he should set about
this last, if the case occurred. " First of all," said
Mohammed, " I should inquire who the shedder of
blood was. I should hear, for instance, that you
had been travelling in the Hauran and had been
killed, but I should not know by whom. I should
then leave Tudmur, and, taking a couple of camels
so as to seem to be on business, should go to the
place where you had died, under a feigned name,
and should pretend to wish to buy corn of the
nearest villagers. I should make acquaintance with
the old women, who are always the greatest talkers,
and should sooner or later hear all about it. Then,
when I had found out the real person, I should
watch carefully all his goings out and comings in,
and should choose a good opportunity of taking him
unawares, and run my sword through him. Then I
should go back to Tudmur as fast as my delúl could
carry me." Wilfrid objected that in England we
thought it more honourable to give an enemy the
chance of defending himself; but Mohammed would
not hear of this. " It would not be right. My
duty," he said, " would be to avenge your blood,
not to fight with the man ; and if I got the oppor-

tunity, I should come upon him asleep or unarmed.
If he was some poor wretch, of no consequence, I
should take one of his relations instead, if possible
the head of his family. I cannot approve of your
way of doing these things. Ours is the best."
Mohammed might have reasoned (only Arabs never
reason), that there were others besides himself concerned in the deed being secretly and certainly
done. An avenger of blood carries not only his
own life but the lives of his family in his hand;
and if he bungles over his vengeance, and himself
gets killed, he entails on them a further debt of
blood. To Mohammed, however, on such a point,.
reasoning was unnecessary. What he had described was the custom, and that was enough.

We are now a little to the south of the village of
Gunayeh where we have sent Abdallah with a delúl
to buy straw. There is no camel pasture here nor
anything the horses can eat. To the east we can
see the blue line of the Hauran range, and to the
west the Syrian hills from Hermon to Ajalon. I
told Mohammed the story of the sun standing still
over Gibeon and the moon over Ajalon, which he
took quite as a matter of course, merely mentioning
that he had never heard it before.

I forgot to say that we crossed the old Roman
road several times to-day. It is in fair preservation,
but the modern caravan track avoids it. Perhaps
in old days wheeled carriages were common and
required a stone road. Now there is no such

necessity. At Ghabaghat, a village we passed about eleven o'clock, we found a tank supplied with water from a spring, and while we were waiting there watering the camels a fox ran by pursued by two greyhounds, who soon came up with and killed him. One of the dogs, a blue or silver grey, was very handsome and we tried to buy him of his owner, a soldier, but he would not take the money. After that we had a bit of a gallop in which we were pleased with our new mares. But we are both tired with even this short gallop, being as yet not in training, and we feel the heat of the sun.

Sunday, December 15.—We have left the Leja country and are now in bare open fields, a fine district for farmers, but as uninteresting as the plains of Germany or northern France. These fields are better watered than the Leja, and we crossed several streams to-day by old stone bridges belonging to the Roman road. The streams run, I believe, eventually into the Jordan, and in one place form a marsh to the right of the road which Mohammed declared to be infested by robbers, men who lurk about in the tall reeds and when they have made a capture run off with their booty into it and cannot be followed. We saw nothing suspicious, however, nor anything of interest but a huge flock of sand grouse, of which we got four as they passed overhead. There were also immense clouds of starlings, and we started a hare. We passed many villages, the principal one being Shemskin, where

there are the ruins of an old town. Our road then
bore away to the right, leaving the Roman road for
good. This goes on straight to Bozra, the chief town
of the Hauran in former days. At Tafazz we stopped to pay a visit to some
Tudmuri settled there, relations of Mohammed's but
not on the Ibn Arûk side, very worthy people
though hardly respectable as relations. Tafazz
from the outside looks like a heap of ruins half
smothered in dunghills. There has been a murrain among the cattle this year, and dead cows
lay about in every stage of decomposition. We
had some difficulty in groping our way through
them to the wretched little mud hovel where the
Tudmuri lived. The family consisted of two
middle-aged men, brothers, with their mother, their
wives, and a pretty daughter named Shemseh (sunshine), some children, and an old man, uncle or
grandfather of the others. These were all presently
clustering round us, and hugging and kissing Mohammed who, I must say, showed a complete
absence of false pride in spite of his fine clothes
and noble appearance. Their welcome to us, poor
people, was very hearty ; and in a few minutes
coffee was being pounded, and a breakfast of un-
leavened loaves, thin and good, an omelette, buttermilk (lebben), and a sweet kind of treacle (dibs),
made of raisins, prepared. While we were at
breakfast a little starved colt looked in at the
door from the yard ; and some chickens and a

pretty fawn greyhound, all equally hungry I
thought, watched us eagerly. The people were
very doleful about the want of rain, and the
loss of their yoke-oxen, which makes their next
year's prospects gloomily uncertain. They told
us, however, that they had a good stock of wheat
in their underground granaries, sufficient for a
year or even more, which shows a greater amount
of forethought than I should have expected of
them. In these countries it is quite necessary to
provide against the famines which happen every
few years, and in ancient times I believe it was a
universal practice to keep a year's harvest in store.

After many entreaties that we would stay the
night under their roof they at last suffered us to
depart, promising that the men of the party would
rejoin us the following day at Mezárib, for Mezárib
was close by. There we arrived about three o'clock
and are encamped on the piece of desert ground
where the fair is held. The view from our tents
is extremely pretty, a fine range of distant hills,
the Ajlun to the south-west, and about a mile off
a little lake looking very blue and bright, with a
rather handsome ruined khan or castle in the fore-
ground. To the left the tents of the Suk, mostly
white and of the Turkish pattern. There are about
a hundred and fifty of them in four rows, making
a kind of street. The village of Mezárib stands
on an island in the lake, connected by a stone
causeway with the shore, but the Suk is on the

mainland. There is a great concourse of people
with horses, and donkeys, and camels, and more
are constantly coming from each quarter of the
compass. They have not as yet paid much attention to us, so that we have been able to make
ourselves comfortable. There is a fresh wind
blowing from the south, and there is a look in
the clouds of something like rain. I have never
before wished for rain on a journey, but I do so
heartily now ; these poor people want it badly.

December 16.—To-day we have done nothing
but receive visits. First there came a Haurani, who
announced himself as a sheykh, and gave us the information that Sotamm ibn Shaalan and the Roala
are somewhere near Ezrak. If this be true it will
be a great piece of good luck for us, but other
accounts have made it doubtful. A more interesting visitor was a young man, a native of Bereydeh
in Nejd, who, hearing that we were on our way to
Jôf, came to make friends with us. Though a well-
mannered youth, he is evidently nothing particular
in the way of position at home, and admits having
been somebody's servant at Bagdad, but on the
strength of a supposed descent from the Beni Laam
in Nejd, he has claimed kinship with Mohammed
and they have been sitting together affectionately
all the morning, holding each an end of Mohammed's rosary. We have cross-questioned him about
Nejd ; but though he knows Haïl and Kasím and
other places, he can give us little real informa-

tion. He seems to have left it as a boy. We are cheered, however, by the little he has had to tell us, as he seems to take it for granted that everybody in Nejd will be delighted to see us, and he has given us the name and address of his relations there. Mohammed went last night to find out whether any of the Beni Sokkhr Sheykhs were at the Suk, for it is to them that we have letters from Mohammed Dukhi, and in the middle of the day Sákhn, a son of Fendi el-Faiz, the nominal head of the tribe, was introduced. He was a not ill-looking youth, and when we had shewn him our letter to his father informed us that the Sheykh had just arrived, so we sent him to fetch him. While Hanna was preparing coffee, the old man came to our tent. In person he is very different from any of the Ánazeh Sheykhs we have seen, reminding one rather of the Jiburi, or other Euphrates Arabs. The Beni Sokkhr are in fact of Shimali or Northern race, which is quite distinct from the Nejdi, to which both Ánazeh and Shammar belong. He is a fine picturesque old man, with rugged features and grey beard and an immense nose, which put us in mind of the conventional Arab types of Scripture picture books, and seemed to correspond with a suggestion I have heard made, that the Beni Sokkhr * are really the Beni Issachar, a lost tribe.

The Sheykh was very much " en cérémonie," and we found it difficult to carry on conversation with

* Sakhr, a stone—the real origin of their name.

him. Either he had not much to say, or did not care to say it to us; and the talk went on principally between his second son Tellál, a Christian merchant (here on business), and Mohammed. We did not, ourselves, broach the subject of our journey; but after coffee had been served, Mohammed had a private conversation with the Sheykh, which resulted in an invitation from him to his tents, which he described as being somewhere near Zerka on the Haj road, from which he will send us on to Maan, and ultimately to Jôf. This plan, however, does not at all suit Wilfrid, who is determined on exploring the Wady Sirhán, which no European has ever done, and he insists that we must go first to Ezrak. Fendi, it appears, cannot take us that way, as he is on bad terms with the Kreysheh, a branch of his own tribe who are on the road. Perhaps, too, he is afraid of the Roala. It is very perplexing, as some sort of introduction we must have at starting, and yet we cannot afford to go out of our way or even wait here indefinitely till Fendi is ready. The Jerdeh people are after all not expected for another two days, and it may be a week before they go on.

Later in the day Sottan, Fendi's youngest son, came to us and offered to accompany us himself to Jôf, but at a price which was altogether beyond our ideas. He had travelled once with some English people on the Syrian frontier, and had got foolish notions about money. Five pounds was the sum we had thought of giving; and he talked about a hundred.

So we sent him away. Later still, came a Shammar from the Jebel, who said he was willing to go for fifteen mejidies, and a Kreysheh who made similar offers. We have engaged them both, but neither could do more than show us the road. They would be no introduction. The difficulty, by all accounts, of going down the Wady Sirhán, is from the Sherarât, who hang about it, and who having no regular Sheykh, cannot easily be dealt with. They are afraid, however, of the Beni Sokkhr Sheykhs, and of course of Mohammed Dukhi and Ibn Shaalan ; and if we could only get a proper representative of one or other of these to go with us, all would be right. But how to get such a one is the question.

It has been very hot and oppressive here to-day, and the appearance of rain is gone. The thermometer about noon stood at 86°.

December 17.—We have decided not to wait here any longer, but to go off to-morrow in the direction of Ezrak, trusting to find some one on the road. We shall have to pass through Bozra, and may have better luck there. Our Shammar seems to think it will be all right ; but the Kreysheh came back this morning with a demand for thirty pounds, instead of the two pounds ten shillings, which he informed Mohammed, Fendi had told him to ask. He seems to be with Fendi, although his branch of the tribe are not on terms with their principal chief. He still talks, however, of coming on the original terms, but that will be without

Fendi's permission. It is quite necessary to be, or appear to be stingy with these people, as throwing money away is considered by them the act of a simpleton.

Mohammed has been sent to the Suk to make some last purchases, and inquire about two more camels. Now that it is decided we are to go by the Wady Sirhán, we shall be obliged to buy two extra camels to carry food for the rest. In ordinary seasons this would not be necessary, but this year everybody tells us we shall find no pasture. *Aliek*, which is the camel food used at Damascus, is made of a sort of grain, like small misshapen peas or lentils, the husk green and the seed red. It is mixed up into dough with wheaten flour and water, and then kneaded into egg-shaped balls five inches long. Six of these balls are a camel's daily ration, which, if he can pick up any rubbish by the way, will be enough to keep him fat. We are carrying barley for the mares.

Aamar and Selim, our Taffazz relations, have come to pay us their promised visit, and will perhaps accompany us to-morrow. They brought with them a measure of *ferikeh*, wheat crushed very fine, a sort of burghul, some bread, and a couple of fowls; also Mohammed's sheepskin coat, which one of the women has been lining for him; and lastly, the little greyhound we saw at their house, all as a present, or very nearly so, after the fashion of the country.

Mohammed has come back with two camels for
our approval, one a very handsome animal, but
rather long-legged, the other short and broad-
chested like a prize-fighter. We have paid ten
pounds and eleven pounds for them. Nothing is
absolutely settled about who is going and who is not
going with us. Nothing but this, that we leave
Mezárib to-morrow.

As I write, an immense hubbub and a cry of
thieves from the Suk. They are ducking a man in
the lake.

SALKHAD.

CHAPTER III.

" Rather proclaim it
That he which hath no stomach to this fight
Let him depart. His passport shall be made."
SHAKESPEARE.

Beating about—Bozra—We leave the Turkish dominions—Mohammed vows to kill a sheep—The citadel of Salkhad and the
independent Druses—We are received by a Druse chieftain—
Historical notice of the Hauran.

December 18.—Our caravan has lost some of its
members. To begin with the two guides, the
Kreysheh and the Shammar have failed to make
their appearance. Then Abd er-Rahman, the little
Agheyl, came with a petition to be allowed to go
home. He was too young, he said, for such a journey,
and afraid he might die on the road. He had
brought a cousin with him as a substitute, who
would do much better than himself, for the cousin
was afraid of nothing. The substitute was then
introduced, a wild picturesque creature all rags and
elf locks and with eyes like jet, armed too with a
matchlock rather longer than himself, and evidently
no Agheyl. We have agreed, however, to take him
and let the other go. Unwilling hands are worse
than useless on a journey. Lastly, the slave Awwad
has gone. Like most negroes he had too good an
opinion of himself, and insisted on being treated as
something more than a servant, and on having a

donkey to ride. So we have packed him too off. He was very angry when told to go, and broke a rebab we had given him to play on, for he could both play and sing well. We are now reduced to our two selves, Mohammed, Abdallah, Hanna, Ibrahim and the substitute—seven persons in all, but the Tafazz people are to go the first two days' march with us and help drive the camels.

We were glad to get clear of the dirt and noise of the Suk, and leaving the Haj road, took a cross track to the south-east, which is to lead us to Bozra. All day long we have been passing through a well-inhabited country, with plenty of villages and a rich red soil, already ploughed, every acre of it, and waiting only for rain. The road was full of people travelling on donkeyback and on foot to Mezárib, singing as they went along. In all the numerous villages we saw the effects of the late murrain in the dead cattle strewed about. I counted seventy carcasses in one small place, a terrible loss for the poor villagers, as each working cow or bullock was worth ten pounds. I asked what disease had killed them, and was told it was "min Allah" (from God). Mohammed, however, calls it *abu hadlan* (father of leanness).

This district is said to be the best corn-growing country anywhere, and looks like it, but unless rain falls soon, the year must be barren. The villages depend almost entirely on rain for their water supply. In each there is an old reservoir hollowed

out of the rock.   It is difficult to understand how
these tanks get filled, for they seem to have no
drainage leading to them, being on the contrary
perched up generally on high ground.   They are
now all dry, and the villagers have to send many
miles for their drinking water.   All this country
belongs to the Hauran, and we are now in a Haurani
village called Ghízeh.   The people are evidently
not pure Arabs, as many of them have light eyes.

We are being hospitably entertained by the
village Sheykh, who is an old acquaintance of
Mohammed's father's, and insists on setting all he
has got before us,—coffee, a plate of rice, barley for
the mares, and, what is more precious just now,
water for them as well as for ourselves.   Hassan,
for such is his name, has a very pretty wife, who
was among the crowd which gathered round us on
our arrival at the village.   She, like the women of
all these villages, made no pretence of shyness, and
was running about unveiled as any peasant girl
might in Italy.   She was evidently a spoilt child,
and required more than one command from Hassan
before she would go home.   The Sheykh has been
spending the evening with us.   He is in great
distress about his village, which is in the last straits
for water.   The cattle, as I have said, have all died,
and now even the beasts of burden which have to
go for the water are dying.   The nearest spring is
at Bozra, twelve miles off ; and if the donkeys
break down the village must die too of thirst.   He

told us that a Frank passed this way two years ago, and had told him that there must be an ancient well somewhere among the ruins of which the village is built, and he has been looking for it ever since. He entreated us to tell him the most likely spot either for finding the old well or digging a new one. We are much distressed at not being engineers enough to do this for him; and I can't help thinking how much a real reformer (not a Midhat) might do in Turkey by attending to such crying wants as these. Ghízeh is within fifty miles from Damascus as the crow flies, and there are scores of villages in like condition throughout the Hauran, which a Syrian governor might relieve at the cost of sending round an engineer. But until tramways and railroads and new bazaars have been made, I suppose there is little chance for mere wells under the present *régime.*

Besides meat and drink, Hassan has given us useful advice. He has reminded Mohammed of another old friend of his father's, who he thinks might be of more service to us than anybody else could be, and he advises us to go first to him. This is Huseyn ibn Nejm el-Atrash, a powerful Druse Sheykh, who lives somewhere beyond the Hauran mountains. He must certainly have relations with some of the Bedouin tribes beyond, for it appears he lives in a little town quite on the extreme edge of the inhabited country towards the Wady Sirhán. We have always heard of this Druse country as

unsafe, but what country is not called unsafe outside the regular Turkish authority? The Ghízeh
Sheykh's suggestion seems worth following, and we
shall make for the Druse town.

The little greyhound Shiekhah (so called from a
plant of that name) is very docile and well-behaved.
She is a regular desert dog, and likes dates better
than anything else. I have made her a coat to
wear at night for she is chilly.

December 19.—Hassan with true hospitality
did not leave his house this morning, but let us
depart quietly. His coming to wish us good-bye
would have looked like asking for a present, and he
evidently did not wish for anything of the sort.
This is the first time we have received hospitality
absolutely gratis in a town, for even when staying
with Mohammed's father at Tudmur, the women of
the family had eagerly asked for money. In the
desert, Hassan's behaviour would not have needed
remark.

Before leaving Ghízeh we went to look at a house
where there is a mosaic floor of old Roman work,
scrolls with orange trees and pomegranates, vines
with grapes on them, vases and baskets, all coloured
on a white ground. It speaks well for the quality
of the workmanship that it has so long stood the
weather and the wear, for it is out of doors, and
forms the pavement in the courtyard of a house.

Three and a half hours of steady marching brought
us to Bozra, where we now are. The entrance of

the town is rather striking, as the old Roman road, which has run in a straight line for miles, terminates in a gateway of the regular classic style, beyond which lie a mass of ruins and pillars, and to the right a fine old castle. A raven was sitting on the gateway, and as we rode through solemnly said " caw."

Bozra is, I have no doubt, described by Mr. Murray, so I won't waste my time in writing about the ruins, which indeed we have not yet examined. They seem to be Roman, and in tolerable preservation. The castle is more modern, probably Saracenic, a huge pile built up out of older fragments. It is occupied by a small garrison of Turkish regulars, the last, I hope, we shall see for many a day, for Bozra is the frontier town of the Hauran, and beyond it the Sultan is not acknowledged. I believe that its occupation is not of older date than fifteen to twenty years ago, the time when Turkey made its last flicker as a progressing state, and that before that time the people of Bozra paid tribute to Ibn Shaalan, as they once had to the Wahhabis of Nejd. The Roala still keep up some connection with the town, however, for a shepherd we met at the springs just outside it assured us that Ibn Shaalan had watered his camels at them not two months ago. It was somewhere not far from Bozra that the forty days' battle between the Mesenneh and the Roala, described by Fatalla,* was fought. Though the

---

* This is a mistake, as the battle was fought on the banks of the Orontes.

details are no doubt exaggerated, Mohammed knows of the battle by tradition. Wilfrid asked him particularly about it to-day, and he fully confirms the account given by Fatalla of the downfall of the Mesenneh. He has added too some interesting details of their recent history. We are encamped outside the town at the edge of a great square tank of ancient masonry, now out of repair and dry. Here would be another excellent occupation for Midhat and his Circassians.

December 20.—We were disturbed all night by the barking of dogs, and the strange echoes from the ruined places round. I never heard anything so unearthly—a cold night—and melancholy too, as nights are when the moon rises late, •and is then mixed up in a haggard light with the dawn.

The Tafazz relations are gone, very sorrowful to wish us good-bye. Selim, the elder of the two, told me that he has been thirty years now in the Hauran, and has no idea of going back to Tudmur. The land at Tafazz is so good that it will grow anything, while at Tudmur there are only the few gardens the stream waters. He is a *fellah* and likes ploughing and sowing better than camel driving. To Tafazz they are gone, Selim on his chestnut mare, old, worn, and one-eyed, but *asil;* Aamar on his bay Kehîleh from the Roala, also old and very lame. They went with tears in their eyes, wishing us all possible blessings for the road.

The consequence is, we have to do more than our share of work, and have had a hard day loading and reloading the camels, for we were among the hills, and the roads were bad. The beasts have not yet become accustomed to each other, and the old camel we bought at Mezárib shows every sign of wishing to return there. He is an artful old wretch, and chose his moment for wandering off whenever we were looking the other way, and wherever a bit of uneven ground favoured his escape. Once or twice he very nearly gave us the slip. He wants to get back to his family, Abdallah says, for we bought him out of a herd where he was lord and master, a sultan among camels. Our road to-day has been very rough. We were told to make our way to Salkhad, a point on the far horizon, just on the ridge of the Hauran, and the only road there was the old Roman one. This went in an absolutely straight line over hill and dale, and as two out of every three of the stones paving it were missing, and the rest turned upside down, it was a long stumble from beginning to end. We had been warned to keep a good look-out for robbers, so Wilfrid and I rode ahead, reconnoitering every rock and heap. We passed one or two ruined villages, but met nobody all day long, still following the pointed hill of Salkhad, which, as we got nearer it, we could see was crowned by a huge fortress.

The country had now become a mass of boulders, which in places had been rolled into heaps, making gigantic cairns, not recently, but perhaps in ancient days, when there were giants in the land. The soil thus uncovered was a rich red earth, and here and there it had been cultivated. There was now a little pasture, for on the hills rain had fallen, and once we saw some goats in the distance.

As we approached Salkhad the road got so bad that Mohammed made a vow of killing a sheep if ever we got safe to Huseyn el-Atrash. We were amused at this and asked him what it meant ; and he told us the story of the prophet Ibrahim who made a vow to kill his son, and who was prevented from doing so by the prophet Musa, who appeared to him and stopped him, and showed him two rams which he said would do instead. These vows the Arabs make are very curious, and are certainly a relic of the ancient sacrifices. Mohammed explained them to us. "The Bedouins," he said, "always do this when they are in difficulties," he could not say why, but it was an old custom ; and when they go back home they kill the sheep, and eat it with their friends. He does not seem to consider it a religious ceremony, only a custom, but it is very singular.

Nine and a half hours' march from seven o'clock brought us to the foot of the conical hill, on which the fortress of Salkhad stands. This is a very ancient building, resembling not a little the fortress of Aleppo, a cone partly artificial and surrounded by a moat, cased with smooth stone and surmounted by walls still nearly perfect. We remarked on some of them the same device as at Aleppo, a rampant lion, the emblem of the Persian Monarchy. The fortress itself, however, is probably of much older date, and may have existed at the time the children of Israel conquered the country. Wilfrid and I, who had gone on in front, agreed to separate here, and ride round the citadel, he to the right, and I to the left, and I was to wait on the top of the ridge till he gave me some signal. This I did and waited so long, that at last the camels came up. He in the meantime had found a little town just under the fortress on the other side and had ridden down into it. At first he saw nobody, and thought the place deserted, but presently people in white turbans began to appear on the house-tops, very much astonished to see this horseman come riding down upon them, for the road was like a stair. He saluted them, and they saluted politely in return, and answered his inquiry for Huseyn el-Atrash, by pointing out a path which led down across the hills to a town called Melakh, where they said Huseyn lived. They asked where he was going, and he said Bussora, Bussora of Bagdad, at which they laughed, and showing him the Roman road, which from Salkhad still goes on in a straight line about south-east, said that that would take him to it. This is curious, for it certainly is exactly the direction, and yet it is impossible there can ever have really been a road there. It probably goes to Ezrak

but we hope to find out all about this in a day or
two. At the bottom of the hill Wilfrid beckoned to
me, and I found him at a large artificial pool or
reservoir, still containing a fair supply of water, and
there, when the rest had joined us, we watered the
camels and horses. Mohammed in the meanwhile
had been also on a voyage of discovery, and came
back with the news that Huseyn el-Atrash was
really at Melakh, and Melakh was only two hours
and a half further on.

Salkhad is a very picturesque town. It hangs
something like a honeycomb under the old fortress
on an extremely steep slope, the houses looking
black from the colour of the volcanic stone of which
they are built. Many of them are very ancient,
and the rest are built up of ancient materials, and
there is a square tower like the belfry of a
church.* The tanks below are at least equally old
with the town, having a casing of hewn stone, now
much dilapidated, and large stone troughs for watering cattle. Its inhabitants, the people in the white
turbans, are Druses, a colony sent I believe from the
Lebanon after the disturbances in 1860.

From Salkhad our road lay principally down hill,
for we had now crossed the watershed of the Jebel

---

* The Hauran was among the first districts conquered by the
Caliph Omar. It shared for some centuries the prosperity of the
Arabian Empire, but suffered severely during the Crusades. There
is no reason, however, to doubt that it continued to be well inhabited until the conquest of Tamerlane in 1400, when all the lands
on the desert frontier were depopulated.

Hauran, and became somewhat intricate, winding about among small fields. The country on this side the hills is divided into walled enclosures, formed by the rolling away of boulders, which give it a more European look than anything we have seen of late. These date I should think from very early times, for the stones have had time to get covered with a grey lichen, so as to resemble natural rather than artificial heaps, and in these dry climates lichen forms slowly. In some of the enclosures we found cultivation, and even vines and fig-trees. It is remarkable how much more prosperous the land looks as soon as one gets away from Turkish administration. The sun was setting as we first caught sight of Melakh, another strange old medi-æval town of black stone, with walls and towers much out of the perpendicular; so leaving the camels to come on under Abdallah's charge and that of a man who had volunteered to guide us, we cantered on with Mohammed, and in the twilight arrived at the house of Huseyn el-Atrash.

Huseyn is a fine specimen of a Druse sheykh, a man of about forty, extremely dark and extremely handsome, his eyes made darker and more brilliant by being painted with kohl. This seems to be a general fashion here. He was very clean and well dressed in jíbbeh and abba; and, unlike most of the Druses, he wore a kefiyeh of purple and gold, though with the white turban over it in place of the aghal. He was sitting with his friends and neighbours on a little terrace in front of his house, enjoying the coolness of the evening, while we could see that a fire had been lit indoors. He rose and came to meet us as we dismounted, and begged us to come in, and then the coffee pots and mortar were set at work and a dinner was ordered. The Sheykh's manners were excellent, very ceremonious but not cold, and though we conversed for an hour about "the weather and the crops," he carefully avoided asking questions as to who we were and what we wanted. Neither did we say anything, as we knew that the proper moment had not come. At last our camels arrived, and dinner was served, a most excellent one, chicken and burghul, horse-radishes in vinegar and water, several sweet dishes, one a purée of rice, spiced tea, cream cheese, and the best water-melon ever tasted. The cookery and the people remind us of the frontier towns of the Sahara, everything good of its kind, good food, good manners, and good welcome. Then, when we had all eaten heartily down to the last servant, he asked us who we were. Mohammed's answer that we were English persons of distinction, on our way to Jôf, and that he was Mohammed, the son of Abdallah of Tudmur, made quite a *coup de théâtre*, and it is easy to see that we have at last come to the right place. We have been, however, glad to retire early, for we have had a hard day's march, nearly twelve hours, and over exceedingly bad ground.

December 21.—The shortest day of the year,
but still hot, though the night was cold.

We spent the morning with Huseyn. His house
has not long been built, but it looks old because it
is built of old stones. Its construction is simple
but good, the main room being divided into sections
with arches so as to suit the stone rafters with
which it is roofed. In front there is a pleasant
terrace overlooking an agreeable prospect of broken
ground, with glimpses of the desert beyond. While
Wilfrid was talking to Huseyn I went to see the
ladies of the establishment. Huseyn has only one
wife ; her name is Wardi (a rose). She is the
mother of a nice little boy, Mohammed, about six
years old and very well behaved, whom we had seen
with the Sheykh ; and of a pretty little girl of two,
named Amina. There are, besides, some older
children by a former husband. Wardi is rather fat,
with a brilliant complexion and well-kohled eyes
and eyebrows ; she has good manners, and received me very cordially in a room opening on to a
terrace, with a beautiful view eastward of some
tells at the edge of the Hamad. She sat surrounded
by dependants and relations, among whom were
Huseyn's mother and her own. The former was
suffering from cough and loss of voice, and another
member of the family complained of a rheumatic
arm ; both wanted me to advise them as to treatment. The ladies would not uncover their faces
until Assad, the Sheykh's secretary, who accompanied

me, had retired. Wardi's concealment of her features
was, however, a mere make-believe, only a corner of
her head veil pulled half across her face. She
talked a great deal about her children of the former
marriage, Mustafa a son of eighteen, who is chief
of a neighbouring village, and a daughter of perhaps
twelve who was present. This young girl seemed
particularly intelligent and had received some
education; enough to read out a phrase from my
Arabic exercise book, and to repeat the first chapter
of the Koran. The pleasure of my visit was somewhat marred by the quantity of sweetmeats and tea
and coffee served; with the tea and coffee I got on very
well, as the cups were of the usual small size, but
the sugar-plums were of so massive a kind that it
was impossible to swallow them. The two small
children fortunately came to my rescue; and by
their zeal in devouring everything I handed to
them, took off their mother's attention from my
shortcomings. At parting Wardi gave me a bunch
of feathers pulled then and there out of an ostrich
skin hanging up against the wall; the skin, she
said, had been brought to her some months before,
from somewhere in the south.

The Druses of the Hauran say that they are
Arabs who came here with the immediate successors
of the prophet from the south; that the Jebel was
at that time inhabited by Rûmi (Greeks), whose
descendants still live here and are Christians. We
saw one of them in Huseyn's house to-day, appa-

rently on excellent terms with the other visitors. He was dressed like an Arab, and was undistinguishable from the ordinary felláhín Arabs one sees in the desert towns. The Druse women, except those of Huseyn's family, go about unveiled. They are particularly well-mannered and civil, with clean fresh complexions and bright coloured cheeks, and always say "Salam aleykum" to travellers. They all kohl their eyes carefully and broadly.

There has of course been much discussion about our further journey. It is rather aggravating to think that a whole week has passed since we left Damascus, and yet we are not, as the crow flies, more than eighty miles on our way. Still there seems a chance now of our really getting forward, for Huseyn promises to send some men with us to Kâf, an oasis in the Wady Sirhán, with which there is occasional communication on this side of the Hauran, as there are salt beds to which the villagers send camels to fetch salt. They say it is about five days' journey from here. The principal difficulty is that there are several Bedouin tribes on the road, and nobody knows which. The Sirdíeh are friends of Huseyn's, and so are the Kreysheh, but there are others whom he does not know, Sherarât Sirhán and Howeysin, the last mere thieves "worse than the Sleb." Any or all of these may be met with, though it is very possible we may meet nobody. Huseyn has sent a man on horseback to Ezrak, the first stage on our way, where there are wells and an old castle, to find out who is there. The Kreysheh we have letters to, from Mohammed Dukhi, and if we can find them there will be no more difficulty, as they are strong enough to give us protection from the rest. At any rate we go on to-morrow. We are anxious to get away to the desert, for life is very fatiguing in these towns ; there are so many people to be civil to, and the children make such a noise. They have been playing hockey all day long just outside our tent, tiresome little wretches. Wilfrid went out for an hour this afternoon, and got some grouse, of which there are immense flocks all about the fields, while I made a picture of the town from behind a wall.

We have at last got a man to go with us as servant, who looks promising. He is a Shammari from Jebel Shammar who, for some reason or other, has left his own tribe (probably for some crime against Bedouin law), and has been settled for the last few years at Salkhad, where he has married a Druse woman. There is some mystery about his profession and way of life, but he has an attractive face, and in spite of very poor clothes a certain air of distinction. We both like him, and Huseyn seems to know something about him. Besides, he has made the whole journey from Nejd already, and has been backwards and forwards between Salkhad and Jôf more than once. He wants now, he says, to go back to his own country. Mohammed has also discovered a red-headed man, a native of Sokhne and as such almost a fellow countryman, who will come as camel driver under Abdallah ; so that our complement of hands is made up to its original number, eight. To-morrow we may hope to sleep in the desert.

Note.—Alas, since this was written, our friends at Melakh have experienced sad reverses. In September, 1879, Midhat Pasha, to signalize his assumption of office at Damascus, and support that reputation of energy which Europe has given him, sent an armed force to coerce the independent Druses. At first these, fighting for their liberty, were successful. They met and defeated the Turkish troops advancing through the Leja, and the expedition returned with a loss of 400 men. A month later, however, Midhat retrieved his fortunes. He bribed or persuaded Mohammed Dukhi to overrun the Eastern Hauran with his Bedouins, and while these were blockading the towns, marched a second column of regular troops through the mountains, and so gained possession of Salkhad, Melakh, and the rest, reducing all to submission. An Ottoman Governor now replaces the native Sheykhs, and the blessings of the Sultan's rule have been extended to every village of the Hauran.

RUN TO EARTH.

CHAPTER IV.

"For all is rocks at random thrown,
 Black walls of crag, black banks of stone."
                                    SCOTT.

We start in earnest—The Harra—A Theory of Mirage—Camp of the
Beni Sokkhr—Wady er Rajel—A Christmas Dinner in the
Desert—Sand storm—We reach Kâf.

December 22.—A white frost, and off at half-
past seven. Huseyn has sent two men with us,
Assad, his head man, and another. We have also
letters from him for Ali el-Kreysheh, and the
Sheykh of Kâf.

Mohammed as we rode away was much elated
at the success of this visit, and related to me the
pretty things Huseyn had said about us. Huseyn
had seen other franjis but none who understood the
shoghl Arab, Arab ways, as we did. They had come
with an escort to see the ruins, but we had come
to see him. "Ah," said Mohammed, "now they
are sitting drinking coffee and talking about us.
They are saying to each other that the Beg and
I are brothers, and we are travelling together, as
is right, in search of relations, and to make friends
all over the world. There is nothing so *asil* (noble)
as to travel and make friends. Once upon a time

there was an old man who had a son, but very
little other property, and when he came to die he
called his son and said to him, " O my son, I am
about to die, and I have nothing to leave behind
me for your good but advice, and my advice is
this : 'Build to yourself houses in every part of
the world.' And the son, who was a child without understanding, wondered how he was to do
this, seeing he had no money to build houses
with, and so set out on a journey in search of a
wise man who could explain to him his father's
last words. And he travelled for many years
and visited every part of the world, and made
friends in each town, and at last he found the
wise man who told him that he had already done
as his father had bidden him, " for," he said, "you
have friends everywhere, and is not your friend's
house your own ? "

We too were in high spirits, as everything now
seemed to be going right. Our course lay nearly
south on the road to Ezrak, and we passed several
ruined villages and some cultivated land. Every
now and then we put up immense packs of sand-
grouse, which were busy feeding on the seeds of the
zueyti, a kind of thistle which grows abundantly on
the fallows. Wilfrid got eight of them at a shot,
and at one of the villages we bought ten partridges
of a man who had been out with a matchlock, so
that we are well supplied with meat for a couple of
days. Assad has got a very handsome greyhound

with him, of the long-haired breed, which has a
wonderful nose for game. His master declares he
sees the birds, for the Arabs do not seem to understand the theory of scent.

After two hours' fair travelling, we stopped at a
village called Metém, where Assad had friends, and
where we were obliged to go through the ceremony
of drinking coffee, losing much time thereby.
Then a new discussion arose as to our road,
somebody having just come in from Ezrak, who
announced that the Sirhan were camped there, and
the Sirhan we knew were friendly with Huseyn el-
Atrash. Assad, and Salman his companion, refused
in consequence to go that way, and were for
stopping the night at Metém to think over it ; but
this we would not listen to. We were determined
to go somewhere, and if not to Ezrak then by some
other route to Kâf. Somebody suggested El
Kreysheh, who was said to be in the Wady er-Rajel,
and others the Sirdíeh, who were camped a day's
journey towards the east. It was difficult to
decide ; but at the well of the village while we
were watering our animals, we met a man and his
wife, who told us they knew where to find the
Sirdíeh, and were themselves on their way to join
them. So this decided us, and we determined on
the Sirdíeh. The Sirdíeh are friends of Huseyn's,
and our Druse guides made no objection to going
that way ; Awwad the Shammari declared also that
it was all right. Accordingly we left the Ezrak road,

and striking off to the east, soon found ourselves out
of the range of cultivation. Metém is to be the last
village we shall see, and the desert is now before us
all the way to Nejd.

We are encamped at the edge of a plateau, from
which there is an immense prospect of hill and
plain, and Wilfrid has been very busy making out
a rough chart of the different landmarks, as they
may be useful to-morrow if we should happen to
miss our way. The man and woman we met at the
well are with us, and know the different points by
name. Awwad too, declares he knows every part of
the desert between this and Kâf, and he has pointed
out a tell, south-east by south, beyond which
it lies. The Druses, like townsmen, are already
nervous at the sight of the desert, and angry with
us for camping away from villages and tents. Our
camp is well concealed in an old volcanic crater,
where also we are sheltered from the wind, which is
very cold. There is a spring just below called Ain
el-Ghiaour (the infidel's spring); according to the
Druses, the scene of a great battle fought by the
Arabs of the first invasion, in which they routed the
Christians. At that time all the country we have
been passing through, and perhaps the broken
ground in front of us, was well inhabited ; and
there is a tell with a ruined convent on it not far
off to the north-west, still known as Ed Deyr.
There is capital pasture here, *rotha*, which the
camels have been making the most of. We too

have dined, and now all is quiet, and the sky is full
of stars. We have been sitting on the edge of the
crater talking over plans for to-morrow. The
Sirdíeh, it now appears, are at a *khabra* or pool,
called Shubboitia, which we could see before the
sun set like a yellow line far away to the north-
east, too far out of our road for us to go there.
Awwad is in favour of going straight to Kâf, and
taking our chance of what Arabs we may meet. El
Kreysheh is somewhere in front of us, and so they
say is Ibn Majil, the Akíd of the Roala, whom we
met last year. At any rate, we must take a good
supply of water with us, and go forward at the first
streak of dawn.

December 23.—As soon as it was light we
climbed up to the top of the crater and looked
over the plain. It was a wonderful sight with
its broken tells and strange chaotic wadys, all
black with volcanic boulders, looking blacker still
against the yellow morning sky. There is always
something mysterious about a great plain, and
especially such a plain as this, where Europeans,
one may say, have never been, and which even the
people of the Hauran know little of. Besides, it
seems to have had a history if only in the days of
Og, king of Basan. But it was not to look at the
view or for any romantic reason that we had come
there ; only to examine the country before us and
see if we could discover traces of Arab encampments. After looking carefully all round we at

last made out a thin column of smoke to the north-east, ten or twelve miles away, and another nearly due east. The first must be the Sirdíeh, the second perhaps the Kreysheh. Satisfied with this we returned to our party, who were just setting the camels in motion, and as the sun rose we began our march.

We have been stumbling about all day among the boulders of the Harra, following little tracks just wide enough for the camels to get along, and making a great circuit in order to find ourselves at last barely twelve miles from where we began. At first we kept company with our new acquaintances, the people going to the Sirdíeh, but when we had arrived at the foot of the hills we found them turning away to the north, and so wished them good-bye, much to the Druses' disgust, who did not at all relish our wild-goose chase of the Kreysheh, and still less the idea of going straight to Káf. They followed, however, when they found that we would listen to no reason, and I must say good-humouredly. One great charm of the Arab character is that it bears no malice, even about trifles. Sulkiness is very rare with them. They did not pretend to know much of the country, so we made Awwad lead the way. Going straight was out of the question, for the Harra is an impracticable country, not only for camels but for horses, on account of the boulders, except just where the paths lead. We had a bleak desolate ride, for a cold wind had sprung up in our faces with a decided

touch of winter. This country must be a furnace,
however, in summer with its polished black stones.
I noticed that these were very regularly weathered ;
one side, that towards the north, being grey with
a sort of lichen, so that as we rode past they
seemed to change colour continually. There was
very little sign of life in this region, only a few
small birds, and no trace of inhabitants or of any
recent passers by. The tracks followed generally
the beds of wadys, and wandered on without any
particular aim or direction. They looked like the
paths made by sheep or camels, only that the
stones were so big it seemed impossible that the
mere passage of animals could have ever made them.
On the whole I think they must be artificial, made
by shepherds in very ancient times for their flocks.
In the spring, we are told, the whole of this Harra is
excellent grazing ground. It is a curious thing that
every here and there in the hollows there is a space
free from stones where water lies after rain, forming
a pool. Why are there no stones there ? The soil
is a dry clay with a highly glazed surface cracked
into very regular squares, so glazed indeed that even
close by it has the appearance of water, reflecting
the light of the sky. This, no doubt, is the way
some of the curious mirage effects are produced in
the desert, for it is to be noticed that the most
perfect delusions are found just in places where one
would naturally expect to find water—that is, where
water has been.

At half-past twelve, we came suddenly on a
level bit of open ground, which we took at first for
one of these khabras, but found it to be part of a
long wady running north and south, with a very
distinct watercourse in the middle, with tamarisk
bushes, and patches of fresh grass, showing that
water had run down it not long ago. Both Awwad
and the Druses recognised this as the Wady-er-
Rajel, where the Kreysheh were reported to be
encamped, and the only question was, whether to
turn up or down it. While we were debating,
however, a flock of sheep was sighted, and presently
a boy, who told us he was a Sirdíeh, but that
the Kreysheh were only a couple of hours further
down the valley. This just suited, as it was exactly
in the right direction for us, and we are now at Ali
el-Kreysheh's camp, and being hospitably entertained by a young relation in the Sheykh's absence.
Ali is away at Mezárib with fifty horsemen, to
escort the Jerdeh on their way to Maan.

We have had some singing to-night, and playing
of the rebab. Among the songs I was pleased to
recognise an old Shammar ballad about Abdul
Kerim and the man who had no mare.

December 24.—The Kreysheh, at whose camp
we now are, belong to the Beni Sokkhr, a large, but
not very warlike tribe, which occupies the whole
of the district from the pilgrim road eastwards to
the extreme edge of the Harra, throughout a
wilderness of stones. To this they are said to owe

their name of Beni Sokkhr, children of the rocks;
and they assure us that they have lived in the
Harra "from all time." They do not come from
Nejd, they say, like the Ánazeh, but are Shimali or
Northern Arabs. We were told the names of ten
divisions into which the Beni Sokkhr have ramified,
each owning a separate Sheykh, though nominally
subject to Fendi el-Faïz, or rather his son Sóttan,
for Fendi is old and has given up practical
authority. These divisions are probably nothing
more than groups of the tribe, as their names are
those of their Sheykhs, the principal being Sóttan,
and next to him El Kreysheh, and next again Ed
Dreybi ibn Zebbed. The Kreysheh have camels as
well as sheep, and seem pretty well off; but they
have no great number of mares, and those not
of the best type. They keep hawks and greyhounds.

They have given us news of the Roala. Ibn Majil,
whom we met last year at Sotamm Ibn Shaalan's,
and who took our side in the negociations for peace
with the Sebaa, has now separated from Sotamm,
and is somewhere down by Jôf, so perhaps we may
meet him; while Sotamm has just marched north
again to attack the Welled Ali. The Kreysheh are
friends with Ibn Majil, but at war with Sotamm,
another curious instance of the inconsistencies of
Bedouin politics. These are, indeed, as changing
as the clouds in the sky, and transform themselves
so rapidly, that in Desert history, if it were written,

ten years would comprise as much incident as a
century in Europe.

While negotiations were going on about arrangements for our further progress, I went to call on
Ali el-Kreysheh's wives. There are two of them,
Hazna and Fassal; but I only saw the latter,
who had the women's tent to herself with her
attendants and three children, two little boys and a
girl, remarkably dirty, and (what is rare among
Bedouins) suffering from sore eyes. Fassal was
plain and uninteresting but sensible, and I daresay
has the advantage over Hazna, who, poor thing, is
childless. She told me she was from a section of
the tribe further north, and took an interest in
Damascus, asking about the new Valy as well as
about Mohammed ibn Smeyr, who is the great
name in these parts. She seemed much pleased
with the box of sugar-plums I gave her, and
when I went away followed me as far as the
end of the tent ropes invoking blessings on my
head.

I found our own tents down and everything
ready for a start; for an arrangement had been
come to with the young man representing our host,
that we were to have a *zellem* (person) to go with
us as far as Kâf for the sum of ten mejidies (forty
shillings). Assad and Salman were just saying
good-bye, for they had to go back to Melakh. They
were made very happy with a Turkish pound apiece,
and Assad has left us his greyhound, the black and

tan dog, who whined piteously when his master went
away. I like the dog for this.

As we left the Kreysheh camp a bitter wind
sprang up from the west-south-west, and continued
all day long, chilling us, in spite of all the furs and
cloaks we could put on, to the bone. Our course
lay nearly across it south-south-east. We are out
of the hills now in a nearly level plain still covered
with the black stones. The only variety during
the day was when we came to a large khabra
(Khabra-el-Gurrthi), a dreary flat of dried up clay
and sand which we took two hours to cross, though
we went at the camels' best pace. The wind drove
great clouds of sand across it, making it one of the
dreariest places I ever saw. We were all too cold
for much talking, and sat huddled up on our delúls
with our backs to the wind, and our heads wrapped
up in our cloaks. We met no one all day long,
except one string of a dozen camels driven by two
very wild-looking Arabs who told us they were
Sherarât, and nothing living except a hare which
got up among the stones, and which the dogs
coursed for some hundreds of yards, over ground
which would have broken every bone of an English
greyhound, apparently without hurting themselves.
About two o'clock we came, to our great delight,
upon the Wady er-Rajel again, an angle of whose
course we had been cutting off. Here we found
beautiful soft ground and grass and pools of water,
for this wady had running water in it last month,

and is not quite drunk up yet. The pasture was too good to be passed, so here we remain for the night. Just as we were unloading, a little troop of gazelles looked over the edge of the wady, perhaps come for water, and Mohammed set off in pursuit with a Winchester rifle. We heard him fire all the twelve shots one after the other, but he came back empty-handed. Our tent is set under the lee of a rough wall of loose stones, such as are set up by the shepherds as a shelter for their flocks. The wind still blows tempestuously, and it is cold as a Christmas Eve need be. But Hanna has made us a capital curry, which with soup and burghul and a plum-pudding from a tin, makes not a bad dinner, while Abdallah has distinguished himself baking bread, and Awwad roasting coffee.

Wednesday, December 25.—Christmas Day. We are out of the Harra at last, and on open ground. That black wilderness had become like a nightmare with its horrible boulders and little tortuous paths, which prevented the camels from doing more than about two miles an hour. Now we are able to push on at three, or three and a quarter.

After floundering down the wady for half an hour, we came to some splendid pools in a narrow cleft of rock, where we stopped to take in water. We have been very fortunate in such a season as this to find the Wady er-Rajel full. The rain which filled it must have been some isolated water-spout on the eastern slope of Jebel Hauran, for not

a drop fell anywhere else ; and there is no autumn
grass except just along its edge.   It is rapidly drying, or rather being drunk up, and the little vegetation is very closely eaten down.   In the smaller
pools there is a very distinct flavour of sheep and
camels in the water ; but at the pools we came to
this morning it is still pure.   The Kreysheh have
been all up this valley, eating and drinking their
way, and leaving not a blade they could help behind them, and we have come upon numerous
tracks of their cattle.   Every here and there we
have passed the traces of their camps, stones set in
line on three sides of a square ; one we saw had
been only just deserted, and we put up a number
of vultures and ravens from the fresh carcase of a
camel lying by it.   There crossed it also the footprint of a horse, which brought on the usual talk
of ghazús and marauders, in which our people
delight.   They, however, have settled it among
them to their satisfaction, that such accidents as
meeting robbers or people of a hostile tribe are
" min Allah " (from God), to be classed with the
rain and fine weather, and sickness and good health,
all which things the Bedouins consider fortuitous.

Having filled our goat skins, we left the Wady er-
Rajel for good, and are to come across no more
water now till we get to Kâf.   The valley takes a
turn here to the west before it reaches the Wady
Sirhán, and would therefore be out of our road.
We have been crossing some rolling downs covered

with light flinty gravel, a delightful change from
the Harra, and have had a gallop or two after
the gazelles, which now and then came in sight.
We thought too of our Christmas dinner, and
how glad we should be to get some addition to the
rice, which was all we had ; but neither greyhounds
nor mares were in good enough condition to run
down their quarry. Once we made a rather
successful stalk, and a charge in among a small
herd, but the dogs could not get hold of anything,
and, though several shots were fired, nothing came
to bag. Then we had a long gallop after Sayad,
the black and tan greyhound, who went on after the
gazelles for a good two miles, so that we were afraid
of losing him ; and then another long gallop to get
back to our camels. This time, we had been three
quarters of an hour away from them, and we found
our people all much alarmed, Abdallah rather angry
at our going so far, for Mohammed was with us.
He was perfectly in the right, and we were to
blame, for we are on a serious journey not a
sporting tour ; and to say nothing of danger from
enemies, there is always a certain risk of missing one another in a country like this where camels
leave no track behind them. A turn to right or
left out of the direct line and a fold in the ground,
and they are lost. So we apologised, and promised
to do so again no more. We were, however, in a
most unexpected manner provided with dinner ; for
while we were still talking, behold a grazing camel

all alone on the plain, not a mile away ; when with a general shout of " a prize," the whole party on horseback and on foot rushed in pursuit. We were naturally the first up, and drove the animal at a canter to the others. The camel was a young one of last spring, in good condition, and at the sight tears rushed into Hanna's eyes—tears of hunger, not of pity. I am afraid indeed that none of the party had much thought of pity, and the scene caused me mixed feelings of compassion for the poor victim, and disgust at ourselves who were waiting to prey upon it. No question was raised as to ownership ; camels found astray in desert places were by acclamation declared the property of the first comer. We were in fact a ghazú, and this was our lawful prize. So the poor little camel was driven on before us.

Dinner is thus secured, and I must see what else can be arranged in honour of the occasion.

December 26.—Mohammed, Abdallah, Awwad, the two Ibrahims and Hanna, all of them, spent the evening in feasting and ate up the whole of the camel except the short ribs, which were set before us, and the shoulders which were kept for to-day. They divided among them the labour of killing, skinning and quartering, and cooking it, for all were equally ready to lend a hand to the work. People talk sometimes of camel meat, as if it were something not only unpalatable, but offensive. But it is in reality very good ; when young it resembles mutton, even when old it is only tough, and never

has any unpleasant taste as far as my experience
goes; indeed if served up without the bones it
could hardly be distinguished from mutton.

The servants having thus feasted were all soon
sound asleep, and even when suddenly, between
two and three in the morning, the wind rose with
a deafening noise, they did not wake, not till their
tent blew down upon them as ours did upon us.
We were awake and might have kept our tent
standing had we not been too lazy to get up and
drive in the pegs. It was too late when the tent
had fallen on us to do anything but lie as well as
we could beneath the ruins and wait for daylight.
Fortunately the main pegs had not drawn, and the
sand, for this hurricane was a sand storm, soon
covered over the edges of the fallen tent, and no
further damage was done. In the morning, the
servants proposed staying where we were; but we
would not hear of this, as we had water for only
two days, and it would have been folly to dawdle,
so after rubbing the sand out of or rather into our
eyes, we set to work packing and loading. The
wind continued violent and bitterly cold, and
carried a great deal of sand with it. It came from
the west-south-west. We had camped under shelter
at a small tell close to the Tell Guteyfi, which proved
to be the same as one pointed out to us by Awwad
from Ain el-Giaour, and once beyond it, we found
ourselves on a perfectly open bit of plain, exposed
to the full fury of the gale, now more violent than

ever. Sand storms are evidently common here, for
the Tell Guteyfi, which is of black volcanic boulders
like the Harra, is half smothered in sand. We saw
it looming near us in the thick air, and soon after
were almost hidden from each other in the increas-
ing darkness. The sun shone feebly at intervals
through the driving sand, but it was all we could
do to keep the caravan together, and not lose sight
of each other. At one moment we had all to stop
and turn tail to the wind, covering our eyes and
heads with our cloaks, waiting till the burst was
over. Nothing could have faced it. Still we
were far from having any idea of danger, for
there really is none in these storms, and had
plenty of time to notice how very picturesque the
situation was, the camels driven along at speed, all
huddled together for protection, with their long
necks stretched out, and heads low, tags and ropes
flying, and the men's cloaks streaming in the wind,
all seen through the yellow haze of sand which
made them look as though walking in the air. The
beasts looked gigantic yet helpless, like antediluvian
creatures overwhelmed in a flood. Still, as I said,
there was no danger, for the wind was steady in its
direction, and our course was directly across it—
that we knew—and by patiently struggling on, we
managed to get over a deal of ground. Suddenly
the sandy plain over which we were travelling,
seemed to sink away in front of us, and at the
bottom of a steep dip we could see clumps of

tamarisk looming through the storm. We knew that a refuge was at hand.

Here then we are comfortably housed under one of these bushes, where there is a delightful lull. The soil is all deep sand, white as snow, and the tent which we have rigged up is already half buried in it, so that we might imagine ourselves at home snowed up on Boxing Day. We have made a fire of tarfa sticks inside the tent, and have been enjoying Hanna's delicious coffee. Where is one ever so much at home as in one's own tent? Awwad surprised us very much to-day by objecting, when we proposed to pitch the tent, that it would be impossible to do so in the sand. If Mohammed or any of the townspeople had done so it would have been natural, but Awwad is a Bedouin born, and must have pitched camp hundreds of times in the Nefúd. Yet he had never heard of burying a tent peg.

One misfortune has happened in the storm. The old rogue of a camel we bought at Mezárib, who has been trying all along to get back to his family, has given us the slip. Taking advantage of the darkness, and knowing that the wind would obliterate his track at once, he decamped as soon as unloaded, and is gone. Mohammed and Awwad, each on a delúl, are scouring the country, but without a chance of finding him ; for at best they can only see things a hundred yards off, and he was not missed for the first half hour. Mohammed has vowed to kill a lamb, but I fear that will do no good.

December 27.—We have arrived at Kâf after a long march, twenty-seven or twenty-eight miles. Course about south-east.

In the night a little rain fell, and the wind moderated. At eight o'clock we started, crossing a wide plain of coarse sand interspersed with low sandstone tells. At noon we came upon a well-marked track, the road of the salt caravans between Bozra and Kâf, which, after crossing a rather high ridge, brought us to a very curious valley; an offshoot, we were told, of the Wady Sirhán. The geological formation of this is singular; the crest of the ridge on either side the valley is of black rock with detached stones of the same—then yellow sandstone, then another black layer, then pure sand, then sand with isolated black stones, then a calcareous deposit, and at the bottom chalk. The actual bed of the wady is a fine white sand sprinkled over with tamarisk and guttub bushes. As we were crossing this our dogs started a jerboa, and, little creature though it is, it gave them much trouble to catch it. Its hops were prodigious, and from side to side and backwards and forwards, so that the dogs always ran over it, and snatching, always missed it; till at last, as if by accident, it jumped into Shiekhah's mouth. Abdallah and the rest were very anxious to eat it, but it was so mauled as to be beyond cooking. At three o'clock we crested another ridge, and from it suddenly came in sight of the great Wady Sirhán, the object of so many of our conjectures. It seems, however, to be no wady, but the bed of an ancient sea. A little black dot on the edge of a *subbka* or salt lake, now dry, and just under a tall black tell, marked the oasis of Kâf, an infinitesimal village of sixteen houses, and a palm garden of about an acre.

I have had the misfortune to sprain my knee, an awkward accident, and very annoying in the middle of a journey. My delúl, always a fidgety animal, gave a bolt just as I was leaning over to arrange something on the off side of the *shedâd*, or saddle, and pitched me off. The pain is indescribable, and I fear I shall be helplessly lame for some time to come. But here we are at Kâf.

KAF.

CHAPTER V.

"Rafi ran after her with his sword drawn, and was just about to strike
off her head, when she cried 'quarter.'"—ABULFEDA.

Kâf and Itheri—More relations—The Wady Sirhán—Locust
hunting—Hanna sits down to die—Tales of robbery and violence—We are surprised by a ghazú and made prisoners—
Sherarât statistics—Jôf.

December 28.—Kâf is a pretty little village,
with a character of its own, quite distinct from anything one sees in Syria. All is in miniature, the
sixteen little square houses, the little battlemented
towers and battlemented walls seven feet high—
seventy or eighty palm trees in a garden watered
from wells, and some trees I took at first for
cypresses, but which turned out to be a very
delicate kind of tamarisk.* Though so small a
place, Kâf has a singularly flourishing look, all is
neat there and in good repair, not a battlement
broken or a door off its hinges, as would certainly
have been the case in Syria. There are also a good
many young palms planted in among the older ones,
and young fig trees and vines, things hardly ever
found in the North. The people are nice looking

* The *Ithel*, a tree grown in every villa e of Central Arabia, but
not, as far as I know, found there wild.

and well behaved, though at first they startled us a
little by going about all of them with swords in
their hands. These they hold either sloped over
their shoulders or grasped in both hands by the
scabbard, much as one sees in the old stone figures
of mediæval martyrs, or in the effigies of crusaders.
Abdallah el-Kamis, Sheykh of the village, to whom
we had letters from Huseyn, received us with great
politeness ; and a room in his house was swept out
for our use. Like all the other rooms, it opened
on to the court-yard, in the middle of which was
tethered a two-year-old colt. Our room had been a
storing place for wood, and was without furniture
of any sort, but we were delighted to find also
without inhabitants. The architecture here is very
simple, plain mud walls with no windows or openings of any kind except a few square holes near the
roof. The roof was of *ithel* beams with cross rafters
of palm, thatched in with palm branches. The
principal room is called the kahwah or coffee room ;
and in it there is a square hearth at the side or in
the middle for coffee-making. There is no chimney,
and the smoke escapes as it can ; but this is not so
uncomfortable as it sounds, for the wood burnt here
burns with a beautiful bright flame, giving out a
maximum of heat to a minimum of smoke. It is
the *ratha* or *ghada.** People sit round the hearth
while coffee is being made, a solemn process occupying nearly half an hour.

* A kind of tamarisk.

As soon as we arrived, a trencher of dates was
brought, dates of the last year's crop, all sticky and
mashed up, but good; and later in the evening, we
had a more regular dinner of burghul and boiled
fowls. We are much struck with the politeness of
everybody. Abdallah, our host, asked us at least
twenty times after our health before he would go on
to anything else ; and it was not easy to find appropriate compliments in return. Everything of course is
very poor and very simple, but one cannot help
feeling that one is among civilized people. They
have been making a great fuss with Mohammed, who
is treated as a sheykh. Tudmur is well known by
name, and at this distance is considered an important
town. Much surprise was expressed at finding a
man of his rank in the semi-menial position Mohammed holds with us, and he was put to some
polite cross-questioning in the evening as to the
motive of his journey. No Franjis have ever been
seen at Kâf before, so the people say ; and they do
not understand the respect in which Europeans are
held elsewhere. Mohammed, however, has explained
his "brotherhood with the Beg," and protested that
his journey is one of honour, not of profit; so that
we are treated with as much courtesy as if we were
Arabs born. Awwad the Shammar has been of
great use to us, as he is well known here, and he
serves as an introduction.

Kâf is quite independent of the Sultan, though it
has twice been sacked by Turkish soldiers, once

under Ibrahim Pasha in 1834, and again only a few
years ago, when the Government of Damascus sent
a military expedition down the Wady Sirhán. We
were shown the ruins of a castle, Kasr es-Saïd, on a
hill above the town which the former destroyed, and
we heard much lamentation over the proceedings of
the latter. The inhabitants of Kâf acknowledge
themselves subjects of Ibn Rashid, the Jebel Shammar
chief, some of whose people were here only a few
days since, taking the annual tribute, a very small
sum, twenty mejidies (£4), which they are glad to
pay in return for his protection. They are very
enthusiastic about "the Emir," as they call him,
and certainly have no reason to wish for annexation
to Syria. The little town of Kâf and its neighbour
Itheri, where we now are, have commercially more
connection with the north than with the south, for
their principal wealth, such as it is, arises from the
salt trade with Bozra. Abdallah el-Kamis seems to
be well off, for he possesses several slaves, and has
more than one wife. But the colt I have mentioned
is his only four-footed possession ; he would have
come with us, he said, if he had owned a delûl. I
noticed a few camels and donkeys and goats about
the village.

Makbul, the Kreysheh, has gone back, and we
now want to find a Sherâri to take us on to Jôf.
We have come on to Itheri, Kâf's twin oasis, two
and a half hours east of it, also in the Wady
Sirhán. This is not marked on many of the modern

maps, though Chesney has it incorrectly placed
on his. We find by the barometer that they are
both on the same level, so that our conjecture seems
confirmed, about the Wady Sirhán having no slope.
The Wady Sirhán is a curious chaotic depression,
probably the bed of some ancient sea like the Dead
Sea, and is here about twelve miles broad if we
can judge by the hills we see beyond it, and which
are no doubt the opposite cliffs of the basin. There
are numerous wells both here and at Kâf, wide and
shallow, for the water is only eight feet below the
surface of the ground. From these the palm gardens
are irrigated. There are wells too outside, all lying
low and at the same level. The water is drinkable,
by no means excellent. We crossed a large salt lake,
now dry, where the salt is gathered for the caravans.

On our road Mohammed entertained us with tales
of his birth and ancestry. The people of Kâf have
heard of the Ibn Arûks, and have told Mohammed
that he will find relations in many parts of Arabia
besides Jôf. They say there is somebody at
Bereydeh, and a certain Ibn Homeydi, whom
Mohammed has heard of as a cousin. Then here at
Itheri, the Sheykh's wife is a member of the Jôf
family. Everything in fact seems going just as we
expected it.

Itheri is a still smaller place than Kâf, but it
boasts of an ancient building and miniature castle
inside the walls, something after the fashion of the
Hauran houses. This, instead of mud, the common

Arab material, is built of black stones, well squared
and regularly placed. On the lintel of the doorway
there is or rather has been, an inscription in some
ancient character, perhaps Himyaritic, which we
would have copied had it been legible, but the
weather has almost effaced it.* Here we are being
entertained by Jeruan, an untidy half-witted young
man, with long hair in plaits and a face like a Scotch
terrier, who is the son of Merzuga, Mohammed's
cousin, and consequently a cousin himself. Though
nothing much to be proud of as a relation, we find
him an attentive host. His mother is an intelligent
and well-bred woman, and it seems strange that
she should have so inferior a son. Her other three
sons, for Jeruan is the eldest of four, have their
wits like other people, but they are kept in the
background. Merzuga came to see me just now
with a large dish of dates in her hand, and stopped
to talk. Her face is still attractive, and she must
have once been extremely beautiful. I notice that
she wears a number of silver rings on her fingers
like wedding rings.

Merzuga tells us we shall find plenty of Ibn Arûk
relations at Jôf. She herself left it young and talks
of it as an earthly paradise from which she has been
torn to live in this wretched little oasis. Itheri is
indeed a forlorn place, all except Jeruan's palm
garden. After a walk in the palm garden, in which

* We were told that this inscription related to hidden treasure,
a common fancy among the Arabs who cannot read.

my lameness prevented me from joining, we all sat
down to a very good dinner of lamb and sopped
bread—the bread tasted like excellent pastry—
served us by Jeruan in person, standing according
to Arab fashion when guests are eating. His
mother looks well after him, and tells him what to
do, and it is evident, though he has the sense to say
very little, that he is looked upon as not quite
" accountable " in his family. Wilfrid describes
the walk in the garden as rather amusing, Mohammed and Abdallah making long speeches of
compliments about all they saw, and telling Jeruan's
head man extraordinary stories of the grandeur and
wealth of Tudmur. Jeruan's garden, the only one
at Itheri, contains four hundred palm trees, many
of them newly planted, and none more than twenty-
five years old. Amongst them was a young tree of
the *héllua* variety, the sweet date of Jôf, imported
from thence, and considered here a great rarity. At
this there was a chorus of admiration. The ithel
trees were also much admired. They are grown for
timber, and spring from the stub when cut down,
a six years' growth being already twenty feet
high.

Two men have arrived from Jôf with the welcome
news that all is well between this and Jôf ; that is,
there are no Arabs yet in the Wady Sirhán ; welcome because we have no introductions, and a
meeting might be disagreeable. The season is so
late and the pasture so bad, that the Wady has

been quite deserted since last spring. There will
be no road now, or track of any kind, and as it is
at least two hundred miles to Jôf, we must have a
guide to shew us the wells. Such a one we have
found in a funny looking little Bedouin, a Sherári,
who happens to be here and who will go with us for
ten mejidies.

December 29.—There was a bitter east wind
blowing when we started this morning, and I observed a peewit, like a land bird at sea, flying hither
and thither under the lea of the palm trees, looking
hopeless and worn out with its long voyage. Poor
thing, it will die here, for there is nothing such
a bird can eat anywhere for hundreds of miles. It
must have been blown out of its reckoning, perhaps
from the Euphrates.

Our course to-day lay along the edge of the Wady,
sometimes crossing stony promontories from the
upper plain, sometimes sandy inlets from the Wady.
The heights of these were always pretty much the
same, 2250 feet above and 1850 below—so these
may be taken as the respective heights of the Hamád
and of the Wady Sirhán. There are besides, here
and there, isolated tells, three hundred to four hundred
feet higher than either. Rough broken ground all
day, principally of sand with slaty grit sprinkled
over it, the vegetation very scanty on the high
ground, but richer in the hollows. In one small
winding ravine leading into the Wady, we found
ghada trees, but otherwise nothing bigger than

shrubs. There Awwad told us that two years ago
he was robbed and stripped by a ghazú from the
Hauran. He had lost six camels and all he possessed. The Haurani were eight in number, his own
party six. I asked him how it was the robbers got
the best of it. He said it was " min Allah" (from
God). The Wady Sirhán seems to be a favourite
place for robbers, and Awwad takes the occur-
rence as a matter of course. I asked him why
he had left his tribe, the Shammar, and come to
live so far north as Salkhad. He said it was
"*nasib,*" a thing fated; that he had married a
Salkhad wife, and she would not go away from
her people. I asked him how he earned his living,
and he laughed. "I have got half a mare," he
said, "and a delúl, and I make ghazús. There
are nine of us Shammar in the Hauran, and we
go out together towards Zerka, or to the western
Leja and take cattle by night." He then showed us
some frightful scars of wounds, which he had got on
these occasions, and made Wilfrid feel a bullet which
was still sticking in his side. He is a curious
creature, but we like him, and, robber or no robber,
he has quite the air of a gentleman. He is besides
an agreeable companion, sings very well, recites
ballads, and is a great favourite everywhere. At
Kâf and Itheri he was hugged and kissed by the
men, old and young, and welcomed by the women
in every house.

We were nearly frozen all the morning, the wind

piercing through our fur cloaks. At half-past twelve, after four hours' marching, we came to some wells called Kurághir, six of them in a bare hollow, with camel tracks leading from every point of the compass towards them. It is clear that at some time of the year the Wady is inhabited; Awwad says by the Roala in winter, but this year there is nobody. The water, like that of Kâf and Itheri, is slightly brackish. Near Kurághir we saw some gazelles and coursed them vainly. It is vexatious, for I have forgotten to bring meat, and unless we can catch or shoot something, we shall have none till we get to Jôf. I ought to have thought of it, for, though provisions are by no means plentiful at Itheri, we could probably have bought a sheep and driven it on with us. The pain of my lameness distracted my attention—a bad excuse, but the only one. I suffer less when riding than at any other time.

We are now, since four o'clock, camped on the sand under some ghada bushes, and the wind has dropped for the moment. It seems always to blow here except for an hour about sunset and another at dawn. We are to dine on beef tea, burghul with curry sauce, and a water-melon, the last of our Hauran store.

December 30.—On the high level all the morning over ground like the Harra with volcanic stones, a fierce south-east wind in our faces, so that we could not talk or hardly think. Our course lay

towards an inhospitable looking range of hills called
El Mizmeh, and when we reached these, to the right
of them, for we travel in anything but a straight line.
Saw great numbers of red locusts which, as the sun
warmed the ground, began to fly about and were
pursued by the men and knocked down with sticks.
Enough have been secured to make a dish for dinner.
When flying, these insects look very like large May
flies, as they have the same helpless heavy flight,
drifting down the wind with hardly sufficient power
of direction to keep them clear of obstacles. Sometimes they fly right against the camels, and at others
drop heavily into the bushes where they are easily
caught. When sitting on the ground, however,
they are hard to see, and they keep a good look-out
and jump up and drift away again as you come near
them. They seem to have more sense, than power
of moving.

At two we came to more wells,—Mahiyeh—most
of them choked up with sand, but one containing a
sufficient supply of brackish water. These wells lay
among clumps of tamarisk, out of which we started
several hares which the greyhounds could not catch,
as they always dodged back to cover. Wilfrid and
I waited behind for this fruitless hunting upon which
our dinner depended, and did not join the rest of the
party for more than a mile. Before we reached
them we came upon Hanna, sitting on the ground
on his *hedûm* (quilt and abba), and Ibrahim standing over him, both shouting, " *Wah ! wah ! wah !* "

We could not conceive what had happened and could get no information from either of them, except that they were going to remain where they were. These two townspeople sitting on their beds all alone in the Wady Sirhán were so absurd a spectacle that, at the moment, we could not help laughing ; but it was not an affair for laughter, and of course it was impossible to leave them there. We insisted on an explanation. There had been a quarrel between Hanna and Abdallah, because the latter had driven on Hanna's delúl fast with the other camels, and refused to let it be made to kneel down and get up again. Abdallah and Awwab were in a great hurry to get as far from Mahiyeh as possible, because Hamdán the Sherári says it is a dangerous spot. But Hanna was angry, and in his anger he dropped his cloak ; upon which he jumped down, pulling his bed after him, and sat down on the ground. There the others left him, wailing and raving, and in this state we found him. He proposed that he and Ibrahim should be left behind to be eaten up by the hyæna whose tracks we had seen. However, Ibrahim, who had only stayed to keep him company, was quite ready to go on, and, seeing this, Hanna was not long in getting up, and, making his brother carry his bedding, he followed us. It was no good inquiring who was right or who was wrong ; we stopped the camels, and, driving back the delúl, insisted on Hanna's mounting, which after some faces he did, and the episode ended. Mohammed has been commissioned to insist with the Arabs on peace, and we have we think prevailed with Hanna to bear no malice. It is absolutely impossible for anybody to go back now without losing his life, and I trust they will all be reasonable ; it is disagreeable to think that there has been discord in our small party, separated as it is from all the rest of the world. We are camped now in a side wady where the camel pasture is good. We saw the place from a great distance, for we are becoming skilful now at guessing likely spots. Wherever you see rocky ground in lines you may be sure pasture will be found. We have seen no sign of recent habitation in the country since leaving Itheri, neither footprint of camel nor of man.

The locusts fried are fairly good to eat.

December 31.—Another long day's march, and here we are at the end of the year in one of the most desolate places in the world. It was so cold last night, that all the locusts are dead. They are lying about everywhere, and being eaten up by the little desert birds, larks, and wheatears. We have got down again into the main bed of the Wady Sirhán, which is still at the same level as before ; it is here nearly flat, and covered with great bunches of guttub and other shrubs, all very salt to the taste ; the soil crumbly and unsound, in places white with saltpetre. Awwad and the Sherári declare that there are quicksands, *hadôda* (literally,

an abyss), somewhere in the neighbourhood, in which
everything that passes over sinks and disappears,
leaving no trace—men, camels, and gazelles ; but of
such we saw nothing. Coasting the edge of the
Wady, we came suddenly on some gazelles, which
led us to higher ground, where we found a stony
wilderness of the Harra type ; and amongst the
stones we saw a hyæna trotting leisurely. We got
nothing, however ; neither him nor the gazelles, and
are still without meat. No other incident occurred
till we came to a palm tree standing by itself in
an open place ; near it, a charming little spring,
quite in among the roots of a thick clump of palm
bushes. The hole is about three feet across, and
two deep, with about a foot of water in it ; the
water rises again as fast as it is taken out, but
never overflows. There were traces of hyænas and
gazelles about, and this, I suppose, is where the
desert animals come to drink, for it is the only water
above ground we have yet seen. This spring is
called Maasreh (little by little)—a pleasant spot
where we should have liked to camp ; but it is
always dangerous to stop near water, lest people
should come. Awwad says there is some tradition
of a town or village having formerly existed here ;
but no ruins are to be seen. The water is sweet
and good, as might be perceived by the insects
which were swimming about in it. The Arabs
always judge of the wholesomeness of water in this
way. There is nothing more suspicious in the

desert than perfectly clear water, free from animal
life.

We are now camped under a low cliff, hollowed
out into caves as if by water, capital dens for
hyænas. There is a beautiful view looking back at
the Mizmeh hills. The evening is still and cold, but
we do not like to make much fire for fear of enemies.
Hamdán, our Sherári guide, an uncouth, savage
creature to look at, has been reciting a very pretty
ballad, which he tells us he made himself. It is in
stanzas of four lines with alternate rhymes, and
relates to an episode in his own family. As he
recited it the rest of the Arabs chimed in, repeating
always the last word of the line with the rhyming
syllable ; it had a good effect. The story was
simple, and told how Hamdán's mother and sister
had a quarrel, and how they brought their grievances
before Obeyd ibn Rashid at Haïl, and how the old
Sheykh settled it by putting a rope round the
daughter's neck, and bidding the mother hold the
end of it, and do so for the rest of their days.
Whereupon the daughter had kissed her mother, and
Obeyd had sent them away with presents, a delúl,
a cloak each, and a hundred measures of wheat, a
present he had continued giving them every year
till he died, and which is given still by his nephew,
Mohammed, the present ruler of Jebel Shammar.
Hamdán has also given us an interesting account of
the Haïl politics, which agrees very closely with what
we remember of Mr. Palgrave's, carrying them on to

a later date. The present Ibn Rashid is not by any
means so amiable a character as his brother Tellál ;
and Hamdán's account of his career is rather startling.
It appears that he has put to death something like a
dozen of his relations, and is more feared than loved
by the Shammar. This is very tiresome, as it may
be a reason for our not going on to Nejd after all.
But we shall hear more when we get to Jôf.

Hamdán's recitative was, as nearly as I could
write the musical part of it, like this :—

January 1, 1879.—A black frost, but still. We
have changed our course, and have been going all
day nearly due south—twenty-five miles, as near as
we can calculate it—and down the middle of the
Wady Sirhán, a level plain of sand and grit, with
here and there mounds of pure white sand covered
with ghada. Our plan is to get up and strike the
tents at the first glimpse of dawn, drink a cup
of coffee, and eat a biscuit or a bit of rusk (kâk),
and then march on till three or four in the afternoon
without stopping for an instant, eating half-a-dozen
dates and some more rusk as we go. Then immediately on stopping, and before the tents are pitched,
we light a fire and make coffee, which carries us on

till dinner is ready, about sunset. It is wonderful
how little food one can do with while travelling.
We have had no meat now for the last four days till
to-day, only beef tea, and burghul, and dates, with
sometimes fried onions, or flour mixed with curry
powder and butter, and baked into a cake. This
last is very good, and easily made. To-day, however, we are in clover, as the dogs coursed a hare, and
we dug her out. The desert hare is very little bigger
than a large rabbit, and is literally too much for one,
and not enough for two ; but Mohammed magnani-
mously foregoes his portion, and says he can wait.

Mohammed has been improving the occasion of a
dispute which arose this evening on a choice of
camp, to tell us some stories of his own adventures
in the desert ; and we have been telling him ours.
He had a younger brother, whom his mother was
very fond of, a regular town boy with " a white
face like a girl," who knew how to read and write
and knew nothing of the desert (Mohammed himself,
like his great namesake, has always been a camel
driver). Now at Tudmur they have constantly had
fights and quarrels for the Sheykhat, and on one
such occasion his brother was sent away by his
parents to Sokhne, the neighbouring village, about
thirty miles from Tudmur ; and there he stayed for
some time with a relation. At last, however, he
got tired of being away from home, and wanted to
see his mother. He started off with another boy of
his own age (about fifteen) to walk back to Tudmur.

It was in the middle of summer, and they lost their way and wandered far down into the Hamád where they died of thirst. Mohammed had gone out to look for them, and found them both dead close together.

On another occasion Mohammed himself was nearly meeting his death. He had gone alone with his camels on the road to Karieteyn, and had fallen in with a ghazú of robbers from the hills. These stripped him of everything except his shirt and a tarbush. His gun he had contrived to hide under a bush, but they left him nothing else, neither food nor water, and it was in the middle of summer. Karieteyn, the nearest place, was about forty miles off, and he was lame with a blow he had received. However, when the robbers were gone, he set out in that direction, and managed to walk on till night and the next day, till he got to a ruin called Kasr el Hayr where he fell down senseless under the shade, and lay for twenty-four hours unable to move, and suffering agonies from thirst. At last, when he had said to himself, "now I shall have to die," a party of camel men from Sokhne came by and found him lying there. At first they took him for a slave, for the sun had burnt him black, and his tongue was dried so that he could not speak. Fortunately one of the party recognised him, and then they gave him water. He still could give no account of himself, but they put him on a donkey and brought him with them to Tudmur.

Our own story was the one of our quarrel with
Abunjad and our rush from Akaba to Gaza, when
we so nearly perished of thirst.

The year would have begun prosperously, but for
a severe cold Wilfrid has caught. He has lost his
voice.

January 2.—A hard frost—water frozen in the
pail. Reached the wells of Shaybeh at half-past
eight and watered the camels—water very brackish
—level by aneroid 1950, depth to surface of water
twelve feet. Got into a sort of track, part of the
morning, but one evidently not frequented. At one
o'clock came to another well, near a curious rock
which at first we took for a castle. We have now
crossed the wady and are on its western bank.
Passed a ruined house of no great antiquity called
Abu Kasr and another well near it, and at half-past
four have encamped under some sand hills, crowned
with ghada, a delightful spot not far from a fourth
well called Bir el-Jerawi—level by barometer 1840.
Wilfrid has recovered his voice but still has a bad
cold. I am as lame as ever, though in less pain. I
sometimes think I shall never be able to walk again.

Friday, January 3.—We have had an adven-
ture at last and a disagreeable one ; a severe lesson
as to the danger of encamping near wells. We
started early, but were delayed a whole hour at
Jerawi taking water, and did not leave the wells till
nearly eight o'clock. Then we turned back nearly
due east across the wady. The soil of pure white

sand was heavy going, and we went slowly, crossing low undulations without other landmark than the tells we had left behind us. Here and there rose little mounds tufted with ghada. To one of these Wilfrid and I cantered on, leaving the camels behind us, and dismounting, tied our mares to the bushes that we might enjoy a few minutes' rest, and eat our midday mouthful—the greyhounds meanwhile played about and chased each other in the sand. We had finished, and were talking of I know not what, when the camels passed us. They were hardly a couple of hundred yards in front when suddenly we heard a thud, thud, thud on the sand, a sound of galloping. Wilfrid jumped to his feet, looked round and called out, "Get on your mare. This is a ghazú." As I scrambled round the bush to my mare I saw a troop of horsemen charging down at full gallop with their lances, not two hundred yards off. Wilfrid was up as he spoke, and so should I have been, but for my sprained knee and the deep sand, both of which gave way as I was rising. I fell back. There was no time to think and I had hardly struggled to my feet, when the enemy was upon us, and I was knocked down by a spear. Then they all turned on Wilfrid, who had waited for me, some of them jumping down on foot to get hold of his mare's halter. He had my gun with him, which I had just before handed to him, but unloaded; his own gun and his sword being on his delúl. He fortunately had on very thick clothes, two abbas one over the other, and

English clothes underneath, so the lances did him no harm. At last his assailants managed to get his gun from him and broke it over his head, hitting him three times and smashing the stock. Resistance seemed to me useless, and I shouted to the nearest horseman, " *ana dahílak* " (I am under your protection), the usual form of surrender. Wilfrid hearing this, and thinking he had had enough of this unequal contest, one against twelve, threw himself off his mare. The *khayal* (horsemen) having seized both the mares, paused, and as soon as they had gathered breath, began to ask us who we were and where we came from. " English, and we have come from Damascus," we replied, " and our camels are close by. Come with us, and you shall hear about it." Our caravan, while all this had happened, and it only lasted about five minutes, had formed itself into a square and the camels were kneeling down, as we could plainly see from where we were. I hardly expected the horsemen to do as we asked, but the man who seemed to be their leader at once let us walk on (a process causing me acute pain), and followed with the others to the caravan. We found Mohammed and the rest of our party entrenched behind the camels with their guns pointed, and as we approached, Mohammed stepped out and came forward. " Min entum ? " (who are you ?) was the first question. " Roala min Ibn Debaa." " Wallah ? will you swear by God ? " " Wallah! we swear."

"And you?" "Mohammed ibn Arûk of Tudmur."
"Wallah?" "Wallah!" "And these are Franjis
travelling with you?" "Wallah! Franjis, friends
of Ibn Shaalan."

It was all right, we had fallen into the hands of
friends. Ibn Shaalan, our host of last year, was
bound to protect us, even so far away in the desert,
and none of his people dared meddle with us,
knowing this. Besides, Mohammed was a Tudmuri,
and as such could not be molested by Roala, for
Tudmur pays tribute to Ibn Shaalan, and the
Tudmuris have a right to his protection. So, as
soon as the circumstances were made clear, orders
were given by the chief of the party to his followers
to bring back our mares, and the gun, and everything which had been dropped in the scuffle. Even
to Wilfrid's tobacco bag, all was restored. The
young fellows who had taken the mares made rather
wry faces, bitterly lamenting their bad fortune in
finding us friends. "Ah the beautiful mares," they
said, "and the beautiful gun." But Arabs are
always good-humoured, whatever else their faults,
and presently we were all on very good terms, sitting
in a circle on the sand, eating dates and passing round
the pipe of peace. They were now our guests.

What struck us as strange in all this was, the
ready good faith with which they believed every word
we said. We had spoken the truth, but why did
they trust us? They knew neither us nor Mohammed; yet they had taken our word that we were

friends, when they might so easily have ridden off
without question with our property.   Nobody would
ever have heard of it, or known who they were.

It appears that Ibn Debaa (hyæna), the Sheykh,
and his friends were a small party in advance of the
main body of the Roala.   They had come on to see
what pasturage there might be in the wady, and had
there camped only a few miles from the wells of El
Jerawi near which we slept last night.   They had
come in the morning for water, and had seen our
tracks in the sand, and so had followed, riding in hot
haste to overtake us.   It was a mere accident their
finding us separated from the rest of the caravan,
and they had charged down as soon as they saw us.
Everything depends on rapidity in these attacks,
and this had been quite successful.   The least
hesitation on their part, and we should have been safe
with our camels.   There they could not have molested
us, for though they were twelve to our eight, they had
only lances, while we carried firearms.   We liked the
look of these young Roala.   In spite of their rough
behaviour, we could see that they were gentlemen.
They were very much ashamed of having used their
spears against me, and made profuse apologies ; they
only saw a person wearing a cloak, and never
suspected but that it belonged to a man.   Indeed
their mistake is not a matter for surprise, for
they were so out of breath and excited with
their gallop, that they looked at nothing except
the object of their desire—the mares.   The loss of

these, however, I fear, was to them a cause of greater
sorrow than the rough handling to which we had
been treated, when, after explanations given and
regrets interchanged, they rode away. Mohammed
was anxious not to detain them, prudently considering that our acquaintance with them had gone
far enough, and it was plain that Awwad was in a
terrible fidget. I fancy he has a good many debts of
blood owing him, and is somewhat shy of strangers.
The others, too, were rather subdued and silent ; so
we wished Ibn Debaa farewell and let him go.

The mares belonging to this ghazú were small,
compact, and active, with especially good shoulders
and fine heads, but they were of a more poneyish
type than our own Anazeh mares. Most of them
were bay. One I saw was ridden in a bit.

When the Rcala were gone we compared notes.
In the first place, Wilfrid's hurts were examined, but
they are only contusions. The thick rope he wears
round his head had received all the blows, and though
the stock of the gun is clean broken, steel and all,
his head is still sound. The lances could not get
through his clothes. As regards myself the only
injury I have received is the renewal of my sprain.
But I could almost forget the pain of it in my anger
at it, as being the cause of our being caught. But
for this we might have galloped away to our camels
and received the enemy in quite another fashion. I
was asked if I was not frightened, but in fact there
was at first no time, and afterwards rage swallowed

up every other feeling. Wilfrid says, but I do not
believe him, that he felt frightened, and was very
near running away and leaving me, but on reflection stayed. The affair seems more alarming now
it is over, which is perhaps natural.

As to the others, Mohammed is terribly
crestfallen at the not very heroic part he took in
the action. The purely defensive attitude of the
caravan was no doubt prudent ; but it seemed
hardly up to the ideal of chivalry Mohammed has
always professed. He keeps on reproaching himself, but we tell him that he did quite right.
It was certainly our own fault that we were surprised in this way, and if the enemy, as they
might have been, had really been robbers and outlaws, our safety depended on our having the caravan
intact as a fortress to return to after being robbed.
To have rushed forward in disorder to help us would
have exposed the whole caravan to a defeat, which
in so desolate a region as this would mean nothing
less than dying of cold and starvation.

We may indeed be very thankful that matters
were no worse. I shall never again dismount while
I remain crippled, and never as long as I live, will I
tie my horse to a bush.

Many vows of sheep, it appears, were made by
all the party of spectators during the action, so we
are to have a feast at Jôf—if ever we get there.

Now all is quiet, and Hamdán the Sherâri is
singing the loves of a young man and maiden who

were separated from one another by mischief-makers, and afterwards managed to carry on a correspondence by tying their letters to their goats when these went out to pasture

January 4.—There was no dawdling this morning, for everybody has become serious, and we were off by seven, and have marched steadily on for quite thirty miles without stopping, at the rate of three-and-a-half miles an hour. We have left the Wady Sirhán for good, and are making a straight cut across the Hamád for Jôf. There is no water this way, but less chance of ghazús. The soil has been a light hard gravel, with hardly a plant or an inequality to interfere with the camels' pace. At one o'clock we came to some hills of sandstone faced with iron, the beginning of the broken ground in which, they say, Jôf stands. We had been gradually ascending all day, and as we reached that, the highest point of our route, the barometer marked 2660 feet. Here we found a number of little pits, used, so Hamdán explained, for collecting and winnowing *semh*, a little red grain which grows wild in this part of the desert, and is used by the Jôf people for food.

A little later we sighted two men on a delúl, the first people we have seen, except the ghazú, since leaving Káf. Wilfrid and Mohammed galloped up to see what they were, and Mohammed, to atone I suppose for his inertness on a recent occasion, fired several shots, and succeeded in frightening them

out of their wits. They were quite poor people,
dressed only in old shirts, and they had a skin of
dates on one side the camel and a skin of water on
the other. They were out, they said, to look for a
man who had been lost in the Wady Sirhán, one of
the men sent by Ibn Rashid to Kâf for the tribute.
He had been taken ill, and had stopped behind his
companions, and nobody had seen him since. They
had been sent out by the governor of Jôf to look for
him. They said that we were only a few hours
from the town.

Meanwhile, I had remained with our camels,
listening to the remarks of Awwad and Hamdán,
both dying with curiosity about the two zellems
from Jôf. At last Awwad could wait no longer,
and begged Hamdán to go with him. They both
jumped down from the camels they were riding,
and set off as hard as they could run to meet the
Jôfi, who by this time had proceeded on their way,
while Wilfrid and Mohammed were returning.
Wilfrid on arriving held out to me a handful of the
best dates I have ever eaten, which the men had
given him. The Sherâri and Awwad presently came
back with no dates, but a great deal of Jôf gossip.

We are encamped this evening near some curious
tells of red, yellow, and purple sandstone, a formation exactly similar to parts of the Sinai peninsula. There is a splendid view to the south, and
we can see far away a blue line of hills * which,

* Jebel el Tawîl.

they tell us, are beyond Jôf, at the edge of the Nefúd !

We have been questioning Hamdán about his tribe, the Sherarât, and he gives the following as their principal sections :—

El Hueymreh.	. . .	Sheykh El Hawi.
El Helesseh	. . .	,, Ibn Hedayaja.
El Khayâli	. . . .	,, Zeyd el Werdi.
Shemalat	. . . .	,, Fathal el Dendeh.

The Sherarât have no horses, but breed the finest dromedaries in Arabia. Their best breed is called *Benat Udeyhan,* (daughters of Udeyhan). With a Bint Udeyhan, he says, that if you started from where we now are at sunset, you would be to-morrow at sunrise at Kâf, a distance of a hundred and eighty miles. A thief not long ago stole a Sherâri delúl at Mezárib, and rode it all the way to Haïl in seven days and nights !

January 5.—A long wearisome ride of twenty-two miles, always expecting to see Jôf, and always disappointed. The ground broken up into fantastic hills and ridges, but on a lower level than yesterday, descending in fact all day. Every now and then we caught sight of the Wady Sirhán far away to the right, with blue hills beyond it, but in front of us there seemed an endless succession of rocky ridges. At last from the top of one of these there became visible a black outline, standing darkly out against the yellow confusion of sandstone hills and barren wadys, which we knew must be the castle of Marid.

It looked a really imposing fortress, though dreary enough in the middle of this desolation. Towards this we pushed on, eager for a nearer view. Then we came to a natural causeway of white rock, which Awwad and Hamdán both affirmed to be a continuation of the Roman road from Salkhad. We should have liked to believe this, but it was too clear that the road was one made by nature. Along this we travelled for some miles till it disappeared. All of a sudden we came as it were to the edge of a basin, and there, close under us, lay a large oasis of palms, surrounded by a wall with towers at intervals, and a little town clustering round the black castle. We were at Jôf.

THE CASTLE OF JÔF.

CHAPTER VI.

And Laban said to him, "Surely thou art my bone and my flesh." And he
abode with him the space of a month.—Book of Genesis.

The Jôf oasis—We are entertained by Ibn Rashid's lieutenant—A
haunch of wild cow—Dancing in the castle—Prayers—We go
on to Meskakeh.

Jof is not at all what we expected. We thought
we should find it a large cultivated district, and
it turns out to be merely a small town. There is
nothing at all outside the walls except a few square
patches, half an acre or so each, green with young
corn. These are watered from wells, and irrigated
just like the gardens inside the walls, with little
water-courses carefully traced in patterns, like a
jam tart. The whole basin of Jôf is indeed barely
three miles across at its widest, and looks, what
it no doubt is, the empty basin of a little inland
sea. How, or when, or why, it was originally
dried up, is beyond me to guess (one can only say
with Mohammed, it is "min Allah"); but the
proofs of its pelagic origin are apparent everywhere.
It looks lower than the rest of the Wady Sirhán,
with which it probably communicates; and we
thought at first that it might have been the last

water-hole, as it were, of the sea when it dried up.
But this is not really the case, as its lowest part is
exactly on a level with all the hollows of the wady.
Its wells are between 1800 and 1900 feet above the
sea. They are shallow, only a few feet from the
surface, and the water is drawn by camels pulling a
long rope with a bucket, which empties itself as it
reaches the surface into a kind of trough. The
town, with its gardens, all encircled by a mud wall
ten feet high, is about two miles long from north to
south, and half a mile across. The rest of the plain
is nearly a dead flat of sand, with here and there a
patch of hard ground, sandy clay, where the water
collects when it rains, and salt is left when it
dries up.

Wherever a well has been sunk, a little garden
has been made, fenced in with a wall, and planted
with palms. There are perhaps a dozen of these
outlying farms occupying two or three acres each.
In one place there are four or five houses with their
gardens together, which have the look of a village.
The whole of the basin, except these oases, is
dazzlingly white, showing the palm groves as black
patches on its surface. Jôf itself contains not more
than six hundred houses, square boxes of mud, clustering, most of them, round the ruin of Marid, but
not all, for there are half a dozen separate clusters
in different parts of the grove. Many of these houses
have a kind of tower, or upper storey, and there are
small towers at irregular intervals all round the

outer wall. The chief feature of the town, besides Marid, is a new castle just outside the *enceinte*, inhabited by Ibn Rashid's lieutenant. It stands on rising ground, and is an imposing building, square, with battlemented walls forty feet high, flanked with round and square towers tapering upwards twenty feet higher than the rest. It has no windows, only holes to shoot from ; and each tower has several excrescences like hoods (machicoulis) for the same purpose.

There is nothing like a bazaar in Jôf, nor even streets, as one generally understands the word, only a number of narrow tortuous lanes, with mud walls on either side. As we rode into the town, we found the lanes crowded with armed men, all carrying swords in the way we had seen at Kâf, dark-visaged and, we thought, not very pleased to see us. They answered our "salaam aleykum" simply, without moving, and let us pass on without any particular demonstration of hospitality. To suppose them indifferent, however, was a mistake ; their apparent coldness was only Arab formality, and when Mohammed began to inquire after the house of his relations, they very civilly pointed out the way, and one or two of them came with us. We were led down a number of narrow byways, and through the palm-gardens to the other side of the town, and then out by another gate beyond to one of the isolated farms we had seen from the cliff. It was close by, not a quarter of a mile, and in a few minutes more we

had dismounted, and were being hospitably entertained in the tidy kahwah of Huseyn's house.

What Huseyn's exact relationship is to Mohammed, I have not yet been able to discover—Mohammed himself hardly knows—but here it is evident
that any consanguinity, however slight, is considered
of high importance. We were no sooner seated by
Huseyn's fire, watching the coffee roasting, than
another relation arrived, attracted by the news
of our arrival, and then another, both loud in their
expostulations at our having accepted Huseyn's
hospitality, not theirs. Mohammed was kissed and
hugged, and it was all he could do to pacify these
injured relatives by promising to stay a week with
each, as soon as our visit to Huseyn should be over.
Blood here is indeed thicker than water. The
sudden appearance of a twentieth cousin is enough
to set everybody by the ears.

A lamb has been killed, and we have each had
the luxury of a bath in our own tent, and a
thorough change of raiment. The tent is pitched
in a little palm garden behind the house, and we
are quite at peace, and able to think over all that
has happened, and make our plans for the future.

January 6.—Last night, while we were sitting
drinking coffee for the ninth or tenth time since our
arrival, two young men came into the kahwah and
sat down. They were very gaily dressed in silk
jibbehs, and embroidered shirts under their drab
woollen abbas. They wore red cotton kefiyehs on

their heads, bound with white rope, and their
swords were silver-hilted. Everyone in the kahwah
stood up as they entered, and we both thought
them to be the sons of the Sheykh, or some great
personage at Jôf. Wilfrid whispered a question
about them to Huseyn, who laughed and said they
were not sons of sheykhs, but "zellemet Ibn Rashid,"
Ibn Rashid's men, in fact, his soldiers. The red
kefiyeh, and the silver hilted sword, was a kind of
uniform. They had come, as it presently appeared,
from Dowass, the acting governor of Jôf, to invite
us to the castle, and though we were sorry to leave
Huseyn's quiet garden and his kind hospitality, we
have thought it prudent to comply. Neither Huseyn
nor anyone else seemed to think it possible we could
refuse, for Ibn Rashid's government is absolute at
Jôf, and his lieutenant's wishes are treated as commands, not that there seems to be ill-feeling between
the garrison and the town ; the soldiers we saw
appear to be on good terms with everybody, and are
indeed so good-humoured, that it would be difficult
to quarrel with them. But Jôf is a conquered
place, held permanently in a state of siege, and the
discipline maintained is very strict. We have
moved accordingly with all our camp to the precincts
of the official residence, and are encamped just
under its walls. The *kasr*, which, as I have said, is
outside the town, was built about twelve years ago
by Metaab ibn Rashid, brother of the Emir Tellál
(Mr. Palgrave's friend), and though so modern a

construction, has a perfectly mediæval look, for
architecture never changes in Arabia. It is a very
picturesque building with its four high towers at
the corners, pierced with loopholes, but without
windows. There is one only door, and that a
small one in an angle of the wall, and it is
always kept locked. Inside it the entrance turns
and twists about, and then there is a small
court-yard surrounded by the high walls, and a
kahwah, besides a few other small rooms, all dark
and gloomy like dungeons. Here the deputy
governor lives with six soldiers, young men from
Haïl, who, between them, govern and garrison and
do the police work of Jôf. The governor himself is
away just now at Meskakeh, the other small town
included in the Jôf district, about twenty miles from
here. He is a negro slave, we are told, but a person
of great consequence, and a personal friend of the
Emir.

Jôf, as far as we have been able to learn through
Mohammed, for we don't like to ask too many
questions ourselves, was formally an appanage of the
Ibn Shaalans, Sheykhs of the Roala, and it still pays
tribute to Sotamm; but about twenty years ago
Metaab ibn Rashid conquered it, and it has ever
since been treated as part of Nejd. There have
been one or two insurrections, but they have been
vigorously put down, and the Jôfi are now afraid of
stirring a finger against the Emir. On the occasion
of one of these revolts, Metaab cut down a great

many palm trees, and half ruined the town, so they
are obliged to wait and make the best of it.   In
truth, the government can hardly be very oppressive.
These six soldiers with the best will in the world
cannot do much bullying in a town of four or five
thousand inhabitants.   They are all strong, active,
good-humoured young fellows, serving here for a
year at a time, and then being relieved.   They are
volunteers, and do not get pay, but have, I suppose,
some advantages when they have done their service.
They seem quite devoted to the Emir.

Four years ago, they tell us, the Turkish Governor
of Damascus sent a military expedition against
Jôf (the same we heard of at Kâf), and held it for a
a few months ; but Ibn Rashid complained to the
Sultan of this, and threatened to turn them out and
to discontinue the tribute he pays to the Sherîf of
Medina if the troops were not withdrawn, so they
had to go back.   This tribute is paid by the Emir
on account of his outlying possessions, such as Kâf,
Teyma, and Jôf, which the Turks have on various
occasions attempted to meddle with.   He is, however,
quite independent of the Sultan, and acknowledges
no suzerain anywhere.   The greatness of Ibn Saoud
and the Wahhabis is now a thing of the past, and
Mohammed ibn Rashid is the most powerful ruler
in Arabia.   We hear a charming account of Nejd,
at least of the northern part of it.   You may travel
anywhere, they say, from Jôf to Kasîm without
escort.   The roads are safe everywhere.   A robbery

has not been known on the Emir's highway for
many years, and people found loafing about near
the roads have their heads cut off. Ibn Rashid
allows no ghazús against travellers, and when he
makes war it is with his enemies. The Ibn Haddal
and Ibn Majil are his friends, but he is on bad
terms with Sotamm and the Sebaa Sheykhs.
There are two twelve pounder cannons of English
make in the castle. They are ancient pieces of no
value, but were used, it appears, in the siege of Jôf
by Metaab.

The Jôfi are of a different race from the Shammar
of Nejd, being as mixed in their origin almost as the
Tudmuri or the villagers of the Euphrates. Huseyn
el-Kelb, our first host here, tells us he belongs to
the Taï, and that others of his neighbours are
Sirhán or Beni Laam. He is not really a cousin of
Mohammed's, but a cousin's cousin ; the real cousins
living at Meskakeh. Though we were very comfortable with him, we are not less well off here ; and
it is more interesting being at the kasr. Dowass,
the deputy governor, is a very amiable man, and
all his soldiers are exceedingly civil and obliging.
They are a cheerful set of people, talking openly
about everything with us, politics and all. They
assure us Ibn Rashid will be delighted to see us,
but we must see Jóhar, the black governor, first.
There are several real slaves in the fort, but no
women. The soldiers leave their wives behind at Haïl
when they go away on service. There are no horses

in Jôf, except one two-year-old colt belonging to
Dubejeh, one of the soldiers, who all admire our
shagra (chestnut mare) amazingly, saying that there
is nothing in Nejd so beautiful. Neither are there
any beasts of burden, not even asses. The few
camels there are in the town are kept for drawing
water ; and the only other four-footed creatures I
have seen are a few goats and three half-starved
cows at the kasr. There is not an atom of vegetation within miles of Jôf, and the camels and these
cows have to eat chopped straw and refuse dates.

Our dinner to-day consisted of a lamb and three
other dishes—one a sort of paste like the paste used
for pasting paper, another merely rancid butter with
chopped onions, and the third, bread sopped in
water—all nasty except the lamb. There was,
however, afterwards an extra course brought to us
as a surprise, a fillet of " wild cow " (probably an
antelope) from the Nefûd, baked in the ashes, one
of the best meats I ever tasted.

In the evening we had an entertainment of
dancing and singing, in which Dowass, as well as
the soldiers, took part. They performed a kind of
sword dance, one performer beating on a drum
made of palm wood and horse hide, while the rest
held their swords over their shoulders and chaunted
in solemn measure, dancing as solemnly. Occasionally
the swords were brandished, and then there was a
scream very like what may be heard in the hunting-
field at home. Once or twice there was a distinct

who-whoop, exactly in the proper key, and with the proper emphasis. The tunes were many of them striking, after the manner of Arabian music. One of them ran thus :—

The dancing ended, a huge bowl of date molasses (dibs) and juice from *trengs* (a gigantic sort of lemon) was mixed ; and surprising quantities of this temperance liquid drunk. Now we are quiet, outside the castle, which is locked up for the night, and are at liberty to write or make sketches by moonlight, things we dare not do in the daytime.

January 7.—Hamdán, our Sherâri guide, who had disappeared, returned this morning furtively for the balance of pay due to him. He says he is afraid of the people at the castle, and cannot stay with us.

A messenger has come from Meskakeh with an invitation from Jóhar for us, so we are going on there to-morrow. We are not, however, to stay with Jóhar, as he has no house of his own there, but with our relations, the Ibn Arûks, who have at last been really discovered. Nassr ibn Arûk, the head of the family, hearing of our arrival, has sent his son with every sort of polite message, and it is to his house we shall go. The young man is modest, and well-mannered, without pretension, honest and straightforward, if one can read any-

thing in faces; and evidently much impressed with
the honour done him by our intended visit.

We have been making calls all the morning, first
on our former host, Huseyn el-Kelb, and the other
relatives, and then on one or two notables of the
town. Huseyn says that the Beyt Habûb, mentioned
by Mr. Palgrave, exists, but that the noblest of all
the families is that of Mehsin ibn Dirra, formerly
Sheykh of Jôf, but now reduced to the condition
of one of the Emir's subjects. Ibn Dirra is not
(Mohammed tells us) by any means pleased at the
political changes in Jôf; but he is afraid to show
more than a half-smothered discontent, for Mohammed ibn Rashid keeps a hostage for his good
conduct in the person of his eldest son. This youth
resides at Haïl, where he is not exactly a prisoner,
but cannot return to his friends. At all the houses
we were fed and entertained, having to drink endless cups of coffee flavoured with cloves (heyl), and
eat innumerable dates, the *helwet el Jôf*, which they
say here are the best in Arabia; they are of excellent
flavour, but too sweet and too sticky for general
use. The people of Jôf live almost entirely on
dates; not, however, on the *helwet*, which are not
by any means the common sort. There are as
many varieties here of dates as of apples in our
orchards, and quite as different from each other.
The kind we prefer for ordinary eating is light
coloured, crisp, and rounder than the helwet; while
these are shapeless, and of the colour of a horse

chestnut. It is a great mistake to suppose that dates are better for being freshly gathered; on the contrary, they mellow with keeping. The sweeter kinds contain so much sugar, that when placed in an open dish they half dissolve into a syrup, in which the sugar forms in large lumps. I have no doubt that regular sugar could be manufactured from them.

The coffee making is much the same process here as among the Bedouins of the north, except that it is more tedious. First, there is an interminable sorting of the beans, which are smaller and lighter in colour than what one gets in Europe; then, after roasting, a long pounding in a mortar, though the coffee is never pounded quite fine; then an extraordinary amount of washing and rinsing of coffeepots, five or six of them; and lastly, the actual boiling, which is done three times. The Jôf mortars are very handsome, of red sandstone, the common stone of the country, and are, I believe, an article of export. I should like to take one away with me but they are too heavy, a quarter of a camel load each. The design on them is simple but handsome, and I should not be surprised if it were very ancient. The only other manufactures of Jôf that I heard of, are cartridge belts and woollen abbas. The former are showy and tipped with silver, and all the servants have purchased them; the latter are made of wool brought from Bagdad. Awwad bought one for six and a half mejïdies.

We next had a look at the castle of Marid, the
only building of stone in Jôf. Its construction
dates, I should say, from mediæval times, certainly
it is not classic, and it has no particular feature to
make it interesting. It looks best at a distance. I
find the map places it a long way from Jôf, but in
reality it is within the walls of the town, on the
western edge. It stands about 2000 feet above
the sea.

While sitting in Ibn Dirra's house, we saw an
instance of Ibn Rashid's paternal government, and
the first sign of Wahhabism. The midday prayer
was called from the roof of the mosque close by, for
there is no minaret in Jôf, but for some time
nobody seemed inclined to move, taking our visit
as an excuse. Then an old man with a sour face
began lecturing the younger ones, and telling them
to get up and go to pray, and finding precept of no
avail, at last gave them the example. Still the
main body of the guests sat on, till suddenly up
jumped the two young soldiers who had come with
us, and shouting "kum, kum," get up, get up, set
to with the flats of their swords on the rest and so
drove them to the mosque, all but our host, whose
position as such made him sacred from assault. It
is very evident that religion is not appreciated here,
and except the sour looking old man nobody seemed
to take the praying seriously, for the soldiers when
they had done their duty of driving in the others,
came back without ceremony from the mosque.

The outward show of religion does not seem natural among the Arabs.

Another sword dance to-night, and another carouse on lemonade.

January 8.—A cloudy, almost foggy morning, and a shower of rain. We wished Dowass and his soldiers good-bye, and they really seemed sorry to part with us. They are extraordinarily good-tempered, honest people, and have treated us with great kindness. Dowass's last attention to me was the present of an enormous treng as big as a large cocoanut. The trengs are sour not sweet lemons, but they have a rind an inch thick, sweet enough to be eaten though very woolly.

Meskakeh, where we have come to-day, is about twenty miles from Jôf, and there is a well-beaten track between the two places. We were a rather numerous party, as several Jôfi came with us for company, and we have Areybi ibn Arûk, Nassr's son, and another Aruk, a cousin of his, and a man with a gun who is by way of going on with us to Haïl. All the party but ourselves were on foot, for the Jôfi never ride, having neither horses nor camels nor even donkeys. One of the men had with him an ostrich eggshell slung in a sort of network, and used like a gourd to hold water. He told me that ostriches are common in the Nefûd, which is now close by. The scenery all the way was fantastic, sometimes picturesque. First we crossed the punchbowl of Jôf to the other side, passing several ruined farms, the ground absolutely barren, and the lowest part of it covered with salt. The whole of this depression is but a mile across. Then our road rose suddenly a hundred feet up a steep bank of sand, and then again a hundred and sixty feet over some stony ridges, descending again to cross a subbkha with a fringe of tamarisks just now in flower, then tracts of fine ironstone gravel, undistinguishable from sheep's droppings. About two hours from Jôf is a large water-hole, which the Jôfi call a spring, the water about eight feet below ground. In the wadys where water had flowed (for it rained here about a month ago), there were bright green bulbous plants with crocus flowers, giving a false look of fertility. In other places there were curious mushroom rocks of pink sandstone topped with iron, and in the distance northwards several fine masses of hill, Jebel Hammamíyeh or the pigeon mountains being the most remarkable. These may have been a thousand feet higher than Jôf. Far beyond, to the north-east and east, there ran a level line of horizon at about an equal height, the edge of the Hamád, for all the country we have been crossing is within the area of the ancient sea, which, we suppose, must have included the Wady Sirhán, Jôf, and Meskakeh.

On one of the rocks I noticed an inscription, or rather pictures of camels and horses, cut on a flat surface about five feet across. We could not, however, under the circumstances, copy it.

Meskakeh, though not the seat of Jóhar's government, is a larger town than Jôf,—seven hundred
houses they say, and palm gardens at least twice as
extensive as the other's. The position of the two
towns is much the same, a broad hollow surrounded
by cliffs of sandstone, but the Meskakeh basin is less
regular, and is broken up with sandhills and outlying
tells of rock. Meskakeh, like Jôf, has an ancient
citadel perched on a cliff about a hundred feet high,
and dominating the town. The town itself is
irregularly built, and has no continuous wall round
its gardens. There are many detached gardens and
groups of houses, and these have not been ruined as
those of Jôf have been by recent wars. Altogether,
it has an exceedingly flourishing look, not an acre
of irrigable land left unplanted. Everything is neat
and clean, the walls fresh battlemented, and every
house trim as if newly built. The little square plots
of barley are surrounded each by its hedge of wattled
palm branches, and the streets and lanes are scrupu-
lously tidy. Through these we rode without stopping,
and on two miles beyond, to Nassr's farm. We are
now in the bosom of the Ibn Arûk family, after all no
myth, but a hospitable reality, receiving us with open
arms, as if they had been expecting us every day for
the last hundred years. They know the Ibn Arûk
ballad and Mohammed's genealogy far better than he
knows it himself, so for the time at least we may hope
to be in clover, and if after all we get no further, we
may feel that we have travelled not quite in vain.

CHAPTER VII.

" And Leah was tender eyed but Rachel was beautiful."—Book of Genesis.

The Ibn Arûks of Jôf—Mohammed contracts a matrimonial alliance
—Leah and Rachel—We cheapen the bride's dower—A negro
governor and his suite—A thunder-storm.

WE stayed three days with Nassr and his sons,
and his sons' wives and their children, in their quiet
farm house. It was a rest which we much needed,
and proved besides to be an interesting experience,
and an excellent opportunity of learning more of
Arab domestic life than we had done on our previous
journeys. Not that the Ibn Arûks of Meskakeh are
in themselves of any particular interest. Like their
relations of Tudmur, they have been too long settled
down as mere townspeople, marrying the daughters
of the land, and adopting many of the sordid town
notions, but they were honest and kind-hearted, and
the traditions of their origin, still religiously preserved, cast an occasional gleam of something like
romance on their otherwise matter of fact lives.
Nassr, the best of the elder generation, resembled
some small Scottish laird, poor and penurious, but
aware of having better blood in his veins than his

neighbours—one whose thought, every day in the
year but one, is of how to save sixpence, but who on
that one day shows himself to be a gentleman, and
the head of a house. His sons were quiet, modest,
and unpretending, and, like most young Arabs,
more romantically inclined than their father. They
even had a certain appreciation of chivalrous ideas ;
especially Turki, the elder, in whom the Bedouin
blood and Bedouin traditions predominated almost
to the exclusion of commercial instincts, while in
his brother Areybi, these latter more than counter-
balanced the former. We liked both the brothers,
of course preferring Turki, with whom Wilfrid made
great friends.

Mohammed is less distantly related to these
people than I had supposed. His ancestor, Ali ibn
Arûk, was one of the three brothers who, in consequence of a blood feud, or, as Wilfrid thinks more
likely, to escape the Wahhabi tyranny of a hundred
years ago, left Aared in Nejd, and came north as
far as Tudmur, where Ali married and remained.
Another brother, Abd el-Kader ibn Arûk, had
stopped at Jôf, settled there, and became Nassr's
grandfather. As to the third, Mutlakh, the descendants of the two former know nothing of his fate,
except that, liking neither Tudmur nor Jôf, he
returned towards Nejd. Some vague report of his
death reached them, but nobody can tell when or
how he died. Nassr came from Jôf to Meskakeh
not many years ago.

Nassr is now the head of the family, at least of
that branch of it which inhabits the Meskakeh oasis.
But there lives in an adjoining house to his, his first
cousin, Jazi ibn Arûk, brother to our friend Merzuga, and father to two pretty daughters. These,
with a few other relations, make up a pleasant
little family party, all living in their outlying farm
together.

Of course our first thought on coming amongst
them was for a wife for Mohammed, at whose
request I took an early opportunity of making
acquaintance with the women of the family. I
found them all very friendly and amiable, and some
of them intelligent. Most of the younger ones were
good looking. The most important person in the
harim was Nassr's wife, a little old lady named
Shemma (candle), thin and wizened, and wrinkled,
with long grey locks, and the weak eyes of extreme
old age ; and, though she can have been hardly
more than sixty, she seemed to be completely worn
out. She was the mother of Turki and Areybi ;
and I had heard from Mohammed that Nassr had
never taken another wife but her. In this, however,
he was mistaken, for on my very first visit, she
called in a younger wife from the adjoining room,
and introduced her at once to me. The second
wife came in with two little boys of two and three
years old, the eldest of whom (for they all have
extraordinary names) is called Mattrak, " stick ; "
in spite of which he seemed an amiable, good-

tempered child. In this he resembled his mother,
whose respectful manner towards her elder, Shemma,
impressed me favourably; she had, besides, a really
beautiful face. The little boy, Mattrak, I recognised
as a boy I had seen in the morning with old Nassr
in our garden, and supposed to be his grandson.
Nassr was doing his best to spoil the child, after the
fashion of old men among the Arabs. I had then
given Mattrak a little red frock, one I had bought
for Sotamm's boy, Mansur, when we thought we
were going to the Roala, and in this the child was
now strutting about, showing off his finery to two
very pretty little girls, his sisters. These two ran
in and out during my visit, helping to bring bowls
of dates, and to eat the dates when brought. Next
appeared Turki's two wives, a pretty one and a
plain one, and Areybi's one wife, pretty, and lately
married. All these seemed to be on better terms
with one another than is usually the case among
mixed wives and daughters-in-law. They were
extremely anxious to please me, and I, of course,
did my best to satisfy their hospitable wishes about
eating. They offered me dates of countless kinds,
—dry ones and sticky ones, sweet and less sweet,
long dried ones, and newer ones, a mass of pulp;
it was impossible for one person to do justice to
them all.

Shemma treated all the young people with the
air of one in authority, though her tone with them
was kind. She, however, spoke little, while the

others talked incessantly and asked all sorts of questions, requiring more knowledge of Arabic than I possessed to answer. In the middle of the visit, Nazzch, Nassr's married daughter, own sister to Turki and Areybi, arrived with her daughter, and an immense bowl of dates. She had walked all the way from the town of Meskakeh, about three miles, carrying this child, a fat heavy creature of four, as well as the dates, and came in, panting and laughing, to see me. She was pleasant and lively, very like her brother Turki in face, that is to say, good-tempered rather than good-looking. Any one of these young ladies, seen on my first visit, might have done for Mohammed's project of marriage, but, unfortunately, they were all either married or too young. I asked if there were no young ladies already " out," and was told that there were none in Nassr's house, but that his cousin Jazi had two grown-up daughters, not yet married ; so I held my peace till there should be an opportunity of seeing them.

Mohammed, in the meantime, had already begun to make inquiries on his own account, and the first day of our visit was not over before he came to me with a wonderful account of these very daughters of Jazi. There were three of them, he declared, and all more beautiful each than the others, Asr (afternoon), Hamú, and Muttra—the first two unfortunately betrothed already, but Muttra still obtainable. I could see that already he was

terribly in love, for with the Arabs, a very little
goes a long way ; and never being allowed to see
young ladies, they fall in love merely through
talking about them. He was very pressing that I
should lose no time about making my visit to their
mother, and seemed to think that I had been
wasting my time sadly on the married cousin.
Mohammed has all along declared that he must be
guided by my opinion. I shall know, he pretends,
at once, not only whether Muttra is pretty, but
whether good-tempered, likely to make a good
wife. He had been calculating, he said, and thought
forty pounds would be asked as her dower. It is a
great deal to be sure, but then she was really " asil,"
and the occasion was a unique one—a daughter of
Jazi !—a niece of Merzuga !—a girl of such excellent
family !—an Ibn Arûk ! and Ibn Arûks were not to
be had every day !—forty pounds would hardly be
too much. He trusted all to my judgment—I had
so much discernment, and had seen the wives and
daughters of all the Anazeh Sheykhs ; I should
know what was what, and should not make a mistake. Still, he would like Abdallah to go with me,
just to spy out things. Abdallah, as a relation,
might be admitted to the door on such an occasion,
though he, Mohammed, of course could not ; he
might, perhaps, even be allowed to see the girl, as
it were, by accident. With us, the Ibn Arûks, the
wives and daughters are always veiled, a custom
we brought with us from Nejd, for we are not

like the Bedouins; yet on so important an occasion as this, of arranging a marriage, a man of a certain age, a dependant, or a poor relation, is sometimes permitted to see and report. I promised that I would do all I could to expedite the matter.

Accordingly, the next day Turki was sent for, and a word dropped to him of the matter in hand, and he was forthwith dispatched to announce my visit to the mother of the daughters of Jasi— Mohammed explaining, that it was etiquette that the mother should be made acquainted with the object of my visit, though not necessarily the daughters. Then we went to Jazi's house, Turki, Abdallah, and I.

Jazi's house is close to Nassr's, only the garden wall dividing them, and is still smaller than his, a poor place, I thought, to which to come for a princess; but in Arabia one must never judge by externals. At the door, among several women, stood Saad, Jazi's eldest son, who showed us through the courtyard to an inner room, absolutely dark, except for what light might come in at the doorway. It is in Arabia that the expression "to darken one's door," must have been invented, for windows there are none in any of the smaller houses. There was a smell of goats about the place, and it looked more like a stable than a parlour for reception. At first I could see nothing, but I could hear Saad, who had plunged into the darkness, shaking something

in a corner, and as my eyes got accustomed to
the twilight, this proved to be a young lady, one
of the three that I had come to visit. It was Asr
the second, a great, good-looking girl, very like her
cousin Areybi, with his short aquiline nose and
dark eyes. She came out to the light with a great
show of shyness and confusion, hiding her face in
her hands, and turning away even from me ; nor
would she answer anything to my attempts at
conversation. Then, all of a sudden, she broke
away from us, and rushed across the yard to
another little den, where we found her with her
mother and her sister Muttra. I hardly knew
what to make of all this, as besides the shyness, I
thought I could see that Asr really meant to be rude,
and the polite manners of her mother Haliyeh and
her little sister Muttra confirmed me in this ide .
I liked Muttra's face at once ; she has a particularly
open, honest look, staring straight at one with her
great dark eyes like a fawn, and she has, too,
a very bright fresh colour, and a pleasant cheerful voice. I paid, then, little attention to Asr's
rudeness, and asked the little girl to walk with
me round their garden, which she did, showing me
the few things there were to be seen, and explaining
about the well, and the way they drew the water.
The garden, besides the palm trees, contained
figs, apricots, and vines, and there was a little
plot of green barley, on which some kids were
grazing. Muttra told me that in summer they

live on fruit, but that they never preserve the
apricots or figs, only the dates. I noticed several
young palm trees, always a sign of prosperity. The
well was about ten feet square at the top, and
carefully faced with stone, the water being only a
few feet below the surface of the ground. Water,
she told me, could be found anywhere at Meskakeh
by digging, and always at the same depth. I was
pleased with the intelligence Muttra showed in this
conversation, and pleased with her pretty ways and
honest face, and decided in my own mind without
difficulty that Mohammed would be most fortunate
if he obtained her in marriage. It was promising,
too, for their future happiness, to remark that
Haliyeh, the mother, seemed to be a sensible
woman; only I could not understand the strange
behaviour of the elder sister Asr. Abdallah, in
the meanwhile, standing at the door, had made
his notes, and come to much the same conclusion
as myself; so we returned with an excellent
report to give to the impatient suitor waiting
outside.

Mohammed's eagerness was now very nearly
spoiling the negociation, for he at once began to
talk of his intended marriage; and the same thing
happened to him in consequence, which happened
long ago to Jacob, the son of Isaac. Jazi, imitating
the conduct of Laban, and counting upon his
cousin's anxiety to be married, first of all increased
the dower from forty pounds to sixty, and then

endeavoured to substitute Leah for Rachel, the
ill-tempered Asr for the pretty Muttra.

This was a severe blow to Mohammed's hopes,
and a general council was called of all the family to
discuss it and decide. The council met in our tent,
Wilfrid presiding; on one side sat Mohammed, with
Nassr as head of the house; on the other, Jazi and
Saad, representing the bride, while between them,
a little shrivelled man knelt humbly on his knees,
who was no member of the family, but, we afterwards learned, a professional go-between. Outside,
the friends and more distant relations assembled,
Abdallah and Ibrahim Kasir, and half a dozen of
the Ibn Arûks. These began by sitting at a
respectful distance, but as the discussion warmed,
edged closer and closer in, till every one of them
had delivered himself of an opinion.

Mohammed himself was quite in a flutter, and
very pale; and Wilfrid conducted his case for him.
It would be too long a story to mention all the
dispute, which sometimes was so warmly pressed,
that negociations seemed on the point of being
broken off. Jazi contended that it was impossible
he should give his younger daughter, while the
elder ones remained unmarried. "Hamú, it was true,
was engaged, and of her there was no question, but
Asr, though engaged too, was really free; Jeruan,
the shock-headed son of Merzuga, to whom she was
betrothed, was not the husband for her. He was an
imbecile, and Asr would never marry him. If a girl

declares that she will not marry her betrothed, she is
not engaged, and has still to seek a husband she likes.
But this would not do. We cited the instance of
Jedaan's marriage with an engaged girl, and the unfortunate sequel, as proving that Jeruan's consent was
necessary for Asr, and Mohammed chimed in, " Ya
ibn ammi, ya Jazi, O Jazi! O son of my uncle how
could I do this thing, and sin against my cousin?
How could I take his bride? Surely this would be
a shame to us all." In fine, we insisted that
Muttra it should be or nobody, and Asr's claim was
withdrawn. Still it was pleaded, Muttra was but a
child, hardly fifteen, and unfit for so great a
journey as that to Tudmur. Where indeed was
Tudmur? who of all the Jôfi had ever been so far?
Mohammed, however, replied that if youth were an
obstacle, a year or two would mend that. He was
content to wait for a year, or two, or even for three
years, if need were. He was an Ibn Arûk, and
trained to patience. As to Tudmur, it was far, but
had we not just come thence, and could we not go
back? He would send one of his brothers at the
proper time, with twenty men, thirty, fifty, to escort
her. So argued, the marriage project was at last
adopted, as far as Muttra was concerned. But the
question of " settlements " was not as easily got over.
Here it was very nearly being wrecked for good and
all. Wilfrid had all along intended to pay the dower
for Mohammed, but he would not say so till the
thing was settled, and left Mohammed to fight out

the question of jointure to as good a bargain as they could make. This Mohammed was very capable of doing, despite the infirmity of his heart, and strengthened by Abdallah, who took a strictly commercial view of the whole transaction, a middle sum was agreed on, and the conference broke up.

Things, however, were not yet to go off quite smoothly. On the day following, when I went with some little presents for the bride to Jazi's house, I was met at the door by Jazi himself, who received me, as I at once perceived, with an embarrassed air, as also did Haliyeh, for both she and a strange relation were sitting in the kahwah. To my questions about Muttra short answers were given ; and the conversation was at once turned on " the weather and the crops," or rather on that Arabian substitute for it, a discussion about locusts. We had had a heavy thunderstorm in the morning, for which all were thankful. It would bring grass in the Nefûd, but the locusts there, never were so numerous as this year. Again I asked about the girls, but again got no reply ; and at last, tired of their idle talk, and quite out of patience, I exclaimed, " O Jazi, what is this ? I trust that you—and you, O Haliyeh,—are pleased at this connection with Mohammed." To which he replied, in a sing-song voice, " Inshallah, inshallah," and Haliyeh repeated " Inshallah," and the stranger. I saw that something must be wrong, for it was no answer to my

question, and rose to go. Then Haliyeh went out
with me into the yard, and explained what had
happened. Asr, it appeared, with her violent temper,
was frightening them all out of their wits. She
would not hear of her sister being married before
herself, or making so much better a match. Jeruan
she despised, though he was Sheykh of Kâf; and
she wanted to marry the Sheykh of Tudmur herself. She had tormented old Jazi into withdrawing
his consent; and Muttra was afraid of her. What
was to be done? I said it was no use arguing
about this over again; that if she and her husband
were really not able to manage their daughters, we
must look out elsewhere for Mohammed; that I
hoped and trusted Asr would not be so foolish as to
stand in the way of her sister's happiness, for it
would not profit her. This bad temper of hers
made it more than ever certain that she could not
marry Mohammed, and, in fine, that the family
must make up their minds, yes or no, about
Muttra, and at once, for we were leaving Meskakeh
presently, and must have the matter settled. I then
saw the two girls, and spoke to them in the same
strain, and with such effect that a few hours later,
Mohammed, who had fallen into low spirits about
the affair, now came with a joyful countenance to
say that the marriage contract would be signed that
evening.

Signed, therefore, it was, though to the last
moment difficulty on difficulty was raised, and a

lamentably haggling spirit displayed by all except
Turki in the matter of the dower. Fifty Turkish
pounds was, however, the sum ultimately fixed on ;
and Wilfrid refused curtly to advance a beshlik
beyond it, even to buy off a cousin who unaccount-
ably appeared on the scene and claimed his right to
Muttra or an equivalent for her in coin. It was
not very dignified this chaffering about price ; and
people do better in England, leaving such things to
be settled by their lawyers.

Everything, however, was at last arranged, the
marriage contract written out and signed, and
everybody made happy. Then the rest of the
evening was spent in jubilation. A kid was
killed and eaten, songs sung, and stories told, nor
was, as might be expected, the Arûk ballad left out
of the programme. Nassr is a poet, and recited an
ode impromptu for the occasion. Among the guests
were two pilgrims from Mecca—so at least they
called themselves—and some men who had run
away from the Turkish conscription in Syria. These
feasted with the rest, as though they too had been
relations. And so ended Mohammed's marriage
negociations. He is to come back next year or send
for Muttra ; but for the present he is to be content
and wait.

While this family arrangement was in progress,
we had also on hand a more important negociation
of our own, and that was to get the governor's
permission for our journey on to Haïl. The first

thing to be done was to make friends with
Jóhar, for all in this despotic country depends
upon his good will and pleasure ; and if he had
chosen to send us back to Kâf by the Wady
Sirhán, I do not know that we could have offered
any resistance. Jôf is not an easy place to get
away from. It is more than three hundred miles
from the nearest point on the Euphrates, and
without the governor's leave no one would have
dared to travel a mile with us. Accordingly, the
day after our arrival at Meskakeh, we called on
Jóhar, who had been warned of our visit, and
received us in state.

Jóhar is a perfectly black negro, with repulsive
African features ; tall, and very fat, and very vain.
He had put on his finest clothes to receive us, a
number of gaudy silk jibbehs one over the other, a
pair of sky-blue trousers—things new to us in
Arabia—a black and gold abba, and a purple kefiyeh. His shirt was stiff with starch, and crackled
every time he moved. He carried a handsome gold-
hilted sword, and looked altogether as barbaric a
despot as one need wish to see. He kept us waiting nearly ten minutes in the kahwah, to add, I
suppose, to his importance, and then came in behind
a procession of armed men, all of them well got up
with silver hilted swords, silver ornamented belts,
and blue and red kefiyehs bound with thick white
aghals. He affected the affable, rather languid air
of a royal personage, passing from one subject of

conversation to another without transition, and
occasionally asking explanations of our remarks or
questions from one or other of his attendants. It
struck me as eminently absurd to see this negro,
who is still a slave, the centre of an adulous group
of white courtiers, for all these Arabs, noble as
many of them are in blood, were bowing down
before him, ready to obey his slightest wink and
laugh at his poorest joke. After the first few
moments of dignified silence, Jóhar, as I have
said, became affable, and began asking the news.
We had come from the north, and could tell him all
about the war. What was Sotamm doing and what
was Ibn Smeyr,—the latter evidently a hero with
the Jôfi or rather with the Haïl people, for they are
not friends with Sotamm, and old Mohammed
Dukhi is considered Sotamm's great rival. We
were glad to be able to say that we had seen Ibn
Smeyr himself at Damascus not a month ago.
Jóhar told us in return of a report recently brought
in to Meskakeh by some Sleb that the Roala had
been beaten in a fight with Mohammed Dukhi, and
that Sotamm was killed—a report we were sorry to
hear.

Then, but in a tone of minor interest, we were
questioned about the Sultan. He had made peace
with the Muscov, Jóhar was glad to hear it.
Peace was a good thing, and now "inshallah es Sultan
mabsutin," " the Sultan, let us hope, was pleased;"
this with a mock sentimental, patronising accent and

a nasal twang in the voice, which was extremely comic. A little whispering then took place between Mohammed and one of the suite, which resulted in their going out together, to hand over to Jóhar the presents we had brought for him. Mohammed was, I believe, cross-questioned as to our position and the objects of our journey, and answered, as it had been agreed beforehand he should do, that we were going to Bussora to meet friends, and that we had come by way of Jôf to avoid the sea-voyage. This, though of course not by any means the *whole* truth, was true as far as it went, and was a story easily understood and accepted by those to whom it was told. Mohammed added, moreover, that as we had happened to pass through the Emir's dominions, the English Beg was anxious to pay his respects to Ibn Rashid at Haïl before going any further, and begged Jóhar to give us the necessary guides. This, after some discussion, and some coyness on the governor's part, he consented to do. His heart had been softened by the handsome clothes we had given him, and I believe a small present in money was also talked of between him and Mohammed.

When we were summoned again to Jóhar's presence, this time on the house-top, we found the negro's face wreathed in smiles, and our journey being discussed as a settled matter. Carpets were then spread, and we all sat down on the roof and had breakfast, boiled meat on rice, with a sharp sauce to pour over the rice, and then after the usual

washings and el hamdu lillahs we retired, extremely
pleased to get away from the flies and the hot sun
of Jóhar's roof; and not a little thankful for the
good turn things had taken with us. As Wilfrid
remarked, when we were well on our mares again
and riding home, Jóhar was just the picture of a
capricious despot, and one who, if he had been in a
bad humour, might have ordered our heads off, with
no more ceremony than he had ordered breakfast.
Our last day at Meskakeh was a quiet one.

January 11.—Every morning since we have been
here there has been a fog, and to-day (Saturday), as
I have already said, it has rained heavily. The rain
came with thunder and lightning, as I believe is
almost always the case in this part of the world. I
am much surprised to learn, in talking of the lightning, that nobody at Meskakeh has heard of people
being killed by it, and Mohammed confirms the
statement made here, by saying that the same is the
case at Tudmur. He seemed astonished when I
asked him, at lightning being thought dangerous, and
says that accidents from it never occur in the desert.
This is strange. The surface soil of Meskakeh is
very nearly pure sand, and the rain runs through
it as quickly as it falls, remaining only in a few
hollows, where there is a kind of sediment hard
enough to hold it.

In the afternoon the weather cleared, and we made
a little expedition to the top of the low tell just outside Nassr's farm. The tell is of sandstone rock,

orange coloured below, but weathered black on the
upper surface. It is not more than a hundred feet
high, but standing alone, it commands a very extensive view, curious as all views in the Jôf district are,
and very pretty besides. In the fore-ground just
below lay the farm, a square walled enclosure of
three or four acres, with its palms and ithel trees,
and its two low mud houses, and its wells, looking
snug and trim and well to do. Beyond, looking
westwards, three other farms were visible, spots of
dark green in the broken wilderness of sand and
sandstone rock, and then behind them Meskakeh,
only its palm-tops in sight, and the dark mass of its
citadel rising over them in fantastic outline. The
long line of the palm grove stretched far away to the
south, disappearing at last in a confused mass of
sand-hills. These specially attracted our notice, for
they marked the commencement of the Nefûd, not
indeed the great Nefûd, but an outlying group of
dunes tufted with ghada, and not at all unlike those
passed through by the Calais and Boulogne railway.
Our route, we know, lies across them, and we are to
start to-morrow.

While I sat sketching this curious view, Wilfrid,
who had climbed to the top of a tall stone, crowning
the hill, came back with the news that he had discovered an inscription. We have been looking out,
ever since our arrival in the sandstone district, for
traces of ancient writing, but have hitherto found
nothing except some doubtful scratches, and a few

of those simple designs one finds everywhere on the sandstone, representing camels and gazelles. Here however, were three distinctly formed letters, Π H, Ϙ, two of them belonging to the Greek alphabet.

It was evident, too, by the colour of the incisions, that they had been there for very many years. On these we have built a number of historical conjectures relating to Meskakeh, and its condition in classical times.

When we came home again, we found that Mohammed had been to make the last arrangements with Jóhar for our journey. The great man had raised objections at one point of the negociations, but these had been settled by a *dahab* or gold piece, and he has now agreed to send a man with us, a professional guide for crossing the Nefûd. It seems that there are two lines by which Haïl may be reached, one of thirteen and the other of ten days' journey. The first is better suited, they say, for heavy laden camels, as the sand is less deep, but we shall probably choose the shorter route, if only for the sake of seeing the Nefûd at its worst. For the Nefûd has been the object of our dreams all through this journey, as the *ne plus ultra* of desert in the world. We hear wonderful accounts of it here, and of the people who have been lost in it. This ten days' journey represents something like two hundred miles, and there are only two wells on the way, one on the second, and another on the eighth day. The

guide will bring his own camel, and carry a couple
of waterskins, and we have bought four more, making
up the whole number to eight. This will have to
suffice for our mares as well as for ourselves, and we
shall have to be very careful. We have laid in a
sufficient stock of dates and bread, and have still
got one of the kids left to start with in the way of
meat, the other has just been devoured as I have
said, and cannot be replaced. Provisions of every
kind are difficult to procure at Meskakeh; it was
only by the exercise of a little almost Turkish bullying that Jóhar has been able to get us a camel load
of corn.

The rain is over and the moon shining. All our
preparations are made for crossing the Nefûd, and
in a few hours we shall be on our way. We shall
want all our strength for the next ten days.

A NEJD SHEEP.

CHAPTER VIII.

" We were now traversing an immense ocean of loose reddish sand, un-
limited to the eye, and heaped up in enormous ridges running parallel to
each other from north to south, undulation after undulation, each swell two
or three hundred feet in average height, with slant sides and rounded crests
furrowed in every direction by the capricious gales of the desert. In the
depths between the traveller finds himself as it were imprisoned in a suffo-
cating sand pit, hemmed in by burning walls on every side ; while at other
times, while labouring up the slope, he overlooks what seems a vast sea of
fire, swelling under a heavy monsoon wind, and ruffled by a cross blast into
little red hot waves."—PALGRAVE.

Mohammed in love—We enter the red sand desert—Geology of the
Nefûd—Radi—The great well of Shakik—Old acquaintance—
Tales of the Nefûd—The soldiers who perished of thirst—The
lovers—We nearly remain in the sand—Land at last.

January 12.—We left the farm this morning
in a thick fog, among the benedictions of the Ibn
Arûks. They have treated us kindly, and we were
sorry to say good-bye to them, especially to Turki
and Areybi, although we are a little disappointed in
our expectations of the family in general. In spite
of their noble birth and their Nejdean traditions,
they have the failings of town Arabs in regard to
money, and it was a shock to our feelings that
Nassr, our host, expected a small present in money
at parting, nominally for the women, but in reality,
no doubt, for himself. No desert sheykh, however
poor, would have pocketed the mejidies. The boys
too asked for gifts, the elder wanted a cloak, because

one had been given to his brother, the younger, a
jíbbeh, because he already had a cloak ; and other
members of the household came with little skins
full of dates or semneh in their hands, in the guise
of farewell offerings, and lingered behind for something in return. All this of course was perfectly
fair, and we were pleased to make them happy with
our money ; but it hardly tallied with the fine
sentiments they had been in the habit of expressing,
in season and out of season, about the duties of
hospitality. Such small disappointments, however,
must be borne, and borne cheerfully, for people
are not perfect anywhere, and a traveller has
no right to expect more abroad than he would find
at home. In England we might perhaps not have
been received at all, while here our welcome had
been perfectly honest at starting, whatever the
afterthought may have been. So Wilfrid solemnly
kissed the relations all round, and exchanged
promises of mutual good-will and hopes of meeting ;
I went in to the harim to say good-bye to the rest
of the family, and fortunately was not expected to
kiss them all round ; and then we set out on our
way.

Our course lay due south over the sand hills we saw
yesterday, and presently these shut out Meskakeh
and its palm groves from our view, and we were
once more reduced to our own travelling party of
eight souls, with Radi our new guide, and fairly on
the road to Haïl. These sand dunes are not really

the Nefûd, and are much like what may be seen
elsewhere in the desert, in the Sahara for instance,
or in certain parts of the peninsula of Sinai. They
are very picturesque, being of pure white sand,
from fifty to a hundred feet high, with intervening
spaces of harder ground, and are covered with
vegetation. The ghada here grows quite into a
tree, with fine gnarled trunks, nearly white, and
feathery grey foliage. We met several shepherds
with their flocks, sent here to graze from the town,
and parties of women gathering firewood. Mohammed amused us very much all the morning,
talking with these wood gatherers. He had managed
to get a glimpse of his bride elect and her sister
before starting, and fancies himself desperately in
love, though he cannot make up his mind which of
the two he prefers. Sometimes it is Muttra, as it
ought to be, and sometimes the other, for no better
reason, as far as we can learn, than that she is taller
and older, for he did not see their faces. His con-
versations to-day with the wood gatherers shewed
a *naïveté* of mind neither of us suspected. He
would ride on whenever he saw a party of these
women, and when we came up was generally to be
found in earnest discussion with the oldest and
ugliest of them on the subject of his heart. He
would begin by asking them whether they were
from Meskakeh, and lead round the conversation
to the Ibn Arûk family, and if he found that the
women knew them, he would vaguely ask how

many daughters there were in Jazi's house, and whether married or unmarried. Then he would hint that he had heard that the eldest one was very beautiful, and ask cautiously after the youngest, ending always by the disclosure that he himself was an Ibn Arûk from Tudmur, and that he was engaged to whichever of the two unmarried ones the old women had seemed to favour in their descriptions. By this process he had quite lost his head about both sisters, sometimes fancying that he was the happiest of men, and sometimes that Jazi had passed off the less valuable of his daughters upon him. On such occasions he would turn to me and beg me to repeat for the hundredth time my description of Muttra's merits, which consoled him until he met somebody else to raise new doubts in his mind.

After about eight miles of travelling through the sand dunes, we came out rather suddenly on the village of Kara, the last that we shall see for many a day. It is commanded by a rocky mound, with a ruin on it, and contains seventy or eighty houses; the palm grove surrounding it is remarkable for the palms and ithel trees. The fog had cleared off, and the sun was hot enough to make us glad to sit down for a few minutes under the mud wall which encloses the oasis. Some villagers came out, and we had a little chat about Kara and its sheykh, while our mares were being watered from a well close by. They told us we

should find a Roala camp not far upon our way,
for the camels from it were watered from this very
well. Formerly Kara, like Jôf and Meskakeh, was
a fief of the Ibn Shaalans, and they still pay a small
tribute to Sotamm, but in return they make the
Bedouins pay for the water they use. There is no
danger of being attacked by the Roala or anyone
else, for we are in Ibn Rashid's country now, where
highway robbery is not allowed. The villagers
were very hospitable in their offers of entertainment
if we would remain at Kara, but there was nothing
in the place sufficiently interesting to detain us, so
we went on. It contains, like Jôf and Meskakeh,
a ruined castle on a low tell, but the ruins are now
not much more than the foundations of old stone
walls made without cement.

Not long after leaving the village, we came upon
a party of Roala, with several hundred camels
coming in to Kara for water. They were unarmed,
and travelling as peaceably as peasants would in
Italy. They told us their camp was out of our
way, and too far off for us to reach to-night, but
that we should find Beneyeh ibn Shaalan, a cousin
of Sotamm's, near the well of Shakik our watering
place for to-morrow. It argued well for the
security of the country, to find parties of villagers,
as we presently did, out in the sand dunes many
miles beyond Kara, with all these Bedouins about.
But really there seem to be law and order in Ibn
Rashid's government. After travelling on for

another two hours and a half in broken ground, we came at last to a steep acclivity which proved, when we had mounted it, to be the further edge of the Meskakeh depression, and above it we found ourselves on a gravelly plain. The view from this edge, looking back, was very interesting, and gave us at once an idea of the geography of the whole country, the great basin of Meskakeh with its tells and sand hills, the long ridge of hill under which the oasis stands, the range of Jebel Hammamiyeh too, all mere islands in the basin, which seems moreover to include Jôf as well as the eastern villages in its main circuit. Wilfrid has little doubt now that Meskakeh and Jôf are really only the tail as it were of the Wady Sirhán or rather its head, for the whole must be in shape something like a tadpole, and this point its nose.

The Hamád or plain where we now were, is three hundred and fifty feet higher than Kara and Meskakeh, or 2220 feet above the sea. It is absolutely level and bare of vegetation, a flat black expanse of gravelly soil covered with small round pebbles, extending southwards to the horizon, and quite unlike anything in the basin below. We were much surprised to find such an open plain in front of us, for we had expected nothing now but sand, but the sand, though we could not see it, was not far off, and this was only as it were the shore of the great Nefûd.

At half past three o'clock we saw a red streak on

the horizon before us, which rose and gathered as we approached it, stretching out east and west in an unbroken line. It might at first have been taken for an effect of mirage, but on coming nearer we found it broken into billows, and but for its red colour not unlike a stormy sea seen from the shore, for it rose up, as the sea seems to rise, when the waves are high, above the level of the land. Somebody called out "the Nefûd," and though for a while we were incredulous, we were soon convinced. What surprised us was its colour, that of rhubarb and magnesia, nothing at all like the sand we had hitherto seen, and nothing at all like what we had expected. Yet the Nefûd it was, the great red desert of central Arabia. In a few minutes we had cantered up to it, and our mares were standing with their feet in its first waves.

January 13.—We have been all day in the Nefûd, which is interesting beyond our hopes, and charming into the bargain. It is, moreover, quite unlike the description I remember to have read of it by Mr. Palgrave, which affects one as a nightmare of impossible horror. It is true he passed it in summer, and we are now in mid-winter, but the physical features cannot be much changed by the change of seasons, and I cannot understand how he overlooked its main characteristics. The thing that strikes one first about the Nefûd is its colour. It is not white like the sand dunes we passed yesterday, nor yellow as the sand is in parts of the

Egyptian desert, but a really bright red, almost crimson in the morning when it is wet with the dew. The sand is rather coarse, but absolutely pure, without admixture of any foreign substance, pebble, grit, or earth, and exactly the same in tint and texture everywhere. It is, however, a great mistake to suppose it barren. The Nefûd, on the contrary, is better wooded and richer in pasture than any part of the desert we have passed since leaving Damascus. It is tufted all over with ghada bushes, and bushes of another kind called *yerta*, which at this time of the year when there are no leaves, is exactly like a thickly matted vine. Its long knotted stems and fibrous trunk give it so much that appearance, that there is a story about its having originally been a vine. The rasúl Allah (God's prophet), Radi says, came one day to a place where there was a vineyard, and found some peasants pruning. He asked them what they were doing, and what the trees were, and they, fearing his displeasure or to make fun of him, answered, these are "yerta" trees, yerta being the first name that came into their heads. "Yerta inshallah, yerta let them be then," rejoined the prophet, and from that day forth they ceased to be vines and bore no fruit. There are, besides, several kinds of camel pasture, especially one new to us called adr, on which they say sheep can feed for a month without wanting water, and more than one kind of grass. Both camels and mares are therefore pleased with the

place, and we are delighted with the abundance of
firewood for our camps. Wilfrid says that the
Nefûd has solved for him at last the mystery of
horse-breeding in Central Arabia. In the hard desert
there is nothing a horse can eat, but here there
is plenty. The Nefûd accounts for everything.
Instead of being the terrible place it has been
described by the few travellers who have seen
it, it is in reality the home of the Bedouins during
a great part of the year. Its only want is water,
for it contains but few wells ; all along the edge,
it is thickly inhabited, and Radi tells us that in
the spring, when the grass is green after rain, the
Bedouins care nothing for water, as their camels are
in milk, and they go for weeks without it, wandering far into the interior of the sand desert.

We have been travelling through the Nefûd
slowly all day, and have occupied ourselves in
studying its natural features. At first sight it
seemed to us an absolute chaos, and heaped up here
and hollowed out there, ridges and cross ridges, and
knots of hillocks all in utter confusion, but after
some hours' marching we began to detect a uniformity
in the disorder, which we are occupied in trying
to account for. The most striking features of the
Nefûd are the great horse-hoof hollows which are
scattered all over it (Radi calls them *fulj*). These,
though varying in size from an acre to a couple of
hundred acres, are all precisely alike in shape and
direction. They resemble very exactly the track of

an unshod horse, that is to say, the toe is sharply
cut and perpendicular, while the rim of the hoof
tapers gradually to nothing at the heel, the frog
even being roughly but fairly represented by broken
ground in the centre, made up of converging
water-courses. The diameter of some of these
fuljes must be at least a quarter of a mile, and
the depth of the deepest of them, which we
measured to-day, proved to be 230 feet, bringing
it down very nearly exactly to the level of the
gravelly plain which we crossed yesterday, and
which, there can be little doubt, is continued underneath the sand. This is all the more probable, as we
found at the bottom of this deepest fulj, and nowhere
else, a bit of hard ground. The next deepest fulj we
measured was only a hundred and forty feet, and was
still sandy at the lowest point, that is to say, just
below the point of the frog. Though the soil composing the sides and every part of the fuljes is of pure
sand, and the immediate surface must be constantly
shifting, it is quite evident that the general outline of
each has remained unchanged for years, possibly for
centuries. The vegetation proves this; for it is not
a growth of yesterday, and it clothes the fuljes like
all the rest. Moreover, our guide, who has travelled
backwards and forwards over the Nefûd for forty
years, asserts that it never changes. No sandstorm ever fills up the hollows, or carries away the
ridges. He knows them all, and has known them
ever since he was a boy. "They were made so by

God." Wilfrid has been casting about, however, for some natural theory to account for their formation, but has not yet been able to decide whether they are owing to the action of wind or water, or to inequalities of the solid ground below. But at present he inclines to the theory of water. We shall be able perhaps to say more of them hereafter, when we have seen more of them, and I therefore reserve my remarks. We have had a long day's journey, plodding up to the camel's fetlocks in sand, and now it is time to look after Hanna, who is busy cooking. Height of our camp 2440 feet; but the highest level crossed during the day was 2560 feet. Nobody seen all day but one Roala on a delúl, who told us there was a camp to our left. We looked for it, but only made out camels at a great distance.

January 14.—Another bright clear morning, but with a cold wind from the south-east. Nothing can be more bright and sparkling than the winter's sun reflected from these red sands. The fuljes have again been the object of our attention. We find that they all point in the same direction, or nearly so, that is to say, with the toe of the horse-hoof towards the west, though the steepest part of the declivity varies a little, sometimes the southerly and sometimes the northerly aspect being more abrupt than that facing east. This would seem to point rather to wind than water as being the original cause of the depressions. At the edge, moreover, of

the large fuljes there is generally a tallish mound of
sand with a ridge, such as one sees on the top of a
snow peak, and evidently caused by the wind, the
lee side being steep and the weather side rounded.
These seem to change with a change of wind and
are generally bare of vegetation, and what is singular,
of a lighter coloured sand than the rest. One can
guess the existence of a deep fulj from a long way
off, by the presence of one of these snowy looking
mounds on the horizon. It is seldom that one can
see very far in the Nefûd, as one is always toiling up
or down sandslopes, or creeping like a fly round the
edges of these great basins. The ground is generally
pretty even, just round the edges, and one goes from
one fulj to another so as to take this advantage of
level. We rode up to the top of one or two of the
highest sand peaks, and from one of them made out
a line of hills about fifteen miles off to the west-
south-west, with an isolated headland beyond, which
we recognized as the Ras el Tawíl pointed out to
us the day we arrived at Jôf. From these heights
too we could observe the lay of the fuljes, and
make out that they followed each other in strings,
not always in a straight line, but as a wady would
go, winding gently about. This made us speculate
on the water theory again. Wilfrid thinks that
there may be a very gradual slope in the plain
beneath the sand, and that whenever rain falls,
as of course it must do here sometimes, it sinks
through to the hard ground and flows under the

sand along shallow winding wadys, and that the
sand in this way is constantly slipping very gradually
down the incline, and wherever there is a slope in
the plain below, there the fulj occurs above it.*
This notion is favoured by what wc have observed
of the bare places, where such occur, for they always
slope down towards the west. Radi assures us that
no water ever collects in the fuljes even after rain.
It runs into them and disappears. While we were
discussing these points of natural history, we
suddenly perceived camels grazing at the edge of a
fulj not half a mile below us, and jumped on to our
mares in a great hurry. I have contrived a bandage
which enables me to mount quickly, and ever since
the ghazú in the Wady Sirhán, we keep a good
look-out for enemies. We then rode down to see
what was to be seen, and presently found half a dozen
people, men and women, in a fulj, and several more
camels grazing near a tent. The tent was a mere
awning with a back to it, and as soon as they saw us
the women ran and pulled it down, while the men
rushed off to the nearest camels, and made them kneel.
They were evidently in a fright, and so quickly was it
all done that by the time we had ridden up, the tent
and tent furniture, such as there was, were loaded
and ready to go. The Arabs take pride in being
able to strike camp and march at almost a moment's
notice, and in this case I think it hardly took three

---

* A diagram, shewing what a section of the Nefûd would be like,
is given in the geographical notes, Vol. ii., page 243.

minutes. They seemed much surprised and puzzled at our appearance when we rode up, and at first said they were Roala, but when our people joined us they confessed that they were of the Howeysin, a very poor tribe despised by the rest of the Bedouins and holding much the same position as the Sleb. They were, however, to our eyes undistinguishable from other Bedouins.

I asked Mohammed after this, how it was that in the desert each tribe seemed so readily recognized by their fellows, and he told me that each has certain peculiarities of dress or features well known to all. Thus the Shammar are in general tall, and the Sebaa very short but with long spears. The Roala spears are shorter, and their horses smaller. The Shammar of Nejd wear brown abbas, the Harb are black in face, almost like slaves, and Mohammed told me many more details as to other tribes which I do not remember. He said that Radi had recognised these people as Howeysin directly, by their wretched tent. He then reminded us of how we had been deceived last year by the ghazú we had met in the Hamád the day we found Jedaan. It was very lucky, he declared, that nothing disagreeable had happened then, for he had found out since that the nine people Wilfrid had ridden up to talk to, were in reality a ghazú of Amarrat, headed by Reja himself, Sheykh of the Erfuddi section of that tribe. Reja had come in not many weeks later to Palmyra to buy corn, and had stayed two days in

Abdallah's house, and had recognized him as the man who was with the Beg that day. These Amarrat had been in the act of discussing how they should attack our caravan when Wilfrid rode up, and the fact of his doing so alone made them imagine that our caravan was a very strong one, so they had decided on leaving us alone. Mohammed and Reja were now friends, Reja having given Mohammed a falcon on going away, and Mohammed the strange present of a winding-sheet. Winding-sheets he explains are much esteemed by the Bedouins, and this one had been made by Mohammed's mother.

Soon after this we came upon a real Roala camp, at least a camp of their slaves. The men were not negroes, though very dark and ill-looking. They explained that they belonged to Beneyeh ibn Shaalan, a cousin of Sotamm's, and the head of the tribe now in the Nefûd. They gave us some fresh camel's milk, the first we have tasted this year. We then began to descend into a long valley, which here intersects the Nefûd, and in which stand the wells of Shakik. Close to one of these we now are, camped on a bit of hard ground, under the first wave of sand beyond the wells. There are four wells known as Shakik; the one where we now are and another near it, and two others, three or four miles distant, up and down the valley. They are all, we hear, of the same depth, two hundred and twenty-five feet, and are apparently very ancient, for this one is lined with cut stones, and the edges

are worn through with long usage of ropes in drawing water. There is, however, here, a little wooden
pulley for the rope to pass over, a permanent
arrangement very unusual in the desert, where
everything removable is as a matter of course removed. A rope or a bucket would have no chance
of remaining a week at any well. There was a dead
camel near the well, on which a pair of vultures and
a dog were at work, but nothing else living.

While we were looking over our ropes, and wondering whether we could make up enough, with all
the odds and ends tied together, to reach to the
water, a troop of camels came flourishing down
upon us, cantering with their heads out, and their
heels in the air, and followed by some men on
delúls. These proved to be Ibn Shaalan's people,
and, to our great surprise and delight, one of them,
a man named Rashid, recognized us as old acquaintances. We had met him the year before at the
Roala camp at Saikal far away north. He had
come, he said, with Abu Giddeli to our tent, and
we remember the circumstance perfectly. It is
pleasant to think of finding friends in such a place
as this, and it shows how far the tribes wander
during the year. Saikal is five hundred miles from
Shakik, as the crow flies. Rashid at once offered to
draw us all the water we wanted, for he had a long
rope with him, and coffee was drunk and dates were
eaten by all the party. Amongst them are two
sons of Beneyeh's, Mohammed and Assad, the

elder a shy boorish youth, but the younger, nine
years old, a nice little boy. To him we entrusted our complimentary message to his father.
Beneyeh ibn Heneyfi ibn Shaalan is the Sheykh of
a large section of the Roala, the very one we heard
of last year as having stayed in Nejd. He is on ill
terms with Sotamm on account of a chestnut mare
Sotamm took from him by force, some years ago.
The children had never seen a European in their
lives, or been further north than the Wady Sirhán.
We should like to pay Beneyeh a visit, but his
tents are many miles out of our way, and we dare
not trifle with the Nefûd.

A camel foal was born to-day by the well. I
went to look at the little creature which was left
behind with its mother, when the rest were driven
home. I noticed that it had none of those bare
places (callosities) which the older camels get on
their knees and chest from kneeling down, and that
its knees were bruised by its struggles to rise. We
helped it up, and in three hours' time it was able to
trot away with its mother.

January 15.—This morning, as I looked out of
of the tent, I saw a halo round the moon, and thought
there would be rain ; but no such luck has come,
though the sky was overcast and the day sultry.
We made a great effort to get off early, and there
was a great deal of " yalla, yalla " from Mohammed
with very little result, for the men had been cele-
brating our passage of the Nefûd, which began

seriously to-day, with a final feast on kid, and were
dull and slow in consequence.   Wilfrid made them
a short speech last night, about the serious nature
of the journey we were undertaking, the hundred
miles of deep sand we have to cross, and the
necessity of husbanding all our strength for the
effort. With the best despatch we can hardly hope
to reach Jobba under five days, and it may be six
or seven. No heavily laden caravan such as ours
is, has ever, if we may believe Radi, crossed the
Nefûd at this point, and if the camels break down,
there will be no means of getting help, nor is there
any well after Shakik. Abdallah has accordingly
been made *sheykh of the water*, with orders to dole
it out in rations every night, and allow nobody to
drink during the day. The Arabs are very childish
about meat and drink, eating and drinking all day
long if they get the chance, and keeping nothing for
the morrow. But here improvidence can only bring
disaster, and we think Abdallah as well as Mohammed are impressed with the situation. There is
something sobering and solemn in these great tracts
of sand, even for the wildest spirits, and we have
begun our march to-day in very orderly fashion.

Radi, the little guide (his name signifies *willing*),
has proved a great acquisition to our party, willing
to give every sort of information when asked, and
not impertinently talkative. He is a curious little
old man, as dry and black and withered as the dead
stumps of the yerta bushes one sees here, the drift-

wood of the Nefûd.   He has his delúl with him, an
ancient bag of bones which looks as if it would
never last through the journey, and on which he
sits perched hour after hour in silence, pointing
now and then with his shrivelled hand towards the
road we are to take.   He is carrying with him on
his camel one of the red sand-stone mortars of the
Jôf for a relation of Ibn Rashid's, and this seems to
balance the water-skin hanging on the other side.
From time to time, however, he speaks, and he has
told us more than one interesting tale of those who
have perished here in former days.   In almost every
hollow there are bones, generally those of camels,
"Huseyn's camels," Radi calls them, and if anybody asks who Huseyn was, there is a laugh.   At
the bottom, however, of one fulj there are bones of
another sort.   Here a ghazú perished, delúls and
men.   They were Roala who had crossed the Nefûd
to make a raid upon the Shammar, and had not
been able to reach Shakik on their way back.   The
bones were white, but there were bits of skin still
clinging to them, though Radi says it happened ten
years ago.   In another place, he shewed us two
heaps of wood, thirty yards apart, which mark
the spot where a Shammar ghazú, which had been
lifting camels in the Wady Sirhán, was overtaken
by their owner, a Sirhán sheykh, who had thrown
his lance these thirty yards at the akid of the
Shammar and transfixed him, mare and all.   Again,
he pointed out the remains of forty Suelmat camel

riders, who had lost their way, and perished of thirst.

The sand, for several miles after leaving the wells, was covered with camel tracks, Roala camels no doubt, and here and there we came across the track of a horse, but the further one gets into Arabia, the rarer horses seem to be. After these first few miles, however, there appeared no trace of living creatures except lizards. Radi took us first in a nearly southerly direction, till he hit a line of landmarks, invisible to us but well known to him, running south-south-east. This he calls *the road*, the road of Abu Zeyd, and told us the following legend in connection with it (there was no more trace of a road than there might have been on the sea). Many years ago, says Radi, there was a famine in Nejd, and the Beni Hellal were without bread. Then Abu Zeyd, sheykh of the tribe, spoke to his kinsmen Merrey and Yunis, and said, "Let us go out towards the west, and seek new pastures for our people," and they travelled until they came to Tunis el-Gharb, which was at that time ruled by an Emir named Znati, and they looked at the land and liked it, and were about to return to their tribe with the news, when Znati put them all into prison. Now Znati had a daughter who was very beautiful, named Sferi, and when she saw Merrey in the dungeon, she fell in love with him, and proposed that he should marry her, and promised that his life and all their lives should be spared. But Merrey did

not care for her and would not at first consent. Still
she persisted in her love, and sought to do them good,
and interceded with her father to spare their lives.
Now Znati began to be perplexed with his prisoners,
hearing from his daughter that they were of noble
birth, and not knowing what to do with them. And
when she told them this, they proposed that one of
them should be released, and sent home to bring a
ransom for his fellows, but in their hearts they were
determined that Abu Zeyd should be the one sent,
and that he should return, not with a ransom, but
with all his people to Tunis, and so set them free.
And Sferi carried the proposal to her father, and
said, "Two of these men are of noble birth, but the
third is a slave, but I know not which it is. Let
then the slave go and get ransom for his masters."
And Znati said, "How shall we discover the slave
amongst them, and distinguish him from the others?"
and she said, "By this. Take them to a muddy
place, where there is water, and bid them pass over
it. And you shall see that whichever is the slave
amongst them will gather up his clothes about him
carefully, while the nobly born will let their clothes
be soiled." And her father agreed, and it happened
so that on the following day the three men were
brought out of their dungeon, and made to pass
through a muddy stream. And Abu Zeyd, being
warned by Sferi, put his abba on his head, and lifted
up his shirt to the waist, while Merry and Yunis
walked through without precaution. So Abu Zeyd

was set free and returned to Nejd, and gathering all
his people together there, he led them across the
Nefûd by this very way, making the road we had
just seen, to enable them to come in safety. He
then marched on to Tunis, and laid siege to the town.

Abu Zeyd beseiged Tunis for a year but could not
enter, and he never would have taken it, but for Sferi
who was plotting for his success outside.   Sferi was
a wise woman.   She could read and write, and knew
magic and could interpret prophecies.   And there
was a prophecy concerning Znati that he could be
killed by no one in battle but by a certain Dib
ibn Ghanim, a robber in the neighbouring desert.
And Sferi sent word of this to Abu Zeyd, who took
this robber into his service, and on the next occasion
sent him against Znati when he came out to fight.
And the Emir was slain.

Then Abu Zeyd became Emir of Tunis and Merrey
married Sferi.

Such is Radi's story, which it may be hoped is not
exactly true as to Sferi's betrayal of her father.   As
to the road legend, it is impossible to say that the
road is there "to witness if he lies."   Road or no
road we have been wandering about in zigzags all
day long, sometimes toiling up steep slopes, at others
making a long circuit to avoid a fulj, and sometimes
meandering for no particular reason yet always on a
perfectly untrodden surface of yielding sand.   The
ground is more broken than ever, the fuljes bigger
and the travelling harder.   But both mares and

camels have marched bravely, and we have got over
about twenty-one miles to-day. Our camp this
evening, though in a fulj, is five hundred and sixty
feet higher than the wells of Shakik.

January 16.—A thunderstorm in the night which
has turned the sand crimson. Radi congratulates
us upon this, as he says now we shall get to Jobba,
inshallah ! He seems to have been a little doubtful
before. But the heavy rain has hardened the ground,
and we have been able to push on at almost as good
a rate as if we had been travelling on gravel. As
we get deeper into the Nefûd, the fuljes are further
apart and the cross ridges lower. The fuljes seem
to run in pretty regular strings from east to west,
or rather from east by south to west by north.
It is interesting to observe the footmarks of
wild animals on the sand, for they are now
clearly marked as on fresh fallen snow. The most
common are those of hares answering in size to our
rabbits at home, and to-day the greyhounds have
put up and coursed several of them, though quite
in vain, for the ghada trees and bushes soon screen
them from the dogs. We have had a gallop or
two, and there is no danger of losing ourselves,
for we only have to go back on our footsteps
to find the caravan. Besides the hares there are
several sorts of small birds, linnets, wrens, desert
larks, wheatears, and occasionally crows. I also saw
a pair of kestrels evidently quite at home. Reptiles
are still much more numerous, the whole surface of

the desert being marked with lizard tracks, while here
and there was the trail of a snake. Our people killed
two to-day of the sort called *suliman*, common in
most parts of the desert, a long, slim, silvery snake,
with a little head, and quite harmless. The warm
sunshine after the rain had brought them out.
We have been inquiring of Radi after the more
dangerous species, and he describes very accurately
the horned viper and the cobra. I was surprised to
hear of the latter, but it is impossible to mistake his
description of a snake which stands on its tail, and
swells out its neck like wings. These, he says, are
only seen in the summer. Gazelles there seem to be
none in the Nefûd, but we crossed the quite fresh
track of two "wild cows" (antelope). This animal,
Radi assures us, never leaves the Nefûd and never
drinks. Indeed there is no water here above ground
anywhere nearer than Jebel Aja, and it must be
able to do without. The slot was about the size
of a red deer fully grown. We are very anxious to
see the beast itself, which they assure us is a real cow,
though that can hardly be. We have also kept a
good look-out for ostriches but without result. In
the way of insects, we have seen a few flies like
houseflies, and some dragonflies and small butterflies.
There is a much better sort of grass in the Nefûd and
more of it than on the outskirts, which I suppose is
from the absence of camels.

I find that Radi makes out his course almost
entirely by landmarks. On every high sand-hill he

gets down from his delúl, and pulls some ghada
branches, which are very brittle, and adds them to
piles of wood he has formerly made. These can be
seen a good way off. We have learned, too, to make
out a sort of road after all, of an intermittent kind,
marked by the dung of camels, and occasionally on
the side of a steep slope there is a distinct footway.
Along this line our guide feels his way, here and
there making a cast, as hounds do when they are
off the scent. Neither he nor Mohammed, nor any
of the Arabs with us, have the least notion of steering
by the sun, and when Wilfrid asked Mohammed if he
thought he could find his way back to Shakik, he
answered, " How could I do so ? Every one of these
sand-hills is like the last."

We have been entertained by Radi with more
blood and bones stories, the most terrible of which
is that of some Turkish soldiers,* who many years
ago were treacherously abandoned in the Nefûd.
They had occupied Haïl in the days of the first Ibn
Rashid, and had been left there as a garrison. But
either the Sultan could not communicate with them
or forgot them, and after a certain time they wished
to go home. Many of them had died at Haïl, and
the remainder of them, about five hundred, easily
agreed to set out for Damascus under the escort of
Obeyd, the Emir's brother, who had resolved to
destroy them. They left Haïl on horseback and

---

* These were no doubt the Egyptians of Ibrahim Pasha's army,
left behind at Aneyzeh.

followed their Shammar guides to this place, who to
all questions as to where they should find wells,
answered, a little further, a little further on. At
last the Bedouins left them. They seem to have
been brave fellows, for the last that was heard of
them was a sort of song or chorus which they sang
as they struggled on, "Nahnu askar ma nahnu atâ-
sha nahnu askar ma benríd moyeh." "We are not
thirsty, we soldiers want no water." But at noon
that day they must have lost heart, and lain down
under the bushes to get a sort of shade, and so they
were afterwards found scattered about in the different
fuljes. Some of their horses made their way back
to Jobba, and became the property of any who could
seize them. They were sold by these lucky people
for a few sheep or goats each. It is a ghastly tale.

A pleasanter one is that of two young lovers who
eloped from Jôf, and were pursued by their relations.
Suspecting that they would be tracked, and to avoid
scandal, they had agreed that instead of walking
together, they would keep parallel lines about a
hundred yards apart and so set out on their journey,
and when they came to a certain fulj, which Radi
pointed out to us, they were too tired and lay down
to die each under his bush. Thus they were found
and fortunately in time, and their discretion so
pleased the relations on both sides, that consent was
given to their marriage, and the nuptials celebrated
with rejoicings.

At half-past ten we suddenly caught sight of the

peaks of Aalem, two conical rocks which jut out of
the sand, and make a conspicuous landmark for
travellers on their way to Jobba.   It was an
immense relief to see them, for we had begun to
distrust the sagaicty of our guide on account of the
tortuous line we followed, and now we knew that
the worst was over, and that if need were, we could
find our way on across the other half of the Nefûd,
with some prospect at least of success.   We left
our camels to follow, and rode on towards the hills.
It still took us several hours to reach them, but we
were by three o'clock touching the stones with our
hands to feel that they were real.   It was as if we
had been lost at sea and had found a desert island.

We had some time to wait while the caravan
laboured slowly on to join us.   I remained with
the mares and kept a look-out while Wilfrid climbed
to the top of the smaller rock.   " What a place to
be buried in," he exclaimed.   " Mount Nebo must
have been like this."   But people who die in the
Nefûd have seldom anyone to bury them.   As he
clambered round the pile of loose stones near the
top of the tell, he found to his great delight a
painted lady butterfly sunning itself in a sheltered
spot.   If, as is probable, there is no vegetation
suited for the caterpillar of this butterfly nearer
than Hebron, this little insect must have travelled
at least four hundred miles.   Here it seemed happy
in the sun.   This smaller rock, or rocky hill, was
just a hundred feet from the level of the plain,

and rose sheer out of it bare and naked as a rock
does at sea.   The barometer at the top of it shewed
3220 feet.   The taller Aalem is perhaps three times
its height.

Aalem, Radi says, is Sheykh of the Nefûd, and
the little tell is his son.   At some miles distance to
the north-east there is a cluster of white sand-hills,
Aalem's "harîm."   The rocks of Aalem are sandstone weathered black, not granite as we had hoped,
and this no doubt is the material from which in the
lapse of years the great red sand heaps have been
formed.   They are not of solid rock but resemble
heaps of stones.   On the top of the one Wilfrid
ascended was a cairn with the remains of some old
letters scratched on the stones, of the same kind as
those to be seen on Sinai, or rather in the Wady
Mokattib.   The view was, by Wilfrid's report,
stupendous, but one impossible to draw or even
attempt to draw.   Here could be seen spread out
as on a map the general features of the Nefûd, the
uniformity of the ocean of sand streaked with the
long lines of its fulges, Aalem itself rising in
their midst like a rock out of a sea streaked with
foam.

We are now encamped about two miles beyond
Aalem.   I have filled a bottle with sand to make
an hour-glass with at home.

January 17.—A white frost, some of which was
packed up with the tents and carried with us all
day.

It is curious that now we have passed Aalem the
vegetation has changed. Up to that point the ghada
reigned supreme, and I could not have believed it
could so suddenly disappear, yet such is the case.
Now not a bush of ghada is to be seen, and its
place is taken by the yerta which before was rare.
It seems impossible to account for this, as there is
no material change of level, and absolutely no
change in the character of the soil. The bushes by
which we camped last night were quite the last
southwards. We are sorry to lose them, as ghada is
the finest firewood in the world. Charcoal made
from it, which one finds here and there where there
has been a camp fire, is finer than the finest charcoal
used for drawing. The yerta is inferior. On the
other hand there is more of the grass called *nassi*
for the camels, and of the *hamar*, a whitish-blue
prickly plant which the mares are very fond of,
while the *adr*, a shrub with stiff green leaves and
brownish yellow flowers, is still the commonest
plant.

The sand has dried again since yesterday, and as
the day grew warmer became very heavy for the
camels. The labour of trudging through the
yielding surface is beginning to tell on them, and
to-day most of our men have walked, Mohammed
giving the example. Every one was cheerful, in
spite of the hard work, and all showed wonderful
strength in running on and playing pranks in the
sand. Wilfrid, who is in fair training, was quite

unable to keep up with them, and I fared still
worse as may be imagined, being as yet very
lame ; we both, however, felt bound to try and
walk at intervals for the sake of our mares.
Ibrahim el-tawíl (the tall as contrasted with
Ibrahim el-kasír, or the short), who has hitherto
been the butt of the party, being sent down on
fools' errands to fetch water from fuljes, and up to
the tops of sand-hills, to see imaginary mountains,
has proved himself to-day most valiant. He,
although a Christian, is a match for any Moslem
of the party, and gives as much as he takes in
the rough games the Arabs indulge in to keep up
their spirits. At one moment he got hold of the
servants' tent pole, a very heavy one, and played at
quarter-staff with it among them to such effect, that
I thought there would have been bones broken.
Abdallah, too, when there is any particularly hard
piece of climbing to do and the rest seem fagged,
generally runs on and stands on his head till they
come up. We encourage this mirth as it makes the
work lighter.

Our water is now running rather short, for we
have had to divide a skin among the mares each
day, but this lightens the loads. Two of the camels
are beginning to flag, Hanna's delúl, which has
hardly had fair play, as he and Ibrahim have been
constantly changing places on its back, and making
a camel kneel and get up repeatedly tires it more
than any weight ; also the beautiful camel we

bought at Mezárib. This last, in spite of his good
looks, seems to be weakly. His legs are a trifle
long, and his neck a trifle short, two bad points for
endurance, and then he is only a three year old and
has not had the distemper, at least so Abdallah says.
A camel can never be depended on till he has had
it. The ugly camel, too, which they call Shenuan,
seems distressed. He has certainly got the mange,
and I wish we had insisted on this point when we
suspected the camels at Damascus, but it is too late
now. The rest are still in fine order, in spite of the
long journey and the absence of fresh pasture, which
at this time of year they require. Nothing green,
has yet appeared, except a diminutive plant like a
nemophila, with a purple flower which is beginning
to show its head above the sand. Fresh grass
there is none, and last year's crop stands white and
withered still without sign of life.

We met a man to-day, a Roala, alone with
twelve camels, yearlings and two year olds, which
he had bought from the Shammar and was driving
home. He had paid twenty-five to thirty-five
mejidies apiece for them, but they were scraggy
beasts. The Nejd camels are nearly all black, and
very inferior in size and strength to those of the
north. When we came upon the man we at first
supposed he might be an enemy, for anybody here
is likely to be that, and Awwad rushed valiantly at
him with a gun, frightening him out of his wits and
summoning him in a terrible voice to give an

account of himself. He was perfectly harmless and unarmed, and had been three nights out already in the Nefûd by himself. He had a skin of water and a skin of dates, and was going to Shakík, a lonely walk.

At half-past three (level 3040 feet) we caught sight of the hills of Jobba, and from the same point could just see Aalem. It was a good occasion for correcting our reckoning, so we took the directions accurately with the compass, and made out our course to be exactly south by east.

To-day all our Mahometans have begun to say their prayers, for the first time during the journey. The solemnity of the Nefûd, or perhaps a doubt about reaching Jobba, might well make them serious; perhaps, however, they merely want to get into training for Nejd, where Wahhabism prevails and prayers are in fashion. Whatever be the cause, Mohammed on the top of a sand-hill was bowing and kneeling towards Mecca with great appearance of earnestness, and Awwad recited prayers in a still more impressive manner, raising his voice almost to a chant.

Talking by the camp fire to night, Radi informs us that the Nefûd extends twelve days' journey to the east of where we now are, and eleven days' journey to the west. At the edge of it westwards, lies Teyma, an oasis like Jôf, where there is a wonderful well, the best in Arabia. We asked him about sand-storms, and whether caravans were ever buried

by them. He said they were not. The sand never
buries any object deeply, as we can judge by the
sticks and bones and camel-dung which always
remain on the surface. The only danger for
caravans is that a storm may last so long that their
provision of water fails them, for they cannot travel
when it is severe. Of the simum, or poisonous wind
spoken of by travellers, he has never heard, though
he has been travelling to and fro in the Nefûd for
forty years. Abdallah, however, says he has heard
of it at Tudmur, as of a thing occurring now and
again. None of them have ever experienced it.

January 18.—A calm night with slight fog, hoar
frost in the morning.

It appears that there was a scout or spy about
our camp in the night from the Shammar. We had
been sighted in the afternoon, and he had crept up
in the dark to find out who we were. At first he
thought we were a ghazú, but afterwards recognised
Radi's voice, and knew we must be travellers going
to Ibn Rashid. He came in the morning and told
us this ; and that he was out on a scouting expedition to look for grass in the Nefûd. He seemed
rather frightened, and very anxious to please ; and
assured us over and over again that Mohammed
Ibn Rashid would be delighted to see us.

It has been another hard day for the camels.
Shenuan has broken down and cannot carry his
load ; and Hanna, like the rest of the men, has had
to walk, for his delúl is giving in. The sand seems

to get deeper and deeper; and though we have been at work from dawn to dusk, we are still ten or fifteen miles from Jobba. But for the hills which we see before us every time we rise to the crest of a wave, it would be very hopeless work. Every one is serious to-night.

Sunday, January 19.—A terrible day for camels and men. Hanna's delúl, Shenuan, and the tall camel they call "Amúd," or the "Pillar," refused their aliek last night, being too thirsty to eat; and to-day they could carry no loads. Shakran, too, who has hitherto been one of our best walkers, lagged behind ; and the whole pace of the caravan has been little over a mile an hour. But for the extraordinary strength of Hatherán, the gigantic camel which leads the procession, and on whom most of the extra loads have been piled, we should have had to abandon a great part of our property ; and, indeed, at one moment it seemed as if we should remain altogether in the Nefûd, adding a new chapter to old Radi's tales of horror. And now that we have escaped such a fate and have reached Jobba, we can see how fortunate we have been. But for the perfect travelling weather throughout our passage of the Nefûd, and the extraordinary luck of that thunderstorm, we should not now be at Jobba. The sand to tired camels is like a prison, and in the sand we should have remained. Mohammed, Abdallah, and the rest all behaved like heroes ; even old Hanna, with stray locks of grey hair hanging from under his kefiyeh, for he has grown grey on the journey, and his feet bare, for it is impossible to walk in shoes, trudged on as valiantly as the most robust of the party. All were cheerful and uncomplaining, though the usual songs had ceased, and they talked but little.

Wilfrid and I were the only ones who rode at all, except Hanna, whom Wilfrid forced to ride his mare from time to time, and we were the gloomiest of the party. We felt annoyed at being unable to do our work on foot with the others; though from time to time we walked or rather waded through the sand, until obliged to remount for lack of breath and strength. Neither of us could have kept up on foot; but a European is no match for even a town Arab in the matter of walking.

To-day the *khall Abu Zeyd* (Abu Zeyd's road) was distinctly traceable, and we begin to think that it may not have been altogether a romance. There are regular cuttings in some places, and the track is often well marked for half a mile together. Radi assures us that there is a road of stone under the sand; of stone brought from Jebel Shammar at, I am afraid to say, what expense of camels and men, who died in the work. I noticed to-day a buzzard and a grey shrike; and a couple of wolves had run along the road, as one could see by their footmarks and the scratchings on the sand.

The level of the Nefûd had been rising all day, and at one o'clock we were 3300 feet above the

sea. From this point we had a large view southwards, sand, all sand still for many a mile ; but
close before us the group of islands we had so long
been steering for, the rocks of Jobba. The nearest
was not two miles off. We could see nothing of
the oasis, for it was on the other side of the hills ;
but we could make out a wide space bare of sand,
which looked like a subbkha, and beyond this a
further group of rocks of exceedingly fantastic outline, rising out of the sand. It was like a scene
on some great glacier in the Alps. Beyond again,
lay a faint blue line of hills. "Jebel Shammar.
Those are the hills of Nejd," said Radi. They were
what we have come so far to see.

We made haste now to get to the rocks, and
reached them at half-past three. They were of the
same character as Aalem, sand and ironstone. There
Wilfrid took a map, and I a sketch, and we waited
till the camels came up ; a doleful string they were
as we looked down from the top of our rocky hill at
them passing below. Shenuan and Amûd toiled on
with only their saddles, and the poor black delúl,
absolutely bare and hardly able to walk, was fifty
yards behind, urged along by Abdallah. We still
had some miles to go to get to Jobba, but on harder
ground and all down hill ; and Mohammed proposed
that we three should ride on, and prepare a place for
the camels in the village. On our way we saw what
we thought was a cloud of smoke moving from west
to east, and the tail of it passed over us. We found

it was a flight of locusts in the red stage of their
existence, which the people here prefer for eating,
but we did not care to stop now to gather them,
and rode on.   It was nearly sunset when we first
saw Jobba itself, below us at the edge of the subbkha,
with dark green palms cutting the pale blue of the
dry lake, and beyond that a group of red rocks
rising out of the pink Nefûd ; in the foreground
yellow sand tufted with adr ; the whole scene transfigured by the evening light, and beautiful beyond
description.

DELÚL RIDER.

CHAPTER IX.

"They went till they came to the Delectable Mountains, which mountains belong to the Lord of that hill of which we have spoken."

PILGRIM'S PROGRESS.

Jobba—An unpleasant dream—We hear strange tales of Ibn Rashid—Romping in the Nefûd—A last night there—The Zodiacal light—We enter Nejd—The granite range of Jebel Shammar.

JOBBA is one of the most curious places in the world, and to my mind one of the most beautiful. Its name Jobba, or rather Jubbeh, meaning a well, explains its position, for it lies in a hole or well in the Nefûd; not indeed in a fulj, for the basin of Jobba is on quite another scale, and has nothing in common with the horse-hoof depressions I have hitherto described. It is, all the same, extremely singular, and quite as difficult to account for geologically as the fuljes. It is a great bare space in the ocean of sand, from four hundred to five hundred feet below its average level, and about three miles wide; a hollow, in fact, not unlike that of Jôf, but with the Nefûd round it instead of sandstone cliffs. That it has once been a lake is pretty evident, for there are distinct water marks on the rocks which crop up out of its bed just above the town; and, strange to say, there is a tradition still extant of there having formerly been water there. The wonder is how this space is kept clear of sand. What force is it that walls out the Nefûd and prevents encroachment? As you look across the subbkha or dry bed of the lake, the Nefûd seems like a wall of water which must overwhelm it, and yet no sand shifts down into the hollow, and its limits are accurately maintained.

The town itself (or village, for it has only eighty houses) is built on the edge of the subbkha, 2860 feet above the sea, and has the same sort of palm gardens we saw at Jôf, only on a very small scale. The wells from which these are watered are seventy-five feet deep, and are worked, like all the wells in Arabia, by camels. The village is extremely picturesque, with its little battlemented walls and its gardens. At the entrance stand half a dozen fine old ithel-trees with gnarled trunks and feathery branches. The rocks towering above are very grand, being of purple sandstone streaked and veined with yellow, and having an upper facing of black. They are from seven hundred to eight hundred feet high, and their bases are scored with old water marks. Wilfrid found several inscriptions in the Sinaïtic character upon them. Jobba is backed by these hills, and by a strip of yellow sand, like the dunes of Ithery, on which just now there are brilliantly green tufts of adr in full leaf. Beyond the subbkha the rocks of

Ghota rising out of the Nefûd remind one of the
Aletsch Glacier, as seen from the Simplon Road.
So much for the outer face of Jobba. The interior
is less attractive. The houses are very poor, and
less smartly kept than those of Kâf and Ithery. I
can hardly call them dirty, for dirt in this region of
sand is almost an impossibility. It is one of the
luxuries of the Nefûd that no noxious insects are
found within its circuit. The Nefûd and, indeed,
Nejd, which lies beyond it, are free from those
creatures which make life a torment in other
districts of the East. Even the fleas on our greyhounds died as soon as they entered the enchanted
circle of red sand. But Jobba would be dirty if it
could; and its inhabitants are the least well-mannered of all the Arabs we saw in Nejd. The fact is,
the people are very poor and have no communication
with the outer world, except when the rare travellers
between Haïl and Jôf stop a night among them.
At the time of our passage through Jobba, the
Sheykh had lately died, and his office was being
held by a young man of two or three and twenty,
who had no authority with his fellow-youths, a
noisy, good-for-nothing set. Ibn Rashid has no
special lieutenant at Jobba, and the young Sheykh
Naïf was unsupported by any representative of the
central government, even a policeman. The consequence was that though entertained hospitably
enough by Naïf, we were considerably pestered by
his friends, and made to feel not a little uncomfort-

able. I quote this as a single instance of incivility
in a country where politeness is very much the rule.

The style of our entertainment at Naïf's house
requires no special mention, as it differed in no
respect from what we had already received elsewhere. There was a great deal of coffee drinking,
and a great deal of talk. Wherever one goes in
Arabia one only has to march into any house one
pleases, and one is sure to be welcome. The kahwah
stands open all day long, and the arrival of a guest
is the signal for these two forms of indulgence,
coffee and conversation, the only ones known to the
Arabs. A fire is instantly lighted, and the coffee
cups in due course are handed round. One curious
incident, however, of our stay at Jobba must be
related.

For some days before our arrival there Mohammed,
who was usually careless enough about the dangers
of the road, had betrayed considerable uneasiness
whenever there was a question of meeting Arabs on
the way or making new acquaintances. He had
dissuaded us more than once from looking about for
tents ; and when we had met the solitary man with
the camels and the man we called the spy, he had
given very short answers to their inquiries of who
we were, and where we were going. It was not till
the evening of our arrival at Jobba that he explained
the cause of his anxiety. It then appeared that
Radi in the course of conversation had mentioned
the name of a certain Shammar Sheykh, one Ibn

Ermal, as being in the neighbourhood, and Mohammed had remembered that many years ago a
Sheykh of that name had made a raid against
Tudmur. There had been some fighting, and a
man or two killed on the Shammar side; and this
was enough to make it extremely probable that a
blood-feud might be still unsettled between his
family and the Ibn Ermals. He therefore begged
us not to mention his name in Jobba, or the fact
that he and Abdallah were Tudmur men. He had
the more reason for this because he had discovered
that Naïf, our host, was himself related to the Ibn
Ermals ; and it was fortunate that Tudmur had not
yet been mentioned by any one in conversation.
Later on in the evening he came to us very radiant,
with the news that we need no longer be under any
apprehension. He had managed ingeniously to lead
the conversation with Naïf to the subject he had at
heart, and had just learned that the blood-feud was
considered at an end. Mohammed ibn Rashid,
before he came to the Sheykhat of Jebel Shammar,
was Emir el-Haj, or Prince of the pilgrimage to
Mecca, a position of honour and profit, under his
brother Tellál, and in that capacity had made
acquaintance with several Tudmuri at the holy
cities, and when he succeeded to the Sheykhat he
had good-naturedly composed their difference with
his people. He had either paid the blood-money
himself, or had used pressure on Ibn Ermal to forego
his revenge, and the blood-feud had been declared

cancelled. Whatever the Emir's reason for acting
thus as peace maker, it was a very fortunate circumstance for us, and now Mohammed and Naïf were
the best of friends. On the morning, however, of our
departure from Jobba (we stayed there two nights),
Naïf, in wishing Mohammed good bye, narrated that
he had had a curious dream that night. He had gone
to sleep, he said, thinking of this old feud; and in
his sleep he thought he heard a voice reproaching
him with having neglected his duty of taking just
revenge on the man who was his guest, and he had
been much distressed between the conflicting duties
of vengeance and hospitality, so that he had got up
in his sleep to feel about for his sword, and had
found himself doing this when he woke. Then he
had remembered that the feud was at an end, and
said El hamdu lillah, and went to sleep again.
"What a dreadful thing it would have been," he
said to Mohammed at the end of this story, "if I
had been obliged to kill you, you, my guest!"
Mohammed, however, maintained to us that even if
the blood-feud had not been settled, Naïf would not
have been bound to do anything, once he had eaten
and drunk with him in his house. Such, at least,
would be the rule at Tudmur, though morals might
be stricter in Nejd.

We only stayed, as I have said, two nights with
Naïf. The young people of the village were in-
quisitive and obtrusive, and we were obliged to
make a sort of scene with our host about it, a thing

which is disagreeable, but sometimes necessary. I
dare say they meant no harm, but their manners
were bad, and there was something almost hostile in
their tone about Nasrani (Nazarenes or Christians),
which it was advisable to check. I am glad to say
that this is the only instance we have had in Arabia
of unpleasant allusions to religion. The Arabs are
by nature tolerant to the last degree on this point,
and national or religious prejudices are exceedingly
rare.

This little episode, however, made us rather
anxious about our possible reception at Haïl. No
European nor Christian of any sort had penetrated
as such before us to Jebel Shammar, and all we
knew of the people and country was the recollection
of Mr. Palgrave's account of his visit there in disguise
sixteen years before. Ibn Rashid, for all we knew,
might be as ill-disposed towards us as these Jobbites
here, and it was clear that, without his countenance
and protection, we should be running considerable
risk in entering Haïl. Still, the die was cast. We
had crossed our Rubicon, the Red Desert, and there
was no turning back. There was nothing to be
done but to put a good face on things and proceed
on our way. We cross questioned Radi as to the
state of affairs at Haïl, and I may as well give here
the whole of the information he gave us, corroborated
and amplified by subsequent narrators. The main
facts we learned from him.

Radi, in the first place, confirmed in general

terms the account we had already heard of the
history of the Ibn Rashid family. About fifty years
ago, Abdallah ibn Rashid, at that time "a mere
zellem," individual, of the Abde section of the
Shammar tribe, took service with the Ibn Saouds of
Upper Nejd, and was appointed lieutenant of Jebel
Shammar, by the Wahhabi Emir. He was a great
warrior, and reduced the whole country to order with
the help of his brother Obeyd, the principal hero of
Shammar tradition. Of Obeyd we heard nothing
to confirm the evil tales mentioned by Mr. Palgrave.
On the contrary, he has left a great reputation
among the Arabs for his hospitality, generosity, and
courage, the three cardinal virtues of their creed.
He was never actually Emir of Jebel Shammar, but
after his brother's death he virtually ruled the
country. It was he that counselled the destruction
of the Turkish soldiers in the Nefûd. He lived to
a great age, and died only nine years ago, having
been paralysed from the waist downwards for some
months before his death. It is related of him that
he left no property behind him, having given away
everything during his lifetime—no property but his
sword, his mare, and his young wife. These he left
to his nephew Mohammed, ibn Rashid, the reigning
Emir, with the request that his sword should remain
undrawn, his mare unridden, and his wife unmarried
for ever afterwards. Ibn Rashid has respected his
uncle's first two wishes, but he has taken the wife
into his own harim.

Abdallah ibn Rashid died in 1843, and was succeeded in the Sheykhat of the Shammar and the
lieutenancy of Haïl, by his son Tellál, who took the
title of Emir, and made himself nearly independent
of the Wahhabi government. There is not much
talk at Haïl now about Tellál. He has left behind
him little of the reputation one would expect from
Mr. Palgrave's account of him. In his time, his
second brother and successor, Metaab, conquered Jôf
and Ithery, and Metaab's name is much more
frequently mentioned than Tellál's. About twelve
years ago Tellál went out of his mind and committed
suicide. He stabbed himself at Haïl with his own
dagger. He left behind him several sons, the eldest
of whom was Bender, and two brothers, Metaab and
Mohammed, besides his uncle Obeyd, then a very
old man, and several cousins. Bender was quite a
boy at the time, and Metaab succeeded Tellál with
the approval of all the family. Metaab, however,
only ruled for three years, and dying rather suddenly,
a dispute arose as to the succession. Mohammed,
who for some years had been acting as Emir el-Haj,
or leader of the pilgrims, was away from Haïl,
settling a matter connected with his office with Ibn
Saoud at Riad, and Bender, being now twenty years
old, was proclaimed Emir. He was supported by
all the family except Mohammed and Hamúd,
Obeyd's eldest son, who had been brought up with
Mohammed as a brother. Mohammed, when he
heard of this, was very angry, and for many days, so

Raḍi told us, sat with his kefiyeh over his face like one in grief, and refused to speak with anyone. He remained at Riad, rejecting all Bender's advances and invitations until Obeyd was dead, when he consented to return to Haïl, and resume his post with the Haj. This post brought him in much money, and he was fond of money. But he plotted all the while for the Sheykhat, intriguing with the Sherarât and other Bedouins under Bender's rule. It was in this way that he ultimately gratified his ambition, for it happened one day that a caravan of Sherarât came to Haïl to buy dates, and placed themselves under Mohammed's protection instead of the Emir's. This made Bender very angry, and he sent for Mohammed, and asked him the meaning of this insolence. "Are you Sheykh," he asked, "or am I?" He then mounted his mare and rode out, threatening to confiscate the Sherarât camels, for they were encamped under the walls of Haïl. But Mohammed followed him, and riding with him, a violent dispute arose, in which Mohammed drew his *shabriyeh* (a crooked dagger they all wear in Nejd), and stabbed his nephew, who fell dead on the spot. Then Mohammed galloped back to the castle, and, finding Hamúd there, got his help and took possession of the place. He then seized the younger sons of Tellál, Bender's brothers, all but one child, Naïf, and Bedr, who was away from Haïl, and had their heads cut off by his slaves in the courtyard of the castle. They say, however, that Hamúd protested against this. But Mohammed was reckless, or wished to strike terror, and not satisfied with what he had already done, went on destroying his relations. He had some cousins, sons of Jabar, a younger brother of Abdallah and Obeyd; and these he sent for. They came in some alarm to the castle, each with his slave. They were all young men, beautiful to look at, and of the highest distinction; and their slaves had been brought up with them, as the custom is, more like brothers than servants. They were shown into the kahwah of the castle, and received with great formality, Mohammed's servants coming forward to invite them in. It is the custom at Haïl, whenever a person pays a visit, that before sitting down, he should hang up his sword on one of the wooden pegs fixed into the wall, and this the sons of Jabar did, and their slaves likewise. Then they sat down, and waited and waited, but still no coffee was served to them. At last Mohammed appeared surrounded by his guard, but there was no "salaam aleykum," and instantly he gave orders that his cousins should be seized and bound. They made a rush for their swords, but were intercepted by the slaves of the castle, and made prisoners. Mohammed then, with horrible barbarity, ordered their hands and their feet to be cut off, and the hands and the feet of their slaves, and had them, still living, dragged out into the courtyard of the palace, where they lay till they died. These ghastly crimes, more ghastly than ever

in a country where wilful bloodshed is so unusual,
seem to have struck terror far and wide, and no one
has since dared to raise a hand against Mohammed.
Now he is said to have repented of his crimes, and
to be " angry with himself " for what he has done.
But Radi is of opinion that Heaven is at least as
angry, for though Mohammed has married over and
over again, he has never been blessed with a son,
nor even with a daughter.   His rule, however, apart
from its evil commencement, though firm, has been
beneficent.   The only other persons, with one exception, who have suffered death during his reign, have
been highway robbers, and these are now extirpated
within three hundred miles of Haïl.   A traveller
may go about securely in any part of the desert with
all his gold in his hand, and he will not be molested.
Neither are there thieves in the towns.   He has
made Jebel Shammar definitely independent of
Riad, and has resisted one or two attempted
encroachments by the Turks.   He is munificent to
all, and exercises unbounded hospitality.   No man,
rich or poor, is ever sent away from his gate unfed,
and seldom without a present of clothes or money ;
and hospitality in Arabia covers a multitude of sins.
Besides, the Arabs easily forget, and Mohammed is
already half forgiven.   " Allah yetowil omrahu," God
grant him long life, exclaimed Radi, after giving
us these particulars.

The one exception I have alluded to was this.
About two years after Mohammed had gained the

Sheykhat, Bedr, the second son of Tellál, who had escaped the massacre of his brothers, began to grow a beard, and in Arab opinion was come of age ; and being a youth of high spirit and high principle, resolved to avenge his brothers' deaths. This was clearly his duty according to Arab law. He was alone and unaided, except by some former slaves of his father's, to whose house at Haïl he returned secretly. With their assistance, he made a plan of falling upon Mohammed one day when he was paying a visit to Hamúd in Hamúd's house next the castle. He went with one slave to the house, and asking admittance was shown into the kahwah, where, if he had found the Emir, he would have drawn his sword and killed him ; but, as it happened, Mohammed had just gone out into the garden, and only Hamúd was present. Hamúd asked him what he wanted, and he said he wished to speak to the Emir, but Hamúd suspecting something, detained him and gave Mohammed warning. When arrested and recognised, Bedr was cross-questioned again, and then declared his intention of avenging his brother Bender's death, nor would he desist from this. Mohammed, it is said, besought him to hear reason, and offered to release him if he would be content to let matters alone. " I do not wish to shed more blood," he said, " but you must promise to leave Haïl." Still the young man refused, and at last in despair, Mohammed ordered his execution. The slave, who accompanied

Bedr, was not ill-used. Indeed, Mohammed sent him away with gifts, and he now resides very comfortably at Samawa on the Euphrates.

After this, Mohammed, who seems to have really felt remorse for his wickedness, sent for Naïf, the remaining son of Tellál, who was still a boy, and took him to live with him, and treated him as his own son. Only a year ago, seeing the boy growing up, he exhorted him to marry, offering him one of his nieces and a fitting establishment. But the boy, they say, hung back. " What ! " he said, " you would treat me as you treat a lamb or a kid which you fatten before you kill it ? " Mohammed wept and entreated, and swore that he would be as a father to Naïf; and the youth still lives honourably treated in the Emir's house. Opinion at Haïl, however, is very decided that as soon as Naïf is old enough, either he or his uncle must die. It will be his duty to follow Bedr in his attempt, and if need be, to end like him.

All this, as may be supposed, was anything but agreeable intelligence to us, as we travelled on to Haïl. We felt as though we were going towards a wild beast's den. In the meantime, however, there were four days before us, four days of respite, and of that tranquillity which the desert only gives, and we agreed to enjoy it to the utmost. There is something in the air of Nejd, which would exhilarate even a condemned man, and we were far from being condemned. It is impossible to feel really distressed or

really anxious, with such a bright sun and such
pure delicious air. We might feel that there was
danger, but we could not feel nervous.

Our last three nights in the Nefûd were devoted
to merriment, large bonfires of yerta, round which
we sat in the clear starlight, feasting on dates bought
at Jobba, and feats of strength and games among the
servants. I will give the journal for one day, the
22nd of January : "We have been floundering
along in the deep sand all day leisurely, and with
much singing and nonsense among the men, for we
are in no hurry now; it is only one day on to Igneh,
the first village of Jebel Shammar. The camels,
though tired, are not now in any danger of breaking
down, and they have capital *nassi* grass to eat ; the
tufts of grass are beginning to get their new shoots.
The Nefûd here is as big as ever, and the fuljes as deep ;
and we crossed the track of a bakar wahash or wild
cow, not an hour before we stopped. At half past
three, we came upon a shepherd driving forty sheep
to market at Haïl. He is a Shammar from Ibn
Rahîs, a sheykh, whose tents we saw to-day a long
way off to the north-east, and he intends selling his
flock to the Persian pilgrims who are expected at
Haïl to-day. The pilgrims, he says, are on their
way from Mecca, and will stay a week at Haïl.
Who knows if we may not travel on with them ?
The sheep, which I took at first for goats, are gaunt,
long legged creatures, with long silky hair, not wool,
growing down to their fetlocks, sleek pendulous ears

and smooth faces. They are jet black with white
heads, spots of black round the eyes and noses,
which look as if they had been drinking ink. They
are as unlike sheep as it is possible to conceive, all
legs, and tail, and face. But they have the merit of
being able to live on adr for a month at a time without needing water. They are, I fancy, quite peculiar
to Nejd. This meeting was the signal for a halt,
and behold a delightful little fulj, just big enough
to hold us, in the middle of a bed of nassí. We
slid our horses down the sand-slope, the camels
followed, Mohammed, the while, bargaining with
the shepherd for the fattest of his flock. Here we
unloaded, and the camels in another ten minutes
were scattered all over the hill-side, for there is a
sand-hill at least a hundred feet high, close by above
us. Ibrahim, the short, was set to watch them while
the rest were busy with the camp. There is an
enormous supply of fire-wood, beautiful white logs
which burn like match wood. We climbed to the
top of the hill to take the bearings of the country,
for there is a splendid view now of Jebel Shammar,
no isolated peak, as Dr. Colvill would have it last
year, but a long range of fantastic mountains,
stretching far away east and west, reminding one
somewhat of the Sierra Guadarama in Spain. There
are also several outlying peaks distinct from the
main chain. Behind us, to the north-west, the
Jobba group, with continuations to the west and
south-west. Eastwards, there is a single point,

Jebel Atwa. Haïl lies nearly south-east, its position marked by an abrupt cliff near the eastern extremity of the Jebel Aja range. The northern horizon only is unbroken. This done, we both went down to measure a fulj half a mile off, and found it two hundred and seventy feet deep, with hard ground below. It is marked very regularly on its steep side with sheep tracks, showing how permanent the surface of the Nefûd remains, for the little paths are evidently of old date.* By the time of our return, Hanna's good coffee was ready with a dish of flour and curry, to stay hunger until the sheep is boiled. Awwad, who delights in butcher's work, has killed the sheep in the middle of our camp, for it is the custom to slaughter at the tent door, and has been smearing the camels with gore. When asked why, he says, "it will look as if we had been invited to a feast. It always looks well to have one's camels sprinkled." He has rigged up three tent poles, as a stand to hang the sheep from, and is dismembering in a truly artistic fashion. Ibrahim el-tawîl and Abdallah are collecting an immense pile of wood for the night. Hanna is preparing to cook. Poor Hanna has been having a hard time of it since Meskakeh, for now that everybody has to walk, he insists upon walking too, "to prevent trouble," he says, and probably he is right. A regular Aleppin Christian like

---

* Query.—May not these be the spiral markings noticed by Mr. Palgrave, and attributed by him to the wind, in his description of a certain maelstrom in the Nefûd?

Hanna, in such a country as this, does best by
effacing himself and disarming envy, unless indeed
he can fraternize, and at the same time inspire
respect, as Ibrahim seems to have done. Hanna is
patient, and does not complain, endeavouring,
though with a rueful countenance, to be cheerful
when the rest tease him. I do my best to protect
him, but he dares not take his own part. Lastly,
Mohammed is sitting darning his shirt, against
making his appearance at Court, and talking to two
Jobbites, who are travelling with us, about the
virtues of Ibn Rashid, and the grandeur of the Ibn
Arûks. The Ibn Arûk legend, like a snowball, is
gathering as it rolls, and we fully expect Mohammed
to appear in the character of a Prince at Haïl. He
talks already of Nejd as his personal property, and
affects a certain air of protection towards us, as that
of a host doing the honours to his guests. His
scare about Ibn Ermal is quite forgotten. Prince or
peasant, however, Mohammed has the great merit
of always being good-tempered, and this evening he
is very amusing. He has been telling us the whole
history of his relations with Huseyn Pasha at Deyr.
which we never quite understood before (and which
I dare not repeat in detail for fear of bringing him
into trouble). He has been two or three times in
prison, but poor Huseyn seems to have been made a
sad fool of. Mohammed also gave us a full, true, and
particular account of Ahmed Beg Moali's death;
and then we had a long discussion about the exact

form in which we are to introduce ourselves at
Haïl. Mohammed will have it that Wilfrid ought
to represent himself as a merchant travelling to
Bussorah to recover a debt, but this we will not
listen to. We think it much more agreeable and
quite as prudent to be straightforward, and we
intend to tell Ibn Rashid that we are persons of
distinction in search of other persons of distinction; that we have already made acquaintance
with Ibn Smeyr and Ibn Shaalan, and all the
sheykhs of the north, and that each time we have
seen a great man, we have been told that these were
nothing in point of splendour to the Emir of Haïl,
and that hearing this, and being on our way to
Bussorah, we have crossed the Nefûd to visit him,
as in former days people went to see Suliman ibn
Daoud, and then we are to produce our presents and
wish him a long life. Mohammed has been obliged
to admit that this will be a better plan; and so it is
settled. Radi, whom we have taken more or less
into our confidence, thinks that the Emir will be
pleased, and promises to sing our praises " below
stairs," and he talks of a Franji having already been
at Haïl, and having gone away with money and
clothes from Ibn Rashid. Who this can be, we
cannot imagine, for Mr. Palgrave was not known there
as a European. So we whiled away the time till
dinner was ready, and when all had well feasted,
Mohammed came to invite us to the servants' fire,
where feats of strength were going on. First,

Abdallah lies flat on the sand, a camel saddle is put
upon his back, and then two gigantic khurjes, weigh-
ing each of them about a hundredweight. With these
he struggles to his knees, and then by a prodigious
effort to his feet, staggers a pace, and topples over.
Mohammed, not to be outdone, lifts Ibrahim kasír,
who weighs at least twelve stone, on the palm of his
hand off his legs. Then they make wheels, such as
are seen at a circus, and play at a sort of leap-frog,
which consists of standing in a row one close behind
the other, when the last jumps on their shoulders
and runs along till he comes to the end, where he
has to turn a somersault and alight as he can on his
head or his heels. This is very amusing, and in the
deep sand hurts nobody. All, except Hanna, join
in these athletic sports, but Awwad, who is a
Bedouin born, goes through the performance with a
rather wry face. Bedouins never play at games
as the town Arabs do, and they have not the
physical strength of the others. Awwad revenges
himself, however, by malignantly hiding bits of hot
coal in the ground, and every now and then somebody steps on these traps with his bare feet, and
there is a scream. Great amusement, too, is caused
by Wilfrid showing them the old game of turning
three times round with the head resting on a short
stick, and then trying to walk straight. This is
considered very funny, and they generally manage
to tumble over Hanna, and when they make him try
it, arrange that he shall run into the fire. The best

game, to my mind, is something like one sometimes
played by sailors on board ship. They all put their
cloaks together in one heap, and one man has to
guard it. Then the rest dance round him, and try
to steal the clothes away without getting touched.
Ibrahim tawîl is great at this sport, and defends
the heap with his huge hands and feet, dealing
tremendous blows on the unwary, and paying off, I
fancy, not a few old scores. Abdallah especially,
who is disliked by the rest on account of his bad
temper, gets shot clean off his legs by a straight
kick almost like a football, and a fight very nearly
ensues. But a diversion is made by the ingenious
Awwad, who steals away with a gun and fires it
suddenly from the top of the fulj, and then comes
tumbling head over heels down the sand to represent
a ghazú. So the evening passes, and as we go back
to our private lair, we see for the first time the
zodiacal light in the western sky."

This was our last night in the Nefûd, and the recollection of it long stood as our standard of happiness, when imprisoned within walls at Haïl, or
travelling in less congenial lands. The next day we
reached Igneh, the first village of Jebel Shammar,
and the day after the mountains themselves, the
"Happy Mountains," which had so long been the
goal of our Pilgrim's progress.

January 23.—It is like a dream to be sitting here,
writing a journal on a rock in Jebel Shammar. When
I remember how, years ago, I read that romantic

account by Mr. Palgrave, which nobody believed, of an
ideal State in the heart of Arabia, and a happy land
which nobody but he had seen, and how impossibly remote and unreal it all appeared; and how, later during
our travels, we heard of Nejd and Haïl and this very
Jebel Shammar, spoken of with a kind of awe by all
who knew the name, even by the Bedouins, from the
day when at Aleppo Mr. S. first answered our vague
questions about it by saying, "It is *possible* to go
there. Why do *you* not go ? " I feel that we have
achieved something which it is not given to every
one to do. Wilfrid declares that he shall die happy
now, even if we have our heads cut off at Haïl. It
is with him a favourite maxim, that every place is
exactly like every other place, but Jebel Shammar is
not like anything else, at least that I have seen in
this world, unless it be Mount Sinaï, and it is more
beautiful than that. All our journey to-day has
been a romance. We passed through Igneh in the
early morning, stopping only to water our animals. It
is a pretty little village, something like Jobba, on the
edge of the sand, but it has what Jobba has not,
square fields of green barley unwalled outside it.
These are of course due to irrigation, which while
waiting we saw at work from a large well, but they
give it a more agricultural look than the walled
palm-groves we have hitherto seen. Immediately
after Igneh we came upon hard ground, and in our
delight indulged our tired mares in a fantasia, which
unstiffened their legs and did them good. The soil

was beautifully crisp and firm, being composed of fine ground granite, quite different from the sandstone formation of Jobba and Jôf. The vegetation, too, was changed. The yerta and adr and other Nefûd plants had disappeared, and in their place were shrubs, which I remember having seen in the wadys of Mount Sinaï, with occasionally small trees of the acacia tribe known to pilgrims as the " burning bush" —in Arabic " talkh "—also a plant with thick green leaves and no stalks called " gheyseh," which they say is good for the eyes. Every now and then a solitary boulder, all of red granite, rose out of the plain, or here and there little groups of rounded rocks, out of which we started several hares. The view in front of us was beautiful beyond description, a perfectly even plain, sloping gradually upwards, out of which these rocks and tells cropped up like islands, and beyond it the violet-coloured mountains now close before us, with a precipitous cliff which has been our landmark for several days towering over all. The outline of Jebel Shammar is strangely fantastic, running up into spires and domes and pinnacles, with here and there a loop-hole through which you can see the sky, or a wonderful boulder perched like a rocking stone on the sky line. One rock was in shape just like a camel, and would deceive any person who did not know that a camel could not have climbed up there. At half-past one we passed the first detached masses of rock which stand like forts outside a citadel, and, bearing away gradually

to the left, reached the buttresses of the main body
of hills. These all rise abruptly from the smooth
sloping surface of the plain, and, unlike the mountains of most countries, with no interval of broken
ground. Mount Sinaï is the only mountain I have
seen like this. In both cases you can stand on a
plain, and touch the mountain with your hand. Only
at intervals from clefts in the hills little wadys issue,
showing that it sometimes rains in Jebel Shammar.
Indeed to-night, we shall probably have a proof of
this, for a great black cloud is rising behind the peaks
westwards, and every now and then it thunders.
All is tight and secure in our tent against rain.
There is a small ravine in the rock close to where
we are encamped, with a deep natural tank full of
the clearest water. We should never have discovered
it but for the shepherd who came on with us to-day,
for it is hidden away under some gigantic granite
boulders, and to get at it you have to creep through
a hole in the rock. A number of bright green plants
grow in among the crevices (capers ?), and we have
seen a pair of partridges, little dove-coloured birds
with yellow bills.

We passed a small party of Bedouin Shammar,
moving camp to-day. One of them had a young
goshawk* on his delúl. They had no horses with
them, and we have not crossed the track of a horse
since leaving Shakik. I forgot to say that yesterday we saw a Harb Bedouin, an ugly little black

* More probably a lanner.

faced man, who told us he was keeping sheep for
the Emir.   The Harb are the tribe which hold the
neighbourhood of Medina, and have such an evil
reputation among pilgrims.

January 24.—Thunderstorm in the night.   We
sent on Radi early this morning, for we had only a
few miles to go, with our letters to Haïl.   It was a
lovely morning after the rain, birds singing sweetly
from the bushes, but we all felt anxious.   Even Mohammed was silent and preoccupied, for none knew
now what any moment might bring forth.   We put
on our best clothes, however, and tried to make our
mares look smart.   We had expected to find Haïl
the other side of the hills, but this was a mistake.
Instead of crossing them, we kept along their edge,
turning gradually round to the right, the ground still
rising.   The barometer at the camp was 3370, and
now it marks an ascent of two hundred feet.

We passed two villages about a mile away to our
left, El Akeyt and El Uta; and from one of them
we were joined by some peasants riding in to Haïl
on donkeys.   This looked more like civilisation than
anything we had seen since leaving Syria.   We were
beginning to get rather nervous about the result of
our message, when Radi appeared and announced that
the Emir had read our letters, and would be delighted
to see us.   He had ordered two houses to be made
ready for us, and nothing more remained for us to do,
than to ride into the town, and present ourselves at
the kasr.   It was not far off, for on coming to the

top of the low ridge which had been in front of us for some time, we suddenly saw Haïl at our feet not half a mile distant. The town is not particularly imposing, most of the houses being hidden in palm groves, and the wall surrounding it little more than ten feet high. The only important building visible, was a large castle close to the entrance, and this Radi told us was the kasr, Ibn Rashid's palace.

In spite of preoccupations, I shall never forget the vivid impression made on me, as we entered the town, by the extraordinary spick and span neatness of the walls and streets, giving almost an air of unreality.

RECEPTION AT HAÏL.

CHAPTER X.

Haïl—The Emir Mohammed Ibn Rashid—His menagerie—His horses—His courtiers—His wives—Amusements of the ladies of Haïl—Their domestic life—An evening at the castle—The telephone.

As we stayed some time at Haïl, I will not give the detail of every day. It would be tedious, and would involve endless repetitions, and not a few corrections, for it was only by degrees that we learned to understand all we saw and all we heard.

Our reception was everything that we could have wished. As we rode into the courtyard of the kasr, we were met by some twenty well-dressed men, each one of whom made a handsomer appearance than any Arabs we had previously seen in our lives. "The sons of Sheykhs," whispered Mohammed, who was rather pale, and evidently much impressed by the solemnity of the occasion. In their midst stood a magnificent old man, clothed in scarlet, whose tall figure and snow-white beard gave us a notion of what Solomon might have been in all his glory. He carried a long wand in his hand—it looked like a sceptre—and came solemnly forward to greet us. "The Emir," whispered Mo-

hammed, as we all alighted.   Wilfrid then gave the
usual "salam aleykum," to which every one replied
"aleykum salam," in a loud cheerful tone, with
a cordiality of manner that was very reassuring.   I
thought I had never seen so many agreeable faces
collected together, or people with so excellent a
demeanour.   The old man, smiling, motioned to
us to enter, and others led the way.   We were
then informed that these were the servants of the
Emir, and the old man his chamberlain.   They
showed us first through a dark tortuous entrance,
constructed evidently for purposes of defence, and
then down a dark corridor, one side of which was
composed of pillars, reminding one a little of the
entrance to some ancient Egyptian temple.   Then
one of the servants tapped at a low door, and exchanged signals with somebody else inside, and the
door was opened, and we found ourselves in a large
kahwah, or reception room.   It was handsome from
its size, seventy feet by thirty, and from the row of
five pillars, which stood in the middle, supporting
the roof.   The columns were about four feet in
diameter, and were quite plain, with square capitals,
on which the ends of the rafters rested.   The room
was lighted by small square air-holes near the roof,
and by the door, which was now left open.   The
whole of the inside was white, or rather, brown-
washed, and there was no furniture of any sort, or
fittings, except wooden pegs for hanging swords to,
a raised platform opposite the door where the

mortar stood for coffee-pounding, and a square hearth in one corner, where a fire was burning. It was very dark, but we could make out some slaves, busy with coffee-pots round the fire. Close to this we were invited to sit down, and then an immense number of polite speeches were exchanged, our healths being asked after at least twenty times, and always with some mention of the name of God, for this is required by politeness in Nejd. Coffee was soon served, and after this the conversation became general between our servants and the servants of the Emir, and then there was a stir, and a general rising, and the word was passed round, "yiji el Emir," the Emir is coming. We, too, got up, and this time it really was the Emir. He came in at the head of a group of still more smartly-dressed people than those we had seen before, and held out his hand to Wilfrid, to me, and to Mohammed, exchanging salutations with each of us in turn, and smiling graciously. Then we all sat down, and Wilfrid made a short speech of the sort we had already agreed upon, which the Emir answered very amiably, saying that he was much pleased to see us, and that he hoped we should make his house our house. He then asked Mohammed for news of the road ; of Jóhar and Meskakeh, and especially about the war going on between Sotamm and Ibn Smeyr. So far so good, and it was plain that we had nothing now to fear ; yet I could not help looking now and then at those pegs on the wall, and thinking of the story of the young Ibn Jabars and their slaves, who had been so treacherously murdered in this very hall, and by this very man, our host.

The Emir's face is a strange one. It may be mere fancy, prompted by our knowledge of Ibn Rashid's past life, but his countenance recalled to us the portraits of Richard the Third, lean, sallow cheeks, much sunken, thin lips, with an expression of pain, except when smiling, a thin black beard, well defined black knitted eyebrows, and remarkable eyes,—eyes deep sunk and piercing, like the eyes of a hawk, but ever turning restlessly from one of our faces to the other, and then to those beside him. It was the very type of a conscience-stricken face, or of one which fears an assassin. His hands, too, were long and claw-like, and never quiet for an instant, incessantly playing, while he talked, with his beads, or with the hem of his abba. With all this, the Emir is very distinguished in appearance, with a tall figure, and, clothed as he was in purple and fine linen, he looked every inch a king. His dress was magnificent; at first we fancied it put on only in our honour, but this we found to be a mistake, and Ibn Rashid never wears anything less gorgeous. His costume consisted of several jíbbehs of brocaded Indian silk, a black abba, interwoven with gold, and at least three kefiyehs, one over the other, of the kind made at Bagdad. His aghal, also, was of the Bagdad type, which I had hitherto supposed were only worn by women, bound up with silk and gold thread, and set high on the forehead, so as to look like a crown. In the way of arms he wore several golden-hilted daggers and a handsome golden-hilted sword, ornamented with turquoises and rubies, Haïl work, as we afterwards found. His immediate attendants, though less splendid, were also magnificently clothed.

After about a quarter of an hour's conversation, Mohammed ibn Rashid rose and went out, and we were then shown upstairs by ourselves to a corridor, where dates and bread and butter were served to us. Then a message came from the Emir, begging that we would attend his *mejlis*, the court of justice which he holds daily in the yard of the palace. We were not at all prepared for this, and when the castle gate was opened, and we were ushered out into the sunshine, we were quite dazzled by the spectacle which met our eyes.

The courtyard, which is about a hundred yards long by fifty broad, was completely lined with soldiers, not soldiers such as we are accustomed to in Europe, but still soldiers. They were, to a certain extent, in uniform, that is to say, they all wore brown cloaks and blue or red kefiyehs on their heads. Each, moreover, carried a silver-hilted sword. I counted up to eight hundred of them forming the square, and they were sitting in a double row under the walls, one row on a sort of raised bench, which runs round the yard, and the

other squatted on the ground in front of them.
The Emir had a raised seat under the main wall,
and he was surrounded by his friends, notably
his cousin Hamúd, who attends him everywhere,
and his favourite slave, Mubarek, whose duty it is
to guard him constantly from assassins.* In front
of the Emir stood half-a-dozen suppliants, and outside the square of soldiers, a mob of citizens and
pilgrims, for the pilgrimage had arrived at Haïl.
We had to walk across the square escorted by a
slave, and the Emir motioned us to take places at
his side, which we accordingly did ; he then went
on with his work. People came with petitions,
which were read to him by Hamúd, and to which
he generally put his seal without discussion, and
then there was a quarrel to settle, the rights of
which I confess I did not understand, for the Arabic
spoken at Haïl is different from any we had hitherto heard. I noticed, however, that though the
courtiers addressed Mohammed as Emir, the poorer
people, probably Bedouins, called him " ya Sheykh,"
or simply " ya Mohammed." One, who was probably a small Shammar Sheykh, he kissed on the
cheek. Some pilgrims, who had a grievance, also
presented themselves, and had their case very sum-
marily decided ; they were then turned out by the
soldiers. No case occupied more than three minutes,

---

* The danger to Mohammed is a personal one on account of the
blood he has shed, not an official one, for, as Emir, he is adored by
his subjects.

and the whole thing was over in half-an-hour. At last the Emir rose, bowed to us, and went into the palace, while we, very glad to stretch our legs, which were cramped with squatting on the bench barely a foot wide, were escorted to our lodgings by the chamberlain and two of the soldiers.

We found a double house provided for us in the main street of Haïl, and not two hundred yards from the kasr—a house without pretence, but sufficient for our wants, and secure from all intruders, for the street door could be locked, and the walls were high. It consisted of two separate houses, as I believe most dwellings in Arabia do, one for men and the other for women. In the former there was a kahwah and a couple of smaller rooms, and this we gave over to Mohammed and the servants, keeping the *harim* for ourselves. This last had a small open court, just large enough for the three mares to stand in, an open vestibule of the sort they call *liwan* at Damascus, and two little dens. In one of these dens we stored our luggage, and in the other, spread our beds. The doors of these inner rooms could be locked up when we went out, with curious wooden locks and wooden keys; the doors were of ithel wood. All was exceedingly simple, but in decent repair and clean, the only ornaments being certain patterns, scratched out in white from the brown wash which covered the walls. Here we soon made ourselves comfortable, and were not sorry to rest at last, after our long journey.

Our rest, however, was not to come yet. It was only one o'clock when we arrived at our house, and before two, the Emir sent for us again. This time the reception was a private one in the upper rooms of the kasr, and we found the Emir alone with Hamúd. He received us with even more cordiality than before, and with less ceremony. We had brought presents with us, the duty of displaying which we left to Mohammed, who expatiated on their value and nature with all the art of a bazaar merchant. As for us, we were a little ashamed of their insignificance, for we had had no conception of Ibn Rashid's true position when we left Damascus, and the scarlet cloth jíbbeh we had considered the *ne plus ultra* of splendour for him, looked shabby among the gorgeous dresses worn at Haïl. We had added to the cloak and other clothes, which are the usual gifts of ceremony, a revolver in a handsome embroidered case, a good telescope, and a Winchester rifle, any one of which would have made Jedaan or Ibn Shaalan open his eyes with pleasure ; but Ibn Rashid, though far too well-bred not to admire and approve, cared evidently little for these things, having seen them all before. Even the rifle was no novelty, for he had an exactly similar one in his armoury. Poor Mohammed, however, went on quite naïvely with his descriptions, while the Emir looked out of window through the telescope, pretending to be examining the wall opposite, for there was no view. Hamúd, his cousin, whose acquaintance we now made, is more *sympathique* than the Emir, though they are ridiculously like each other in face, but Hamúd has the advantage of a good conscience, and has no vengeance to fear. They were dressed also alike, so that it was difficult at first to know them apart ; perhaps there is a motive in this, as with the Richmonds of Shakespeare. The Emir's room was on the same plan as the kahwah, but smaller, and boasting only two columns, the coffee place in the right-hand corner as you enter, and the Emir's fireplace, with a fire burning in it, on an iron plate in front. Persian carpets were spread, and there were plenty of cushions to lean against by the wall. We were invited to sit down to the left of the Emir and Hamúd, who never seems to leave his side. Mohammed had a place on the right, between them and the door. Coffee, and a very sweet tea, were handed round in thimblefuls, and a good deal of conversation ensued. We had brought a letter from our old friend the Nawab Ikbal ed-Dowlah, who had been at Haïl about forty years ago, in the time of Abdallah ibn Rashid.* The Emir remembered his coming, though he must have been a child at the time, and said some pretty things in compliment of him. He then asked Mohammed about his Arûk relations in Jôf, and said that they had

---

* The Nawab was in fact detained a prisoner at Haïl for about two months. But this we did not at the time know; nor was any allusion made by Ibn Rashid to the circumstance.

always been faithful to him. They had taken the
Emir's part, it would seem, in some revolt which
took place there a few years ago. There was also
an Ibn Arûk in Harík, a Bedouin sheykh, who the
Emir said was a friend of his ; at least, he was on
bad terms with Ibn Saoud and the Wahhabis, and
this is a title to favour at Haïl. Ibn Rashid is very
jealous of Ibn Saoud, and now that the Wahhabi
empire is broken up, fosters any discontent there
may be in Aared. I believe many of the Bedouin
sheykhs of Upper Nejd have come over to him.
Mohammed, thus encouraged, launched out into his
favourite tales, and repeated the Ibn Arûk legend,
which, I confess, I am beginning to get a little tired
of, and then went on to describe the wonders of
Tudmur, of which he now implied, without exactly
stating it in words, that he was actual Sheykh.
The house he lived in at home, he said, had
columns of marble, each sixty feet in height, and
had been built originally by Suliman ibn Daoud.
There were two hundred of these columns in and
around it, and the walls were twenty feet thick.
The Emir, who seemed rather perplexed by this,
appealed to us for confirmation, and we told him
that all this really existed at Tudmur ; indeed, there
was no gainsaying the fact that Mohammed's father's
house had some of the objects named on the pre-
mises, though the house itself is but a little square
box of mud. The city wall, in fact, makes one
side of the stable, and a column or two have been

worked into the modern building; but this we did not think it necessary to explain. Mohammed's reputation rose in consequence, and I already began to fear that the Emir's civilities had turned his head. I heard him whisper to Hamúd that the silver-hilted sword he is wearing, and which is the one Wilfrid gave him at Damascus, was an ancestral relic; it had been, he said, "min zeman," from time immemorial, in the Arûk family. He had also established a fiction, in which he privately entreated us to join, that we started from home with a hawk (for all the best falcons come from Tudmur), and lost it on the journey.*

While we were discussing these important matters, the call to prayer was heard, and the two Ibn Rashids, begging us to remain seated, rose and went out.

They were absent a few minutes, and on their return the Emir, to our great delight, proposed to show us his gardens, and immediately led the way down tortuous passages and through courts and doors into a palm grove surrounded by a high wall. Here we were joined by numerous slaves, some black, some white, for there are both sorts at Haïl. A number of gazelles were running about, and came up quite familiarly as we entered. These were of two varieties, one browner than the other, answering, I believe, to what are called the "gazelle des

* To travel with a hawk is a sign of nobility.

bois," and the "gazelle des plaines," in Algeria.
There were also a couple of ibexes with immense
heads, tame like the gazelles, and allowing themselves to be stroked. The gazelles seemed especially at home, and we were told that they breed here
in captivity. The most interesting, however, of all
the animals in this garden were three of the wild
cows (bakar wahhash), from the Nefûd, which we
had so much wished to see. They proved to be, as
we had supposed, a kind of antelope,* though their
likeness to cows was quite close enough to account
for their name. They stood about as high as an
Alderney calf six months old, and had humps on
their shoulders like the Indian cattle. In colour
they were a yellowish white, with reddish legs
turning to black towards the feet. The face was
parti-coloured, and the horns, which were black,
were quite straight and slanted backwards, and fully
three feet long, with spiral markings. These wild
cows were less tame than the rest of the animals, and
the slaves were rather afraid of them, for they seemed
ready to use their horns, which were as sharp
as needles. The animals, though fat, evidently
suffered from confinement, for all were lame, one
with an enlarged knee, and the rest with overgrown
hoofs. When we had seen and admired the menagerie, and fed the antelopes with dates, we went on
through a low door, which we had almost to creep
through, into another garden, where there were

* Oryx beatrix.

lemon trees (treng), bitter oranges (hámud), and pomegranates (roman). The Emir, who was very polite and attentive to me, had some of the fruit picked and gave me a bunch of a kind of thyme, the only flower growing there. We saw some camels at work drawing water from a large well, a hundred to a hundred and fifty feet deep, to judge by the rope. The Emir then crept through another low door and we after him, and then to our great satisfaction we found ourselves in a stable-yard full of mares, tethered in rows each to a manger. I was almost too excited to look, for it was principally to see these that we had come so far.

This yard contained about twenty mares, and beyond it was another with a nearly equal number. Then there was a third with eight horses, tethered in like manner ; and beyond it again a fourth with thirty or forty foals. I will not now describe all we saw, for the Emir's stud will require a chapter to itself. Suffice it to say, that Wilfrid's first impression and mine were alike. The animals we saw before us were not comparable for beauty of form or for quality with the best we had seen among the Gomussa. The Emir, however, gave us little time for reflection, for with a magnificent wave of his hand, and explaining with mock humility, " The horses of my slaves," he dragged us on from one yard to another, allowing us barely time to ask a few questions as to breed, for the answers to which he referred us to Hamúd. We had seen enough, how-

ever, to make us very happy, and Hamúd had promised that we should see them again. There was
no doubt whatever that, in spite of the Emir's dis-
claimer, these were Ibn Rashid's celebrated mares,
the representatives of that stud of Feysul ibn Saoud,
about which such a romance had been made.

An equally interesting spectacle, the Emir thought
for us, was his kitchen, to which he now showed the
way. Here, with unconcealed pride, he displayed
his pots and pans, especially seven monstrous
cauldrons, capable each, he declared, of boiling
three whole camels. Several of them were actually
at work, for Ibn Rashid entertains nearly two
hundred guests daily, besides his own household.
Forty sheep or seven camels are his daily bill of
fare. As we came out, we found the hungry
multitude already assembling. Every stranger
in Haïl has his place at Ibn Rashid's table,
and towards sunset the courtyard begins to fill.
The Emir does not himself preside at these feasts.
He always dines alone, or in his harim ; but the
slaves and attendants are extraordinarily well-drilled,
and behave with perfect civility to all comers, rich
and poor alike. Our own dinner was brought to us at
our house. Thus ended our first day at Haïl, a day of
wonderful interest, but not a little fatiguing. " Ya
akhi," (oh my brother), said Mohammed ibn Arûk
to Wilfrid that evening, as they sat smoking and
drinking their coffee, " did I not promise you that
you should see Nejd, and Ibn Rashid, and the mares

of Haïl, and have you not seen them?" We both
thanked him, and, indeed, we both felt very grate-
ful. Not that the favours were all on one side ;
for brotherly offices had been very evenly balanced,
and Mohammed had been quite as eager to make
this journey as we had. But, alas! our pleasant
intercourse with Mohammed was very near its end.

The next few days of our life at Haïl may be
briefly described. Wilfrid and Mohammed went
every morning to the mejlis, and then paid visits,
sometimes to Hamúd, sometimes to Mubarek, sometimes to the Emir. A slave brought us our breakfast daily from the kasr, and a soldier came to
escort us through the streets. Mohammed had now
made acquaintances of his own, and was generally
out all day long. I stayed very much in doors, and
avoided passing through the streets, except when
invited to come to the castle, for we had agreed
that discretion was the better part of valour with
us. That there was some reason for this prudence
I think probable, for though we never experienced
anything but politeness from the Haïl people, we
heard afterwards that some among them were not
best pleased at the reception given us by the Emir.
Europeans had never before been seen in Nejd ; and
it is possible that a fanatical feeling might have
arisen if we had done anything to excite it.
Wahhabism is on the decline, but not yet extinct at
Haïl ; and the Wahhabis would of course have been
our enemies. In the Emir's house, or even under

charge of one of his officers, we were perfectly safe, but wandering about alone would have been rash. The object, too, would have been insufficient, for away from the Court there is little to see at Haïl.

With Hamúd and his family we made great friends. He was a man who at once inspired confidence, and we had no cause to regret having acted on our first impression of his character. He has always, they say, refused to take presents from the Emir; and has never approved of his conduct, though he has sided with him politically, and serves him faithfully as a brother. His manners are certainly as distinguished as can be found anywhere in the world, and he is besides intelligent and well informed. The Emir is different; with him there was always a certain *gêne.* It was impossible to forget the horrible story of his usurpation; and there was something, too, about him which made it impossible to feel quite at ease in his presence. Though he knows how to behave with dignity, he does not always do so. It is difficult to reconcile his almost childish manner, at times, with the ability he has given proofs of. He has something of the spoiled child in his way of wandering on from one subject to another; and, like Jóhar, of asking questions which he does not always wait to hear answered, a piece of ill-manners not altogether unroyal, and so, perhaps, the effect of his condition as a sovereign prince. He is also very naïvely

vain, as most people become who are fed constantly
on flattery; and he is continually on the look-out
for compliments about his power, and his wisdom,
and his possessions. His jealousy of other great
Sheykhs whom we have seen is often childishly
displayed. Hamúd has none of this. I fancy he
stands to his cousin Mohammed somewhat in the
position in which Morny is supposed to have stood
to Louis Napoleon, only that Morny was neither so
good a man nor even so fine a gentleman as Hamúd.
He gives the Emir advice, and in private speaks his
mind, only appearing to the outer world as the
obsequious follower of his prince. Hamúd has
several sons, the eldest of whom, Majid, has all his
father's charm of manner, and has, besides, the
attraction of perfectly candid youth, and a quite
ideal beauty. He is about sixteen, and he and his
brother and a young uncle came to see us the morning after our arrival, sent by their father to pay
their compliments. He talked very much and
openly about everything, and gave us a quantity of
information about the various mares at the Emir's
stable, and about his father's mares and his own.
He then went on to tell us of an expedition he had
made with the Emir to the neighbourhood of Queyt,
and of how he had seen the sea. They had made a
ghazú on the felláhín of the sea-coast, and had then
returned. He asked me how I rode on horseback,
and I showed him my side-saddle, which, however,
did not surprise him. " It is a shedad," he said;

" you ride as one rides a delúl." This young Majid,
though he looks quite a boy, is married ; and we
were informed that here no one of good family puts
off marriage after the age of sixteen. I made
acquaintance with his wife Urgheyeh, who is very
pretty, very small in stature, and very young ; she
is one of Metaab's daughters, and her sister is
married to Hamúd, so that father and son are
brothers-in-law.

Mubarek, the Emir's chief slave, was one of our
particular acquaintances.   He inhabits a very handsome house, as houses go in Haïl ; and there
Wilfrid paid him more than one visit.   His house
is curiously decorated with designs in plaster of
birds and beasts—ostriches, antelopes, and camels.
Though a slave, Mubarek has not in appearance the
least trace of negro blood ; and it is still a mystery
to us how he happens to be one.   He is a well-bred
person, and has done everything in his power to
make things pleasant for us.

On the second day after our arrival, after the
usual compliments and some conversation, I asked
the Emir's permission to pay a visit to the harim.
Mohammed ibn Rashid appeared gratified by my
request, which he immediately granted, saying that
he would send to the khawatin (ladies) to inform
them, and desire them to prepare for my reception.
He accordingly despatched a messenger, but we sat
on talking for a long time before anything came of
the message ; I had grown quite tired of waiting,

and was already wondering how soon we should be
at liberty to return home, where I might write my
journal in secret, when the servant re-appeared,
and brought us word that Amusheh, the Emir's chief
wife, was ready to receive me. I fancy that ladies
here seldom dress with any care unless they want to
display their silks and jewels to some visitor; and
on such special occasions their toilet is a most elaborate one, with kohl and fresh paint, and takes a long
time. The Emir at once put me in charge of a black
slave woman, who led the way to the harim.
Hamúd's wives as well as Mohammed's live in the
palace, but in separate dwellings. The kasr is almost a town in itself, and I and my black guide
walked swiftly through so many alleys and courts,
and turned so many corners to the right and to the
left, that if I had been asked to find my way back
unassisted, I certainly could not have done it. At
last, however, after crossing a very large courtyard,
we stopped at a small low door. This was open,
and through it I could see a number of people sitting round a fire within, for it was the entrance to
Amusheh's kahwah. This room had two columns
supporting the ceiling, like all other rooms I had
seen in the palace, except the great kahwah, which
has five. The fire-place, as usual, an oblong hole in
the ground, was on the left as one entered, in the
corner near the door; in it stood a brazier containing the fire, and between it and the wall handsome
carpets had been spread. All the persons present

rose to their feet as I arrived. Amusheh could easily
be singled out from among the crowd, even before she
advanced to do the honours. She possesses a certain
distinction of appearance and manner which would
be recognised anywhere, and completely eclipsed
the rest of the company. But she, the daughter of
Obeyd and sister of Hamúd, has every right to out-
shine friends, relatives, and fellow wives. Her face,
though altogether less regularly shaped than her
brother's, is sufficiently good-looking, with a well-
cut nose and mouth, and something singularly
sparkling and brilliant. Hedusheh and Lulya, the
two next wives, who were present, had gold brocade
as rich as hers, and lips and cheeks smeared as red
as hers with carmine, and eyes with borders kohled
as black as hers, but lacked her charm. Amusheh
is besides clever and amusing, and managed to keep
up a continual flow of conversation, in which the
other two hardly ventured to join. They sat looking pretty and agreeable, but were evidently
kept in a subordinate position. Lulya shares with
Amusheh, as the latter informed me, what they consider the great privilege of never leaving town, thus
taking precedence of Hedusheh, on whom devolves
the duty of following the Emir's fortunes in the
desert, where he always spends a part of the year in
tents. The obligation of such foreign service is
accounted derogatory, and accordingly objected to
by these Haïl ladies. They have no idea of amusement, if I may judge from what they said to me,

but a firm conviction that perfect happiness and
dignity consist in sitting still.

This happiness Amusheh and I enjoyed for some
time. We sat together on one carpet spread over a
mattress, cushions being ranged along the wall
behind us for us to lean against, and the fire in
front scorching our faces while we talked. On my
right sat Hedusheh ; beyond her Lulya and the rest
of the company, making a circle round the fireplace.
Before long, Atwa, a pretty little girl, who was
introduced to me as the fourth wife, came in and
took her place beyond Lulya. She looked more
like a future wife than one actually married, being
very young; and indeed it presently appeared that
she had merely been brought to be looked at and
considered about, and that the Emir had decided to
reject her as too childish and insignificant.* He
was, in fact, casting about in his mind for some
suitable alliance which should bring him political
support, as well as an increase of domestic comfort.
That these were the objects of his new matrimonial
projects I soon learned from his own mouth, from
the questions he asked me about the marriageable
daughters of Bedouin Sheyks. What could, indeed,
be more suitable for his purpose than some daughter
of a great desert sheykh, whose family should be valuable allies in war, while she herself, the ideal fourth
wife, unlike these ladies of the town, should be

---

* I heard nothing of the fate of Obeyd's widow, and could not
inquire.

always ready to accompany her husband to the
desert, and should indeed prefer the desert to the
town ?

Among other persons present were several oldish
women, relatives, whose names and exact relationship have slipped my memory ; also a few friends
and a vast number of attendants and slaves, these
last mostly black. They all squatted round the fire,
each trying to get into the front rank, and to
seize every opportunity of wedging in a remark, by
way of joining in the conversation of their betters.
None of these outsiders were otherwise than plainly
dressed in the dark blue or black cotton or woollen
stuffs, used by ordinary Bedouin women in this part
of Arabia, often bordered with a very narrow red
edge, like a cord or binding, which looks well. The
rich clothes worn by Amusheh and her companion
wives are somewhat difficult to describe, presenting
as they did an appearance of splendid shapelessness.
Each lady had a garment cut like an abba, but
closed up the front, so that it must have been put
on over the head ; and as it was worn without any
belt or fastening at the waist, it had the effect of a
sack. These sacks or bags were of magnificent
material, gold interwoven with silk, but neither
convenient nor becoming, effectually hiding any
grace of figure. Amusheh wore crimson and gold,
and round her neck a mass of gold chains studded
with turquoises and pearls. Her hair hung down
in four long plaits, plastered smooth with some

reddish stuff, and on the top of her head stuck a
gold and turquoise ornament, like a small plate,
about four inches in diameter. This was placed
forward at the edge of the forehead, and fastened
back with gold and pearl chains to another ornament resembling a lappet, also of gold and turquoise,
hooked on behind the head, and having flaps which
fell on each side of the head and neck, ending in
long strings of pearls with bell-shaped gold and
pearl tassels. The pearls were all irregularly shaped
and unsorted as to size, the turquoises very unequal
in shape, size, and quality, the coral generally in
beads. The gold work was mostly good, some of it
said to be from Persia, but the greater part of Haïl
workmanship. I had nearly forgotten to mention
the nose-ring, here much larger than I have
seen it at Bagdad and elsewhere, measuring an
inch and a half to two inches across. It consists
of a thin circle of gold, with a knot of gold and
turquoises attached by a chain to the cap or lappet
before described. It is worn in the left nostril, but
taken out and left dangling while the wearer eats
and drinks. A most inconvenient ornament, I
thought and said, and when removed it leaves an
unsightly hole, badly pierced, in the nostril, and
more uncomfortable-looking than the holes in
European ears. But fashion rules the ladies at
Haïl as in other places, and my new acquaintances
only laughed at such criticisms. They find these
trinkets useful toys, and amuse themselves while

talking by continually pulling them out and putting
them in again. The larger size of ring seemed
besides to be a mark of high position, so that the
diameter of the circle might be considered the
measure of the owner's rank, for the rings of all in-
feriors were kept within the inch.

Amusheh was very communicative, but told me
so many new names, that I could not remember all
the information she volunteered about the Ibn
Rashid family and relationships. She remarked
that neither she nor any of Mohammed's wives had
any children, a fact which I already knew, and not
from Radi alone ; for it is the talk of the town and
tribe that this is a judgment for the Emir's crimes.
She spoke with great affection of her nephew Majid
and of her brother Hamúd, and with veneration of
her father Obeyd, but I cannot recollect that she
told me anything new about any of them. She
spoke too of Tellál, but of course made no mention
of Bender. Indeed, anxious as I was for any information she might give, I knew too much of the
family history and secrets to venture on asking
many questions; besides, any show of curiosity
might have made her suspect me of some unavowed
motive. I therefore felt more at ease when the
conversation wandered from dangerous topics to safe
and trivial ones, such as the manners and customs
of different countries. " Why do you not wear your
hair like mine ? " said she, holding out one of her
long auburn plaits for me to admire; and I had

to explain that such short locks as mine were not sufficient for the purpose. " Then why did I not dress in gold brocade?" "How unsuitable," I replied, " would such beautiful stuffs be for the rough work of travelling, hunting, and riding in the desert." When we talked of riding, Amusheh seemed for a moment doubtful whether to be completely satisfied about her own lot in life—she would like, she said, to see me on my mare; and I promised she should, if possible, be gratified; but the opportunity never occurred, and perhaps the supreme authority did not care that it should. Even she might become discontented. Thus conversing, time slipped away, and the midday call to prayer sounded. My hostess then begged me to excuse her, and added, " I wish to pray." She and the rest then got up and went to say their prayers in the middle of the room. After this she returned and continued the conversation where we had left it off.

Some slaves now brought a tray, which they placed before me. On it was a regular solid breakfast : a large dish of rice in the middle, set round with small bowls of various sorts of rich and greasy sauces to be eaten with the rice. I excused myself as well as I could for my want of appetite, and said that I had this very morning eaten one of the hares sent to us by the Emir. Of course I was only exhorted all the more to eat, and obliged to go through the form of trying ; but fortunately there were other hungry mouths at hand, and eager eyes watching till the dishes should be passed on to them, so I got off pretty easily.

Amusheh afterwards invited me to go upstairs, that she might show me her own private apartment, on the floor above the kahwah. I followed her up a steep staircase, of which each step was at least eighteen inches in height. It led nowhere, except to a single room, the same size as the one below, and built in the same way, with two columns supporting the roof, and with a window in a recess corresponding to the door beneath. This apartment was well carpeted, and contained for other furniture a large bed, or couch, composed of a pile of mattresses, with a velvet and gold counterpane spread over it; also a kind of press or cupboard, a box (sanduk) rather clumsily made of dark wood, ornamented by coarse, thin plaques of silver stuck on it here and there. The press stood against the wall, and might be five feet long and two to three feet high, opening with two doors, and raised about two feet from the floor on four thin legs. Underneath and in front of it were three or four rows of china and crockery of a common sort, and a few Indian bowls, all arranged on the carpet like articles for sale in the streets. Amusheh asked what I thought of her house, was it nice? And after satisfying herself of my approbation, she conducted me down again, and we sat as before on the mattress between the brazier and the wall.

During my stay, the Emir paid two visits to the

kahwah, and each time that he appeared at the
door the crowd and the wives, except Amusheh,
rose and remained standing until he left. Amusheh
only made a slight bow or movement, as if about to
rise, and kept her place by me while her husband
stood opposite to us talking. He addressed himself
almost entirely to me, and spoke chiefly in the
frivolous, almost puerile, manner he sometimes
affects. He inquired my opinion of his wives,
whether they were more beautiful and charming
than Ibn Shaalan's wife, Ghiowseh, the sister of El
Homeydi ibn Meshur, or than his former wife,
Turkya, Jedaan's daughter, who had left him and
returned to her father's tent. In the forty-eight
hours since my arrival at Haïl, the Emir had already
asked me many questions about these two ladies,
and I now answered for the hundredth time that
Turkya was pretty and nice, and that Ghiowseh was
still prettier, but very domineering. He was, however, determined on a comparison of the two
families, and it was fortunate that now, having
seen Amusheh, Hedusheh, and Lulya and Atwa, I
could say with truth they were handsomer, even
the poor little despised Atwa, than their rivals. He
was rather impatient of Atwa being classed with
the others, and said, " Oh, Atwa, I don't want
her ; she is worth nothing." His character is, as
I have already said, a strange mixture of remarkable ability and political insight on the one hand,
and on the other a tendency to waste time and

thought on the most foolish trifles, if they touch
his personal vanity. Of his ability I judge by his
extremely interesting remarks on serious subjects,
as well as by the position he has been able to seize
and to keep. Of his energy no one can doubt, for he
has shown it, alas, by his crimes ; but he is so eaten
up with petty personal jealousies, that I sometimes
wonder whether these would influence his conduct
at an important political crisis. I think, however,
that at such a moment all little vanities would be
forgotten, for he is above all things ambitious, and
his vanity is, as it were, a part and parcel of his
ambition. He is personally jealous of all other
renowned chiefs, because here in Arabia personal
heroism is, perhaps more than anywhere else in the
world since the age of chivalry, an engine of
political power. He would, I doubt not, make
alliance with Sotamm, if necessary to gain his ends ;
nevertheless, he could not resist talking to me about
Ibn Shaalan at this most inappropriate moment,
evidently hoping to hear something disparaging of
his rival. I confess I found it embarrassing to
undergo an examination as to the merits of
Ghiowseh and Turkya in the presence of Mohammed's own wives, who all listened with wide
open eyes, breathless with attention. My embar-
rassment only increased when, after the Emir was
gone, Amusheh, on her part, immediately attacked
me with a volley of questions. While he remained
he had persisted in his inquiries, especially about

Turkya, till I, being driven into a corner, at last
lost patience, and exclaimed, " But why do you ask
me these questions? Why do you want to hear
about Turkya? What is it to you whether she is
fair or kind? You never have seen her, nor is it
likely you ever will see her!" "No," he replied, "I
have never seen her. Yet I want to know something about her, and to hear your opinion of her.
Perhaps some day I may like to marry her. I
might take her instead of this little girl," pointing
to Atwa, " who will never do for me, and whom I
will not have. She is worthless," he repeated,
" worthless." Poor little Atwa stood listening, but
I think with stolid indifference, for I watched her
countenance, and could not detect even a passing
shade of regret or disappointment. Indeed, of all
the wives, Amusheh alone seemed to me to have any
personal feeling of affection for the Emir. She, the
moment he had left, fell upon me with questions.
" Who is Turkya?" she asked, almost gasping for
breath. It surprised me that she did not know, for
she knew who El-Homeydi ibn Meshur was. I had
to explain that his sister Ghiowseh had married
Sotamm ibn Shaalan, and to tell her the story of
Sotamm's second marriage; and of how Ghiowseh
had determined to get rid of her rival, and succeeded
in making the latter so uncomfortable, that she had
left, and had since refused to return. Amusheh
certainly cares about Ibn Rashid, and I thought she
feared lest a new element of discord should be

brought into the family. As to her own position, it could hardly be affected by the arrival of a new wife ; she, as Hamúd's sister, must be secure of her rank and influence, and the Emir, with his guilty conscience, would never dare, if he ever wished, to slight her or Hamúd, to whose support he owes so much.

From Amusheh's house I went with a black slave girl to another house also within the kasr, that of Hamúd's wife, Beneyeh, a daughter of Metaab. There I saw Urgheyeh, her sister, married to Majid, son of Hamúd ; also another wife of Hamúd's. This last person I found was not considered as an equal, and on asking about her birth and parentage, was told, " She is the daughter of a Shammar." " Who ? " I inquired. " Ahad " (one). " But *who* is he ? " " Ahad,—fulan min Haïl min el belad " (some one, a person of the town). She was hardly considered as belonging to *the* family. The third and fourth wives, whom I afterwards saw, are, like the first, relations, one a daughter of Tellál, and the other of Suleyman, Hamúd's uncle on the mother's side (khal). These four are young ; Majid's mother, whose name I never heard, died, I believe, several years ago. Hamúd, like the Emir, keeps up the number of his wives to the exact figure permitted by the law of the Koran, any one who dies or fails to please being replaced as we replace a servant.

Beneyeh met me at her door, and we went

through a little ante-room or vestibule into her
kahwah. Here we remained only a few moments
till, to my surprise, three arm-chairs were brought
and placed in the ante-room. On these I and
Beneyeh and the second class wife sat, drinking tea
out of tea-cups, with saucers and tea-spoons. The
cups were filled to the brim, and the tea in them
then filled to overflowing with lumps of sugar.
It was, however, good. A pile of sweet limes
was then brought; slaves peeled the fruits, and
divided them into quarters, which they handed
round. After these refreshments Beneyeh wished
to show me her room upstairs. It was reached, like
Amusheh's private apartment, by a rugged staircase
from the kahwah, and was built in the same style,
with two columns supporting the rafters, only it
had no outlook, being lighted only by two small
openings high up in the wall. It was, however,
more interesting than Amusheh's room, for its walls
were decorated with arms. There were eighteen or
twenty swords, and several guns and daggers,
arranged with some care and taste as ornaments.
The guns were all very old-fashioned things, with
long barrels, but most of them beautifully inlaid
with silver. Two of the daggers we had already
seen in the evening, when the Emir sent for them to
show us as specimens of the excellence of Haïl gold-
smiths' work. The swords, or sword-hilts, were of
various degrees of richness, the blades I did not see.
Unfortunately at the moment I did not think of

Obeyd and his three wishes, and so forgot to ask
Beneyeh whether Obeyd's sword was among these ;
it would not have done to inquire about the widow,
but there would have been no impropriety in asking
about the sword, and I afterwards the more regretted
having omitted to do so, because this proved to be
my only opportunity. It would have been curious
to ascertain whether Obeyd wore a plain unjewelled
weapon in keeping with Wahhabi austerity. He
would surely have disapproved, could he have fore-
seen it, of the gold and jewels, not to mention silks
and brocaded stuffs now worn by his descendants ;
for his own children have none of the severe
asceticism attributed to him, although they inherit
his love of prayer.

Hamúd came upstairs while I was there with
Beneyeh, but he only stayed a few minutes. They
seemed to be on very good terms, and after he left
she talked a great deal about him, and seemed very
proud of him. " This is Hamúd's, and this, and
this," said she, " and here is his bed," pointing to a
pile of mattresses with a fine coverlid. There were
several European articles of furniture in the room,
an iron bedstead with mattresses, several common
looking-glasses, with badly gilt frames, and a clock
with weights. Urgheyeh now joined us, and
Beneyeh particularly showed me a handsome neck-
lace her sister wore of gold and coral, elaborately
worked. " This was my father's," she told me,
adding that the ornament came from Persia.

Beneyeh is immensely proud of her son, Abdallah,
a fine boy of four months old. She and her sister
were so amiable and anxious to please, that I could
willingly have spent the rest of the afternoon with
them. But it was now time to pay my next visit.
After many good-byes and good wishes from both
sisters, my black guide seized hold of my hand, and
we proceeded to the apartments of another wife of
Hamúd, Zehowa, daughter of Tellál. She is sympa-
thetic and intelligent, extremely small and slight,
with the tiniest of hands. Like the other ladies,
she wore rings on her fingers, with big, irregular
turquoises. We sat by the fire and ate sweet limes
and trengs and drank tea. Zehowa sent for her
daughter, a baby only nine months old, to show me,
and I told her I had a daughter of my own, and
that girls were better than boys, which pleased her,
and she answered, "Yes, the daughter is the mother's,
but the son belongs to the father."

Presently one of the guards, a tall black fellow,
all in scarlet, came with a message for me, a request
from the Beg that I would join him in the Emir's
kahwah, where he was waiting for me. Zehowa,
like her cousins, begged hard that I would stay, or
at least promise to visit her again as soon as possible,
and I, bidding her farewell, followed the scarlet and
black swordsman through courts, alleys, and passages to the kahwah, where I found Wilfrid. He
was being entertained by an elderly man with coffee
and conversation. This personage was Mubarck,

already mentioned as the chief of the slaves, and he had been giving Wilfrid a vast deal of interesting information about horses, especially the dispersion of Feysul ibn Saoud's stud, and the chief sources from which that celebrated collection was obtained. It had been originally got together, he said, entirely from the Bedouins, both of Nejd and of the north, by purchase and in war.

I never saw Zehowa, Beneyeh, or Amusheh again, for the next few days were fully occupied, and afterwards, owing to our finding ourselves involved in a network of mystery, and subject to an adverse influence, the pressure of which made itself felt without our being able at first to lay hold of anything tangible, or even to conjecture the cause, it became more than ever an object to us to remain quiet and unobserved. But I am anticipating circumstances to be detailed further on.

About three days later I paid a visit to the harim of Hamúd's uncle. This gentleman, Suleyman, we were already acquainted with, from seeing him at Court on several occasions. He had sent me an invitation to visit his family, and two black slaves came to escort me to their house, one of the dependencies of the palace. In a kahwah opening out of a small yard, I found the old man waiting to receive me. He dyes his beard red, and loves books, amidst a pile of which he was sitting. I was in hopes that his conversation would be instructive, and we had just begun to talk when, alas, his wife came in with a rush, followed by a crowd of other women, upon which he hastily gathered up all his books and some manuscripts which were lying about, and putting some of them away in a cupboard, carried off the rest and made his escape.

Ghut, his wife, was the stupidest person I had seen at Haïl, but very talkative, and hospitable with dates, fresh butter floating in its own buttermilk, and sugar-plums. The many-coloured crowd of white, brown, and black attendants, slaves, and children, were not in much awe of her, and chattered away without a check to their hearts' content. All were, however, respectful and attentive to me. Ghut's daughter, another Zehowa, presently arrived with a slave carrying her son, Abderrahman, a child about a year old. This Zehowa was good-looking, but nearly as stupid and tiresome as her mother. She was very much taken up with showing me her box of trinkets, which she sent for on purpose to display before me its contents. These were of the usual sort, gold ornaments for head and arms and ankles, set with turquoises and strings of pearls. The furniture of the room, which she and her mother specially pointed out for my admiration, was also like what I had already seen—presses or boxes on legs, and ornamented with rude silver plaques.

The conversation was dull. Here is a sample : *I.* " What do you do all day long ? *Zeh.* ".We live in the kasr." *I.* " Don't you go out at all ? " *Zeh*

"No ; we always stay in the kasr." *I.* "Then you
never ride" (I always ask if they ride, to see the
effect) "as we do?" *Zeh.* "No, we have no mares
to ride." *I.* "What a pity ! and don't you ever go
into the country outside Haïl, the desert?" *Zeh.*
"Oh, no, of course not." *I.* "But, to pass the time,
what do you do?" *Zeh.* "We do nothing." Here
a sharp black boy interrupted us, "O, khatûn,
these are daughters of sheykhs, they have no work
—no work *at all* to do, don't you understand?"
I. "Of course, I understand perfectly ; but they
might amuse themselves without doing work," and
turning to Zehowa I added, "Don't you even look
at the horses?" *Zeh.* "No, we do nothing." *I.* "I
should die if I did nothing. When I am at home
I always walk round the first thing in the morning
to look at my horses. How do you manage to
spend your lives?" *Zeh.* "We sit." Thus supreme
contentment in the harim here is to sit in absolute
idleness. It seems odd, where the men are so active
and adventurous, that the women should be satisfied
to be bored ; but such, I suppose, is the tyranny of
fashion.

Every evening after dinner we used to receive a
message from the Emir, inviting us to spend the
evening with him. This was always the pleasantest
part of the day, for we generally found one or two
interesting visitors sitting with him. As a sample
of these I give an extract from my journal :

"We found the Emir this evening in high good

humour. News had just come from El-Homeydi
ibn Meshur, a Roala sheykh of the faction opposed
to Sotamm, that a battle was fought about a month
ago between the Roala and the Welled Ali, and that
Sotamm has been worsted. Sotamm, at the head
of a ghazú numbering six hundred horsemen, had
marched against Ibn Smeyr at Jerud, but the latter
refused to come out and fight him, and so Sotamm
retired. On his way back home, however, he fell in
with an outlying camp of Welled Ali, somewhere to
the east of the Hauran, and summoned it to surrender.
These, numbering only a hundred and fifty horsemen, at first entered into negotiation, and, it is said,
offered to give up their camp and camels if they
were permitted to retire with their mares (the
women and children would of course not have been
molested in any case), and to this Sotamm wished
to agree. But the younger men of his party, and
especially the Ibn Jendal family, who had a death
to avenge, would not hear of compromise, and a
battle ensued. It ended, strangely enough, in
favour of the weaker side, who succeeded in killing
four of the Roala, and among them Tellal ibn
Shaalan, Sotamm's cousin and heir presumptive.
Sotamm himself is said to have been saved only by
the speed of his mare. Though the forces engaged
were so disproportionate, nobody here seems surprised at the result, for victory and defeat are " min
Allah," " in the hand of God ; " but everybody is
highly delighted, and the Emir can hardly contain

himself for joy. " What do you think now of
Sotamm ? " he said ; " has he head, or has he no
head ? "   " Not much, I am afraid," I answered,
" but I am sorry for him. He is weak, and does
not know how to manage his people, but he has a
good heart." " And Ibn Smeyr, what do you say
to Ibn Smeyr ? " " He has more head than heart,"
I said. This delighted the Emir. " Ah," he
replied, " it is you, khatûn, that have the head.
Now what do you say to me ? have I head, or not
head ? " " You have head," I answered. " And
Hamúd ? " " You all of you have plenty of head
here, more of course than the Bedouins, who are
most of them like children." " But we are Bedouins
too," he said, hoping to be contradicted. " I like
the Bedouins best," I replied ; " it is better to have
heart than head." Then he went on to cross-
question me about all the other sheykhs whose
names he knew. " Which," he asked, " is the best
of all you have met with ? " " Mohammed Dukhi,"
I said, "is the cleverest, Ferhan ibn Hedeb the best-
mannered, but the one I like best is your relation
in the Jezireh, Faris Jerba." I don't think he was
quite pleased at this. He had never heard, he said,
good or bad of Ibn Hedeb, who belonged to the
Bisshr. He was not on terms with any of the
Bisshr except Meshur ibn Mershid, who had paid
him a visit two years ago. We told him that both
Meshur and Faris were Wilfrid's "brothers." Meshur
he liked, but Faris Jerba was evidently no favourite

of his. I fancy the Emir has taken Ferhan's part
in the family quarrel. It is certain that when
Amsheh, Sfuk's widow and Abdul Kerim's mother,
came with her son Faris to Nejd, he would see
neither of them. They stayed in the desert all the
time they were here, and never came to Haïl.
Rashid ibn Ali, too, is Faris's friend, and of course in
no favour at this court.* He then asked about
Jedaan, touched rather unfeelingly on the idiotcy of
Turki, Jedaan's only son, and then cut some jokes
at the expense of our old acquaintance, Smeyr ibn
Zeydan. "An old fool," the Emir exclaimed,
"why did they send him here? They might as
well have sent a camel!" This is the Smeyr who
came to Nejd a year and a half ago to try and get
Ibn Rashid's assistance for Sotamm, and arrange a
coalition against Jedaan and the Sebaa. We knew
his mission had failed, but the fact is Ibn Rashid is
eaten up with jealousy of anyone who has the least
reputation in the desert. We are surprised, however, to find him so well informed about everything
and everybody in the far north, and we are much
interested, as he has solved for us one of the problems
about Nejd which used to puzzle us, namely, the
relations maintained by the tribes of Jebel Shammar
with those of the north. The Emir has told us that
the Shammar of the Jezireh and his own Shammar
still count each other as near relations. "Our

---

* The Ibn Alis were formerly Sheykhs of the Shammar, but were
displaced by the Ibn Rashids fifty years ago.

horses," he said, "are of the same blood." With
the Roala he has made peace, and with Ibn Haddal;
but the Sebaa and the rest of the Bisshr clan are
out of his way. They never come anywhere near
Nejd, except on ghazús, and that very rarely.
Once, however, a ghazú, of Fedaan, had got as far
as Kasím, and he had gone out against them, and
captured a Seglawi Jedran mare of the Ibn Sbeni
strain. He promised to show it to us. We then
talked a good deal about horses, and our knowledge
on this head caused general astonishment. Indeed,
I think we could pass a better examination in the
breeds than most of the Ibn Rashids. By long
residence in town they have lost many of the
Bedouin traditions. Hamúd, however, who takes
more interest in horses than the Emir, has told us
a number of interesting facts relating to the stud
here, and that of the late Emir of Riad, Feysul ibn
Saoud, solving another problem, that of the fabulous
Nejd breed ; but we are taking separate notes about
these things.

We had not been talking long with the Emir
and Hamúd, when a fat vulgar-looking fellow was
introduced and made to sit down by us. It was
evident that he was no Haïl man, for his features
were coarse, and his manners rude. He talked
with a strong Bagdadi accent, and was addressed
by everyone as " ya Hajji." It was clear that he
belonged to the Haj, but why was he here ? The
mystery was soon cleared up, for after a whispered

conversation with Hamúd, the new visitor turned
to Wilfrid, and began addressing him in what we at
first took to be gibberish, until seeing that we made
no answer, he exclaimed in Arabic, " There, I told
you he was no Englishman ! " Wilfrid then cross-
questioned him, and elicited the fact that he had been
a stoker on board one of the British India Company's
steamers on the Persian Gulf, and that the language
he had been talking was English. Only two
phrases, however, we succeeded in distinguishing,
" werry good," and " chief engineer "—and having
recognised them and given their Arabic equivalents,
our identity was admitted. The fellow was then
sent about his business, and a very small, very
polite old man took his place. He was conspicuous
among these well-dressed Shammar by the plainest
possible dress, a dark brown abba without hem or
ornament, and a cotton kefiyeh on his head, un-
bound by any aghal whatsoever. He was treated
with great respect, however, by all, and it was easy
to see that he was a man of condition. He entered
freely into conversation with us, and talked to
Mohammed about his relations in Aared, and it
presently appeared that he was from Southern
Nejd. This fact explained the severity of his
costume, for among the Wahhabis, no silk or gold
ornaments are tolerated. He was, in fact, the
Sheykh of Harík, the last town of Nejd towards
the south, and close to the Dahna, or great southern
desert. This he described to us as exactly like the

Nefûd we have just crossed, only with more vegetation. The ghada is the principal wood, but there are palms in places.

It is not the custom of Haïl to smoke, either from Wahhabi prejudice, or, as I am more inclined to think, because tobacco has never penetrated so far inland in quantities sufficient to make the habit general. No objection, however, has been made to Wilfrid's pipe, which he smokes when and where he chooses, and this evening when the call to prayer sounded, and the Emir and Hamúd had gone out to perform their devotions, the old man I have just mentioned, Nassr ibn Hezani, hinted without more ceremony that he should like a whiff. He has quarrelled with Ibn Saoud, and probably hates all the Wahhabi practices, and was very glad to take the opportunity of committing this act of wickedness. He was careful, however, to return the pipe before the rest came back. He, at any rate, if a Wahhabi, is not one of the disagreeable sort described by Mr. Palgrave, for he invited us very cordially to go back home with him to Harík. The Emir, however, made rather a face at this suggestion, and gave such an alarming account of what would happen to us if we went to Riad, that I don't think it would be wise to attempt to go there now. We could not go in fact without the Emir's permission. I do not much care, for town life is wearisome ; we have had enough of it, and I have not much curiosity to see more of Nejd, unless we can go among the Bedouins there. If Ibn Saoud still had his collection of mares the sight of them would be worth some risk, but his stud has long since been scattered, and Nassr ibn Hezani assures us that there is nothing now in Arabia to compare with Ibn Rashid's stud. Ibn Hezani, like everybody else, laughs at the story of a Nejd breed, and says, as everybody else does, that the mares at Riad were a collection made by Feysul ibn Saoud in quite recent times.

Later in the evening, a native goldsmith was introduced, with a number of articles worked by him at Haïl. They were pretty, but not specially interesting, or very unlike what may be seen elsewhere, dagger hilts and sheaths, and a few ornaments. It was this man, however, who had made the gold hilts which all the princely family here wear to their swords. These we examined, and found the work really good.

The most amusing incident of the evening, however, and one which we were not at all prepared for, was the sudden production by the Emir of one of those toys called telephones, which were the fashion last year in Europe. This the Emir caused two of his slaves to perform with, one going into the courtyard outside, and the other listening. The message was successfully delivered, the slave outside, to make things doubly sure, shouting at the top of his voice, "Ya Abdallah weyn ente? yeridak el Emir." "O Abdallah, where are you? the Emir wants you," and other such phrases. We expressed great surprise, as in duty bound; indeed, it was the first time we had actually seen the toy, and it is singular to find so very modern an invention already at Haïl.

At about ten o'clock, the Emir began to yawn, and we all got up and wished him good-night. He very kindly sent for, and gave me, a number of trengs and oranges, which he gave orders should be conveyed to our house, together with a new-laid ostrich's egg, the "first of the season," which had just been brought to him from the Nefûd.

EVENING WITH THE EMIR.

CHAPTER XI.

"I shall do well:
The people love me, and the Desert's mine ;
My power's a crescent, and my auguring hope
Says it will come to the full."

SHAKESPEARE.

Political and historical—Shepherd rule in Arabia—An hereditary
policy—The army—The law—Taxation—The finances of Jebel
Shammar—Ibn Rashid's ambition.

THE following is the result of our inquiries made
while at Haïl into the political condition and resources of the country. It has no pretension to
rigid accuracy, especially in the figures given, but it
will serve to convey an idea of the kind of government found in Arabia, and of the capacity for self-
rule of the Arab race.

The political constitution of Jebel Shammar is
exceedingly curious ; not only is it unlike anything
we are accustomed to in Europe, but it is probably
unique, even in Asia. It would seem, in fact, to
represent some ancient form of government indi-
genous to the country, and to have sprung
naturally from the physical necessities of the land,
and the character of its inhabitants. I look upon
Ibn Rashid's government as in all likelihood
identical with that of the Kings of Arabia, who
came to visit Solomon, and of the Shepherd Kings,

who, at a still earlier date, held Egypt and
Babylonia ; and I have little doubt that it owes its
success to the fact of its being thus in harmony
with Arab ideas and Arab tradition. To understand it rightly, one ought to consider what Arabia
is, and what the Arab character and mode of life.
The whole of the peninsula, with the exception,
perhaps, of Yemen, and certain districts of Hadra-
mant within the influence of the monsoon winds, is
a rainless, waterless region, in every sense of the
word a desert. The soil is a poor one, mainly of
gravel or of sand, and except in a few favoured
spots, unsuited for cultivation ; indeed, no cultivation is possible at all in Nejd, except with the help
of irrigation, and, as there is no water above ground,
of irrigation from wells. Even wells are rare.
The general character of the central plateaux, and of
the peninsula, is that of vast uplands of gravel, as
nearly destitute of vegetation as any in the world,
and incapable of retaining water, even at a great
depth. It is only in certain depressions of the
plain, several hundred feet lower than the general
level, that wells as a rule are found, and wherever
these occur with a sufficient supply of water, towns
and villages with gardens round them, have sprung
up. These, however, are often widely apart, showing
as mere spots on the map of Arabia, and uncon-
nected with each other by any intervening district
of agricultural land. Indeed, it is not too much to
say, that Nejd contains no agricultural region, as

we understand agriculture, and that all its production is garden produce. From this state of
things, it happens that there is also no rural class,
and that each town is isolated from its neighbours
to a degree impossible with us. The desert surrounds
them like a sea, and they have no point of contact
one with the other in the shape of intervening fields
or villages, or even intervening pastures. They are
isolated in the most literal sense, and from this fact
has sprung the political individuality it has always
been their care to maintain. Each city is an
independent state.

Meanwhile the desert outside, though untenanted
by any settled population, is roamed over by the
Bedouin tribes, who form the bulk of the Arab race.
These occupy for the most part the Nefûds, where
alone pasture in any abundance is found; but they
frequent also every part of the upland districts, and
being both more warlike and more numerous than
the townsmen, hold every road leading from town
to town, so that it depends upon their good will
and pleasure, to cut off communication for the
citizens entirely from the world.

The towns, as I have said, are for the most part
self-supporting; but their production is limited to
garden produce, and the date. They grow no
wheat and rear no stock, so that for bread and
meat they are dependent on without. They
require also a market for their industries, the
weaving of cloth, the manufacture of arms and

utensils, and it is necessary, at least in Jebel Shammar,
to send yearly caravans to the Euphrates for corn.
Thus security of travelling outside their walls is
essential to the life of every town in Arabia, and on
this necessity the whole political structure of their
government is built. The towns put themselves
each under the protection of the principal Bedouin
Sheykh of its district, who, on the consideration of
a yearly tribute, guarantees the citizens' safety
outside the city walls, enabling them to travel
unmolested as far as his jurisdiction extends, and
this, in the case of a powerful tribe, may be many
hundred miles, and embrace many cities. The
towns are then said to "belong" to such and such a
tribe, and the Bedouin Sheykh becomes their
suzerain, or Lord Protector, until, from their
common vassalage, and the freedom of intercourse
it secures them with each other, the germs of
federation spring up, and develop sometimes into
nationality.

This has, I believe, been always the condition of
Arabia.

A farther development then ensues. The Bedouin
Sheykh, grown rich with the tribute of a score of
towns, builds himself a castle close to one of them,
and lives there during the summer months. Then
with the prestige of his rank (for Bedouin blood is
still accounted the purest), and backed by his power
in the desert, he speedily becomes the practical
ruler of the town, and from protector of the citizens

becomes their sovereign. He is now dignified by
them with the title of Emir or prince, and though
still their Sheykh to the Bedouins, becomes king of
all the towns which pay him tribute.

This form of government, resting as it does on a
natural basis, has always been reverted to in Arabia,
whenever the country has, after an interval of
foreign or domestic tyranny, succeeded in eman-
cipating itself. Of very early Arabia little is
known ; neither the Persian nor the Macedonian
nor the Roman Empires embraced it, and it is
probable that Nejd at least existed till the time of
Mahomet exclusively under the system of government I have described. Then for a short time it
became part of the Mussulman Empire, and shared
in the centralised or semi-centralised administration
of the Caliphs, which substituted a theocratic rule
or the simpler forms preceding it. But though
the birthplace of Islam, no part of the Arabian
Empire was sooner in revolt than Arabia itself. In
the second century of the Mahometan era, nearly
all the peninsula had reverted to its ancient independence, nor, except temporarily, has Nejd itself
ever been since included in the imperial system of a
foreign king or potentate. In the middle of last
century, however, just as Mahomet had asserted his
spiritual authority over the peninsula, the Wahhabi
Emir of Aared once more established a centralized
and theocratic government in Arabia. The Bedouin
Princes were one after another dispossessed, and

a new Arabian Empire was established. This included not only the whole of Nejd, but at one time Yemen, Hejaz, and Hasa, with the northern desert as far north as the latitude of Damascus. For nearly sixty years the independence of the towns and tribes of the interior was crushed, and a system of imperial rule substituted for that of old Arabia. The Ibn Saouds, "Imâms of Nejd," governed neither more nor less than had the first Caliphs, and with the same divine pretensions. But their rule came to an end in 1818, when Nejd was conquered by the Turks, and the reigning Ibn Saoud made prisoner and beheaded at Constantinople. Then, on the retirement of the Turks, (for they were unable long to retain their conquest,) shepherd government again asserted itself, and the principality of Jebel Shammar was founded.

The Shammar tribe is the most powerful of Northern Nejd, and the towns of Haïl, Kefar, Bekaa, and the rest, put themselves under the protection of Abdallah ibn Rashid, who had succeeded in gaining the Shammar Sheykhat for himself. He seems to have been a man of great ability, and to him is due the policy of rule which his descendants have ever since pursued. He took up his residence in Haïl, and built the castle there, and caused himself to be recognized as Emir, first in vassalage to the Ibn Saouds, who had reappeared in Aared, but later on his own account. His policy seems to have been first to conciliate or subdue the other Bedouin tribes of Nejd, forcing them to become tributary to his own tribe, the Shammar, and secondly to establish his protectorate over all the northern towns. This was a simple plan enough, and one which any Bedouin Sheykh might have devised ; but Abdallah's merit consists in the method of its application. He saw that in order to gain his object, he must appeal to national ideas and national prejudices. The tribute which he extracted from the towns, he spent liberally in the desert, exercising boundless hospitality to every sheykh who might chance to visit him. To all he gave presents, and dazzled them with his magnificence, sending them back to the tribes impressed with his wealth and power. Thus he made numerous friends, with whose aid he was able to coerce the rest, his enemies or rivals. In treating with these he seems always to have tried conciliation first, and, if forced to arms, to have been satisfied with a single victory, making friends at once with the vanquished, and even restoring to them their property, an act of generosity which met full appreciation in the desert. By this means his power and reputation increased rapidly, as did that of his brother and right-hand man Obeyd, who is now a legendary hero in Nejd.

Another matter to which the founder of the Ibn Rashid dynasty paid much attention was finance. Though spending large sums yearly on presents and entertainments, he took care that these should not exceed his revenue, and at his death he left, according to common report, a house full of silver pieces to his son. Nor have any of his successors been otherwise than thrifty. It is impossible of course to guess the precise amount of treasure thus saved, but that it represents a fabulous fortune in Arabia is certain ; the possession of this, with the prestige which in a poor country wealth gives, is an immense source of power.

Lastly Abdallah, and all the Ibn Rashid family, have been endowed with a large share of caution. No important enterprise has been embarked on in a hurry ; and certainly at the present day affairs of state are discussed in family council, before any action is taken. It seems to have been always a rule with the Ibn Rashids to think twice, thrice, or a dozen times before acting, for even Mohammed's violent deeds towards his nephews were premeditated, and thought over for many months beforehand. In their conduct with the Ibn Saouds and the Turkish Sultans, they have always waited their opportunity, and avoided an open rupture. It is very remarkable that so many members of this family should be superior men, for it is difficult to say who has been the ablest man of them, Abdallah, Obeyd, Tellál, Mohammed, or his cousin Hamúd. Nor is the rising generation less promising.

Having united into a sort of confederation all the Bedouin tribes of Northern Nejd, Abdallah became naturally supreme over the towns ; but he was not

satisfied merely with power, he aimed at making
his rule popular. It is much to his credit, and to
that of his successors, that none of them seem to
have abused their position. Liberality and conciliation, combined with an occasional display of
power, have been no less their policy with the
townsmen than with the Bedouins, and they have
thus placed their rule on its only secure basis,
popularity. In early days the Ibn Rashids had to
fight for their position at Haïl, and later in Jôf and
at Meskakeh. But their rule is now acknowledged
freely everywhere, enthusiastically in Jebel Shammar. It strikes a traveller fresh from Turkey as
surpassingly strange to hear the comments passed
by the townspeople of Haïl on their government,
for it is impossible to converse ten minutes with
any one of them without being assured that the
government of the Emir is the best government in
the world. " El hamdu lillah, ours is a fortunate
country. It is not with us as with the Turks and
Persians, whose government is no government. Here
we are happy and prosperous. El hamdu lillah."
I have often been amused at this chauvinism.

In the town of Haïl the Emir lives in state,
having a body-guard of 800 or 1000 men dressed in a
kind of uniform, that is to say, in brown cloaks and
red or blue kefiyehs, and armed with silver-hilted
swords. These are recruited from among the young
men of the towns and villages by voluntary enlist-
ment, those who wish to serve inscribing their

names at the castle, and being called out as occasion requires. Their duties are light, and they live most of them with their families, receiving neither pay nor rations, except when employed away from home on garrison duty in outlying forts and at Jôf. Their expense, therefore, to the Emir is little more than that of their clothes and arms. To them is entrusted any police work that may be necessary in the towns, but it is very seldom that the authority of the Emir requires other support than that of public opinion. The Arabs of Nejd are a singularly temperate race, and hardly ever indulge in brawling or breaches of the peace. If disputes arise between citizens they are almost always settled on the spot by the interference of neighbours; and the rowdyism and violence of European towns are unknown at Haïl. Where, however, quarrels are not to be settled by the intervention of friends, the disputants bring their cases to the Emir, who settles them in open court, the *mejlis*, and whose word is final. The law of the Koran, though often referred to, is not, I fancy, the main rule of the Emir's decision, but rather Arabian custom, an authority far older than the Mussulman code. I doubt if it is often necessary for the soldiers to support such decisions by force. Thieving, I have been repeatedly assured, is almost unknown at Haïl; but robbers or thieves taken redhanded, lose for the first offence a hand, for the second their head.

In the desert, and everywhere outside the precincts

of the town, order is kept by the Bedouins, with whom the Emir lives a portion of each year. He is then neither more nor less himself than a Bedouin, throws off his shoes and town finery, arms himself with a lance, and leads a wandering life in the Nefûd. He commonly does this at the commencement of spring, and spring is the season of his wars. Then with the extreme heat of summer he returns to Haïl. The tribute paid by each town and village to the Emir is assessed according to its wealth in date palms, and the sheep kept by its citizens with the Bedouins. Four khrush for each tree is, I believe, the amount, trees under seven years old being exempt. At Haïl this is levied by the Emir's officers, but elsewhere by the local sheykhs, who are responsible for its due collection. At Jôf and Meskakeh, which are still in the position of territory newly annexed, Ibn Rashid is represented by a vakil, or lieutenant, who levies the tax in coin, Turkish money being the recognised medium of exchange everywhere. Without pretending to anything at all like accuracy we made a calculation that the Emir's revenue from all sources of tribute and tax may amount to £60,000 yearly, and that the annual passage of the pilgrimage through his dominions may bring £20,000 to £30,000 more to his exchequer.

With regard to his expenditure, it is perhaps easier to calculate. He pays a small sum yearly in tribute to the Sherif of Medina, partly as a religious offering, partly to insure immunity for his outlying

possessions, Kheybar, Kâf and the rest, from Turkish
aggression. I should guess this tribute to be £3,000
to £5,000, but could not ascertain the amount.
The Emir's expenditure on his army can hardly
be more, and with his civil list and every expense of
Government, should be included within £10,000.
On his household he may spend £5,000, and on his
stable £1,000. By far the largest item in his
budget must be described as entertainment. Mohammed ibn Rashid, in imitation of his predecessors,
feeds daily two to three hundred guests at the
palace ; the poor are there clothed, and presents of
camels and clothes made to richer strangers from a
distance. The meal consists of rice and camel
meat, sometimes mutton, and there is besides a
constant "coulage" in dates and coffee, which I
cannot estimate at less than £50 a day, say £20,000
yearly, or with presents, £25,000. Thus we have
our budget made up to about £45,000 expenditure,
as against £80,000 to £90,000 revenue—which
leaves a handsome margin for wars and other
accidents, and for that amassing of treasure which
is traditional with the Ibn Rashids. I must say,
however, once more, that I am merely guessing my
figures, and nobody, perhaps, in Jebel Shammar,
except the Emir himself and Hamúd, could do
more.

It will be seen from all this that Jebel Shammar
is, financially, in a very flourishing state. The curse of
money-lending has not yet invaded it, and neither

prince nor people are able to spend sixpence more
than they have got. No public works, requiring
public expenditure and public loans, have yet been
undertaken, and it is difficult to imagine in what
they would consist. The digging of new wells is
indeed the only duty a "company" could find to
execute, for roads are unnecessary in a country all
like a macadamised highway; there are no rivers to
make canals with, or suburban populations to
supply with tramways. One might predict with
confidence, that the secret of steam locomotion will
have been forgotten before ever a railway reaches
Jebel Shammar.

With regard to the form of government, it is
good mainly because it is effective. It is no doubt
discordant to European ideas of political propriety,
that the supreme power in a country should be
vested in Bedouin hands. But in Arabia they are
the only hands that can wield it. The town cannot
coerce the desert; therefore, if they are to live at
peace, the desert must coerce the town. The Turks,
with all their machinery of administration, and
their power of wealth and military force, have
never been able to secure life and property to
travellers in the desert, and in Arabia have been
powerless to hold more than the towns. Even the
pilgrim road from Damascus, though nominally in
their keeping, can only be traversed by them with
an army, and at considerable risk. Ibn Rashid, on
the other hand, by the mere effect of his will, keeps

all the desert in an absolute peace. In the whole
district of Jebel Shammar, embracing, as it does,
some of the wildest deserts, inhabited by some of
the wildest people in the world, a traveller may go
unarmed and unescorted, without more let or
hindrance than if he were following a highway in
England. On every road of Jebel Shammar, townsmen may be found jogging on donkey-back, alone,
or on foot, carrying neither gun nor lance, and with
all their wealth about them. If you ask about the
dangers of the road, they will return the question,
" Are we not here in Ibn Rashid's country?" No
system, however perfect, of patrols and forts and
escorts, could produce a result like this.

In the town, on the other hand, the Bedouin prince,
despotic though he may be, is still under close
restraint from public opinion. The citizens of Jebel
Shammar have not what we should call constitutional
rights; there is no machinery among them for the
assertion of their power; but there is probably no
community in the old world, where popular feeling
exercises a more powerful influence on government
than it does at Haïl. The Emir, irresponsible as
he is in individual acts, knows well that he cannot
transgress the traditional unwritten law of Arabia
with impunity. An unpopular sheykh would cease,
ipso facto, to be sheykh, for, though dethroned by no
public ceremony, and subjected to no personal ill-
treatment, he would find himself abandoned in
favour of a more acceptable member of his family.

The citizen soldiers would not support a recognised tyrant in the town, nor would the Bedouins outside. Princes in Arabia have, therefore, to consider public opinion before all else.

The flaw in the system, for in every system there will be found one, lies in the uncertainty of succession to the Sheykhat or Bedouin throne. On the death of an Emir, if he have no son of full age and acknowledged capacity to take up the reins of government, rival claimants, brothers, uncles, or cousins of the dead man, dispute his succession in arms, and many and bitter have been the wars in consequence. Such, quite lately, was the quarrel which convulsed Aared on the death of Feysul ibn Saoud, and led to the disintegration of the Wahhabi monarchy, and such, one cannot help fearing, may be the fate of Jebel Shammar, on Mohammed's. He has no children, and the sons of Tellál, the next heirs to the throne, have a formidable rival in Hamúd. The Emir, however, is a young man, forty-five, and may live long ; and if he should do so, seems to have the succession of the Wahhabi monarchy in his hands. He has effected, he and his predecessors, the union of all the Bedouin sheykhs, from Meshhed Ali to Medina, under his leadership, and is in close connection with those of Kasim and Aared. His authority is established as far north as Kâf, and he has his eye already on the towns still further north, if ever they should shake off the Turkish bondage. I look forward to the day when the Roala too, and the Welled Ali, shall have entered into his alliance, possibly even the Sebaa and Ibn Haddal ; and though it is neither likely nor desirable that the old Wahhabi Empire should be re-established on its centralised basis, a confederation of the tribes of the north may continue its best traditions. Hauran and the Leja, and the Euphrates towns, were once tributary to the Ibn Saouds, and may be again one day to the Ibn Rashids. This is looking far afield, but not farther than Mohammed himself looks.

NOTE.—That Mohammed ibn Rashid does not limit his ambition to Nejd has been very recently proved. In the month of April last, 1880, he marched with an army of 5000 men from Haïl, passed up the Wady Sirhán, surprised Mohammed Dukhi ibn Smeyr in the Harra and sacked his camp, and then went on to the Hauran. The citizens of Damascus were not a little startled at learning one morning that the Emir was at Bozra not 60 miles from the capital of Syria, and there was much speculation as to his object in coming so far northwards, no army from Nejd having been seen in the Pashalik since the days of the Wahhabi Empire. Then it was whispered that he had made friends with Ibn Smeyr, that the quarrel between them had been a mistake, and that a Sherari guide, held responsible for the blunder, had been beheaded ; lastly, that an enormous feast of reconciliation had been given by Ibn Rashid to the Northern tribes, at which 75 camels and 600 sheep had been slaughtered, and that after a stay of some weeks at Melakh the Emir had returned to Nejd.

Without pretending to know precisely what was in Mohammed's mind in making this ghazú, or all that really happened, it seems to me not difficult to guess its main object. Ibn Smeyr's success over Ibn Shaalan, already alluded to, had placed him in a leading position with the tribes of the North; and his raid against the Druses of the Hauran, a district once tributary to the Emirs of Nejd, pointed him out for Mohammed's resentment. It is part of the Ibn Rashid policy to strike a blow and then make peace ; and by thus humbling their most successful chief, and becoming afterwards his host, Mohammed achieved exactly that sort of reputation he most valued with the Northern tribes. He has asserted himself as supreme, where he chooses to be so, in the desert, and has moreover reminded the frontier population in Syria of the old Wahhabi pretensions to Eastern Syria. It is conceivable that having coerced or persuaded the Anazeh to join his league, he may, in the coming break-up of the Ottoman Empire, succeed to that part of its inheritance, and be recognised as sovereign in all the lands beyond Jordan.

OUR HOUSE AT HAÏL.

A

PILGRIMAGE TO NEJD.

CHAPTER XII.

"Je ne trouvai point en eux ces formes que je m'attendais à retrouver dans
la patrie de Zeid el Kheil."—GUARMANI.

Nejd horses—Their rarity—Ibn Saoud's stud—The stables at Haïl
Some notes of individual mares—The points of a Nejd head—
The tribes in the Nefûds and their horses—Meaning of the
term "Nejdi"—Recipe for training.

A CHAPTER on the horses we saw at Haïl has
been promised, and may as well be given here.

Ibn Rashid's stud is now the most celebrated in
Arabia, and has taken the place in public estimation
of that stud of Feysul ibn Saoud's which Mr. Palgrave saw sixteen years ago at Riad, and which he
described in the picturesque paragraphs which have
since been constantly quoted. The cause of this
transference of supremacy from Aared to Jebel
Shammar, lies in the political changes which have
occurred since 1865, and which have taken the
leadership of Central Arabia out of the hands of the
Ibn Saouds and put it into those of the Emirs of
Haïl.

Mohammed ibn Rashid is now not only the most powerful of Bedouin sheykhs, but the richest prince in Arabia; and as such has better means than any other of acquiring the best horses of Nejd, nor have these been neglected by him.

The possession of thoroughbred mares is always among the Arabs a symbol of power; and with the loss of their supreme position in Nejd, the Ibn Saouds have lost their command of the market, and their stud has been allowed to dwindle. The quarrels of the two brothers, Abdallah and Saoud, sons of Feysul, on their father's death, their alternate victories and flights from the capital, and the ruin wrought on them both by the Turks, broke up an establishment which depended on wealth and security for its maintenance; and at the present moment, if common report speaks true, hardly a twentieth part of the old stud remains at Riad. The rest have passed into other hands.

That Feysul's stud in its day was the best in Arabia is probable, and it may be that no collection now to be found there has an equal merit; but there seems little reason for supposing that it differed in anything but degree from what we ourselves saw, or that the animals composing it were distinct from those still owned by the various Bedouin tribes of Nejd. All our inquiries, on the contrary (and we spared no occasion of asking questions), tend to show that it is a mistake to suppose that the horses kept by the Emirs of Riad were a

special breed, preserved in the towns of Aared from
time immemorial, or that they differed in any way
from those bred elsewhere in Central Arabia. They
were, we were repeatedly assured, a collection recruited from the various tribes of the Nefûds,—a
very fine collection, no doubt, but still a collection.
Every Bedouin we have asked has laughed at the
idea of there being a special *Nejd breed*, only
found in Aared. In answer to our questions we
were informed that in Feysul's time emissaries from
Riad were constantly on the look-out for mares
wherever they could find them ; and that the Emir
had often made ghazús against this and that tribe,
with no other object than the possession of a particular animal, of a particular breed. The tribe
from which he got the best blood, the Hamdani
Simri and the Kehilan el-Krush, was the Muteyr
(sometimes called the Dushan), while the Beni Khaled,
Dafir, Shammar, and even the Ánazeh, supplied
him with occasional specimens. Abdallah ibn Saoud,
his successor, still retains a few of them, but the bulk
of the collection was dispersed, many of the best passing into the hands of Metaab and Bender, Mohammed ibn Rashid's predecessors. Mohammed himself
follows precisely the same system, except that he
does not take by force, but on payment. He
makes purchases from all the tribes around, and
though he breeds in the town, his collection is constantly recruited from without. Were this not the
case, no doubt, it would soon degenerate, as town-

bred horses in Arabia, being stall-fed and getting no sort of exercise, are seldom fit for much. There is a false notion that the oases, such as those of Jebel Shammar and Aared, are spots especially adapted for the rearing of horses, and that the sandy wastes outside contain no pasture. But the very reverse of this is the case. The oases in which the towns stand, produce nothing but date palms and garden produce, nor is there a blade of grass, or even a tuft of camel pasture in their neighbourhood. The townspeople keep no animals except a few camels used for working the wells, and now and then a donkey. Even these must be fed either on corn or dates, which none but the rich can afford. Horses are a luxury reserved only for princes, and even the richest citizens do their travelling from village to village on foot. Longer journeys are performed on dromedaries brought in from the desert for the purpose, which are either the property of Bedouins or held with them by the citizens on shares.

The Nefûds, on the other hand, contain pasture in abundance, not only for camels, but for sheep and horses, and it is in the Nefûds that all these are bred. Ibn Rashid goes every spring with the bulk of his live stock to the desert, and leaves them during part of the summer with the tribes, only a few animals being reserved for use in the town. It cannot be too strongly insisted upon, that the upper plateaux of Nejd, where the towns and villages

are found, are a stony wilderness almost entirely
devoid of vegetation, while the Nefûds afford
an inexhaustible supply of pasture. The want
of water alone limits the pastoral value of these,
for the inhabited area is necessarily confined
to a radius of twenty or thirty miles round each
well,—and wells are rare. These facts have not,
I think, been hitherto sufficiently known to be
appreciated.

With regard to Ibn Rashid's collection at Haïl
we looked it over three or four times in the stables,
and saw it out once on a gala day, when each
animal was made to look its best. The stables
consist of four open yards communicating with each
other, in which the animals stand tethered each to a
square manger of sun-dried brick. They are not
sheltered in any way, but wear long heavy rugs
fastened across the chest. They are chained by one
or more feet to the ground, and wear no headstalls.
It being winter time and they ungroomed, they were
all in the roughest possible condition, and, as has
been mentioned, our first impression was one of disappointment. When at Haïl they are given no
regular exercise, remaining it would seem for weeks
together tied up thus, except for a few minutes in
the evening, when they are led to drink. They
are fed almost entirely on dry barley. In the
spring only, for a few weeks, they eat green
corn grown on purpose, and then are taken
to the Nefûd or on ghazús. It is surprising that

they should be able to do their work under such
conditions.

The first yard one enters in going through the
stables, contained, when we saw them, from twenty-
five to thirty mares.   In the second were twenty
more, kept in a certain kind of condition for service
in case of necessity ; but even these get very little
exercise.   As they stand there in the yard, slovenly
and unkempt, they have very little of that air of
high breeding one would expect ; and it requires
considerable imagination to look upon them as indeed
the *ne plus ultra* of breeding in Arabia.   We made
the mistake, too common, of judging horses by condition, for, mounted and in motion, these at once
became transfigured.

Here may follow some descriptions of particular
animals, written after one of our visits to the stud ;
these will give a better idea of them than any
general remarks.   In our notes I find :—

"1.   A chestnut Kehîlet el-Krush with three white
feet (mutlak el-yemĭn), 14 hands, or 14·1, but very
powerful.   Her head is plainer than most here—it
would be thought a good head in England—lean
and rather narrow.   She has too heavy a neck,
but a very fine shoulder, a high wither, legs like
steel, hind quarter decidedly coarse, much hair
at the heels.   More bone than breeding, one is
inclined to say, seeing her at her manger, though
moving, and with the Emir on her back, one must

be very captious not to admire. She is Mohammed's favourite charger, and of the best blood in Nejd. Ibn Rashid got this strain from Ibn Saoud's stables at Riad, but it came originally from the Muteyr."

"2. A bay Hamdanieh Simri, also from Ibn Saoud's collection, a pretty head, but no other distinction. N.B. This mare is of the same strain as our own mare Shcrifa, but inferior to her."

"3. A grey Seglawieh Sheyfi, extremely plain at first sight, with very drooping quarters, and a head in no way remarkable, but with a fine shoulder. This Seglawieh Sheyfi has a great reputation here, and is of special interest as being the last of her race, the only descendant of the famous mare bought by Abbas Pasha, who sent a bullock cart from Egypt all the way to Nejd to fetch her, for she was old, and unable to travel on foot. The story is well known here, and was told to us exactly as we heard it in the north, with the addition that this mare of Ibn Rashid's is the only representative of the strain left in Arabia." *

"4. A dark bay Kehîlet Ajuz, quite 14·2, one white foot, really splendid in every point, shoulder quarter and all; the handsomest head and largest eye of any here. She has ideal action, head and

---

* Abbas Pasha's Seglawieh is reported to have had two foals while in Egypt; one of them died, and the other was given to the late King of Italy, and left descendants, now in the possession of the present king.

tail carried to perfection, and recalls Beteyen ibn Mershid's mare, but her head is finer. She belongs to Hamúd, who is very proud of her, and tells us she came from the Jerba Shammar. It surprises us to find here a mare from Mesopotamia; but we are told that interchange of horses between the southern and northern Shammar is by no means rare."

" 5. A dark brown Kehîlet Ajuz, no white except an inch in breadth just above one hoof, lovely head and thoroughbred appearance, and for style of galloping perhaps the best here, although less powerful than the Emir's chestnut and Hamúd's bay. It is hard to choose among the three."

" Of the eight horses, the best is a Shueyman Sbah of great power, head large and very fine. He reminds us of Faris Jerba's mare of the same strain of blood; they are probably related closely, for he has much the same points, forequarter perfect, hindquarter strong but less distinguished. He was bred, however, in Nejd."

" A grey Seglawi Jedran, from Ibn Nedéri of the Gomussa Ánazeh, is a poor specimen of that great strain of blood; but the Bedouin respect for it prevails here though they have now no pure Seglawi Jedrans in Nejd. It is interesting to find this horse valued here, as the fact proves that the Ánazeh horses are thought much of in Nejd. The more one sees of the Nejd horses here, the more is one convinced of the superiority of those of the Ánazeh in

the points of speed, and, proud as every one here is
of the 'kheyl Nejdi,' it seems to be acknowledged
that in these points they are surpassed by the
Ánazeh horses."

"Our own Ánazeh mares are looked upon as
prodigies of speed.

"In comparing what we see here, with what we
saw last year in the north, the first thing that strikes
us is that these are ponies, the others horses. It is
not so much the actual difference in height, though
there must be quite three inches on an average, as
the shape, which produces this impression. The
Nejd horses have as a rule shorter necks and shorter
bodies, and stand over far less ground than the
Ánazehs. Then, although their shoulders are undoubtedly good and their withers higher than one
generally sees further north, the hind-quarter is
short, and if it were not for the peculiarly handsome
carriage of the tail would certainly want distinction.
Their legs all seem to be extremely good ; but we
have not seen in one of them that splendid line of
the hind leg to the hock which is so striking in' the
Ánazeh thoroughbreds. Of their feet it is difficult
to judge, for from long standing without exercise,
all the Emir's mares have their hoofs overgrown.
Their manes and tails are thicker than one would
expect.

"In their heads, however, there is certainly a
general superiority to the Ánazeh mares, at least in
all the points the Arabs most admire, and we we

both struck, directly we saw them, with the difference."

As I may fairly assume that few persons out of
Arabia have an idea what are there considered the
proper points of a horse's head, I will give here a
description of them :
First of all, the head should be large, not small.
A little head the Arabs particularly dislike, but the
size should be all in the upper regions of the skull.
There should be a great distance from the ears to
the eyes, and a great distance from one eye to the
other, though not from ear to ear. The forehead,
moreover, and the whole region between and just
below the eyes, should be convex, the eyes themselves standing rather " *à fleur de tête.*" But there
should be nothing fleshy about their prominence,
and each bone should be sharply edged ; a flat forehead is disliked. The space round the eyes should
be free of all hair, so as to show the black skin
underneath, and this just round the eyes should be
especially black and lustrous. The cheek-bone should
be deep and lean, and the jaw-bone clearly marked.
Then the face should narrow suddenly and run down
almost to a point, not however to such a point as
one sees in the English racehorse, whose profile
seems to terminate with the nostril, but to the tip of
the lip. The nostril when in repose should lie flat
with the face, appearing in it little more than a
slit, and pinched and puckered up, as also should the

mouth, which should have the under-lip longer than
the upper, "like the camel's," the Bedouins say.
The ears, especially in the mare, should be long,
but fine and delicately cut, like the ears of a
gazelle."

It must be remarked that the head and the tail
are the two points especially regarded by Arabs in
judging of a horse, as in them they think they can
discover the surest signs of his breeding. The tails
of the Nejd horses are as peculiar as their heads,
and are as essential to their beauty. However
other points might differ, every horse at Haïl had
its tail set on in the same fashion, in repose
something like the tail of a rocking horse, and
not as has been described, "thrown out in a
perfect arch." In motion the tail was held high
in the air, and looked as if it could not under any
circumstances be carried low. Mohammed ibn
Aruk declared roundly that the phenomenon was an
effect, partly at least, of art. He assured us that
before a foal is an hour old, its tail is bent back
over a stick and the twist produces a permanent
result. But this sounds unlikely, and in any case
it could hardly affect the carriage of the tail in
galloping.

With regard to colour, of the hundred animals in
the Haïl stables, there were about forty greys or
rather whites, thirty bays, twenty chestnuts, and
the rest brown. We did not see a real black, and
of course there are no roans, or piebalds, or duns,

for these are not Arab colours. The Emir one day
asked us what colours we preferred in England, and
when we told him bay or chestnut he quite agreed
with us. Nearly all Arabs prefer bay with black
points, though pure white with a very black skin
and hoofs is also liked. In a bay or chestnut, three
white feet, the off fore-foot being dark, are not
objected to. But, as a rule, colour is not much regarded at Haïl, for there as elsewhere in Arabia a
fashionable strain is all in all.

"Besides the full grown animals, Ibn Rashid's
yards contain thirty or forty foals and yearlings,
beautiful little creatures but terribly starved and
miserable. Foals bred in the desert are poor
enough, but these in town have a positively sickly
appearance. Tied all day long by the foot they
seem to have quite lost heart, and show none of the
playfulness of their age. Their tameness, like that
of the "fowl and the brute," is shocking to see.
The Emir tells us that every spring he sends a
hundred yearlings down to Queyt on the Persian
Gulf under charge of one of his slaves, who sells them
at Bombay for £100 apiece. They are of course
now at their worst age, but they have the prospect
of a few months' grazing in the Nefûd before
appearing in the market."

"On the whole, both of us are rather disappointed
with what we see here. Of all the mares in the
prince's stables I do not think more than three or
four could show with advantage among the Go-

mussa, and, in fact, we are somewhat alarmed lest the Emir should propose an exchange with us for our chestnut Ras el-Fedawi which is greatly admired by every one. If he did, we could not well refuse."

With regard to Nejd horses in general, the following remarks are based on what we saw and heard at Haïl, and elsewhere in Arabia.

First, whatever may have been the case formerly, horses of any kind are now exceedingly rare in Nejd. One may travel vast distances in the Peninsula without meeting a single horse or even crossing a horse track. Both in the Nefûd and on our return journey to the Euphrates, we carefully examined every track of man and beast we met; but from the time of our leaving the Roala till close to Meshhed Ali, not twenty of these proved to be tracks of horses. The wind no doubt obliterates footsteps quickly, but it could not wholly do so, if there were a great number of the animals near. The Ketherin, a true Nejd tribe and a branch of the Beni Khaled, told us with some pride that they could mount a hundred horsemen, and even the Muteyr, reputed to be the greatest breeders of thoroughbred stock in Nejd, are said to possess only 400 mares. The horse is a luxury with the Bedouins of the Peninsula, and not, as it is with those of the North, a necessity of their daily life. Their journeys and raids and wars are all made on camel, not on horse-back; and at most the Sheykh mounts his mare at the

moment of battle. The want of water in Nejd
is a sufficient reason for this. Horses there are
kept for show rather than actual use, and are
looked upon as far too precious to run unnecessary
risks.

Secondly, what horses there are in Nejd, are bred
in the Nefûds. The stony plateaux of the interior
contain no suitable pasture except in a very few
places, while the Nefûds afford grass, green or dry,
the whole year round. The Muteyr, the Beni
Khaled, the Dafir, and the Shammar, are now the
principal breeders of horses in Nejd, but the Ánazeh
are regarded as possessing the best strains, and
the Ánazeh have disappeared from Nejd. They
began to migrate northwards about two hundred
years ago, and have ever since continued moving by
successive migrations till all have abandoned their
original homes. It may be that the great name
which Nejd horses undoubtedly have in the East,
was due mainly to these very Ánazeh, with whose
horses they are now contrasted. The Bisshr Ánazeh
were settled in the neighbourhood of Kheybar, on
the western edge of the Nefûd, the Roala south of
Jôf, and the Amarrat in the extreme east. These
probably among them supplied Nejd horses in
former times to Syria, Bagdad, and Persia, and
some sections of the tribe may even have found
their way further south ; for the Ibn Saouds
themselves are an Ánazeh family. So that then,
probably, as now, the best strains of blood were

in their hands. To the present day in the north the Ánazeh distinguish the descendants of the mares brought with them from Nejd as "Nejdi," while they call the descendants of the mares captured from the tribes of the North, "Shimali" or Northerners.

The management and education of horses seems to differ little in Nejd from what it is elsewhere among the Arabs. But we were surprised to find that, in place of the Bedouin halter, the bit is used at Haïl. At first we fancied that this was in imitation of Turkish manners; but it is more likely to be an old custom with town Arabs. Indeed the Bedouins of the Sahara, no less than the Turks, use the ring bit, which may after all have been an invention of Arabia. Bad as it is for the mouth, it is certainly of use in the fancy riding indulged in at Haïl, the jerid play and sham fighting. Among the Bedouins of Nejd the halter alone is used.

Of anything like racing we could learn nothing. Trials of speed are no longer in fashion, as they must have been once, and skill in turning and doubling is alone of any value. That some tradition, however, of training still exists among the Arabs, the following recipe for rearing a colt seems to prove. It was given us in answer to our description of English racing and racehorses, and probably represents a traditional practice of Arabia as old as the days of Mahomet.

ARAB RECIPE FOR REARING A COLT.

"If," said our informant, "you would make a colt run faster than his fellows, remember the following rules :—

"'During the first month of his life let him be content with his mother's milk, it will be sufficient for him. Then during five months add to this natural supply goat's milk, as much as he will drink. For six months more give him the milk of camels, and besides a measure of wheat steeped in water for a quarter of an hour, and served in a nose-bag.

"'At a year old the colt will have done with milk ; he must be fed on wheat and grass, the wheat dry from a nose-bag, the grass green if there is any.

"'At two years old he must work, or he will be worthless. Feed him now, like a full-grown horse, on barley ; but in summer let him also have gruel daily at midday. Make the gruel thus :—Take a double-handful of flour, and mix it in water well with your hands till the water seems like milk ; then strain it, leaving the dregs of the flour, and give what is liquid to the colt to drink.

"'Be careful from the hour he is born to let him stand in the sun ; shade hurts horses, but let him have water in plenty when the day is hot.

"'The colt must now be mounted, and taken by his owner everywhere with him, so that he shall see

everything, and learn courage. He must be kept
constantly in exercise, and never remain long at his
manger. He should be taken on a journey, for work
will fortify his limbs.

"'At three years old he should be trained to
gallop. Then, if he be of true blood, he will not be
left behind. Yalla!'"

HAMÚD IBN RASHID.

CHAPTER XIII.

" Babel was Nimrod's hunting box, and then
A town of gardens, walls, and wealth amazing,
Where Nabuchodonosor, king of men,
Reigned till one summer's day he took to grazing."
                                        BYRON.

"   .   .   .   .   Oh how wretched
Is that poor man that lives on princes' favours."
                                        SHAKESPEARE.

Mohammed loses his head—A ride with the Emir—The mountain
fortress of Agde—Farewell to Haïl—We join the Persian Haj—
Ways and manners of the pilgrims—A clergyman of Medina.

I HAVE hinted at a mystification in which we
found ourselves involved a few days after our
arrival at Haïl, and which at the time caused us no
little anxiety. It had its origin in a piece of child-
ishness on Mohammed's part, whose head was
completely turned by the handsome reception given
him as an Ibn Arûk by the Emir, and a little
too, I fear, by our own spoiling. To the present
day I am not quite sure that we heard all that
happened, and so forbear entering upon the matter
in detail; but as far as we could learn, Mohammed's vanity seems to have led him to aggran-
dise his own position in the eyes of Ibn Rashid's
court, by representing us as persons whom he
had taken under his protection, and who were in

some way dependent on him ; boasting that the
camels, horses, and other property were his own,
and our servants his people.   This under ordinary
circumstances might have been a matter of small
consequence, and we should not have grudged him a
little self-glorification at our expense, conscious as
we were of having owed the success of our journey
hitherto, mainly to his fidelity.   But unfortunately
the secondary *rôle* which he would thus have assigned to us, made our relations with the Emir not
only embarrassing, but positively dangerous.   Our
reception at first had been cordial to a degree that
made it all the more annoying to find, that when we
had been four days at Haïl, we no longer received
the attentions which had hitherto been paid us. The
presents of game ceased, and the lamb, with which
we had hitherto been regaled at dinner, was replaced
by camel meat.   Instead of two soldiers being sent
to escort us to the palace, a slave boy came with a
message.   On the fifth day we were not invited to
the evening party, and on the sixth Wilfrid, calling
at the palace, was told curtly that the Emir was not
at home.   We could not imagine the cause of this
change, and Mohammed, usually so cheerful and so
open-hearted, had become moody and embarrassed,
keeping almost entirely with the servants in the
outer house.   Hanna, the faithful Hanna, began to
hint darkly that things were not well, and Abdallah
and the rest of the Mussulman servants seemed
unwilling to do their duty.   We remembered

that we were among Wahhabi fanatics, and we
began to be very much alarmed. Still we were far
from guessing the real reason, and it was not till we
had been a week at Haïl that Wilfrid, happening
to meet the Emir's chief slave Mubarek, learned
from him how matters stood. It was no use being
angry; indeed Mohammed's conduct was rather
childish than disloyal, and the *dénouement* would
have not been worth mentioning except as an
illustration of Arab manners and ways of thought,
and also as explaining why our stay at Haïl was cut
shorter than we had originally intended it to be ;
and why, instead of going on to Kasim, we joined
the Persian pilgrimage on their homeward road to
Meshhed Ali.

Matters of course could not rest there, and on
returning home from his interview with Mubarek,
Wilfrid upbraided Mohammed with his folly, and
then sent to the palace for Mufurraj, the master of
ceremonies, and the same dignified old gentleman
who had received us on our arrival, and having explained the circumstances bade him in his turn explain
them to the Emir. The old man promised to do this,
and I have no doubt kept his word, for that very evening we were sent for once more to the palace, and received with the old cordiality. It is, too, I think
very creditable to the arrangements of the Haïl court,
that no explanations of any sort were entered into.
Mohammed, though put in his proper place, was
still politely received ; and only an increase of

amiable attentions made us remember that we had
ever had cause to complain. As to Mohammed, I
am bound to say, that once the fumes of his vanity
evaporated, he bore no kind of malice for what we
had been obliged to do, and became once more the
amiable, attentive and serviceable friend he had
hitherto been. Ill-temper is not an Arab failing.
Still the incident was a lesson and a warning, a
lesson that we were Europeans still among Asiatics,
a warning that Haïl was a lion's den, though fortunately we were friends with the lion. We began
to make our plans for moving on.

I have said little as yet about the Persian pilgrimage which, encamped just outside the walls of Haïl,
had all along been a main feature in the goings on
of the place. On a certain Tuesday, however, the
Emir sent us a message that he expected us to come
out riding with him, and that he would meet us at
that gate of the town where the pilgrims were. It
was a fortunate day for us, not indeed because we
saw the pilgrims, but because we saw what we would
have come the whole journey to see, and had almost
despaired of seeing,—all the best of the Emir's
horses out and galloping about. We were delighted
at the opportunity, and made haste to get ready. In
half an hour we were on our mares, and in the
street. There was a great concourse of people all
moving towards the camp, and just outside the town
we found the Emir's cavalcade. This for the moment
absorbed all my thoughts, for I had not yet seen

any of the Haïl horses mounted. The Emir, splendidly dressed but barefooted, was riding a pretty little white mare, while the chestnut Krushieh followed him mounted by a slave.

All our friends were there, Hamúd, Majid and the two boys his brothers, with a still smaller boy, whom they introduced to us as a son of Metaab, the late Emir, all in high spirits and anxious to show off their horses and their horsemanship ; while next the Emir and under his special protection rode the youth with the tragical history, Naïf, the sole remaining son of Tellál, whose brothers Mohammed had killed, and who, it is whispered, will some day be called on to revenge their deaths. Mubarek too, the white slave, was there, a slave in name only, for he is strikingly like the princely family in feature and is one of the richest and most important personages in Haïl. The rest of the party consisted of friends and servants, with a fair sprinkling of black faces among them, dressed in their best clothes and mounted on the Emir's mares. Conspicuous on his beautiful bay was Hamúd, who, as usual, did us the honours, and pointed out and explained the various persons and things we saw. It was one of those mornings one only finds in Nejd. The air brilliant and sparkling to a degree one cannot imagine in Europe, and filling one with a sense of life such as one remembers to have had in childhood, and which gives one a wish to shout. The sky of an intense blue, and the hills in front of us carved out of sapphire, and the plain, crisp and even as a billiard table, sloping gently upwards towards them. On one side the battlemented walls and towers of Haïl, with the palace rising out of a dark mass of palms almost black in the sunlight; on the other the pilgrim camp, a parti-coloured mass of tents, blue, green, red, white, with the pilgrims themselves in a dark crowd, watching with curious half-frightened eyes the barbaric display of which we formed a part.

Presently the Emir gave a signal to advance, and turning towards the south-west, our whole party moved on in the direction of a clump of palm-trees we could see about two miles off. Hamúd then suddenly put his mare into a gallop, and one after another the rest of the party joined him in a sham fight, galloping, doubling, and returning to the Emir, who remained alone with us, and shouting as though they would bring the sky about their ears. At last the Emir could resist it no longer, and seizing a jerid or palm stick from one of the slaves, went off himself among the others. In a moment his dignity and his town manners were forgotten, and he became the Bedouin again which he and all his family really are. His silk kefiyehs were thrown back, and bare-headed with his long Bedouin plaits streaming in the wind and bare-legged and bare-armed, he galloped hither and thither; charging into the throng, and pursuing and being pursued, and shouting as if he had never felt a care, and never committed a crime in his life.

We found ourselves alone with a strange little personage whom we had already noticed riding beside the Emir, and who seemed even more out of place in this fantastic entertainment than ourselves. I hope at least that we looked less ridiculous than he did. Mounted on a sorry little kadish, and dressed in the fashion of European children fifty years ago, with a high waisted coat, well pleated at the skirt, trousers up to his knees, and feet shod with slippers, a little brown skull cap on his head, and a round shaven face, sat what seemed an overgrown boy, but what in reality was a chief person from among the Persian pilgrims. It was Ali Koli Khan, son of the great Khan of the Bactiari, who for his father's sake was being treated by the Emir with all possible honour. He, with the rest of the Haj, was now on his way back from Mecca, and it was partly to impress him with the Emir's magnificence that the present party had been arranged.

We did not long stay alone, for in a few minutes the galloping ceased, and we then went on sedately as before, and in due time arrived at the palm trees, which, it turned out, were the Emir's property, and contained in a garden surrounded by a high wall. Here we were invited to dismount, and a carpet having been spread under the trees, we all sat down. Slaves were soon busy serving a luncheon of sweetmeats,—boys were made to climb the lemon trees, and shake down the fruit, and coffee was handed round. Then all the party said their prayers except ourselves and the Persian, who, as a Shiah, could not join in their devotions, and we mounted again and rode home. This time we too joined in the galloping, which speedily recommenced, our mares fully enjoying the fun, and in this way we scampered back to Haïl.

On the following day Wilfrid called on Ali Koli Khan in his tent, going there with Mohammed, now once more a reasonable companion and follower. Indeed in the Persian camp assumptions of nobility on Mohammed's part would have been quite thrown away, for the Persians care nothing for Arabian nobility, and treat all alike as Bedouins and barbarians. Ali Koli, though only a younger son, was travelling in state, having his mother with him, and a multitude of servants, male and female, besides his *hemeldaria* or contractor, and the Arabs managing his beasts. His major-domo and interpreter was a magnificent personage, and his followers, dressed in felt tunics and skull caps, gave him the appearance of being an important chief. His tent was of the Turkish pattern, well lined and comfortable, with fine Persian carpets on the floor, and a divan. There Wilfrid found him sitting with a friend, Abd er-Rahim, the son of a merchant of Kermanshah, who is also British consular agent there. The young Persians were very amiable; but the contrast of their manners with those of the ceremonious Arabs

struck Wilfrid at once. There were none of those
elaborate compliments and polite inquiries one gets
used to at Haïl, but rather a European *sans gêne* in
the form of reception. They made Wilfrid comfortable on the divan, called for tea, which was served in
a *samovar*, and at once poured out a long history of
their sufferings on the pilgrimage. This they did in
very broken Arabic, and with an accent irresistibly
absurd, for the Persians speak with a drawl in their
intonation, wholly foreign to that of the Arabs.
Ali's natural language, he says, is Kurdish, but being
an educated person, and an officer in the Shah's
army, he talks Persian equally well. In Persia, Arabic
plays much the part in education which Latin did in
Europe before it was quite a dead language. Both
he and Abd er-Rahim were loud in complaints of
everything Arabian, and in spite of Mohammed's
presence, abused roundly the whole Arab race, the
poverty of the towns, the ignorance of the citizens,
and the robberies of the Bedouins, also the
extortionate charges of the Arab hemeldarias,
contractors for camels, and the miseries of desert
travelling. "Was ever anything seen so miserable as the bazaar at Haïl; not a bag of sweetmeats to be had for love or money, the Arabs
were mere barbarians, drinkers of coffee instead of
tea." Every now and then, too, they would break out
into conversation in their own language. Wilfrid,
however, liked Ali Koli, and they parted very good
friends, with an invitation from both the young

Persians to travel on with them to Meshhed on the
Euphrates, where the Persians always end their
pilgrimage by a visit to the shrines of Ali and
Huseyn. This seemed an excellent opportunity, and
having consulted the Emir, who highly approved of
the plan, we accordingly decided to travel with the
Haj as soon as it should start.

Our last days at Haïl were by no means the least
pleasant. As a final proof of his goodwill and
confidence, the Emir announced that we might pay
a visit to Agde, a fortress in the mountains some
miles from Haïl, and which he had never before
shown to any stranger. I do not feel at liberty to
say exactly where this is, for we were sent to see it
rather on parole, and though I hope Ibn Rashid
runs no danger of foreign invasion, I would not
give a clue to possible enemies. Suffice it to say
that it lies in the mountains, in a position of great
natural strength, made stronger by some rude
attempts at fortification, and that it is really one of
the most curious places in the world.

One approaches it from the plain by a narrow
winding valley, reminding one not a little of the
wadys of Mount Sinai, where the granite rocks rise
abruptly on either hand out of a pure bed of sand.
On one of these is engraved an inscription in Arabic
which we copied and which though not very legible
may be read thus :—

"Hadihi kharâbat Senhârîb."
"This (is) the ruin of Senacherib ('s building)."

Such at least is its meaning in the opinion of Mr.
Sabunji, a competent Arabic scholar, though I will
not venture to explain on what occasion Senacherib
made his way to Nejd, nor why he wrote in Arabic
instead of his own cuneiform.

Inside the defences, the valley broadens out into
an amphitheatre formed by the junction of three or
four wadys in which there is a village and a palm
garden. Besides which, the wadys are filled with wild
palms watered, the Arabs say, "min Allah," by Providence, at least by no human hand. They are
very beautiful, forming a brilliant contrast of green
fertility with the naked granite crags which over-
hang them on all sides. These are perhaps a
thousand feet in height, and run down sheer into the
sandy floor of the wadys, so that one is reminded in
looking at them of that valley of diamonds where
the serpents lived, and down which the merchants
threw their pieces of meat for the rocs to gather, in
the tale of Sinbad the Sailor. No serpents however live in Agde, but a population of very honest
Shammar, who entertained us with a prodigality
of dates and coffee, difficult to do justice to. We
had been sent in the company of two horsemen
of the Emir's, Shammar, who did the honours, as
Agde and all in it are really Ibn Rashid's private
property. These and the villagers gave us a deal
of information about the hills we were in, and
showed us where a great battle had been fought by
Mohammed's father and his uncle Obeyd against

the Ibn Ali, formerly Emirs of the Jebel. It would
seem that Agde was the oldest possession of the Ibn
Rashids, and that on their taking Haïl the Ibn Alis
marched against them, when they retreated to their
fortress, and there gave battle and such a defeat to
the people of Kefar that it secured to the Ibn
Rashids supreme power ever after. They also
showed us with great pride a wall built by Obeyd
to block the narrow valley, and made us look at
everything, wells, gardens, and houses, so that we
spent nearly all the day there. They told us too of
a mysterious beast that comes from the hills by
night and climbs the palm trees for sake of the
dates. "As large as a hare, with a long tail, and
very good to eat." They describe it as sitting on
its hind-legs, and whistling, so that Wilfrid thinks
it must be a marmot. Only, do marmots climb?
They call it the Webber.

We had a delightful gallop home with the two
Bedouins, (Mohammed was not with us,) of whom
we learned one of the Shammar war songs, which
runs thus :—

> " Ma arîd ana erkobu delul,
>   Lau zeynuli shedadeha,
>   Arîdu ana hamra shenuf,
>   Hamra seryeh aruddeha."

thus literally translated :—

> " I would not ride a mere delul,
>   Though lovely to me her shedad (camel-saddle);
>   Let me be mounted on a mare,
>   A bay mare, swift and quick to turn."

They were mounted on very pretty ponies, but could not keep up with us galloping. If we had been in Turkey, or indeed anywhere else but in Arabia, we should have had to give a handsome tip after an expedition of this kind ; but at Haïl nothing of the sort was expected. Both these Shammar were exceedingly intelligent well mannered men, with souls above money. They were doing their duty to the prince as Sheykh, and to us as strangers, and they did it enthusiastically.

The level of Agde is 3,780 feet above the sea, that of Haïl 3,500.

This was, perhaps, the pleasantest day of all those we spent at Haïl, and will live long with us as a delightful remembrance. On the following day we were to depart. Mohammed, while we were away, had been making preparations. Two new camels had been bought, and a month's provision of dates and rice purchased, in addition to a gift of excellent Yemen coffee sent us by the Emir. Our last interview with Ibn Rashid was characteristic. He was not at the kasr, but in a house he has close to the Mecca gate, where from a little window he can watch unperceived the goings on of the Haj encamped below him. We found him all alone, for he has lost all fear of our being assassins now, at his window like a bird of prey, calculating no doubt how many more silver pieces he should be able to make out of the Persians before they were well out of his clutches. Every now and then he

would lean out of the window, which was partly
covered by a shutter, and shout to one of his
men who were standing below some message with
regard to the pilgrims.   He seemed to be enjoying the pleasure of his power over them, and it is
absolute.

To us he was very amiable, renewing all his
protestations of friendship and regard, and offering
to give us anything we might choose to ask for,
dromedaries for the journey, or one of his mares.
This, although we should have liked to accept the
last offer, we of course declined, Wilfrid making a
short speech in the Arab manner, saying that the only
thing we asked was the Emir's regard, and wishing
him length of days.   He begged Mohammed ibn
Rashid to consider him as his vakil in Europe
in case he required assistance of any kind, and
thanked him for all the kindness we had
received at his hands.   The Emir then proposed
that we should put off our departure, and go with
him instead on a ghazú or warlike expedition he
was starting on in a few days, a very attractive
offer which might have been difficult to refuse had
it been made earlier, but which we now declined.
Our heads, in fact, had been in the jaws of the
lion long enough, and now our only object was to
get quietly and decorously out of the den.   We
therefore pleaded want of time, and added that our
camels were already on the road ; we then said
good-bye and took our leave.

There was, however, one more visit to be paid, this time of friendly regard more than of ceremony. As we rôde through the town we stopped at Hamúd's house and found him and all his family at home. To them our farewells were really expressions of regret at parting, and Hamúd gave us some very sound advice about going on with the Haj to Meshhed Ali, instead of trying to get across to Bussora. There had been rain, he said, on the pilgrim road, and all the reservoirs (those marked on the map as the tanks of Zobeydeh) were full, so that our journey that way would be exceptionally easy, whereas between this and Bussorah, we should have to pass over an almost waterless region, without anything interesting to compensate for the difficulty. But this we should see as we went on—the first thing, as I have said, was to get clear away, and it would be time enough later to settle details about our course.

Majid was there, and received from Wilfrid as a remembrance a silver-handled Spanish knife, whereupon he sent for a black cloth cloak with a little gold embroidery on the collar and presented it to me. It was a suitable gift, for I had nothing of the sort, indeed no respectable abba at all, and this one was both dignified and quiet in appearance. Majid at least, I am sure, regrets us, and if circumstances ever take us again to Haïl, it would be the best fortune for us to find him or his father on the throne. They are regarded as the natural heirs to

the Sheykhat, and Ibn Rashid's does not look like a
long life.

After this we mounted, and in another five
minutes were clear of the town. Then looking
back, we each drew a long breath, for Haïl with all
the charm of its strangeness, and its interesting
inhabitants, had come to be like a prison to us, and
at one time when we had had that quarrel with
Mohammed, had seemed very like a tomb.

We left Haïl by the same gate at which we had
entered it, what seemed like years before, but instead
of turning towards the mountains, we skirted the
wall of the town and further on the palm gardens,
which are its continuation, for about three miles
down a ravine-like wady. Then we came out on the
plain again, and at the last isolated group of ithel
trees, halted for the last time to enjoy the shade,
for the sun was almost hot, before joining the
pilgrim caravan, which we could see like a long line
of ants traversing the plain between us and the
main range of Jebel Shammar.

It was, without exception, the most beautiful
view I ever saw in my life, and I will try to
describe it. To begin with, it must be understood
that the air, always clear in Jebel Shammar, was
this day of a transparent clearness, which probably
surpasses anything seen in ordinary deserts, or in
the high regions of the Alps, or at the North
Pole, or anywhere except perhaps in the moon.
For this is the very centre of the desert, four

hundred miles from the sea, and nearly four
thousand feet above the sea level. Before us
lay a foreground of coarse reddish sand, the
washing down of the granite rocks of Jebel Aja,
with here and there magnificent clumps of ithel,
great pollards whose trunks measure twenty and
thirty feet* in circumference, growing on little
mounds showing where houses once stood—just as
in Sussex the yew trees do—for the town seems to
have shifted from this end of the oasis to where it
now is. Across this sand lay a long green belt of
barley, perhaps a couple of acres in extent, the
blades of corn brilliantly green, and just having
shot up high enough to hide the irrigation furrows.
Beyond this, for a mile or more, the level desert
fading from red to orange, till it was again cut by
what appeared to be a shining sheet of water
reflecting the deep blue of the sky—a mirage of
course, but the most perfect illusion that can be
imagined. Crossing this, and apparently wading in
the water, was the long line of the pilgrim camels,
each reflected exactly in the mirage below him with
the dots of blue, red, green, or pink, representing
the litter or tent he carried. The line of the
procession might be five miles or more in length ;
we could not see the end of it. Beyond again rose
the confused fantastic mass of the sapphire coloured
crags of Jebel Aja, the most strange and beautiful

---

* We measured one, a pollard, thirty-six feet round the trunk
at five feet from the ground.

mountain range that can be imagined —a lovely vision.

When we had sufficiently admired all this, and I had made my sketch of it, for there was no hurry, we got on our mares again and rejoicing with them in our freedom, galloped on singing the Shammar song, " Ma arid ana erkobu delúl lau zeynoli sheda-deha, biddi ana hamra shenûf, hamra seriyeh arruddeha," a proceeding which inspired them more than any whip or spur could have done, and which as we converged towards the Haj caravan, made the camels caper, and startled the pilgrims into the idea that the Harb Bedouins were once more upon them. So we went along with Mohammed following us, till we reached the vanguard of the Haj, and the green and red banner which goes in front of it. Close to this we found our own camels, and soon after camped with them, not ten miles from Haïl in a bit of a wady where the standard was planted.

Our tents are a couple of hundred yards away from the Haj camp, which is crowded together for fear of the dangers of the desert. The pilgrim mueddins have just chanted the evening call to prayers, and the people are at their devotions. Our mares are munching their barley, and our hawk (a trained bird we bought yesterday for six mejidies of a Bedouin at Haïl), is sitting looking very wise on his perch in front of us. It is a cold evening, but oh how clean and comfortable in the tent !

February 2.—It appears after all that only about
half the Haj left Haïl yesterday. There has been a
difficulty about camels some say, others that Ibn
Rashid will not let the people go, an affair of money
probably in either case. So we had hardly gone
more than two miles before a halt was ordered by
the emir el-haj, one Ambar, a black slave of Ibn
Rashid's, and the camels and their riders remained
massed together on a piece of rising ground for the
purpose we think of being counted. The dervishes,
however, and other pilgrims on foot went on as
they liked, and so did we, for we do not consider
ourselves bound by any of the rules of the Haj
procession, and Abdallah has orders to march our
camels well outside the main body. There was no
road or track at all to-day, and we went forward on
the look-out for water which we heard was somewhere on ahead, crossing some very rough ground
and wadys which were almost ravines. We have
become so used to the desert now, that from a long
distance we made out the water, guessing its
position from the white colour of the ground near
it. The whiteness is caused by a stonelike deposit
the water makes when it stands long anywhere;
and in this instance it lay in a sort of natural
reservoir or series of reservoirs in the bed of a
shallow wady. These must have been filled some
time during the winter by rain, and we hurried on
to fill our goat skins at them while they were still
clean, for the pilgrims would soon drink up and

pollute them. They are but small pools. We found Awwad already there, he having been sent on in front with a delúl to make sure of our supply, and the process of filling the skins was hardly over before the dervishes who always march ahead of the Haj began to arrive. They have an unpleasant habit of washing in the water first, and drinking it afterwards, which we are told is part of their religious ritual.

The wind has been very violent all day with a good deal of sand in it, but it has now gone down. Our course since leaving Haïl has been east by north, and is directed towards a tall hill, Jebel Jildiyeh, which is a very conspicuous landmark. Our camp to-night is a pleasanter one than yesterday's, being further from the pilgrims, and we have a little wady all to ourselves, with plenty of good firewood, and food for the camels.

February 3.—Though fires were lit this morning at four o'clock as if in preparation of an early start, no move has been made to-day. Half the pilgrimage they tell us is still at Haïl, and must be waited for. Wilfrid went to-day into the camp to find our friend Ali Koli Khan, but neither he nor Abd er-Rahim, nor anyone else he knew had arrived.

The Persian pilgrims, though not very agreeable in person or in habits (for they are without the sense of propriety which is so characteristic of the Arabs), are friendly enough, and if we could talk to them, would, I dare say, be interesting, but on a superficial

comparison with the Arabs they seem coarse and
boorish.   They are most of them fair complexioned,
and many have fair hair and blue eyes ; but their
features are heavy, and there is much the same
difference between them and the Shammar who
are escorting them, as there is between a Dutch
cart-horse and one of Ibn Rashid's mares.   In spite
of their washings, which are performed in season and
out of season all day long, they look unutterably
dirty in their greasy felt dresses, as no unwashed
Arab ever did.   Awwad and the rest of our people
now and then get into disputes with them when
they come too near our tents in search of firewood,
and it is evident that there is no love lost between
Persian and Arab.

My day has been spent profitably at home re-
stuffing my saddle, which was sadly in want of it.
Mohammed has become quite himself again, no airs
or graces of any kind, and, as he says, the air of
Haïl did not agree with him.   He seems anxious
now to efface all recollection of the past, and has
made himself very agreeable, telling us histories connected with the Sebaa and their horses, all of them
instructive, some amusing.

February 4.—Another day's waiting, the pilgrims
as well as we ourselves impatient, but impatience is
no good.   Wilfrid, by way of occupying the time,
went off on a surveying expedition by himself, with
his mare and the greyhounds.   He went in a straight
line northwards, towards a line of low hills which

are visible here from the high ground. They are about twelve miles off. He met nobody except a couple of Bedouins on delûls, going to Atwa, where they told him there is a well. They looked on him and his gun with suspicion, and did not much like being cross-questioned. After that he found the desert absolutely empty of life, a succession of level sandy plains, and rough ridges of sandstone. The hills themselves, which he reached before turning back, were also of yellow sandstone, weathered black in patches, and from the top of the ridge he could make out the Nefûd, like a red sea. He galloped to the ridge and back in three hours. The ride was useful, as it enabled him to get the position of several of the principal hills, Yatubb, Jildiyeh, and others, and to mark them on his chart. He did not say where he intended to go, but as it happened, he returned before there was time for me to become anxious.

In the meanwhile, Awwad and Abdallah had been giving the falcon a lesson with a lure they have made out of one of the nosebags. The bird seems very tame, and comes to Awwad when he calls it, shouting "Ash'o, ash'o," which he explains is the short for its name, Rasham, a corruption of the word *rashmon*, which means shining like lightning. We may hope now with Rasham's assistance to keep ourselves supplied with meat, for hares are in plenty.

In the afternoon visitors came, some Shammar Bedouins of the Ibn Duala family, who have

preferred to camp beside us, as more congenial
neighbours to them than the Persians. They are on
their way from Haïl to their tents in the Nefûd with
a message from the Emir that more camels are
wanted ; and they are going on afterwards with the
Haj as far as Meshhed Ali, or perhaps to Samawa
on the Euphrates, to buy rice (tummin), and wheat.
It is only twice a year that the tribes of Jebel
Shammar can communicate with the outside world ;
on the occasion of the two Haj journeys, coming and
going. It is then that they lay in their provision
for the year. The eldest of these Ibn Duala, a man
of sixty, is very well-mannered and amiable. He
dined with Mohammed and the servants in their
tent, and came to sit with us afterwards in ours.
We are in half a mind to leave this dawdling Haj,
and go on with him to-morrow. But his tents lie
some way to the left out of our road.

Besides the Ibn Dualas, there are some poor
Bedouins with their camels crouched down in our
wady to be out of sight. They are afraid of being
impressed for the Haj, and at first it was difficult to
understand why, if so, they should have come so
close to it. But they explained that they hoped to
get lost in the crowd, and hoped to have the advantage of its company, without having their camels
loaded. They, like everybody else, are on their way
to Meshhed to buy corn.

There is a report that the Emir is coming from
Haïl to-morrow, and will travel three days with the

pilgrimage, going on afterwards, nobody knows where, on a ghazú. This would be tiresome, as now we have wished him good-bye we only want to get away.

February 5.—We have moved at last, but only another ten miles, to a larger wady, which seems to drain the whole country, and which they call Wady Hanasser (the valley of the little fingers), why so called I cannot say. Here there are numerous wells, and a large tract of camel pasture, of the sort called *rimh*. There are a good number of hares in this cover, and we have had some coursing with our greyhounds, aided by a sort of lurcher who has attached himself to us. The servants call him "Merzug," which may be translated a "windfall" literally a gift from God, an unattractive animal, but possessed of a nose.

Two hours after starting we came to a curious tell standing quite alone in the plain. It is, like all the rest of the country now, of sandstone, and we were delighted to find it covered with inscriptions,*

---

* Mr. Rassam, who has been digging at Babylon, informs me that these inscriptions are in the ancient Phœnician character. It would seem that the Phœnicians, who were a nation of shopkeepers, were in the habit of sending out commercial travellers with samples of goods all over Asia ; and wherever they stopped on the road, if there was a convenient bit of soft rock, they scratched their names on it, and drew pictures of animals. The explanation may be the true one, but how does it come that these tradesmen should choose purely desert subjects for their artistic efforts—camels, ostriches, ibexes, and horsemen with lances. I should have fancied rather that these were the work of Arabs, or of whoever

and pictures of birds and beasts of the sort we had already seen, but much better executed, and on a larger scale. The character, whatever its name, is a very handsome one, as distinct and symmetrical as the Greek or Latin capitals, and some of the drawings have a rude, but real artistic merit. They cannot be the work of mere barbarians, any more than the alphabet. It is remarkable that all the animals represented are essentially Arabian, the gazelle, the camel, the ibex, the ostrich. I noticed also a palm tree conventionally treated, but nothing like a house, or even a tent. The principal subject is a composition of two camels with necks crossed, of no small merit. It is combined with an inscription very regularly cut. That these things are very ancient is proved by the colour of the indentations. The rock is a reddish sandstone weathered black, and it is evident that when fresh, the letters and drawings stood out red against a dark back-ground, but now many of these have been completely weathered over again, a process it must have taken centuries in this dry climate to effect.

We were in front of the Haj when we came to this tell (Tell es Sayliyeh), and we waited on the top of it while the whole procession passed us, an hour or more. It was a curious spectacle. From the height where we were, we could see for thirty or forty miles back over the plain, as far as Jebel Aja,

represented the Arabs, in days gone by, anyhow of people living in the country. But I am no archæologist.

at the foot of which Haïl lies. The procession,
three miles long, was composed of some four
thousand camels (nor was this the whole Haj), with
a great number of men on foot besides. In front
were the dervishes, walking very fast, almost
running ; wild dirty people, but amiable, and quite
ready to converse if they know Arabic ; then, a
group of respectably dressed people walking out of
piety, a man with an immense blue turban, we
believe to be an Afghan ; a slim, very neat-looking
youth, who might be a clerk or a shopkeeper's
assistant, reading as he walks a scroll, and others
carrying leather bottles in their hands containing
water for their ablutions, which they stop every now
and then to perform. Sometimes they chant or
recite prayers. All these devotees are very rude to
us, answering nothing when we salute them, and
being thrown into consternation if the greyhounds
come near them lest they should be touched by
them and defiled. One of them, the youth with the
scroll, stopped this morning at our fire to warm his
hands as he went by, and we offered him a cup
of coffee, but he said he had breakfasted, and turned
to talk to the servants, his fellow Mussulmans, but
the servants told him to move on. Among Arabs,
to refuse a cup of coffee is the grossest offence, and
is almost tantamount to a declaration of war. The
Arabs do not understand the religious prejudices of
the Shiyite Persians.

Some way behind these forerunners comes the *berak,*

or banner, carried in the centre of a group of mounted dromedaries magnificently caparisoned and moving on at a fast walk. These most beautiful creatures have coats like satin, eyes like those of the gazelle, and a certain graceful action which baffles description. Not even the Arabian horse has such a look of breeding as these thorough-bred camels. They are called *naamiyeh*, because one may go to sleep while riding them without being disturbed by the least jolting.

The berak, Ibn Rashid's standard, is a square of purple silk with a device and motto in white in the centre, and a green border. It is carried by a servant on a tall dromedary, and is usually partly furled on the march. Ambar, the negro emir el-Haj, generally accompanies this group. He has a little white mare led by a slave which follows him, and which we have not yet seen him ride.

After the berak comes the mass of pilgrims, mounted sometimes two on one camel, sometimes with a couple of boxes on each side, the household furniture. The camels are the property of Bedouins, mostly Shammar, but many of them Dafir, Sherârat, or Howeysin. They follow their animals on foot, and are at perpetual wrangle with the pilgrims, although, if they come to blows, Ibn Rashid's police mounted on dromedaries interfere, deciding the quarrel in a summary manner.

A Persian riding on a camel is the most ridiculous sight in the world. He insists on

sitting astride, and seems absolutely unable to
learn the ways and habits of the creature he rides ;
and he talks to it with his falsetto voice in a language
no Arabian camel could possibly understand. The
jokes cut on the Persians by the Arabs never
cease from morning till night. The better class of
pilgrims, and of course all the women except the
very poor, travel in *mahmals* or litters—panniers,
of which a camel carries two—covered over like a
tradesman's van with blue or red canvas. One or
two persons possess *tahteravans,* a more expensive
kind of conveyance, which requires two mules or
two camels, one before and one behind, to carry it.
In either of these litters the traveller can squat or
even lie down and sleep. The camels chosen for
the mahmals are strong and even-paced ; and some
of these double panniers are fitted up with a certain
care and elegance, and the luxuries of Persian rugs
and hangings. A confidential driver leads the camel,
and servants sometimes walk beside it. One of the
pilgrims keeps a man to march in front with his
narghileh, which he smokes through a very long
tube sitting in the pannier above. There are a few
horses, perhaps about half a dozen. One, a white
Kehîlan Harkan, was bought the other day by a
rich pilgrim from a Shammar Bedouin of the escort.
This horse seems to be thoroughbred as far as can
be judged from his head, tail, and pasterns ; the
rest of him is hidden by a huge *pallan,* or
pack-saddle, with trappings, in which his new

owner rides him. I have seen no others worth
mentioning.

The whole of this procession defiled before us as
we sat perched on the Tell es Sayliyeh just above
their heads.

We have made some new acquaintances, Hejazis
from Medina, who came to our tent to-day and sat
down in a friendly way to drink coffee with us.
The Hejazi, though accounted pure Arabs, are
almost as black as negroes, and have mean squat
features, very unlike those of the Shammar and other
pure races we have seen. They are also wanting in
dignity, and have a sort of Gascon reputation in
this part of Arabia. These were extremely out-
spoken people. The chief man among them, one
Saleh ibn Benji, is keeper of the grand mosque
at Medina, and is now travelling to collect alms in
Persia for the shrine. He told us that although
quite willing to make friends with us here and
drink our coffee, he could not advise us to go to
Medina. Not but what Englishmen as Englishmen
were in good repute there ; but it was against their
rule to allow any except Mussulmans inside the
town. If we came as Mussulmans it would be all
very well, but as Nasrani it would not do. He
himself would be the first to try and compass our
deaths. They had found a Jew in Medina last year
and executed him ; and the people were very angry
because the Sultan had sent a Frank engineer to
survey the district, and had given out that he was

a Moslem. The rule only applied to the two holy cities, Mecca and Medina, not to the rest of the country. The Mussulman subjects of the Queen who came from India were (even though Shias) always well received ; so should we be if we conformed to Islam. The Persians, though tolerated by the Hejazi, were disliked as Persians as well as heretics, and often got beaten in Medina. He (Saleh) was going to collect money from them, as they were fools enough to give it him, but he did not care for their company. He would sooner travel with us. We might all go together on this tour through Persia. One thing he could not understand about the English Government, and that was, what earthly interest they had in interfering with the slave trade. We said it was to prevent cruelty. But there was no cruelty in it, he insisted. " Who ever saw a negro ill-treated ? " he asked. We could not say that we had ever done so in Arabia ; and, indeed, it is notorious that with the Arabs the slaves are like spoiled children rather than servants. We had to explain that in other countries slaves were badly used ; but as Saleh remained unconvinced, we could only wind up with a general remark, that this inter-ference with the slave trade was a " shoghl hukm," a matter concerning the Government, and no affair of ours. He seemed pretty well informed of what was going on in the world, having heard of the Russian war, though not the full circumstances of its termination ; and of the cession of Cyprus, as to which he remarked, that the English Queen has been given Kubros as a bakshish by the Sultan. His last words were, "Plain speaking is best. I am your friend here ; but, remember, not in Medina, on account of religion."

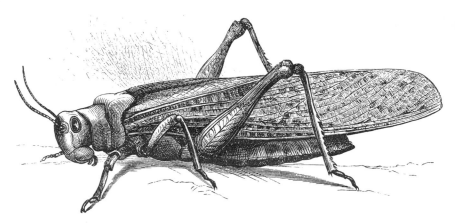

EDIBLE LOCUST.

CHAPTER XIV.

"Come, Myrrha, let us go on to the Euphrates."—BYRON.

We go in search of adventures—Taybetism—An hyæna hunt—How to cook locusts—Hawking—The reservoirs of Zobeydeh—Tales and legends—A *coup de théâtre*—Mohammed composes a kasíd.

February 6.—We are tired of loitering with the Haj, and besides, do not care to see more of Ibn Rashid, who is expected to-day. It is always a good rule not to outstay your welcome, and to go when you have once said good-bye. So, finding no indication of a move in the pilgrim camp this morning, we decided on marching without them. We have not gone far ; indeed, from the high ground where we are camped we can see the smoke of the camp rising up at the edge of the plain. There is capital pasture here ; and we have a fine wide prospect to the south and west ; Jebel Jildiyeh being now due south of us, and Jebel Aja west by south, Haïl perhaps forty miles off ; to the north the Nefûd, and behind us to the east from the ridge above our camp, we can look over a subbkha six or seven miles distant, with the oasis of Bekaa or Taybetism (happy be its name) round its shores. The place had always been called Bekaa, we are told, till a few years ago, when the name was thought unlucky, and changed, though I cannot quite understand why, for the word means a place where water can collect.

We flew our falcon to-day, and, after one or two disappointments, it caught us a hare. The wadys are full of hares, but the dogs cannot see them in the high bushes, and this was the only one started in the open. We have encamped early, and are enjoying the solitude. The moon will be full to-night; and it is provoking to think how much of its light has been wasted by delay. The moon is of little use for travelling after it is full.

February 7.—Though we did not move our camp to-day, we had a long ride, and got as far as the village of Taybetism, which is worth seeing. It is a very curious place, resembling Jobba as far as situation goes. Indeed, it seems probable that most of the towns of Nejd have in common this feature, that they are placed in hollows towards which the water drains, as it is in such positions that wells can be dug without much labour. Like Jobba, Taybetism has a subbkha, but the latter is altogether a more important oasis, for the palm-gardens reach nearly round the lake, and though not quite continuous, they must have an extent of four or five miles. The houses seem to be scattered in groups all along this length, and there is no special town.*

* It was to Taybetism that Abdallah ibn Saoud fled ten years ago when he was driven by his brother out of Aared, and from it that he sent that treacherous message to Midhat Pasha at Bagdad which brought the Turks into Hasa and broke up the Wahhabi Empire.

The geology of the district is most interesting. At
the edge of the subbkha the sandstone rocks form
strange fantastic cliffs, none more than fifty feet
high, but most fanciful in form. Some, shaped like
mushrooms, show that the subbkha must at one
time have been an important lake, instead of the
dry semblance of a lake it now is. We measured
the largest of these, and found it was forty feet in
length by twenty-five in width at top, with a stalk
of only five feet, the whole mass resting on a high
pedestal. Other rocks looked as though they had
been suddenly cooled while boiling and red hot,
with the bubbles petrified as they stood. There
were broad sheets of rose-coloured stone like straw-
berry cream with more cream poured into it and
not yet mixed, streaked pink and white. Here and
there, there were patches of Nefûd sand with the
green Nefûd adr growing on them, and clusters
of wild palms and tamarisks with a pool or two
of bitter water. The subbkha, although quite
dry, looked like a lake, so perfect was the mirage,
of clear blue water without a ripple, reflecting
the palms and houses on the opposite shore. We
went round to some of these, and found beautiful
gardens and well-to-do farms with patches of green
barley growing outside. These were watered from
wells about forty-five feet deep, good water, which
the people drew for our mares to drink. We passed,
but did not go into a large square kasr belonging to Ibn Rashid, where a dozen or so of dervishes

from the Haj were loafing about. They asked us for news—whether the Emir had come, and whether the Haj was still waiting. These were most of them not Persian dervishes, though Shias, but from Bagdad and Meshhed Ali, people of Arab race.

On our way back we crossed a party of Shammar Bedouins, with their camels come for water from the Nefûd, which is close by. They gave us some lebben to drink, the first we have tasted this year. There were women with them. We also met a man alone on a very thin delûl. Mohammed made some rather uncomplimentary remarks about this animal, whereupon the owner in great scorn explained that she was a Bint Udeyhan, the very best breed of dromedaries in Arabia, and that if Mohammed should offer him a hundred pounds he would not sell her, that she was the camel always sent by Ibn Rashid on messages which wanted speed. He then trotted off at a pace which, though it appeared nothing remarkable, soon took him out of sight.

Awwad and Ibrahim Kasir have been back to the Haj camp for water, and have brought news that the Emir has actually arrived, and a message from him, that if we go on to the wells of Shaybeh he will meet us there.

February 8.—We have marched fifteen miles to-day from point to point, making a circuit round Taybetism and are now encamped at the top of the Nefûd. A Shammar boy of the name of Izzar with three delûls came back from the Haj camp yester-

day with Awwad, and he undertakes to show us the
way if we want to go on in front. He would sooner
travel with us than with the Haj, as his beasts are
thin, and he is afraid of their being impressed for
the pilgrims. He wants to drive them unloaded to
Meshhed, so that they may grow fat on the way, and
then load them for the home voyage with wheat.
He talks about six or seven days to Meshhed ; but
Wilfrid insists that we are not twenty miles nearer
Meshhed than when we left Haïl, as we have been
travelling almost due east, instead of nearly due
north, and there must be four hundred miles more
to go. This should take us twenty days at least.
But the servants will not believe. We shall see who
is right. They and Mohammed are very unwilling
to go on before the Haj, but now that we have got
this boy Izzar we are determined not to wait. If
we delay we shall run short of provisions, which
would be worse than anything. Already, Awwad
says, the pilgrims are complaining loudly that they
shall starve if they are kept longer waiting in this
way. They have brought provisions for so many
days and no more, and there is no place now where
they can revictual. " The Haj," added Awwad, " is
sitting by the fire, very angry."

Our march to-day was enlivened by some hunting,
though with no good result. Sayad and Shiekha
coursed a herd of gazelles, and succeeded in turning
them, but could not get hold of any, though one
passed close to Mohammed, who fired without effect.

They made off straight for the Nefûd. The falcon was flown at a houbara (frilled bustard), but the bustard beat him off, as he is only a last year's bird, and not entered to anything but hares. Rasham, however, is an amusement to us and sits on his perch at our tent door. This spot is pleasant and lonely, within a hundred yards of the edge of the Nefûd.

February 9.—Having sent Izzar to a high point for a last look back for the Haj and in vain, we have given them up and now mean to march straight on without them. It is however annoying that we are still going east instead of north, coasting the Nefûd I suppose to get round instead of crossing it ; but we dare not plunge into it against Izzar's positive assurance that the other is the only way. Soil sprinkled with *jabsin* (talc), and in places with the fruit of the wild poisonous melon. Passed the well of Beyud (eggs) thirty feet deep. and travelled six and a half hours, perhaps eighteen miles, to our present camp absolutely without incident. Looking at the stars to-night, Mohammed tells me they call Orion's belt "mizan" (the balance), and the pole star " el jiddeh " (the kid). We now have milk every day from Izzar's she-camel, a great luxury.

February 10.—At eight o'clock we reached the wells of Shaybeh. There are forty of them close together in the middle of a great bare space, with some hills of white sand to the north of them. The

wind was blowing violently, drifting the sand, and
the place looked as inhospitable a one as could well
be imagined, a good excuse for over-ruling all
notions of stopping there, " to wait for the Emir."

Shaybeh stands on the old Haj road which passes
east of Haïl, making straight for Bereydeh in
Kasîm, and the reason of our travelling so far east
is thus explained. Now we have turned at right
angles northwards, and there is a well-defined track
which it will be easy enough for us to follow, even if
we lose our Shammar guide. After leaving the wells,
we travelled for some miles between ridges of white
sand, which the wind was shaping "like the snow
wreaths in the high Alps." The white sand, I
noticed, is always of a finer texture than the red,
and is more easily affected by the wind. It carries,
moreover, very little vegetation, so that the mounds
and ridges are less permanent than those of the
Nefûd. While we were watching them, the wind
shifted, and it was interesting to observe how the
summits of the ridges gradually changed with it, the
lee side being always steep, the wind side rounded.
We gradually ascended now through broken ground
to the edge of a level gravelly plain, beyond which
about four miles distant we could see the red line of
the real Nefûd. We had nearly crossed this, when
we sighted an animal half a mile away, and
galloped off in pursuit, Mohammed following. I
thought at first it must be a wolf or a wild cow, but
as we got nearer to it, we saw that it was a hyæna,

and it seemed to be carrying something in its mouth. The dogs now gave chase, and the beast made off as fast as it could go for the broken ground we had just left, and where it probably had its den, dropping in its hurry the leg of a gazelle, the piece of booty it was bringing with it from the Nefûd. The three greyhounds boldly attacked it, Sayad especially seizing it at the shoulder, but they were unable to stop it, and it still went on doggedly intent on gaining the broken ground. It would have escaped had not we got in front and barred the way. Then it doubled back again, and we managed to drive it before us towards where we had left our camels. I never saw so cowardly a creature, for though much bigger than any dog, it never offered to turn round and defend itself as a boar or even a jackal would have done, and the dogs were so persistent in their attacks, that Wilfrid had great difficulty in getting a clear shot at it, which he did at last, rolling it over as it cantered along almost under the feet of our camels. Great of course were the rejoicings, for though Mohammed and Awwad affected some repugnance, Abdallah declared boldly and at once, that hyæna was " khosh lahm," capital meat. So it was flayed and quartered on the spot. I confess the look of the carcass was not appetising, the fat with which it was covered being bright yellow, but hyænas in the desert are not the ghoul-like creatures they become in the neighbourhood of towns, and on examination

the stomach was found to be full of locusts and fresh
gazelle meat. Wilfrid pronounces it eatable, but I,
though I have just tasted a morsel, could not bring
myself to make a meal off it. I perceive that in spite
of protestations about unclean food, the whole of
this very large and fat animal has been devoured
by our followers. I am not sure whether Mohammed kept his resolution of abstaining.

Locusts are now a regular portion of the day's
provision with us, and are really an excellent article
of diet. After trying them in several ways, we have
come to the conclusion that they are best plain
boiled. The long hopping legs must be pulled off,
and the locust held by the wings, dipped into salt
and eaten. As to flavour this insect tastes of vegetable rather than of fish or flesh, not unlike green
wheat in England, and to us it supplies the place of
vegetables, of which we are much in need. The red
locust is better eating than the green one.* Wilfrid
considers that it would hold its own among the
hors d'œuvre at a Paris restaurant; I am not so
sure of this, for on former journeys I have resolved
that other excellent dishes should be adopted at
home, but afterwards among the multitude of luxuries, they have not been found worth the trouble of
preparation. For catching locusts, the morning is
the time, when they are half benumbed by the cold,
and their wings are damp with the dew, so that they

---

* Red is said to be the female and green the male, but some say
all are green at first and become red afterwards.

cannot fly ; they may then be found clustered in hundreds under the desert bushes, and gathered without trouble, merely shovelled into a bag or basket. Later on, the sun dries their wings and they are difficult to capture, having intelligence enough to keep just out of reach when pursued. Flying, they look extremely like May flies, being carried side-on to the wind. They can steer themselves about as much as flying fish do, and can alight when they like ; in fact, they very seldom let themselves be drifted against men or camels, and seem able to calculate exactly the reach of a stick. This year they are all over the country, in enormous armies by day, and huddled in regiments under every bush by night. They devour everything vegetable; and are devoured by everything animal : desert larks and bustards, ravens, hawks, and buzzards. We passed to-day through flocks of ravens and buzzards, sitting on the ground gorged with them. The camels munch them in with their food, the greyhounds run snapping after them all day long, eating as many as they can catch. The Bedouins often give them to their horses, and Awwad says that this year many tribes have nothing to eat just now but locusts and camels' milk ; thus the locust in some measure makes amends for being a pestilence, by being himself consumed.

We are encamped to-night once more in the Nefûd, amongst the same herbage, and at the edge of one of the same kind of fuljes, we were accus-

tomed to on our way from Jôf. This Nefûd, however, is intermittent, as there are intervening tracts
of bare ground, between the ridges of sand which
here very distinctly run east and west. The sand
is not more than eighty feet deep, and the fuljes are
insignificant compared with what we saw further
west.

February 11.—Some boys with camels joined us
last night, Bedouins from the Abde tribe of
Shammar, on their way to meet the Haj, as they
have been ordered up by Ibn Rashid. They have
given us some information about the road. Ibn
Duala is five days' journey on ; but we shall find
the Dafir, with their Sheykh, Ibn Sueyti, on the
second day. Ibn Sueyti, they say, has a kind of
uttfa like Ibn Shaalan's, but it is pitched like a
tent when a battle is to be fought. The Ajman,
near Queyt, have a real uttfa with ostrich feathers
and a girl to sing during the fighting.* They also
narrated the following remarkable tale.

There is, they say, in the desert, five days' march
from here to the eastwards, and ten days from Suk
es Shiôkh on the Euphrates, a kubr or tomb, the
resting-place of a prophet named Er Refay. It is
called Tellateyn el Kharab (the two hills of the
ruins), and near it is a birkeh or tank always full of
water. The tomb has a door which stands open,
but round it there sleeps all day and all night a
huge snake, whose mouth and tail nearly meet,

* Compare Mr. Palgrave's account.

leaving but just room for anyone to pass in. This it prevents unless the person presenting himself for entrance is a dervish, and many dervishes go there to pray. Inside there is a well, and those who enter are provided (" min Allah") for three days with food, three times a day, but on the fourth they must go. A lion is chained up by the neck inside the kubr.

The birkeh outside is always full of water, but its shores are inhabited by snakes, who spit poison into the pool so that nothing can drink there. But at evening comes the ariel (a fabulous antelope), who strikes the water with his horns, and by so doing makes it sweet. Then all the beasts and birds of the desert follow him, and drink. The Sheykh of the Montefyk is bound to send camels and guides with all dervishes who come to him at Suk-es-Shiôkh to make the pilgrimage to Refay. The boys did not say that they had themselves seen the place.

We are not on the high road now, having left it some miles to the right, and our march to-day has been mostly through Nefûd. The same swarms of locusts everywhere, and the same attendant flocks of birds, especially of fine black buzzards, one of which Abdallah was very anxious to secure if possible, as he says the wing bones are like ivory, and are used for inlaying the stocks of guns and stems of pipes. But he had no success, though he fired several times. Wilfrid was more fortunate, however, in getting what we value more, a bustard,

and the very best bird we ever ate. Though they
are common enough here, it is seldom that they
come within shot, but this one was frightened by
the hawk, and came right overhead. About noon, we came to a solitary building,
standing in the middle of the Nefûd, called Kasr
Torba. It is square, with walls twenty feet high,
and has a tower at each corner. It is garrisoned by
four men, soldiers of Ibn Rashid's, who surlily
refused us admittance, and threatened to fire on us
if we drew water from the well outside. For a
moment we thought of storming the place, which
I believe we could have done without much difficulty, as the door was very rotten and we were all
very angry and thirsty, but second thoughts
are generally accepted as best in Arabia, and on
consideration, we pocketed the affront and went on.

Soon afterwards, we overtook a young man and
his mother, travelling with three delúls in our
direction. They were on the look-out, they said,
for their own people, who were somewhere in the
Nefûd, they didn't quite know where. There are
no tracks anywhere, however, and they have stopped
for the night with us. Very nice people, the young
fellow attentive and kind to his mother, making her
a shelter under a bush with the camel saddles.
They are Shammar, and have been on business to
Haïl.

February 12.—Our disappointment about water
yesterday, has forced us back on to the Haj road

and the wells of Khuddra, thirteen or fourteen miles east of last night's camp. We had, however, some sport on our way. First, a hare was started and the falcon flown. The Nefûd is so covered with bushes, that without the assistance of the bird the dogs could have had no chance, for it was only by watching the hawk's flight that they were able to keep on the hare's track. It was a pretty sight, the bird above doubling as the hare doubled, and the three dogs below following with their noses in the air. We made the best of our way after them, but the sand being very deep they were soon out of sight. Suddenly we came to the edge of the Nefûd, and there, a few hundred yards from the foot of the last sand-bank, we saw the falcon and the greyhounds all sitting in a circle on the ground, watching a large hole into which the hare had just bolted. The four pursuers looked so puzzled and foolish, that in spite of the annoyance of losing the game, we could not help laughing. Hares in the desert always go to ground. Mohammed and Abdallah and Awwad were keen for digging out this one, and they all worked away like navvies for more than half an hour, till they were up to their shoulders in the sandy earth (here firm ground), but it was in vain, the hole was big enough for a hyæna, and reached down into the rock below. Further on, however, we had better luck, and having run another hare to ground, pulled out not only it, but a little silver grey fox, where they were both

crouched together. I do not think the hares ever
dig holes, but they make use of any they can find
when pressed. We also coursed some gazelles.

There are fourteen wells at Khuddra, mere holes
in the ground, without parapet or anything to mark
their position, and as we drew near, we were rather
alarmed at finding them occupied by a large
party of Bedouins. It looked like a ghazú, for
there were as many men as camels, thirty or forty
of them with spears ; and the camels wore shedads
instead of pack saddles. They did not, however,
molest us, though their looks were far from agreeable. They told us they were Dafir waiting like
the rest for the Haj ; that their Sheykh, Ibn Sueyti,
was still two days' march to the eastwards, beyond
Lina, which is another group of wells something
like these ; and they added, that they had heard of
us and of our presents to the Emir, the rifle which
fired twelve shots, and the rest. It is extraordinary
how news travels in the desert. I noticed that
Mohammed when questioned by them, said that he
was from Mosul, and he explained afterwards that
the Tudmur people had an old standing blood feud
with the Dafir in consequence of some ghazú made
long before his time, in which twenty of the latter
were killed.* This has decided us not to pay Ibn
Sueyti the visit we had intended. It appears that
there has been a battle lately between the Dafir

* Compare Fatalla's account of the war between the Mesenneh
and the Dafir near Tudmor at the beginning of the present century.

and the Amarrat (Ánazeh), in which a member of the Ibn Haddal family was killed. This proves that the Ánazeh ghazús sometimes come as far south as the Nefûd. These wells are seventy feet deep, and the water when first drawn smells of rotten eggs ; but the smell goes off on exposure to the air.

The zodiacal light is very bright this evening ; it is brightest about two hours after sunset, but though I have often looked out for it, I have never seen it in the morning before sunrise. It is a very remarkable and beautiful phenomenon, seen only, I believe, in Arabia. It is a cone of light extending from the horizon half-way to the zenith, and is rather brighter than the Milky Way.

February 13.—We have travelled quite twenty-four miles to-day, having had nothing to distract our attention from the road, and have reached the first of the reservoirs of Zobeydeh.

To my surprise this, instead of being on low ground, is as it were on the top of a hill. At least, we had to ascend quite two hundred feet to get to it, though there was higher ground beyond. It is built across a narrow wady of massive concrete, six feet thick, and is nearly square, eighty yards by fifty. The inside descends in steps for the convenience of those who come for water, but a great rent in the masonry has let most of this out, and now there is only a small mud-hole full of filthy water in the centre. We found some Arabs there with their camels, who went away when they saw us, but we

sent after them to make inquiries, and learnt that
they were Beni Wáhari, a new artificial compound
tribe of Sherârat, Shammar and others, made up by
Ibn Rashid with a slave of his own for their Sheykh.
They are employed in taking care of camels and
mares for the Emir. They talk of eight days'
journey now to Meshhed Ali, but Wilfrid says it
cannot be less than fifteen or sixteen.

Mohammed, who has been very anxious to make
himself agreeable, now he is quite away from Haïl
influences, has been telling us a number of stories
and legends, all more or less connected with his
birthplace Tudmur. He has a real talent as
a narrator, an excellent memory, and that most
valuable gift, the manner of a man who believes
what he relates. Here is one of his tales, a fair
specimen of the extraordinary mixture of fable and
historic tradition to be found in all of them :

Suliman ibn Daoud (Solomon, son of David) loved
a Nasraniyeh (a Christian woman), named the Sitt
Belkís,* and married her. This Christian lady
wished to have a house between Damascus and Irak
(Babylonia), because the air of the desert was good,
but no such a house could be found. Then Solomon,
who was king of the birds as well as king of men,
sent for all the birds of the air to tell him where he
should look for the place Belkís desired, and they all
answered his summons but one, Nissr (the eagle),

---

* Belkís is the name usually given by tradition to the Queen of
Sheba.

who did not come. And Solomon asked them if
any knew of a spot between Damascus and Irak, in
the desert where the air was good. But they
answered that they knew of none. And he counted
them to see if all were there, and found that the
eagle was missing. Then he sent for the eagle, and
they brought him to Solomon, and Solomon asked
him why he had disobeyed the first summons. And
Nissr answered, that he was tending his father, an
old eagle, so old that he had lost all his feathers, and
could not fly or feed himself unless his son was
there. And Solomon asked Nissr if he knew of the
place wanted by Belkís ; and Nissr answered that
his father knew, for he knew every place in the
world, having lived four thousand years. And
Solomon commanded that he should be brought
before him in a box, for the eagle could not fly.
But when they tried to carry the eagle he was so
heavy that they could not lift him. Then Solomon
gave them an ointment, and told them to rub the
bird with it and stroke him thus, and thus, and
that he would grow young again. And they did
so, and the feathers grew on his back and wings,
and he flew to Solomon, and alighted before the
throne. And Solomon asked him, " where is the
palace that the Sitt Belkís requires, between
Damascus and Irak, in the desert where the air is
good ? " and the eagle answered, " It is Tudmur,
the city which lies beneath the sand." And he
showed them the place. And Solomon ordered the

jinns to remove the sand, and when they had done
so, there lay Tudmur with its beautiful ruins and
columns.

Still there was no water. For the water was
locked up in a cave in the hills by a serpent twenty
thousand double arms' length long, which blocked
the mouth of the cave. And Solomon called on the
serpent to come out. But the serpent answered
that she was afraid. And Solomon promised that
he would not kill her. But as soon as she was half
way out of the cave (and they knew it by a black
mark on her body which marked half her length),
Solomon set his seal upon her and she died. And
the jinns dragged her wholly out and the water ran.
Still it was poisonous with the venom of the
serpent, and the people could not drink. Then
Solomon took sulphur (kubrit) and threw it into
the cave, and the water became sweet. And the
sulphur is found there to this day.

Mohammed says also that ghosts (afrit) are very
common among the ruins at Tudmur—also (more
curious still) that there is a man at Tudmur more
than a hundred years old, and that when he reached
his hundredth year he cut a complete new set of
teeth, and is now able to eat like a young man.*
So he beguiled the evening.

February 14.—We have passed more birkehs in
better repair than the first, and being now in the

---

* I have since been told by dentists that the fact of a third set
of teeth being cut in old age is not unknown to science.

neighbourhood of water, find a good many Bedouins on the road. Jedur (the Shammar with the mother, with whom we are still travelling, and whom we like particularly) knows everybody, and it is well that he is with us, as some of these Bedouins are rough looking fellows with hang-dog countenances (especially the Dafir and the Sellem), which we don't quite like. To-day, as Wilfrid and I were riding apart from our caravan, a number of men ran towards us without any salaam aleykum and began calling to us to stop. But we did not let them get within arm's length, and bade them ask their questions from a distance. We shall have to keep watch to-night. The road is now regularly marked out with a double wall, which we are told was built by Zobeydeh to hang an awning from, so that the pilgrims might travel in the shade. But this must be nonsense. It is more likely that it is merely the effect of the road having been cleared of the big stones which here cover the plain.

*   *   *   *   *

Since writing this a curious thing has happened. We encamped early inside a ruined birkeh and had just got all in order for the night, when we perceived six men on dromedaries riding down from the north-east, straight towards us. There was much speculation of course amongst us, as to who they might be, honest men or robbers, Shammar or Dafir.

They evidently were not a mere party of camels for
the Haj, as each delúl was mounted by a man with
a lance, and they came on at a trot. They rode
straight to where we were, made their camels kneel
down, took off khurjs and shedads and then
arranged their bivouac for the night. Then they
came up to our tents and accosted Mohammed and
the servants, who of course invited them to sit down
and drink coffee. Mohammed presently came to us
and whispered that he felt convinced they were
Dafir, but that we should presently know for certain.
They sat down and began talking on general subjects,
as the custom is till coffee has been served, but
afterwards Mohammed asked them whence they had
come and whither they were going. They answered
that they were Ketherin, sent by their Sheykh to
Haïl on business, and explained further that their
object was to find a certain relative of their Sheykh's
whom he had heard of as being a guest at Ibn
Rashid's and to invite him to their tents. Perhaps
we might have heard of him, his name was Mohammed ibn Arûk. And their Sheykh's name?
Muttlak ibn Arûk! Here is a *coup de théâtre!*
Mohammed's long-lost relation, the third brother of
the three who left Aared in the eighteenth century
and parted company at Jôf, has been discovered in
his descendant, whose servants are at this moment in
our camp. Imagine the joy of Mohammed and the
triumph of so appropriate an occasion for reciting
once more the kasíd Ibn Arûk. The rhymes of

that well-known legend, recited by Mohammed and
responded to by the new comers in chorus, were
indeed the first intimation we had of what had
happened.   Then the Ketherin ambassadors were
brought to our tent and their story told.   Now
all ideas of Bussorah and Meshhed Ali and the
Haj are abandoned, and, for the moment, there
is no other plan for any of us but an immediate
visit to these new relations.   One of the Ketherin has already started off homewards to announce
the joyful event, and the rest will turn back with us
to-morrow. Muttlak's tents are not more than a day's
journey from where we now are, and we shall see
these long-lost cousins to-morrow before the sun
goes down.   " Yallah," exclaimed Mohammed, beam-
ing with joy and pride.

February 15.—We made a late start, for Mohammed has lost his head again and is playing the fine
gentleman, as he did at Haïl, afraid or ashamed to
be seen by his new acquaintances doing any sort of
work.   Instead of helping to pack or load the
camels, he would do nothing but sit on the ground
playing with his beads, and calling to Awwad to
saddle his delúl,—airs and graces which, I am glad
to see, are thrown away on the Ketherin, who, as
Bedouins, care little for the vanities of life.   Even
when started, we did not get far, for it began to
thunder and lighten, and presently to rain heavily,
so that Wilfrid ordered a halt at half-past ten.
We have now come to the great birkehs which

are full of water. They stand in a valley called
the Wady Roseh, from a plant of that name
which grows in it, and is much prized as pasture
for both camels and horses. There are two tanks
near us, one round, the other square, and both
of the same fashion as the first we saw. We have
been examining the construction and find that the
walls were originally built hollow, of stone, and
filled up with concrete. This is now as hard as
granite, and has a fine polish on the surface. The
water is beautifully clear and good. The largest of
the tanks is sixty-four yards by thirty-seven, and
perhaps twelve feet deep. There is a ruined khan
of the same date close by, and Wilfrid has discovered
an immense well ten feet wide at the mouth and
very deep. All these were constructed by Zobeydeh,
the wife of the Caliph Haroun er-Rashid, who nearly
died of thirst on her way back from Mecca and so
had the wells and tanks dug. Wilfrid believes that
no European has visited them before, though they
are marked vaguely on Chesney's map. A wild
day has ended with a fine sunset. Dinner, not of
stalled ox, nor of herbs, but of boiled locusts and
rice, with such bread as we can manage to make of
flour well mixed with sand.

Mohammed, who has been in the agonies of poetic
composition for a week past, has at last delivered
himself of the following kasíd or ballad, which I
believe is intended as a pendant to the original Ibn
Arûk kasíd, with which he sees we are bored.

KASÍD IBN ARÚK EL JEDÍDE.

Nahárrma min esh Sham, el belád el bayíde,
Némshi ma el wudiân wa el Beg khaláwa.
Wa tobéyt aéla Jôf, dar jedíde.
Yaáz ma tílfi ubrobok khaláwi.
Nahárret 'Abu Túrki, aálumi bayíde,
Dábakha lil khottár héyle semáne.
Ya marhába bil Beg wa es Sitt Khatún.
Talóbbt bíntu gal jaátka atíye.
Wa siághahu min el Beg khámsin mía.
Khatún, ya bint el akrám wa el juwádi.
Khatún, ya bint el Amáva wa el kebár.
Ya Robb, selémli akhúi el Beg wa es Sitt Khatún.
Ya Robb, wasálhom diyar essalámi,
Wa dar el Ajjem wa belad hade Hanûd,
Wa yetóbb aál bahûr sébba khaláwi,
Wa yetóbb aála Lóndra wa yekéllem efnún,
Wa yehágg el sahíbe aála ma sar jári.

NEW BALLAD OF IBN ARÚK.

I went out from Damascus, the far-off country.
I marched through the lone valley, with the Beg alone.
I lighted down at Jôf, at a new built dwelling.
Dear are the souls it shelters. " Guests," he said, " sit down."
" See, Abu Turki, see," I called, " thy kinsmen."
" Bring first for these," he cried, " a fatted lamb.
" Welcome, O Beg, welcome O Lady Khatún,
" Welcome, O distant kinsman, to your home."
I asked him for his daughter. " Take her dowerless."
" Her dower be these, five thousand," said the Beg.
Lady, O daughter of the great the generous !
Lady, O daughter of a princely line !
O Lord, keep safe my brother and the Khatún.
Grant them to reach the dwellings of repose.
Guide them through Persia and far Hind and lead them
By all the seven seas in safety home.
Let them once more behold their friends and London.
Let them relate the things that they have done.

CHAPTER XV.

" Here lie I down, and measure out my grave,
Farewell, kind master."—SHAKESPEARE.

Muttlak Ibn Arûk and the Ketherin—Their horses—We are
adopted by the tribe—The Haj again—Ambar sends round the
hat—A forced march of one hundred and seventy miles—
Terrible loss of camels—Nejef.

February 16.—Two Aslan Shammar of the
Jezireh came last night, and recognised us as
having been in Ferhan Pasha's camp, last year, in
Mesopotamia,—a very pleasant meeting, though we
have no distinct recollection of either of them.
They gave us all the latest Jezireh news in politics.
Ferhan and his brother Faris are now at open war,
though Ferhan is no fighter himself, and leaves the
conduct of affairs to his eldest son, Aassa. All the
Shammar of the Jezireh are with Faris, except
Ferhan's own tail, and the Abde, and the Asslan,
Muttany's men, and our old friend Smeyr ibn-
Zeydan. It is true also that Faris is now friends
with Jedaan. All this we are glad to hear.

This morning, Jedur and his mother left us, as
they are not going any further our way. I like
them both, and should have been glad to give the
mother some small remembrance of our journey
together, but, as Arabs do, they went away without

saying good-bye. Our march to-day was a short one, nine or ten miles, still down the Wady Roseh, where water has actually been running since the late storm, and where there are pools still here and there, and a large swamp full of ducks, storks, and snipe,—the first water above ground we have seen since the Wady er-Rajel, nearly two months ago. There is capital grass, too, in the wady, a few inches high, which our hungry mares enjoy thoroughly. As we were stopping to let them and the camels graze on a particularly inviting spot, suddenly we perceived about thirty delúl riders coming over the hill to our right. Although it was probable that this was Muttlak, we all prepared for defence, making the camels kneel down, and seizing each his best weapon,—Wilfrid the rifle, I the gun, and Mohammed his large revolver. Awwad stood ready, sword in hand, and Abdallah squatted with his long gun pointed towards the new-comers; the rest, except Izzar, who possesses a sword, had only sticks, but made a formidable appearance.

There was no need, however, for alarm, for, presently, one of the approaching party detached himself from the rest, and trotting his dromedary towards us, saluted us in a loud voice, and we saw that it was Hazzam, the man who had gone on to announce our coming to Muttlak. In another five minutes the Sheykh himself had dismounted. There was of course a great deal of kissing and embracing between Mohammed and his new found relations, and Wilfrid came in for a share of it. Muttlak is a charming old man, very quiet and very modest, but possessed of considerable dignity. He has an expression of extreme kindness and gentleness which is very attractive, and we already like him better than any of Mohammed's Jôf relations. Unlike the Ibn Arûks of Jôf and Tudmur, this branch of the family has remained Bedouin, and unmixed by any fellahin alliances. Mohammed's rather vulgar pretensions to birth and dignity have fallen, ashamed before the simplicity of this good old man, the true representative of the Ibn Arûks of Aared, and though the kasíd has been trotted out once more, and the family genealogy stated and compared, it has been with modesty and decorum, and the sadness which befits decayed fortunes. There can be no question here who shall take the upper place, the Sheykh himself being always ready to take the lowest. To us he is charming in his attentions, and without false dignity in his thanks for the small presents* we have made him. He is to stay with us to-night, and then he will take us to his tents to-morrow.

Muttlak has brought us three sheep for a present. He has with him a very handsome falcon, a lanner like ours, but larger.

February 17.—We left our camp in the Wady Roseh, where Muttlak told us there was better pasture than we should find with him, and rode off

---

* Presents of honour always given to a sheykh.

on our mares to pay him a morning visit and return
at night. Muttlak has with him his own little
mare, the counterpart of himself, old and without
other pretension than extreme purity of descent.
She is a kehîlet Omm Jerass (mother of bells), and
was once in Ibn Saoud's stables. It is difficult to
describe her, for her merits are not on the surface ;
I am sure nine out of ten English dealers would pass
her over, if they saw her at Tattersall's or Barnet
Fair, as an insignificant little pony. She is very
small, hardly over 13 hands, for even Mohammed's
mokhra looks tall beside her, chestnut with four
white feet and a blaze, a good but not a pretty head,
and, but for a proud carriage of the tail, no style or
action ; an old brood mare never ridden except on
state occasions like the present, for on ordinary occasions no Arab of Nejd thinks of riding anything
but a delúl. As Muttlak said, very gravely, " When
God has given you a mare that is *asil*, it is not that
you should ride, but that *she* should breed foals."
The old man stuck to his delúl, and the little mare
was ridden by his cousin Shatti, who went with us,
and gave us some valuable information by the way.
The Ketherin, like all the tribes of Nejd, were formerly under Ibn Saoud. They are a branch of the
Beni Khalid, who, in their turn, are a branch of the
Beni Laam, an ancient and noble tribe, of which
the main stock is still found between Aared and
Katîf, while another branch settled some centuries
ago beyond the Tigris, on the Persian frontier. The

Ketherin are now few in number and decayed in circumstances, but Shatti informed us, with some pride, they can still turn out a hundred khayal on occasion ; that is to say, if they are attacked and obliged to fight. This shows more than anything the small number of horses possessed by the tribes of Nejd. I asked Shatti which of the tribes still under Ibn Saoud are now most in repute as breeders of horses ; and he told me the Muteyr or Dushan (for it seems they have both names), who could turn out four hundred horsemen. Their best breeds are Kehîlan Ajuz, Kehîlan el-Krush, Abeyan Sherrak, Maneghy Hedruj, and Rabdan Kesheyban, They have no Seglawis at all; the Krushiehs of Ibn Rashid came originally from them, Feysul having bought them from the tribe. It must not, however, be supposed, he said, that all the Dushan mares were asil. The Dushan, like every other tribe in Nejd and elsewhere, has "mehassaneh," or half-breds, what the Ánazeh would call "beni" or "banat hossan ; " that is to say, animals with a stain in their pedigree, and therefore not asil, though often nearly as good and as good-looking. Their own breeds (that is to say, the Ketherin's) are principally Wadnan, Rishan, Rabdan, and Shueyman. As we got near the Ketherin tents we met two men on a delúl, leading a lovely little bay colt, one of the prettiest I ever saw, which Shatti told us was a Wadnan Horsan.

After nearly three hours' riding we arrived at

the *buyut shaar* (houses of hair), and were soon being hospitably entertained. It is the custom here, as it is in the Sahara, that the Sheykh should receive illustrious strangers, not in his own tent, but in a special tent set up for the purpose. It was a poor place, little more than an awning, but the welcome was hearty and sincere. Here all the principal people of the tribe assembled as soon as the news of our arrival spread, and a feast was prepared of tummin and fresh butter, and naga's milk. The Arabs never kill a lamb except for the evening meal.

After this entertainment I went to visit Muttlak's family, and on my return I found Wilfrid inspecting the mares which we had already seen grazing near the tents. There were half-a-dozen of them, fair average animals, but nothing first-rate, or so handsome as the Wadnan colt, nor any over fourteen hands high. We were looking at these rather disappointedly, when Hazzam ibn Arûk, Muttlak's brother, rode up on a really beautiful mare, which he told us was a Seglawieh Jedran, the only one left in Nejd. He added that they had been obliged to conceal the name of her breed for some years on account of the danger incurred of her being taken by force. In former times, when the Wahhabis were all powerful, any famous mare ran great risk of being seized for the Riad stables. Ibn Saoud would declare war with a tribe merely as an excuse for robbing it of its mares. Ibn Rashid, at the present day, put great pressure on the owners of valuable mares to make them sell ;

but he paid for what he took. This mare had been often asked about both for Ibn Rashid, and for Nassr el-Ashgar, Sheykh of the Montefyk, who (or rather his brother Fahad now) has the best collection of horses after Ibn Rashid and Ibn Saoud. She is a fine bright bay, muttlak-el-yemin, snip on the nose; has a splendid way of moving when ridden, action like Hamúd's mare at Haïl, *handsome* rather than *racing.* The head is good, the eye bright and large, the forehead rather flat, the jowl deep; the wither high and back short, quarters round, like all the Nejd horses, sinews good, and hoofs large and round.

Hazzam's mare is under fourteen hands, but stands over much ground, and ought to be up to weight, being wonderfully compact. We had some hopes at one moment of being able to purchase her, and for a good price and money down I think it might have been done, for they are all most anxious to oblige us. But we have no money and our cheque on Bagdad would be difficult for them to cash. The Ketherin are this year in great distress, as there was no autumn rain, and until a month ago nothing that horses can eat. They are without corn or even dates, and but for the locusts, which have been abundant all the winter, they must have starved. Indeed locusts are still their main article of food, for man as well as beast. Great piles of these insects, dried over the fire, may be seen in every tent.

Amid a general chorus of good wishes, we at last took our leave of these good people. "You," they said to Wilfrid, "shall be our Sheykh whenever you return to us. Muttlak will not be jealous. We will make war for you on all your enemies, and be friends with your friends." Muttlak himself has promised that there shall be a general council to-night to decide whether the tribe shall move north-wards as has been proposed, or not, and that if it is decided that it shall be so, he will join us to-morrow morning, and travel with us to Meshhed to make arrangements with the intervening tribes, whose con-sent must first be obtained. It is strange what friendship we have made with these simple-hearted people in a few hours. We are the first Europeans they have seen, and they look upon us as beings of a superior world.

As we came back to the crest of the hill over-looking Wady Roseh, we saw away to the south a smoke rising—the Haj.

February 18.—We had walked down to the birkeh to try and stalk some ducks when the first runners of the Haj arrived, and presently the Haj itself, now swelled to double its former size, swept past us down the Wady. At the same moment Muttlak appeared on his delúl ready to go with us. This gave us great pleasure. He has got the con-sent of his tribe, and what is of more importance of the women of his family, to go with us to Meshhed Ali, and see what arrangements can be made with the Ánazeh Sheykhs for a migration of the Ketherin northwards. Such migrations have, I fancy, taken

place in all ages among the Bedouins of Arabia,
the want of pasture constantly driving them out-
wards from Central Arabia to the richer deserts of
Syria and Mesopotamia. In this way the Shammar and the Ánazeh obtained their present inheritance of the Hamád and the Jezireh, and thus in
still earlier times the Taï abandoned Nejd.

Muttlak's equipment for the journey is of the
simplest kind, the clothes in which he stands. He
and a single attendant are mounted together on an
old black dromedary, the Sheykh perched on the
saddle, and his man kneeling behind, their only
weapon a stick, and they guide the delúl with a
rope passed through a hole in his nostril, a primitive
arrangement. "There," we said to Mohammed,
"that is how your ancestors left Nejd." The old
man is very pious; unlike the Ánazeh and other
tribes of the north, these Bedouins of Nejd say their
prayers regularly, and profess the Mussulman creed,
and Muttlak's first act on dismounting this evening
in camp, was to go apart with his attendant and
pray. Mohammed and Abdallah still say their
prayers occasionally, though with less and less
fervour as the distance from Haïl grows greater.
Awwad's devotion is of a very varying quality,
sometimes quite imperceptible, at others almost
alarming. I have noticed that any special stress
of work in loading the camels of a morning, or
pitching the tents at night, is sure to call forth a
burst of spiritual fervour. At such times his la-

ilaha-illa-llah goes on for a prodigious length of time, and may be heard a quarter of a mile off.

Ambar, the negro emir-el-haj, has brought a polite message for us from Ibn Rashid. He came with the Haj as far as Khuddra, and then went back to Haïl, so we have lost nothing by not going with him on his intended ghazú.

Having camped early we sent Abdallah and Hanna to the Haj to find out our Persian friends there, and invite them to dine with us, as we had killed a sheep, and just before sunset they arrived, Ali Koli Khan, Huseyn Koli Khan, and Abd er-Rahim of Kermanshah. We seated them all on a carpet outside our little tent, for it is a warm evening, and then the dinner was served. But much to our vexation, for we had carefully arranged the entertainment, they refused to eat anything, first saying that they had already dined, and afterwards admitting that the Mollahs in whose company they were travelling, had forbidden their eating with us during the Haj. They were very polite, however, and made all sorts of apologies, and even took one mouthful each to avoid being positively rude. Ali said that but for his mother's Mollah, he would have asked us to dine with him, for he has a good cook, but under the circumstances it cannot be. Huseyn, who is the son of an ex-vizier, pretended to speak French, but the only complete phrase which he had at command, and which seemed borrowed from a copy-book, was, "L'Arabe est charlatan." This he

repeated in and out of season, whenever there was a
pause in the conversation. These Persians were as
loud as ever in their complaints against the Arabs,
and being now out of his dominions, did not spare
the Emir, whom they accused of having plundered
them terribly. They also had much to tell of the extor-
tions of the hemeldaria, or contractors for the Haj.

It appears that each pilgrim, when he starts for
Mecca, puts himself into the hands of an Arab contractor, generally a native of Meshhed Ali, who
undertakes to provide him with transport, either in
the shape of riding dromedaries, or litters, or even
in some cases, mules or horses. He does this for a
sum of money down, accepting all risks, and is bound
to replace any animal that breaks down or dies on the
road, with another at a moment's notice. It is a very
speculative business, as if all goes well with the Haj,
the hemeldaria makes a fortune, whereas if things go
badly, he may lose one. In some years great
numbers of camels die, and then the contractors are
ruined; but generally they make a very good thing out
of it, as their charges are enormous. At any rate
they seem very rich, and ride about themselves on the
finest dromedaries in the Haj, and wear the finest
clothes. There are twenty of these contractors now
with the Haj, who divide the two thousand Persian
pilgrims amongst them. Besides the Persians there
are about a hundred Shias from Bagdad and Bussorah,
but these do not mix much with the Persians, and
a body-guard of about a thousand Bedouins, Ibn

Rashid's people. In all, over three thousand persons, with five thousand camels. It must be like the journey of the children of Israel to Mount Sinai.

Ali Koli Khan left Haïl with the Emir, nearly a week after we did, so we did not need to be in any hurry, but I think we were right to get clear away while we could.

February 19.—An early start before sunrise, though there were stragglers till seven o'clock. We were the last to go, but we had sent our camels on as there was good grass, and we wanted our mares to have a comfortable feed. Occasionally one of the pilgrims would come and sit down a moment by our fire to warm his hands. We have now quite left the Nefûd, and are travelling over broken stony ground. The Haj marches fast, quite three miles an hour, and there is no stopping on the way. We are halted this evening at the last of the reservoirs of Zobeydeh, the Birkeh Jemaymeh (Jemima's pool). Here there are considerable ruins and a very large well.

The boy Izzar has left us, I am sorry to say, and he is sorry too. He was very serviceable and pleasant, and we lose with him his naga's milk, which we have been drinking fresh every morning. (N.B. We will never travel again without a she camel for milk.) But his delûls have been impressed for the Haj. We gave him three mejidies (about ten shillings) for his ten days' service, which brought down blessings on our heads. I do not think he expected anything.

February 20.—Again the Haj has come to a stand-still, to the renewed wrath of the pilgrims. It is now twenty days since they left Haïl and not more than half the journey has been accomplished. There are two hundred miles more of road, and their provisions, calculated for three weeks, are all but run out. What makes this new delay the more aggravating to them is that it has been ordered by the negro Ambar, so that he may send the hat round for a private contribution to his own benefit. He has made it known that two mejidies a head is what he expects, and that he will not move till the sum is forthcoming. This will be a nice little purse for him, something like eight hundred pounds, and we maintain a fleet in the Red Sea to suppress the slave trade, out of motives of humanity! The Persians are powerless to resist, for without the black man's order, not a camel would move. We, as Ibn Rashid's guests, are exempted from all toll or tax whatever, but we want to get on. Fortunately we laid in a whole month's provisions at Haïl.

The day has been a very hot one, and we have had the tent propped up all round, so that it resembles a gigantic umbrella. It is pitched on a hill overlooking the Haj, and has attracted a good many visitors. The first of them was a certain Seyd Mustafa, a native of Shustar in Persia, but speaking Arabic well. He is travelling as interpreter with Ali Koli Khan, and has given us some

information about the country between Bagdad and
his own town.   Ali Koli has several times proposed
that we should go on with him from Bagdad, to pay
a visit to his father in the Bactíari mountains, and
Wilfrid is very much bent on doing this.

He himself is going round by the river to Bussorah, and then up the Karun to Shustar, a plan
which would not suit us; but Seyd Mustafa says
he will go with us by land, though it is a very
difficult country to get through.   The frontier
between Turkey and Persia is occupied by the Beni
Laam who recognise neither the Sultan nor the Shah.
The Beni Laam however, ought to receive us well
from our connection with the Ibn Arûks, and a visit
to them would almost complete our acquaintance
with the Arab tribes north of Nejd.

Next two poor women came, an old and a young
one, dressed alike in white rags.   They are from
Bagdad, and have made the pilgrimage barefoot
and begging their bread.   One of them carries a tin
mug, into which somebody had just thrown a handful of barley.   I gave them a loaf of bread, with
which they went away invoking blessings on me.
They seem perfectly contented and happy.

Then we had a visit from some Bagdadis; one
had been a soldier, the others shopkeepers.   They
were pilgrims, however, now, and not *on business,*
as most of the Arabs here are.

Next a Ḍafir boy, with a lamb and a skin of
fresh butter to sell, the butter mixed up with date-

skins and hair, and coloured yellow with a plant called saffron. After much haggling (for stinginess in a purchaser inspires respect) we bought the lamb and the butter for a mejidie—four shillings.

Next a Jinfaneh Shammar, with a bay horse, also for sale, a Kehîlan Ajuz fourteen hands, with good jowl, good shoulder, and tail well carried, but rather small eye, thick nose, and coarse hind quarter— altogether strong with plenty of bone—aged, very much aged ! We do not want him.

Then an Ibn Duala, with a Wadneh mare, also bay, thirteen hands three inches, or fourteen hands— pretty head, with projecting forehead, very good jowl, good shoulder, but thick nose and coarse hind-quarter, rather high on the legs, with a good deal of hair on the fetlocks. They all seem to have the same faults.

I asked the Jinfaneh Shammar about the well of Wakisa, marked on Chesney's map as eight hundred feet deep, but he laughed and said, " forty of these," holding out his arms, and Muttlak confirmed the statement ; this would make it two hundred and forty, a much more probable depth.

Wilfrid in the meanwhile had been with Seyd Mustafa and Mohammed to the Haj, and had had tea with Huseyn Koli Khan. They also called on Ambar and Ali Koli Khan ; but both were out. Most of the pilgrims were lying on their backs asleep in the sun. It was very hot.

Ambar's little white mare has been brought to

graze near our tents, for as usual we have chosen
the best pasture for our camp. The slave with her
says she is a Krushieh. She is a flea-bitten grey,
very old and very small, but for her size powerful,
with a good head, though not a handsome one, a very
fine shoulder with high wither, the usual Nejd hind-
quarter and manner of carrying the tail, legs like
iron. To complete the picture, I must mention one
knee swelled, all four feet much out of shape with
long standing in the yard at Haïl, and very hairy
heels. There are with the Haj several yearling
colts bought by the hemeldaria for sale at Bagdad,
scraggy little things more like goats than horses.

The sun has brought out a huge tarantula from the
sand close to our tent. It is the first venomous
reptile I have seen on the journey.

February 21.—Ambar seems determined to
make up for lost time, and he has hurried the Haj
on all day so that we have done over thirty miles.
Our road has been through broken ground, the Wady
el-Buttn (the valley of the stomach), where we saw
a fox and some hares. One of these last the dogs
caught after a long course, and another was run
to ground. Abd er-Rahim, the Kermanshahi, rode
with us a part of the day, mounted on the most
lovely delúl that was ever seen ; she is of a bright
chestnut colour, with a coat like satin, a light
fine mane rather darker than the rest, eyes more
beautiful than those of the gazelle, and a style
of going which I have not seen equalled by any

other camel. This delúl can canter and gallop as
well as trot, and kept up with us very fairly when
we were chasing the hare, though of course she could
not really command a horse's pace. Abder-Rahim
and Ali Koli Khan now both ride delúls, and have
dressed themselves up in Arab fashion, all silk and
gold, the mean-looking little Kurd being thus trans-
formed into a fine gentleman. Their saddles,
bridles, and trappings are also very gay, got up
regardless of expense. They hired their delúls of
Ibn Rashid for the journey, I forget exactly for
what sum, but it was a good deal of money. The
Persians will not eat hare ; and Ali Koli Khan,
who is travelling with a private chaplain, would not
join us in our sport. Indeed he seems now to keep
rather aloof from us, but Abd er-Rahim has no such
scruples. We hear that a sermon was preached
yesterday in camp, against the sin of holding intercourse with kaffirs.

This has been a long, tedious march, two of our
camels being tired. We have come to the end of
our provision of flour for them, and there is really
very little they can eat on the road. Wilfrid makes
it still a hundred and forty miles to Meshhed.

February 22.—We travelled yesterday through a
low-lying district, bounded by cliffs a little in the
style of Jôf (it is all called *el buttn*, the stomach),
and this morning, soon after starting, we reached the
end of it, and had to ascend two or three hundred
feet, the last *akabah* or ascent being very steep.

Here there was a great confusion, as the road was narrowed to a single track, and the Haj had to go almost in single file, instead of in line, its usual way of travelling. The steepness of the cliff proved too much for more than one camel, tired as they were with yesterday's march and want of food. Among them poor Shenuan, the ugly camel of our string, gave in. He is not old, but has long been ailing, and for the last week has carried nothing but his pack-saddle, and been nothing but a trouble to us, still it cost us a pang to abandon him. He has had mange from the very beginning of our journey; in fact, he was the only camel of those originally purchased by Mohammed for us, to which we demurred at the outset. Our objections were over-ruled by Mohammed's arguments, that Shenuan's youth and strength would enable him to get over the effects of mange, but he never prospered, and did not recover from the fatigue of the Nefûd. Poor fellow, he was very loath to be left behind, and struggled on till he came to this hill, which was too much for him. We left him, I am glad to say, in a bit of wady where there was some grass, but I fear his chance is a small one. Camels seldom recover when they get past a certain stage of exhaustion. They break their hearts, like deer, and die. Poor Shenuan! I shall not easily forget his face, looking wistfully after his companions as they disappeared over the crest of the hill. He is the first of our small party that has fallen out of the

ranks, and we are depressed with the feeling that
he may not be the last.

At the top of the cliff we came to a perfectly
level plain, strewn with fine flints, and across this
we have travelled all day. Its height above the
sea is 1460 feet, and we find that ever since leaving
Shaybeh, where the road turned north, we have
been descending at an average rate of about ten
feet per mile, but the descent is not regular, because
of these cliffs which we have come to, which have
all been, in a sense, contrary to the general declivity
of the ground. About mid-day we came to a great
pool of rain-water, at which the camels drank and
the goat-skins were filled, a very welcome accident.
Our march to-day was twenty-four miles.

February 23.—The flinty plain is called Mahamiyeh, and with the Buttn forms a neutral ground
between the Shammar and the Ánazeh, who are
here represented by the Amarrat, their Sheykh Ibn
Haddal. It was somewhere about here that the
battle was fought the other day, in which the
Dafir got the best of it, and some of the Ibn
Haddal were killed. The consequence of its being
thus neutral is, that the Mahamiyeh is covered with
dry grass of last year, uneaten by any flocks, a
great boon to us ; for there is no fresh grass yet.

Beyond the Mahamiyeh we came again to hills,
amongst which we found the wells of Sherab, and
beyond this again the ground sloped downwards
until we came to a regular valley, which we

followed in its windings all the afternoon. This is
the Wady Shebekkeh, which narrows in one place
almost to a ravine. There water had evidently
flowed not long ago, and we found some beautiful
clear pools, beside which the Haj is camped. We
ourselves are some two miles further on, where
there is better pasture. The Haj camels are getting
terribly thin. These forced marches (we came
twenty-eight miles to-day) are telling on them, and
their owners are complaining loudly. The pilgrims
having only hired the camels, of course care nothing
for their welfare, and will not let them graze as
they go, because riding a camel which eats as it
goes is rather tiresome. Then in the evening the
tents have to be pitched in some spot where a large
camp can stand altogether, irrespective of considera-
tions of pasture, the poor camels often having to go
two or three miles to their food. We manage
better, and always choose our spot for their sakes
more than our own. Two of our camels nevertheless are tired, but our camels are loaded far more
heavily than those of the pilgrimage.

To-night we have had a long and serious talk
with Muttlak about the Ketherin tribe, in which
we now consider we have an interest. He promises
that he will really come north as soon as he can
make arrangements with the Sebaa, and we have in
return promised him that we will set up a "house
of hair" with them, and keep a few nagas and a
mare or two, and a small flock of sheep. This

would be very agreeable, and serve as a *pied à terre*
in the desert, quite independent of all the world.

February 24.—Another *akabah* had to be climbed
to-day—another long winding road followed across
another open plain. The wonder is why the road
should wind where there is no obstacle to avoid
and no object to reach by a circuit. But such is
always the case. Everybody seemed cross with the
hard work, enlivened only by an occasional course,
in which the hare sometimes ran right in among the
pilgrims, when there was a scrimmage with the
dervishes for possession of the quarry. The dervishes, who are mostly from Bagdad, are ready
to eat hare or anything else they can get, indeed
everybody is at starvation point. The only cheerful
one of our party is the stalwart Ibrahim, who has
come out again now as a wag. To-day, as we were
marching along, we passed a fat Persian on a very
little donkey, whom Ibrahim began chaffing, but
finding the Persian did not understand him, he ran
up, and seizing hold, lifted donkey and man in his
arms. I could not have believed it possible, had I
not seen that the donkey's four legs were off the
ground. The Persian did not seem to understand
this joke better than the rest, but they are stolid
people, and have had a long breaking in and
experience in patience during the last four months.

We have found a peaceful spot for the night,
with plenty of pasture and plenty of " jelleh " for
fuel. The sun has set, but in the clear cold sky

there is a nearly new moon, which gives a certain amount of light.

Wilfrid is making plans for spending the spring in Persia, and the summer in India, regardless of such news as may meet us at Bagdad from England or elsewhere. Such plans, however pleasant as they are in the planning, cannot be counted on. Much may have happened in the three months since we have been cut off from all communication with Europe, or indeed any part of the world out of Arabia, and even the traveller most detached from all affections or thoughts of his distant home is liable to be seized by a sudden longing for green fields with buttercups and daisies. The passing note of a bird or the scent of a flower may be enough to upset a most admirably contrived plan.

February 25.—Twenty-seven miles of march yesterday, and thirty to-day.

The camels cannot last at this pace, but the Haj is pushing on now because the men are starving. It is said that to-morrow we may reach Kasr Ruheym, the first outpost of the Euphrates district, and there they may find supplies, but it must still be a long distance off, if our reckoning is not altogether incorrect. Wilfrid has kept a dead reckoning now ever since we left Damascus, calculating the direction by the compass, and the distance of each day's march by the pace of the camels, and in the thousand miles we have travelled, it may well be a little out—but according to it we should now be forty-seven miles from Meshhed Ali, which should be to the north-west, not to the north of our present position.

The weather has become cold, and all day long a bitter wind blew in our faces. The vegetation has changed. In one place we saw some acacias, the first trees since we left Haïl, and some of those broom bushes which bear a flower smelling sweet like the flower of the bean, and called here by the Arabs, "*gurrteh.*" The acacias have given their name to the wady, Wady Hasheb (the Valley of timber).

We had a good view of the berak unfurled to-day, and a respectable-looking pilgrim, who lives, he tells us, in the mosque of Abd-el-Kader at Bagdad, pointed out to us the motto and device in the centre of it ; the sword, he says, is the sword of God, and under it is written " La ilaha ila'llahi, wa Mohammed rasuluhu (There is no God but God and Mohammed is his prophet). On the other side of the flag is written " Nasron min Allahi wa fathon karîbon (Victory is from God and success is near).

February 26.—This has been a long and hard day, over ten hours, and the whole time beating against a wind which cut through everything, the sky darkened with sand, driving right in our faces. We have however reached Kasr Ruheym, and all our camels are still alive. Many of the pilgrims' camels, sixty or some say seventy, lay down and died on the road. The beautiful thoroughbred

delúls cannot stand the cold, which is very unusual
at this latitude so late in the season, and their
owners are in despair. All the Haj is furious with
Ambar, not the Persians only, but the Bedouin
escort and the camel owners, for his dawdling
marches at first, and his forced ones afterwards. In
the last six days we have marched a hundred and
seventy miles, the greater part of the Haj on foot,
and almost fasting. What would an English army
say to that ? Yet not one of the men—nor even of
the poor women—who have had to trudge along
thus, has been left behind. For ourselves we have
had no extra fatigue, for the change from camel-back
to horse-back and back again is of itself a rest.
Khrer, my delúl, has very even paces, so that one is
not soon tired riding him.

We are here in clover, not actually at the Kasr,
but in sight of it, encamped at the edge of a running
stream ! The stream rises here and is said to be
perennial. There is a quantity of coarse sword grass
growing beside it, and everything looks green and
pretty to eyes wearied of desert scenes. A pair
of francolins, disturbed by the sudden invasion of
their resting-place, which they doubtless thought
safely secluded from the world, are flying backwards
and forwards, put up continually by the grazing
camels, and are calling to each other from the bushes.
This shows that we are approaching the Euphrates.

There is a village near the Kasr, about two miles
from where we are ; and a good many felláhín on

donkeys and horses have arrived with provisions for sale, but they have not brought a twentieth part of what is wanted for the Haj. A cry of "stop thief" already announces that we have returned to the Turkish Empire! It has not been heard since we left Mezárib.

February 27.—No abatement of the wind, but less sand. It appears that our acquaintances, Ali Koli Khan and Abd er-Rahim are missing, lost in yesterday's storm. They rode with us part of the afternoon, and then, hearing that Ruheym was not far off, they started away on their delúls in front of the Haj at a trot, and of course being Persians, lost their way, for the Persians are helpless people in the desert. The sand was very thick at the time, and they must have got out of the track. Ambar has sent people to look all over the country for them, but without result. They never reached Ruheym, and it is feared that they may have perished of cold in the night.

This delayed the Haj from starting early, and at one time it was given out that no move at all would be made to-day, which would have suited us well, as there was plenty of camel pasture at Ruheym, and two of our animals were quite at the end of their strength. But at eight o'clock the drum beat, and we were obliged to load and be off, for now that we had entered Turkish territory, there was danger on the road, and all must keep together. Ibn Rashid's protection would no longer avail.

The march was tedious, on account of the weariness of the camels, though cheered by the sight of the gilt dome of Meshhed Ali, shining like a star across the blue sea of Nejef, itself a lovely apparition. The sea of Nejef (or as the Arabs call it, the Sheríet-Ibn Haddal), is the counterpart of the Birket el-Korn in the Egyptian Fayum, an artificial lake, formed by cutting a canal from the Euphrates ; it is about twenty miles long, by six or seven broad. It is probably of Babylonian origin, though the Arabs say it was made by an Ibn Haddal ancestor of the present Amarrat Sheykhs, so that his camels might have a drinking pool. The Ibn Haddal were, till comparatively lately, lords of the whole of this district, and levied tribute on Meshhed Ali and Huseyn. The town stands upon the eastern shore above a fine line of limestone cliffs, and remained in sight all day long, as we wound slowly round the lake. It was a beautiful sight as far as nature was concerned, but made horrible by the sufferings of the poor dying camels, which now lay thick upon the road, with their unfortunate owners, poor Bedouins perhaps with nothing else in the world, standing beside them, luggage and bedding strewn about, which the pilgrims were trying to carry off on their heads, seeing the journey so nearly over.

Many of the camels had rushed into the lake, to drink, and lain down there, never to get up again. Others could just move one foot before the other, following at the rate of perhaps a mile an hour, with

hopeless glazed eyes, and poor emaciated bodies
bare of all burden, even of the shedad. We who
started late because we were not ready, and had
thought to remain quiet at Ruheym, passed all
these, amongst others our friend Izzar, the
Shammar boy, who was weeping over his delúls—
two out of the three were dead. All were loud in their
execrations of Ambar, and one or two of Ibn Rashid
himself, whom they held responsible for part of the
delay. Ibn Rashid's government is less popular in
the desert than in the towns, especially on account
of his conduct of the Haj. He impresses the camels
and men at a fixed rate, ten mejidies, and gives no
compensation for losses. They say, however, that
Ambar runs some risk of losing his head, when all
his mismanagement becomes known at Haïl, and I
confess I think he deserves it.

At last we got to the *akabah*, or ascent, where
the road leads up the cliff, and here the camels lay
down by scores, among the rest our beautiful camel,
Amud (the pillar), so called from his great height.
He was younger than the rest, except poor Shenuan,
and had been out of sorts for several days past. A
camel that lies down under such circumstances, seldom
rises again. It is not the labour, but the want of
food that kills ; and unless food can be brought to
the exhausted animal, he never gets strength to rise.
Between five and six hundred must have perished
thus to-day.

At the top of the *akabah* Meshhed Ali lay

close before us, a long line of magnificent old walls
with twelve round towers, all of burnt brick, the
only building appearing over them being the mosque
with its cupola of burnished gold, and its four
minarets. The whole was reddened by the afternoon sun, and the dome looked like a sun itself.

Through a crowd of dirty children perched on the
tombs of the vast burying-ground which, on this
side, stretches for some distance from the walls of
the city ; we approached the gate of Meshhed Ali.
These disorderly ragamuffins shouted jeers and
rude remarks at the pilgrims, and threw stones at
our dogs, and we were glad when, turning an angle
of the wall, we reached the camping ground, a
short distance from the north-eastern corner of the
city, and found ourselves at peace, with leisure to
reflect that our pilgrimage is over.

PERSIAN PILGRIMS IN FRONT OF THE HAJ.

CHAPTER XVI.

The Shrines of the Shias—Bedouin honesty—Legend of the Tower of Babel—Bagdad—Our party breaks up.

MESHHED ALI (the shrine of Ali), or Nejef as it is more correctly called, is an ideal Eastern City, standing as it does in an absolute desert and bare of all surroundings but its tombs. It is nearly square, and the circuit of its walls is broken by only one gate. These walls are of kiln-burnt brick, and date from the time of the Caliphs, and are still in excellent preservation. They are strengthened at intervals by round towers, all very massive and stately. So high are they, that they completely hide every building inside them, with the single exception of the great Mosque of Ali, whose glittering dome of gold shows like a rising sun above them.

Inside, the houses are closely packed; but there is more symmetry in their arrangement than in most Asiatic towns, as the bazaar leads in a straight line from the gate to the Mosque, which stands in the centre of the town. The shops are good, or appeared so to our eyes unused to the things of cities. I did not myself venture far inside, as the streets were very crowded, and we did not wish to attract unnecessary notice just then at the time of the pilgrimage ; but Wilfrid describes the façade of the Mosque as the richest he has seen, a mass of gold and mosaic work like some highly chased reliquary. He would not go inside for fear of offending our pilgrim friends, and left it to the rest of our party to recount the splendours of the tomb.

This tomb of Ali is held by the Shias as at least as holy as the Caaba at Mecca, and it is an article of pious belief with them that any Moslem buried within sight of the dome is certain of salvation. The consequence is that pilgrims from all parts of the Shia world, and especially from Persia, come to Nejef to die, and that immense numbers of corpses are sent there for interment. Burial fees in fact constitute the chief revenue of the place.

This city and Kerbela, where there is the sister shrine of Huseyn, are inhabited by a number of Mahometan subjects of Her Majesty, from India, who have settled in them from religious motives, but remain under the protection of the British Resident at Bagdad. They live on good terms with the Arabs, but do not mix much or intermarry with them, and retain their own language. As is natural in cities of pilgrimage, all classes are ostentatiously religious, and we were amused at listening to the devout exclamations of the blacksmith who came to shoe our horses. " Ya Ali, ya Huseyn, ya Ali, ya Mohammed," at every stroke of the hammer. They are all, moreover, bitterly hostile to Turkish rule, having the double motive of national and religious antipathy to support them. Both Meshhed Ali and Kerbela are kept strongly garrisoned, but in spite of everything have constantly revolted within the last forty years. When we were at Meshhed, the Turkish Caimakam had four companies of infantry under his orders ; and the garrison of Kerbela, the head quarters of the district, was far larger.

Kerbela, which lies fifty miles north of Meshhed Ali, is physically quite unlike its rival. It is un-fortified, and instead of standing in the desert, is surrounded by palm gardens, like the towns of Nejd. It is a richer and more populous city than Meshhed, but to a traveller it is less interesting as having nothing distinctive in its appearance. The Hindieh canal, which supplies it with water from the Euphrates, makes it the centre of the most considerable agricultural district of the Bagdad pashalik. Meshhed, on the other hand, has little besides its shrine to depend on.

We were now very nearly at the end of our resources, both of money, and strength, and patience ; and, without more delay than was absolutely necessary to refit our caravan, we set out for Bagdad. On the evening preceding our departure, a curious incident occurred.

A young Bedouin came to our tent and introduced himself as a Shammar from the Jezireh, one of

Faris's men whom we had met the year before on the Khabur. He hailed the "Beg" at once as brother to his master, and mentioned the incident of the loan of ten pounds made by us to Faris. This sum he offered on his own responsibility to repay us now, and, seeing that we were rather out at elbows, he pulled out the money from his sleeve and almost forced it upon us. He had been sent by Faris to buy a mare from the Montefyk, and had the purchase money with him,—he knew Faris would wish him to repay the debt. Though we would not take the money, the honesty and good feeling shown greatly pleased us, and we were glad of an opportunity to send messages to Faris, Tellál, and Rashid ibn Ali, who it appeared was still with the northern Shammar.

This same night, too, Muttlak left us. It was a grief to us to say good-bye, and he, more visibly touched even than we were, shed tears. He had found, he said, men of the Amarrat at Meshhed, who had promised to arrange his business with the Sebaa for him, and so he would go home. He had come quite two hundred miles with us, and we could not ask him to do more. He had, however, something behind the reasons which he gave us for his going ; Mohammed, his cousin, had grown jealous of his position with us, and, we have reason to suspect, made things uncomfortable for the old Sheykh when we were not present, in a way we could not prevent. Besides this, there was a story of a blood-feud between the Ketherin and the Maadan, a tribe which

lives between Nejef and Kerbela; this may have
helped to deter Muttlak from going on with us, for
he is essentially a man of peace, but there could have
been no danger for him in our company. Be it as it
may, he came that night to dine with us for the last
time, and could eat nothing, and when we asked
him why, he said it was from sorrow, and that he
must say good-bye. It was evident that he spoke
the truth, and I am sure that no word of the
blessings which he heaped upon our heads, and of
his promises to keep our memory green in his heart,
was more than what he felt. Muttlak is not a
man of words. Wilfrid kissed the old Sheykh, and
his servant kissed our hands, and they got on their
old black delúl, and rode quietly away the way they
came, and we saw them no more.

Three days of easy travelling brought us to Kerbela,
for we did not care to push on fast, and four days
more to Bagdad. One incident only of our route
need be mentioned. As we were passing the neighbourhood of Birs Nemrud, the reputed tower of Babel,
we stopped for the night at some tents belonging to
the Messaoud, a half fellahín tribe of the left bank
of the Euphrates, where they were growing barley
on some irrigated land. The Sheykh, Hajji et-Teyma
was away, but his son Fuaz entertained us, and after
dinner related the history of Nimrod, the founder of
the tower. Nimrod, he said, was an impious man,
and thought that the sun was God. And in order
to make war on him he built this tower, but finding

that he could not reach him thus, he had a platform constructed with a pole in the middle, and to each corner of the platform he chained an eagle, and on the pole he hung a sheep, and the eagles wishing to reach the sheep, flew up with the platform and Nimrod who was standing on it. And when Nimrod thought himself near enough, he shot an arrow at the sun. And God to punish him destroyed the tower. The Yezidis worship Nimrod and Shaytan there to this day.

Beyond Kerbela our road lay through cultivated land till we reached the Euphrates, which we crossed by the bridge of boats at Musseyib. Then we found ourselves among Babylonian mounds, canals, and abandoned fields, the unvarying features of Irak. These brought us at last to Bagdad, where by a strange fatality we arrived once more in floods of rain, and where, again, we were welcomed in the hospitable four walls of the Residency. On the 6th of March we slept once more in beds, having been without that luxury for almost three months.

Here, therefore, ends our pilgrimage to Nejd, which, in spite of some difficulties and some hardships, was accomplished successfully without any really disagreeable incident, and here, if we had been wise, our winter's adventures would have ended too. We had been lucky beyond our expectations in seeing and doing all we had proposed as the objects of our journey, and hardly a day of the

eighty-four we had spent in Arabia had been uninteresting or unromantic. What followed was
neither profitable nor agreeable, and might well
have been left undone.

At Bagdad our party necessarily broke up.
Among the letters awaiting us at the Consulate, was
one for Mohammed ibn Arûk which obliged his
instant return to Tudmur. Great events had occurred
there in his absence, and for a moment we felt a pang
of regret at having kept him so long away from his
duties and his interests at home. The politics of
Tudmur are a little complicated. Mohammed's father,
Abdallah, is not the legitimate Sheykh of the town,
the true head of the Ibn Arûk family there being
his cousin Faris. Abdallah, however, has for some
years past enjoyed Government support, and is the
Turkish nominee. The town has consequently been
divided into two factions,* headed respectively by
Faris and Mohammed, the latter representing his
father, who is too old for such quarrels, and as long as
the Turks were supreme at Tudmur, Mohammed's
party had it all their own way. Not, however, that
either faction wished any good to the Sultan, for
during the Russian war Mohammed was one of the
foremost in refusing the contingent demanded of
the Tudmuri for the Turkish army, but family
quarrels are fierce among the Arabs, and they take
advantage of all the help they can get alike from

---

* An incomplete account of this state of things is given in
"Bedouin Tribes of the Euphrates."

friend or enemy. So Mohammed supported Turkish
policy in his native town, and was in turn supported
by the Turks. But after the surrender of Plevna,
and the destruction of the Sultan's army in the
Balkans, Tudmur was abandoned to its own devices,
and Faris once more asserted his right to the
sheykhat, though parties were so evenly balanced
that nothing serious for some time occurred, and
only on one occasion Faris and Mohammed exchanged shots, without serious result. It was in
defiance of remonstrances on the part of his father
and all his friends that Mohammed had come with
us, and the moment he was gone war had broken
out. A messenger, it appears, had arrived to recall
him not a week after he started with us from
Damascus, and now another letter announced that
blood had been shed. This was sufficient reason for
our journey together coming to an end, and Mohammed, though piously ready to accept accomplished facts with an "Allah kerim," was evidently
in a hurry to be off. Even if we had wished it, we
could not ask him to go further with us now. But we
did not wish it. The episode of his foolish behaviour
at Haïl, forgive it as we would, had left a certain
gêne between us, which he was conscious of as well
as ourselves, and, though he had done much since
then to atone for it, we all felt that it was best to
part. Still there was something mournful in his
leaving us on so forlorn an errand, and he, as Arabs
do, shed tears, owning that he had behaved in that

instance ungratefully to us, and protesting his devotion. We on our side made him as comfortable as we could with letters of recommendation to Valys and Consuls, whose protection he might have need of, and with what arms and ammunition we could spare. And so he and Abdallah, and Awwad the robber, went their way on four of our delúls, which we gave them for the journey, and we saw them no more.

We had hoped to induce Hanna to go on with us, for he in all our difficulties had never failed us, and with his cousin the Tawíl had helped us loyally when others had been cross or unwilling—but Hanna was home-sick, and the Tawíl would not desert him. So one day they joined a caravan of muleteers on the point of starting for Mosul, and left us with many tears and blessings ; and the little army with which we had crossed the desert was finally dispersed.

Note. We heard nothing of Mohammed for nearly a year, and then heard that he was in prison. Prompted by a conscientious motive, of which those who have read thus far will need no explanation, he rendered himself liable to the action of Ottoman justice. A man of the Faris faction was found slain at Tudmur, and the relations of the deceased pointed out Mohammed's as the hand which had fired the shot. The Turks had just re-occupied the town and were anxious to make an example, so Mohammed was put in chains and sent to Deyr. There he found means to send us news of his misfortune, and Wilfrid had the satisfaction of being able to fulfil his brotherly obligation by interceding with the Pasha on his behalf, and eventually by procuring his release.

PART II.

OUR PERSIAN CAMPAIGN.

OUR PERSIAN CAMPAIGN.

CHAPTER I.

"Duo illum sequor? In Persas."—PLAUTUS.

"Halas! diséit-elle, faut-il que je périsse sous les pattes d'une araignée, moi qui viens de me tirer des griffes d'un lion? "—FABLES D'ÉSOPE.

New plans and new preparations—We leave Bagdad for Persia —Wild boar hunting in the Wudian—A terrible accident— We travel with a holy man—Camps of the Beni Laam—An alarm.

AMONGST the letters awaiting our arrival at Bagdad, we had found an invitation from Lord and Lady Lytton to spend the summer, or part of it, with them at Simla. It seemed that this would be an opportunity, which might never again occur, of going on to India by land, a plan which might be made to include a visit to the Bactiari mountains, where our acquaintance of the pilgrimage, Ali Koli Khan, had his home. Ali had often talked to us of his father, and of a wonderful stud of thoroughbred Arabians possessed by his family, and the prospect of seeing these, and a tribe reputed to be the most powerful in Persia, was an attraction that could not be denied. He had indeed proposed to travel three

with us, and introduce us himself to his people, and
if circumstances had been propitious, no doubt we
might have accomplished this part of our journey
comfortably enough.   Unfortunately, when we took
leave of the Haj at Meshhed Ali, our friend was not
there for us to concert arrangements with him, nor
even to wish him good-bye.   He had been lost in
the sandstorm, already mentioned as having occurred
on the last day but one of the pilgrimage ; and
though before going on to Kerbela we had received
news of his safety, we had no opportunity of meeting him.   The consequence was that he neither
came with us, nor gave us so much as a letter to
his father ; and in the end we started alone, a
mistake we had ample reason to repent.   The plan
of travelling from Bagdad to India by land appeared
to me of doubtful wisdom under the circumstances ;
but Wilfrid's thirst for exploration was not yet
slaked.   He argued that spring was just beginning,
and a spring journey through Persia must of necessity be the most delightful thing in the world, and
that we could at any moment get down to some
port of the Persian Gulf, if the weather became too
hot for us.   Our means of transport were ready.
We should find some difficulty in disposing of our
camels at Bagdad, and had better make use of
them ; and though we were now without servants,
servants might easily be found.   Thus, in an evil
day, and without due consideration of the difficulties and dangers which were before us, we deter-

mined to go on. A final circumstance decided the matter beyond recall. Captain Cameron, the African traveller, arrived at Bagdad, with the object of surveying a line for an Indo-Mediterranean railway from Tripoli to Bushire, and thence to the Indus, having already made the first stages of his survey; and Wilfrid now proposed to assist him in the more serious part of his undertaking. It was agreed between them that they should take different lines from Bagdad, and meet again either at Bushire or Bender Abbas, thus comparing notes as to the most practicable railway line from the Tigris to the Persian Gulf. Captain Cameron was to follow the left bank of the river as far as Amara, and then to strike across the marshy plains to Ahwas and Bender Dilam, while we should keep further east, skirting the Hamrin and Bactiari hills. So presented, the project sounded useful, if not agreeable, and acquired a definite object, which, if it ran us into unnecessary dangers, served also to carry us through them afterwards. The expedition was accordingly a settled thing.

Our preparations were made, unfortunately, with as little reflection as the decision. On arriving at Bagdad, we had, as has been mentioned, said good-bye to Mohammed and the camel-men, and had, moreover, allowed Hanna and Ibrahim, who were homesick, or tired of travelling, to depart. The difficulty now was how to replace them. It is always a dangerous experiment to begin a serious journey with untried followers, and it was our first

misfortune that we were obliged to do this. Colonel
Nixon, as he had done last year, kindly lent us a
cavass ; but, alas ! Ali, the intelligent fat man who
had been of such assistance to us in our Mesopotamian tour, was not fit to leave Bagdad. He was
lying ill of a fever, and could not be disturbed. The
cavass given us was consequently a stranger, and
might be good or bad, useful or useless, for anything
we knew. It was necessary, too, that somebody
should know Persian, and we engaged a Persian
cook, Ramazan by name, highly recommended, but
equally untried. A young Bagdadi next volunteered
as groom, and, lastly, the Sheykh of the Agheyls, an
old friend, sent two of his men as camel-drivers.

None, however, of these attendants, the two last
excepted, had seen each other before, nor knew anything of our way of travelling or our way of life.
We did not even start together, as it would have
been wise to do. The country round Bagdad is
bare of pasture for many miles, and we thought to
better matters for our camels by sending them on
some marches down the river, intending to join
them later with our baggage by boat, a most
unfortunate arrangement, for the men being stupid
timorous fellows, seem, when left to themselves, to
have lost their heads, and instead of obeying their
orders, which were to travel slowly, pasturing the
animals as they went, drove them without halting
to the village we had named as a meeting-place, and
kept them there, half-starved in dirty stables, till we

came, a piece of negligence which cost us dear.
When we joined them, one, the black delúl, was
already missing, dead they informed us; and a
second, Shayl, a camel which, when we left Damascus, had been a model of strength and good
looks, was so reduced as to be unfit for further
travelling, while the remaining six were but a shadow
of their former selves. Only Hatheran, the giant
leader, who had saved our fortunes in the Nefûd,
was still fit for a full load; and to him once more we
had mainly to trust during all that was to come.

It is difficult for those who have never owned
camels to imagine how much attached one becomes
to these animals on a long journey, and what
a variety of character they possess. Each one
of ours had its name, which it knew well, and
its special quality of courage, or caution, or
docility. Wilfrid's white delúl, "Helweh" (sweet-
meat), was gentle and obedient; the Meccan,
"Hamra," thoughtless and vain; "Ghazal," affec-
tionate, but rude and inclined to buck (poor thing,
she was far from bucking now); "Hatheran,"
especially, was a camel of character. He was
evidently proud of his strength and his superior
understanding, and possessed a singular independence of opinion which compelled respect. It
was his pride to march ahead of the rest, who accepted him as guide, and followed his lead on all
doubtful occasions. He cared little for the beaten
track, choosing his ground as seemed best to him,

and always for good reasons.   He was never impatient or put out, and in difficulties never lost his head.   He could carry twice the load of the others, and could walk faster, and go longer without water. At the same time, he considered himself entitled to extra rations when we made up the evening meal, and would leave us no peace till he was satisfied. I mention these things now, for feeding and driving and tending these camels was to be our chief occupation during the rest of our journey, and on them depended the safety of our march, and, in great measure, of our lives.   I say it with no little vanity, that, starting under the unfavourable circumstances we did, we nevertheless marched our camels without accident five hundred miles over mountain and plain, through swamps and streams never before traversed by camels, and across nine large rivers, one of them bigger than the Rhine ; and that we brought them in to their journey's end fat and well.   I must not, however, forestall matters.

On the 20th of March, having thus sent on our camels with the Agheyls, we embarked on board an English river steamer, with our servants, our horses, our greyhounds, and Rasham, the falcon who had followed our march from Haïl, and were taken down about eighty miles to a point of the river below Kut, where several streams run into the Tigris from the east, thus giving the district the name of Wudian (streams).

It was a cheerless start, for all down the river we

steamed through driving rain, till at last the steamer was brought to, amid the downpour, in front of a bare round bank, and we were invited to descend. There was nothing but mud and a few bushes to be seen for miles, and it seemed impossible we should step out of the luxury of a civilised English cabin into what seemed a mere slough, and that without means of transport further than the bank, for of camels and men there was nothing at all to be seen. But the die was cast; this was the place we had agreed on, and, without more ado, we landed, first our horses and then our baggage, and then ourselves. While this was in operation, some Arabs had appeared on the scene, and to one of them, an old man in a green turban, Captain Clements, before he said good-bye, confided us. Seyd Abbas, he told us, was an old acquaintance, and an honest man; and though the rest, it was easy to see, were of the lowest order of fellahin Arabs, we were fain to be content with this assurance and make what friends we could, at least with the old man. Sitting disconsolately on our camel bags in the rain, we then made our last farewell to all on board, and having watched the steamer till it steamed out of sight, set ourselves in earnest to the work that was before us.*   I resume my journal:

"The tent was soon rigged up on a piece of

---

* Just a year afterwards, poor Captain Clements, being in command of the Kalifeh, was attacked off Korna by an Arab ghazú, and while gallantly defending his vessel, was shot through the lungs.

sounder ground than the rest, and the horses fettered and turned out to graze. My new mare, Canora, so called after the Canora or Nebbuk tree which grows in the Residency yard, is certainly a great beauty, and attracts much, too much, attention, from the rather thievish-looking people of this place. Wilfrid has been to the encampment, which is about half a mile off, with Seyd Abbas, and has made friends with their chief people, but he has no agreeable impression of those he has seen. They appear to be, he says, a mixed collection of fellahín from all the Iraki tribes, and can lay no claim at all to good birth. Their Sheykh alone, for Seyd Abbas is not their Sheykh, claims gentility as coming from the Beni Laam, but we do not like his looks. The Beni Laam, Seyd Abbas tells us, are three days' journey from here, and there is war going on amongst them just now, owing to a quarrel between their Sheykh, Mizban, and one of his brothers. He gives rather a terrible picture of them, and has been trying to dissuade us from going further; but we think that with the letters we have for Mizban, there can be no difficulty. The Beni Laam are, at any rate, a true Bedouin tribe, not fellahín, like the people here. Old Hajji Mohammed (the cavass) stayed with me while Wilfrid was away. He was once in the army, and insisted on standing sentry in the rain in spite of all I could do to make him sit down under the flap of the tent. He has evidently small confidence in the people here.

Some fowls have been brought from the camp, and there are sticks enough to make a fire. Now we shall see what our Persian cook can do. If the camels were here, our being detained would not so much matter. We heard of them at Kut as we passed by in the steamer, but that is twenty-five miles off, and with this rain it is impossible to say when they may arrive.

March 22.—The weather has cleared, and we can see the Hamrin hills to the east, not so very far off. The country is less hideous than it seemed yesterday in the rain. This place is a sort of peninsula or island, formed by two rivers, which come from the Hamrin hills and fall into the Tigris. These seemed to be joined higher up by a canal, so that the space inside is cut off from the desert. It is partly a swamp, partly a thicket of guttub bushes, with here and there patches of cultivation made by felláhín. These call themselves Saadeh, but Seyd Abbas says they come from all parts. He himself is brother to the Sheykh of Ali Ghurbi, a village on the other side of the Tigris. There are no villages at all on this side after Kut, and this island of Wudian is the only inhabited spot. The felláhín are very poor, and complain bitterly of the government, which ruins them. They are completely under the thumb of the Turks, now that the government has steamers on the river, and the tax-gatherers take (if we may believe them), about two-thirds of their crops. They have also to pay ten beshliks (francs)

for each tent, half a beshlik for each sheep, two
beshliks for each buffalo they keep, and a capitation
tax of two and a half beshliks besides. Moreover,
they are visited now and then by zaptiehs, who take
their horses from them if they do not manage to hide
them away, on the pretence that they cannot afford
to keep them, while Mizban makes them pay tribute
for protection too, or rather for the right of being
left alone. The government does absolutely nothing
in return for what it takes. They are indeed in a
wretched plight, and one wonders why they take all
this trouble of cultivation for so little, but perhaps it
is a choice between that and starvation.

The great feature of Wudian is its wild-boars.
These literally swarm in the fields, trotting about
in open day-light, and doing exactly as they like.
The people are afraid of them, and keep out of their
way, and no wonder, for they are gigantic beasts.
A man who was at our tents to-day, shewed us a
terrible wound he had received from one which
charged him quite without provocation. The people
have only their short spears to protect themselves
with. The beasts come almost inside the camp, and
Wilfrid found one this afternoon fast asleep under a
bush, within ten yards of the path which leads to
the tents. The people passing along, went a long
way round so as not to disturb it, for it lay quite
exposed to view. Seyd Abbas begged him to
destroy some of them, and Wilfrid has ridden out on
Ariel, and taken the Winchester rifle to see what he

can do. I have felt feverish, and have stayed at home drying the things which had got wet.

The people here are all Shias, and very fanatical, and Seyd Abbas as a descendant of the Prophet enjoys a high position among them. Among the Ánazeh and Shammar, the Bedouins think nothing of saints and seyyids, but here they have everybody at their feet. Bashaga, the Sheykh, though a Beni Laam and, as such, a "gentleman," is not nearly so important as the old man in the green turban. The latter has been talking to me this morning and promises to take us to Mizban's camp, if we insist on going, though he advises strongly not. He says that with him we shall be safe, as they also have a great respect for Seyyids, and besides he has married into Mizban's family. Seyyid or not, he eats and drinks with us freely; so we feel a certain amount of confidence in him.

Wilfrid has returned triumphant. He was not more than two hours and a half away, and he has killed five boars and a sow. Ariel behaved wonderfully, following the pigs without any need of urging, and without flinching when they charged. It seems to have been splendid sport. Amongst the victims was the old boar that had been seen asleep, and which charged most viciously. It is lucky the dogs were not taken, as they would certainly have got hurt. The Arabs are highly delighted at the result, and we hope it may put us on better terms with them. They have dragged one of the corpses, a disgusting object, to the bank of the river, intending, they say, to send it to the British Resident at Bagdad by the next steamer. No news, alas, of the camels.

March 23.—A fearful storm in the night, and the whole place under water. Wilfrid went out early to try and get news of the camels, riding Job, the grey horse we bought of Col. Nixon. He did not get far, for the streams are so swollen that they are impassable, at least for one who does not know the fords ; and Job is a rather timid horse to get into difficulties with. He is young, and fairly bolted when a pig jumped up from out of a bush near him. We are both going out now for some more boar-hunting. I should enjoy it better if I was sure we should ever get away from this swampy place.

* * * * *

We have had a great misfortune. Ariel is badly wounded. We went out to-day, a large party, people on foot with spears and hoes, and one or two on sorry little mares. It was a beautiful day after the rain, birds singing in all the bushes, francolins calling, hoopoes flying about, and woodcocks starting from guttub thickets. The island was half under water, and droves of pigs, boars, sows and little ones, turned out of the bushes, where they generally lie in the day-time, were grunting and trotting and splashing about everywhere. We singled out a great red boar, and all gave chase, but the ground was heavier than yesterday, and we had a longish

gallop to come up to him. It was difficult, too, to
keep to the boar we had chosen, where there were
so many. At last he charged, and was hit, but not
enough to stop though it turned him, and then we
had another gallop, and another shot rolled him over.
The people on foot, who were following them, rushed
in, but just as they got near him up he jumped, and
bolted towards some deep water, where there was a
high guttub bush. I was in front, and Wilfrid
shouted to me to turn him, which I would have done
if I could, but instead, he turned me, coming at me
with a savage grunt and a toss of his head which I
knew was dangerous. Then he plunged into the deep
water, but instead of going on, suddenly changed his
mind, and came back to where the bush was on the
land, and before we were aware, had charged right
in among us. Wilfrid turned his mare, but, alas,
not fast enough, firing as he turned. To my horror,
I saw the hideous beast catch Ariel and give her a
toss, such as I have seen in the bull-ring given by a
bull. He seemed to lift horse and rider clean off the
ground. Ariel staggered away, while the boar lay
down, and was soon after dispatched by the Arabs.

We meanwhile had torn off our kefiyehs and
scarfs, and were trying to staunch a ghastly wound
in the poor mare's leg. The leg was ripped up
inside from the hock to the stifle, and an artery had
been cut. For a long while it was all in vain.
We could not stop the flow, and no words can describe our misery as we watched the blood pouring

fast upon the ground. We were in despair, for besides the fact of her being thus precious in race, we are much attached to the mare for her own sake, as who would not be, for Ariel is the noblest and best and gentlest creature that ever was. She has a pathetic look in her eyes, and is absolutely patient under her suffering. We have now some hope of her recovery, but Wilfrid fears she must be abandoned, for the sinew is cut bare, and she cannot put her foot to the ground.

While we were engaged in tending her, suddenly the camels appeared. It would have given us immense pleasure a few hours ago. Now all seemed indifferent. Their presence, however, enabled us to bring our camp here, where the mare is.

March 24.—This certainly is an ill-starred journey. The stupid Agheyls have so neglected our camels that Abdeh is dead, and Shayl unable to go further. Nor are the rest in much better case. We had some discussion this morning about giving up our present plan, and taking the next steamer which passes by for Bussora where we could make a fresh start. This would have been the best chance of saving the mare. But we decided to push on, and accordingly we left Wudian this morning, fording the canal, which is about four feet deep, fortunately without accident, and marching slowly in a south-east direction across a perfectly level plain. Ours is a melancholy caravan, for poor Ariel walks with great difficulty, her leg being terribly swollen ; but

she has such courage that we hope she may yet pull
through. It was a choice of evils, bringing or leaving
her; for leaving her would mean that we should never
see her again. Bashaga could not be trusted with
her, nor any of the Arabs of Wudian except Seyd
Abbas, and he has come with us. Seyd Abbas is
mounted on a sorry little white kadish, and his son
Hassan, who has come too, marches on foot. Wilfrid is mounted now on Job, and Hajji Mohammed
on the hamra. Thus we have travelled about ten
miles. The plain is here for the most part absolutely bare alluvial soil, like that of Irak, bu
mixed with saltpetre, and so producing nothing.
Here and there, however, there is a swamp, with a
little show of verdure, and we have encamped in the
middle of a patch of thistles, the first bit of pasture
we have come to. We have met no one, but there
are some tents now at a distance, with camels feeding, supposed to belong to the Beni Laam. Hajji
Mohammed has been to the tents, but he does not
seem to know how to manage among the Bedouins,
and has come back empty-handed, declaring that
the owners were rude to him. We ought, I suppose, to have gone ourselves, but we are in such distress about the mare that we do not like to leave
her. We have been dressing her wounds with
Holloway's ointment, as she lies on her side at our
tent door. The thistles are of the spotted sort, and
all the animals, including Ariel, seem to enjoy them.

March 25.—We hoped that Ariel was better ,

she had eaten well over-night, and though very
stiff this morning, was able to start with us ; but
after travelling a couple of miles, she staggered and
fell down, and though she got up again, she again
fell. The third time she refused to move, the
pain being too great, and there she lay on her
side as if dead. It was useless to try to bring her
further, and as we happened to be passing within
half a mile of the tents we had seen yesterday, it was
agreed that Hassan, Seyd Abbas' son, should stop
with her and get her gradually to them, and so back
to Wudian. We have promised him a handsome
reward if he succeeds in recovering her and sending
her back to Bagdad, and he has protested he will do
everything he can. All the same, I do not doubt
that we have bid good-bye to Ariel for ever. She
lifted up her beautiful head as we took leave of her,
and seemed to understand what was happening, for
Arab horses understand things as people do. Wilfrid brought her a bucket of water, which she drank,
and then she laid her head upon the ground again,
and we went away.*

Travelling without her to-day has seemed unnatural. It is impossible to enjoy looking at the
sunshine or the Hamrin hills, though these have been

* What became of Ariel we shall never know. At first reports
came to Bagdad that she was alive and recovering; then news that
she was dead ; and then, when someone was sent to inquire, it
was discovered that Seyd Abbas and Bashaga and all the Arabs
had deserted and were gone. We hope still she may be with
them.

very beautiful. We are again encamped in the open
plain not ten miles from these hills, and three or
four perhaps from the river, which we have been
marching almost parallel with.

A new complication has arisen in the behaviour
of Ramazan, the cook, who has proved so insubor-
dinate that he is to be sent about his business.
Seyd Abbas is to go to-morrow to Ali Ghurbi on
the river, to make purchases of rice and dates for
us, and he will take Ramazan with him, as also the
groom, who declares he has got fever, caught in the
Wudian swamps, and will go no further. Thus our
party is melting away at the outset ; but we are
in the meanwhile to go on, with a young man Seyd
Abbas brought with him from last night's tents, to
a large camp of the Beni Laam, which is said to be
just under the hills, and wait there till the Seyyid
joins us.

March 26.—Four hours' march has brought us
to the hills. As we got near them, we found the
usual signs of a Bedouin encampment, distant
flocks of sheep and then shepherds, all moving
with that exaggerated, mysterious appearance of
speed the mirage gives. We galloped on to reconnoitre from a tall tell in front of us, and soon
made out the camp. There was a stream of water
just below, and the tell and the plain near it were
covered with something like turf, while the hill
sides were visibly green with grass. A shepherd
told us that the camp was Musa's, the sheykh we

were in search of ; and, waiting till the camels came up with us, we went on there.

Musa ibn Sollal was absent, and we were directed to his brother Akul's tent. We found him fast asleep in a corner of the tent, but he woke up when we entered, and received us politely. He told us that the Sheykh had gone to Amara, at a summons from the mutesserif of that town, to meet his brother Mizban, and have their quarrel made up. It seems that Musa, Akul and Homeydi, all sons of one mother, are making war against their half-brother, Mizban, who is head of the Ibn Sollal family, as well as principal Sheykh of all the Beni Laam ; and the quarrel is now a serious affair, for Mizban has killed one of Musa's sons. There can be little chance of its being patched up by Turkish intervention, for the present mutesserif is weak "like a lady," they say, and not at all the man to deal with a blood-feud.

Akul is an elderly man, with a grey beard, and devoted to children. He has been doing his best to entertain us, as well as to amuse a little group of small children who came clustering around him when he awoke. His tent is a poor one, small and hot like a stewpan ; and we escaped from it the moment we could with propriety go to our own, pitched only a few yards off—too few, alas ! for comfort, for the people here, though well-behaved, cannot resist their curiosity to " farraj."

These Beni Laam must be counted as true Bedouins, as none of them are fellahín, or would lift a finger to till the ground, for which purpose they employ such low tribes as our friends the Saadeh and the Abiad. But they are quite different from any other true Bedouins I have visited, not only in manners but in looks ; and there seems to be among them a great mixture of races. Seyd Abbas has told us that they intermarry with Persian and Kurdish tribes, and that they also receive and adopt into their own tribe vagabonds from no one knows where ; and this account is fully borne out by their appearance. Mixed descent may be read in their faces. Neither do they, as far as I can make out, lay much claim to good breeding, except in the ruling family, Ibn Sollal, which is proud of its ancestry in the male line. Akul and his brother Homeydi, who visited us in the evening, talked a great deal about their Nejdean descent. According to their own account they (the Ibn Sollal) came from Nejd twelve generations ago ; and I do not doubt the correctness of the tradition ; but their Arabian blood has since become so much diluted with foreign additions, that in Nejd itself they would not be accepted as nobly born. They do not deny their marriages with the daughters of the neighbouring lands, but seem to think it a matter of no consequence. They will even marry with townspeople and Bagdadis ; and we heard on board the steamer of a relative of Mizban's married to a certain Jazin Sabunji, a tradesman in

Bagdad. His brother, Ahmet Sabunji, had, on the strength of the connection, given us a letter to add to our packet of introductions to Mizban.

The horses here seem to be of small account. Fifteen or twenty mares, wearing the usual iron shackles, are grazing about a mile off, some with foals by their sides, all standing in water above their fetlocks. We walked round to examine them, and saw one good-looking white mare that may be thoroughbred, and also a bay somewhat better than the rest, but they are inferior animals. A foal was born last night, and was being removed with its mother, a wretched little creature, to the dry ground at the camp. There were no camels to be seen. They and the sheep are at pasture at a considerable distance.

A couple of Bagdad sheep-dealers have come by with a large flock just purchased from Mizban's people. Their description is glowing of the wealth and grandeur, and excellent reception to be met with at the great Sheykh's tents. They are travelling quietly, and apparently without precaution or fear of being attacked by the ghazús, so much talked about. But I suppose they know what they are doing.

Several women came to see me, accompanied by some children, two or three of whom were really beautiful, one little boy especially. Their visit soon attracted a crowd, for everybody who passed stopped to join the circle in front of our tent. They were good-humoured and rather encroaching and forward, but kept in check by a middle-aged man with a big stick, who undertook the office of master of the ceremonies. His method was rough and ready ; every now and then to effect a complete dispersion of the party by rushing into the midst of them and dealing out blows on every side without distinction of age or sex. The visitors then ran away in all directions laughing, and almost immediately returned more gay and merry than before. One young lady, Basha by name, proposed to accompany us on our journey, and my answer, " Marhaba, fetch your mare and come," brought down on her endless chaff.

A few small presents have made Musa very amiable, and he has sent us a guard for our tents. There is, it would seem, some apprehension of attack on the part of the hostile section of the tribe who are not far off, and a ghazú from Mizban is much talked of. So the conference of the two brothers at Amara does not prevent their followers from carrying on the war.

March 27.—Nothing worse happened during the night than a thunderstorm. Wilfrid started early on Job to try and find old Seyd Abbas, of whom nothing was heard yesterday. He went alone, and cantered for about ten miles in the direction of the river, but finding a large marsh between him and it, and, moreover, that Ali Ghurbi was beyond the river, he returned. He met, he tells me, a number of Arabs whom he believes to have been Mizban's people. They made some show of trying to circum-

vent him, but were too ill-mounted to be dangerous.
At midday the Seyyid arrived with two donkey
loads of provisions from the village. We had all
but given him up for lost, and in our dearth of
friends, we now begin to feel something like affection
for him, seeing him return.

We have made so little progress this week that
we could not consent to stay another night with
Musa, and have come on, in spite of tempestuous
skies and alarming rumours of a ghazú, which is
said to be on the march from Mizban's. We have,
however, hitherto, escaped all these dangers. The
thunderstorms, though rattling like artillery, right,
left, in front, and behind us, spared us overhead;
and we have seen no living soul all the afternoon. It is a wild, strange piece of country, but
covered in places with excellent pasture, so that
we have the satisfaction of seeing our dear camels
growing fat beneath our eyes. We have stopped
for the night at the edge of an enormous red
morass, the haunt of innumerable birds. There
are two little tells close by, and a pool of rain
water good to drink. We have now left the neighbourhood of the Tigris for good, so that these
swamps have nothing to do with it. They seem
to be caused by small streams running from the
Hamrin Hills, and caught in this great flat plain.
The railway, in Wilfrid's opinion, if it is ever made,
ought to run along the foot of the hills where the
ground is sounder. It is difficult, however, to ima-

gine the use of a railway in such an uninhabited
country.

The tells where we are, are called Doheyleh ; but
there is nothing in the shape of a village anywhere
this side the Tigris, nor are there any Bedouins
except these Beni Laam.

March 28.—A good morning's march has brought
us safely to Mizban's. It seems that after all we
ran some danger last night, for a ghazú was really
out between the two Beni Laam camps, and we
find Mizban's people in commotion. A few miles
from the camp we were met by a body of horsemen
advancing in open order, who, as soon as they saw
us, galloped at full speed towards us, and seemed
as if intending to attack. But Seyd Abbas rode
forward to meet them on his old grey kadish and
waved his cloak and shouted to them to stop. " It
is I," he called, " Seyd Abbas." Whereupon the
horsemen pulled up, and dismounting, kissed the
old man's hand. They were a ghazú, they told us,
from Lazim, Mizban's eldest son, and they were
following on the track of some robbers from Musa's,
who had carried off seventeen camels in the night.
They cross-questioned Seyd Abbas as to Musa's
whereabouts, but the old man would not let out the
secret. It would have been a breach of the hospitality he had just received from Musa. They did
not stop long, however, to talk, but went on their
way, leaving a couple of the party only to show us
to Mizban's tent.

The tents of the Beni Laam are peculiar. Instead of being, like every other Arab tent we have seen, set on a number of poles each of different height, these are shaped like regular pent-houses, with gable roof and walls. Such, at least, is Mizban's *mudíf*, a construction corresponding with the *kahwah* of a town house, and used only for reception. The living tents are smaller, and the word *beyt* house here applies only to the harim. The mudíf is a fine airy room, very pleasant in the hot weather we are beginning to have. It is pitched close to the river Tibb in the middle of a very large camp, several hundred tents, and looks imposing enough. The country all round is very bare and trodden down, having been exposed last night to a fearful hail storm, which has wrecked all the vegetation. The hailstones, they say, were as big as dates.

The Tibb is much swollen, and flowing through a deep cutting, looks anything but easy to cross,—a turbid yellow river cutting its way through the alluvial plain without valley of any sort, so that you do not know it is there until you come close to it. It is about fifty yards wide.

At the door of the mudíf we alighted, and presently made the acquaintance of our host—not Mizban, for he, as we heard before, is away at Amara, but his son Beneyeh—a rather handsome but not quite agreeable looking youth, whose forward, almost rude manners show him to be, what he no doubt is, a spoilt child. We have been

rather reserved with him in consequence, and have
left to Hajji Mohammed the task of explaining our
name and quality, and delivering the letters which
we have with us for his father. Beneyeh is not the
eldest son, and I do not quite understand why he
does the honours of his father's tent instead of
Lazim. It is difficult to know exactly how to treat
him ; but we think it better to be on the side of
politeness, so we have sent him the cloak intended
for the Sheykh, and have added to it a revolver, with
which he seems pleased. We are so completely in
his hands for our further progress, that we must do
what we can to secure his good will. I have paid
a visit to the harim, and have been well received by
Beneyeh's mother, Yeddi, a fat jovial person, young-
looking for her age. She is very proud of her son,
and the evident cause of his spoiling. Her step-
daughter Hukma, and daughter-in-law Rasi, are both
rather pretty ; though the latter, like the mother-in-
law, shows signs of foreign blood, being inclined to
fat, and being red-haired and fair complexioned.
The occasion of my visit to them was a distressing
one. We had hardly retired to our own tent when a
loud explosion was heard, and immediately afterwards
a man came running to us to beg us to come, for an
accident had happened. In the storm last night some
gunpowder belonging to Beneyeh had got wet, and
a slave had been set to dry it at the fire in the
women's tent, with the result of a blow up and
fearful burning of the unfortunate creature. They

wanted us, of course, to cure him ; and we gave
what advice we could, but with little chance of
success. The poor slave lay groaning there behind
a matting all the time I was in the tent, but Yeddi
and the rest chattered, and laughed, and screamed,
regardless as children. Sick people get little peace
in the Desert.

      *   *   *   *   *

Wilfrid believes he has arranged matters with
Beneyeh, who came to dine with us this evening,
and talked matters over afterwards with Seyd Abbas
He declared at first that a journey across the frontier
into Persia was out of the question, that nobody had
ever been that way, that the Beni Laam were at war
with the Ajjem (Persians) and could not venture into
the neighbourhood of Dizful, or any town of Persia,
and that his father was away, and he had no men
to spare as escort. After much talking, however,
and persuasion on the Seyyid's part, he has agreed
to start with us to-morrow with thirty horsemen and
see us safely to the camp of one Kerim Khan, chief
of a Kurdish tribe, which lives on the river Karkería, beyond which Persia proper begins, and
that he will take £10 for his trouble. The sum
is hardly excessive if he fulfils his part of the
bargain, for the country between Turkey and
Persia has the reputation of being quite impracticable, not only from the robber bands which inhabit
it, but from the rivers which must be crossed. Hajji
Mohammed is very gloomy about the whole matter.

In the middle of our conversation a fearful hubbub arose in the camp round, followed by some shots and the galloping of horses, and Beneyeh exclaiming, " A ghazú, a ghazú ! " jumped up and rushed out of the tent. Our first thought was to put out the candle, and our second to stand to our arms and look outside. In the dim starlight we could see what seemed to be a fight going on inside and round the mudíf ; and though night attacks are very unusual in the desert, we were convinced an enemy was sacking the camp. Though the quarrel was no affair of ours, and we should probably be in little danger had it been daylight, now in the darkness we could not help feeling alarmed. Wilfrid served out cartridges, and gave the order that all should kneel down so as to be prepared for action if the tide of battle should come our way, an arrangement which resulted only in Hajji Mohammed's letting off his gun by accident, and very nearly shooting one of the Agheyls. The mares had their iron fetters on, and with the keys in our pockets we knew they could not be lost. Still it was an anxious moment. At the end of a quarter of an hour, however, Beneyeh came back in great excitement to say that a ghazú had come from Musa's, and that some camels had been driven away ; that the hubbub in the tent was not fighting, but preparation to fight ; and that he was come to borrow a rifle as he and his friends were starting in pursuit. Wilfrid gave him one of the guns and offered to ride with him on his expedition, but Seyd Abbas, who had all the time been cheering us with an assurance that "it was not our affair," would not hear of this ; and, after a long discussion, it was decided that we should all stay together, as indeed is only prudent. I do not believe the ghazú has been anything very serious ; for, though Beneyeh and some of his men have galloped off in the supposed direction of the enemy, by far the greater number have remained, preferring shouting and singing to actual fighting. They are now chaunting in chorus " Aduan—Mizban (enemies—Mizban)—Aduan—Mizban," and striking their spears on the ground to beat time. A great fire has been lit and is blazing in the mudíf, and the dark figures passing and repassing in front of it make the whole thing wild and savage in the extreme.

ARIEL, AN ÁNAZEH MARE.

CHAPTER II.

Gloucester. " 'Tis true that we are in great danger,
The greater therefore should our courage be."
SHAKESPEARE.

"La plus mauvaise rencontre dans le désert est celle de l'homme."
GUARMANI.

We are betrayed into the hands of robbers—Ghafil and Saadun—
We diplomatise—A march across "No-man's-land"—Night
terrors—We claim protection of a Persian prince.

March 29.—The event of last night, though in
truth it was less alarming than it seemed, made us
anxious not to remain longer at Mizban's than could
be helped. Wilfrid accordingly no sooner saw
Beneyeh this morning, than he began to urge our departure on him, as it had been arranged over-night.
The young man was in a bad humour, his pursuit of
the ghazú having been either unsuccessful, or, as
we suspect, never seriously made; and at first
he would hear of nothing but that we should go
back to Amara, instead of crossing the frontier,
which he again declared to be impracticable. He
was put out, moreover, because we did not allow
him to keep the gun which he had borrowed in
the night; and but for old Seyd Abbas, whom
he is bound to treat with respect, I doubt if he
would have kept to his bargain with us. I begin

to regret now that he at last allowed himself to be persuaded, for we seem to have got into a very awkward pass.

Our troubles to-day began early.   First of all we had to say farewell to Seyd Abbas, our last connecting link with respectability.   The old man said he dared not go further ; that in the country where we were going his condition as a seyyid would not be respected, nor could he do more for us than wish us well through it.   He washed his hands, in fact, of the whole proceeding, and protested that he had gone farther than he ought in bringing us thus far. We could not indeed find fault with him for wishing to return, and thanking him heartily for all, and so recommending him once more to see to Ariel, we let him go.   Since then all has gone wrong.   We had first the river to cross, a not very easy proceeding, for the banks were of mud, and the water up to our horses' shoulders.   Still, nothing untoward happened till we had all got over. Then the two Agheyls, our camel-drivers, declared that they too would go no further.   The journey into Persia frightened them, they said, as well as Seyd Abbas, and though they gave a variety of reasons besides, it always came back to this, that they did not like to die in a foreign land.   It was no use arguing with them that they should not die, and that we would provide handsomely for their return to Bagdad by sea ; no offers could move them, nor even the threat of their Sheykh's displeasure, which we held *in terrorem* over them. It was impossible to be really angry, yet our case is a forlorn one without them. To-day we and Hajji Mohammed have had to load and drive the camels ourselves, for he is the only servant left us, and Beneyeh and his Arabs would do nothing, contenting themselves with galloping about and shouting out their unasked-for advice. It was very annoying.

Beneyeh's manner has changed alarmingly. Finding us practically in his power, now we have crossed the Tibb and cannot retreat, he has become most insolent, trying all day to pick a quarrel with us about the revolver we gave him, and which he has put out of order by his clumsiness, and asking for one thing and another belonging to us exactly like a rude, ill-bred child. Wilfrid was obliged to speak sharply to him and bid him be ashamed of himself, as his manners are those of an Iraki fellah, not of a Sheykh's son. Still he went on, now asking for Wilfrid's sword, now proposing to buy my mare, impertinences both, till, on being told he was a fool, he rode on in a huff with his men. There were nine of them, and one only remained with us, an older man who seemed ashamed of his young chief, and with whom we got on more pleasantly. Still it is a disagreeable prospect to have to travel with such rascals all the way to Persia. The party are tolerably mounted, the Beni Laam having a few asil mares, principally of the Wadnan breed, and at Mizban's camp there was a horse which they called a Nusban, a name new to us.

The country, after passing the Tibb, is a fine rolling down, with capital pasture in the hollows, so that to our other difficulties we are fortunately spared that of anxiety about our camels. It is worth something to see them feeding on rich green grass as they go, making up at last for their long winter's fast.

At two o'clock we sighted some tents, where we found Beneyeh with his men, waiting for a dinner of lamb which was being prepared. Hungry as we were, we should have much preferred passing on unfeasted, for we are now suspicious of our host, and feel anxious when away from our horses. Still there was no refusing, or seeming to doubt or be afraid, and we joined with as good a grace as we could in the rather rude entertainment. The meal lasted upwards of an hour, and when we were ready to start there were still delays, so that it was dark before we reached the camp which was to be our resting-place for the night. The late rains have put much of the low-lying country under water, and we are now in a broad valley, formerly, one may guess, a rich agricultural district, but long deserted. We passed about sunset the mounds of an ancient city, which are not marked on any of our maps, and which the people here call Jeréysiat; and near these we came upon the camp where we now are.

What its inhabitants are we do not yet know.

Dakher, the chief man, is, it would seem, a Beni
Laam, but the rest have more the appearance of
outlaws than of respectable Bedouins. They have
the most evil countenances of any people we have
met on any of our travels, and Hajji Mohammed
says roundly they are Kurdish robbers. Dakher
and his brother Ghafil look capable of any treachery.
They have a soft manner, with great flabby faces, and
a black look in their eyes, which, with their rows of
glittering white teeth, give one a shudder. They
received us at first with some show of hospitality
in their " mudíf," which was a large one ; but
though a fire of logs was blazing in the middle,
and pots were standing round, nobody gave us
coffee, a very disagreeable omen ; and when I asked
just now for water, they would not bring it me
in one of their own pans, but took ours. They are
Shias, probably, and rude on principle. We have
pitched our tent the best way we could in the dark,
and piled up all our luggage inside, for every
man here looks like a thief—I might say like a
murderer.

March 30.—Last night, before we lay down to
sleep, Beneyeh came to our tent with Dakher, and
began bullying again and begging, but Wilfrid would
give him nothing except the sum of £10 agreed on,
for which he promised, and Dakher promised, that
thirty khayal should go on with us to Dizful, a
distance of about ninety miles. Beneyeh himself
refused to go, saying that Ajjem (Persia) was not

his country, but Dakher should go for him, or Ghafil. This was a distinct breach of agreement, but we were only too pleased to get rid of him, and Wilfrid, after some show of expostulation, accepted the substitute. Then Beneyeh made a pretence of writing letters to certain khans or chiefs of the frontier tribes, but I suspect these are not worth much, for having no seal of his own with him, the young jackanapes signed the letters with a seal lent him by a bystander, an irregular and rather suspicious proceeding, but we made no remark, being thankful at any price to be freed from his company. With the grimace of one who has played a successful trick he pocketed the money, and then, without saying good-bye, mounted and rode off, our only friend, the middle-aged man, to our sorrow following him.

We were now left alone with Dakher and his crew, who sat round us while with infinite labour we loaded our camels. Poor old Hajji Mohammed in his rusty uniform, with his sword dangling between his legs, was anything but an efficient camel-man, and in spite of the best will in the world things proceeded slowly. It was as much as we could get out of Dakher that he should tell one of his sulky fellows to lend an occasional hand to the work, and keep the rest from getting in our way. The help was given grudgingly, and in obedience rather to Wilfrid's command, for he was now obliged to talk loud, than of good-will. Dakher, however,

kept up a semblance of politeness, being still our
host, a position sacred even in the eyes of the most
abandoned, and when his brother Ghafil appeared,
announcing himself as our escort, we were suffered
to depart.

Once on our horses, and with the camels driven
in front of us, we felt more at ease ; yet all were not
a little anxious. We should, I think, have turned
back now but for the recollection of Beneyeh and
the river Tibb behind us, evils we knew of while
the unknown evils before us seemed preferable.
For a while, too, we flattered ourselves with the
idea that Ghafil was to be our only company,
and for a mile or two the illusion lasted, and we
were reassured. There is something, besides, in a
very bright morning's march through a beautiful
country, for we were close to the hills, which prevents one feeling anxious, and whatever its inhabitants may be, this frontier-land of Persia looks
like a Garden of Eden, with its grass and flowers
knee deep in every hollow.

Ghafil is another and a worse edition of Dakher,
having, over and above his brother's vices of countenance, a most abominable squint. His face looks
always like a thunder-cloud, and the smiles on it
(for he smiles sometimes, showing a wonderful set
of white teeth from ear to ear) are like the smiles
of a wild beast. He has, too, a sort of cat's
manner, soft and cowardly, but very offensive. At
starting, and as long as he was alone with us, he

seemed amiable enough, but at the end of about an
hour we came up with the rest of the party in whose
company we were to travel, and then his demeanour
changed.   These were not horsemen, or an escort
at all, but a collection of the most extraordinary
vagabonds we have ever seen.   There were about
forty of them, with about twice as many beasts,
camels, and oxen, which they were driving before
them loaded with empty sacks.   Amongst them
were two women on foot, and there was a single
horseman heading the procession, mounted on a
little white mare.   We asked them where they
were going, and they answered, " To Dizful, to
buy corn," and then in return plied us with a
hundred questions.   Many of these were not a
little impertinent, but by parrying some, and affect-
ing not to understand the rest, we managed to
hold our own, even returning some of their small
wit with interest on themselves.   Hajji Mohammed,
however, poor man, was soon singled out as a
special butt for their mirth.   His old uniform coat
they found supremely absurd, and he was as merci-
lessly chaffed about his tailor as if he had been
amongst a party of roughs on the Epsom Downs,
while he had not the sense always to keep his
temper.   There was, besides, something more than
mere high spirits in their wit.   He was a Suni, and
they were Shias, and religious bitterness made them
bitter.   From words at last they seemed rapidly
coming to blows, when Wilfrid interfered, making his

horse curvet amongst them, and dispersing them for
a while. But they soon returned, and it was all we
could do to prevent the poor cavass from being
maltreated. One called on him to dismount and
give him a ride, another to let him have a shot
with his gun, and a third to fill him a pipe of
tobacco, to none of which demands the unfortunate
Hajji knew how to give the proper refusal. "Ya
Hajji," "Ya Hajji," was the perpetual cry all the
morning long; "Where is your pipe? where is your
tobacco? Quick, I am thirsting for a smoke."
Ghafil in the meanwhile would do nothing or could
do nothing in the way of control, sitting on his
camel gloomily in silence, or talking in an under-
tone with a great one-eyed rascal, more villainously
hideous than himself. The position was often
almost unbearable, and only the doctrine of patience
which we had learned in Arabia, and a constant
show of good humour to the crowd, made it tolerable. In the course of the afternoon, however, we
managed to get upon some sort of friendly terms
with two or three of the rabble, so that by the evening, when we stopped, we had established a little
party among them in our favour. This, I believe,
was the means of preventing a worse disaster,
for it is nearly certain that Ghafil and the more
serious of the party meant us deliberate mischief.

About an hour before sunset we came to a broad
river, broader and deeper than the Tibb, and here
Ghafil decreed a halt. If we had been a strong

enough party to shift for ourselves, and if we could
have crossed the river alone, we should now have
gone on and left our persecutors behind; but in
our helpless state this was impossible, and we had
no choice but to dismount. It was an anxious
moment, but I think we did what was wisest in
showing no sign of distrust, and we had no sooner
stopped than we gave one a horse to hold, and another
a gun, while we called on others to help us unload
the camels, and get out coffee and provisions for a
general feast. This seemed to most of them too
good an offer to be declined, and we had already
distributed a sack of flour and a sack of rice
amongst them, which the two women had promised
to bake into loaves for the whole party, when
Ghafil and the one-eyed man, who had been down
to look for a ford, arrived upon the scene. They
were both very angry when they saw the turn
things had taken, and were at first for forbidding
the people to eat with us, alleging that we were
kaffirs (infidels), so at least the people informed us
later, but this was more than they could insist on.
They would not, however, themselves eat with us
or taste our coffee, and remained apart with those
of the party which had not made friends with us.
The women were on our side, and the better sort of
the young men. Still it was a terribly anxious
evening, for even our friends were as capricious as
the winds, and seemed always on the point of
picking an open quarrel. Later, they all went

away and left us to our own devices, sitting round
a great bonfire of brushwood they had built up,
" to scare away lions," they said.   We managed to
rig up our tent, and make a barricade of the camel-
bags in such a way that we could not be surprised
and taken at a disadvantage.   I did not shut my
eyes all night, but lay watching the bonfire, with my
hand on my gun.   Hajji Mohammed once in the darkness crept out and got near enough to overhear something of their talk, and he assures us that there was
a regular debate as to whether and when and how
we should be murdered, in which the principal
advocate of extreme measures was the one-eyed
man, a great powerful ruffian who carried a sort
of club, which he told us he used to frighten the
lions, beating it on the ground.   The noise, he
declared, sounded like a gun and drove them away.
With this tale of horror Hajji Mohammed returned to comfort us ; nor was it wholly a delusion, for in the middle of the night, Wilfrid being
asleep, and Hajji Mohammed, whose watch it was,
having fallen into a doze, I distinctly saw Ghafil,
who had previously come under pretext of lions or
robbers to reconnoitre, prowl stealthily round, and
seeing us all as he thought asleep, lift up the flap of
the tent and creep under on Wilfrid's side.   I had
remained motionless, and from where I lay I could
see his figure plainly against the sky.   As he
stooped I called out in a loud voice, " Who goes
there ? " and at the sound he started back, and

slunk away. This woke Hajji Mohammed, and nobody slept again, but I could see Ghafil prowling like an hyæna round us the best part of the night.*

Hajji Mohammed has behaved very well, though he owns himself much frightened. So am I, only I conceal my alarm better than he does. Indeed I am sure that putting on a bold face is our only chance of safety, for nothing but cowardice now prevents Ghafil and his set from attacking us. We are well armed, and he knows he could not do it with impunity. As long as we are on horseback, I believe we run no great risk, but the night is a disagreeable time. If we had only open desert in front of us we could set them all at defiance.

March 31.—The morning broke tempestuously, and we were afraid the river might have risen in the night, a complication which would have probably decided our fate ; but though the clouds lay black and heavy on the hills there was no flood. After trying several places, all of which proved too deep, our akid, the man on the white mare, found a ford, if such it can be called, for the water was over his mare's back, and all the party followed him. The robbers, for so I now call them, passed easily enough, for their camels were unloaded, but ours barely managed it. The current was very strong, and though Hatheran and the strongest of them came on boldly, two of them stopped in the middle

---

* This part of the journal was written at irregular moments when order was not possible. It has been pieced together since.

and seemed on the point of turning down and being
swept away, when Wilfrid rode back below them,
into the deep water, and drove them on. It was
nervous work to watch them, seeing nothing of rider
and horse but their heads, but Job swam very well,
and the camels were saved and all got safely over.
This incident proved a fortunate one, for it impressed
the better sort of the robbers with an idea of our
determination, and there was again a party in our
favour. It was fortunate that it was so, for we
were no sooner across than Ghafil and the one-
eyed monster, Saadun, came forward with a more
menacing manner than they had yet dared to
show, and said we should proceed no further. It
was plain enough what they meant, but we affected
not to understand them, and declaring in a
cheerful tone that it was a charming spot to
stay in, with plenty of grass and water for the
beasts, at once consented to a halt. Wilfrid begged
Ghafil to sit down and smoke a pipe with him, and
when the man sulkily demurred, insisted on it.
" Now, Ghafil," he said, " here you are my guest, as
we have been yours ; what can I do for you to make
you happy ?" " Wallah, ya Beg," interposed Saadun,
" you have done nothing for him or any of us, and
now you must." " Must ? Indeed, I shall be too
delighted. Tell me only in what I can assist you—
what it is that Ghafil wants." Ghafil then began a
long history about his dignity as Sheykh of the
expedition, and the disgrace it was to him to have

received no cloak of honour from the Beg, and the insult that he had thus received from us—at all which Wilfrid expressed the greatest possible pain and surprise.* "There has been some mistake here," he said ; "I would not for the world that anyone should be treated with less respect than was his due by me. The disgrace would be mine ;" and he made a show of taking off his own cloak to give him ; still Ghafil seemed dissatisfied. "No, no, it is not that," said Saadun, in a stage whisper, "what the Sheykh wants is money—money, do you see ?—money for all of us." "And is it possible," exclaimed Wilfrid, "that you have all remained unpaid ?—that Beneyeh gave you nothing of what he received from me ?—that you have been working for me, 'balash,' for nothing ? This is indeed a disgrace. Come, Saadun, let us talk this matter over and repair the mistake." He then took the one-eyed man by the arm and led him aside for a private conference, while Ghafil sat on gloomily with me. Wilfrid's first care, when he got the Kurd alone, was to square him with a present of ten krans (francs) for his own account, and a promise of twenty more when we got to the Kerkha, judging rightly that this fellow was in fact our most dangerous enemy. Then he intrusted him with negociating the rest of the black mail with Ghafil. We were prepared now for

* We trust this duplicity may be pardoned us in consideration of the straits we were in.

almost any demand, for we were completely in
their power, and had a sum of nearly £100 with
us, besides property to the value of perhaps as
much more. We were consequently no little
relieved when Saadun returned with a demand of one
hundred krans, and a silk abba, in return for Ghafil's
protection. This, after much affected reluctance to
part with so enormous a sum, and a declaration
at one moment that rather than pay we would stay
where we were for a month, we at last produced—
giving the robber the very silk abba which had
been one of Ibn Rashid's presents to us in Nejd—
a white silk one, embroidered with gold, but the
only one we had ; which being done we were suffered
to proceed. The truth of the matter probably is
that Ghafil dared not drive us to extremities,
partly from physical fear, for we soon had proof
sufficient of his cowardice, and partly because many
of his men would not have joined him in a deed of
violence. Bloodshed is a thing no Arab willingly
consents to, however low his morality, especially
where a guest, or one who has been a guest, is in
question ; and though the mongrel Kurds and
Persians, who made up more than half the band,
would have abetted him, the rest would not. One
of the women, too, was Ghafil's wife, and the women
were openly friends with us. Another consideration
may have been that we were entering now upon an
enemy's country, for the Dueri is the limit of Beni
Laam authority, and our men were too miserable

cowards not to count upon us for something in case of attack. Part of our agreement with Ghafil was that we were to fight for him in case of need against the Persians, a promise we readily gave. The atmosphere now was somewhat cleared, and we started afresh under rather better conditions. The teasing of Hajji Mohammed continued, but we ourselves were treated with respect, and the one-eyed Kurd even occasionally lent a hand in driving the camels, in company with a youth clothed in green, who had hitherto been one of our worst persecutors.

The whole party proceeded cautiously, avowing without the slightest shame their immense fear of the Ajjem (the Persians), whom they expected to meet at every turn of the road. Beyond the Dueri we found ourselves in a beaten track, which winds up and down over an undulating bit of desert, the last ripple of the Hamrin hills which are now behind us. The akid usually rode on in front to spy out possible enemies, and all had orders to keep together. Ours, however, was such a noisy party, that one would have thought its passage could have been heard for miles round. The bullocks were getting tired and required a great deal of driving, and the shouting and screaming reminded one of an Irish fair. So we went on without a halt till three o'clock, when a halt was ordered in a hollow, where we were out of sight of enemies, and where there was a quantity of wild celery, and another edible

plant called "hakallah," which we found good, for
we had eaten nothing all day. Not far off were
some sand mounds, with tufts of what looked very
like ithel, but we dared not leave our camels to
inspect them. The halt was only for half-an-
hour ; then with shouts of "Yalla yalla, erkob,
erkob," the mob went on.

We stopped again suddenly about an hour before
sunset, and this time in alarm. The akid, who
had ridden to the top of a low hill, was seen waving,
as he came back, his abba, and instantly the cry
arose, " El Ajjem, el Ajjem." In an instant everybody was huddled together in a hollow place, like a
covey of partridges when they see a hawk, and we
were entreated, commanded to dismount. A few
hurried words with the akid confirmed the terrible
news of danger to the band, and all seemed at their
wits' end with terror. " How many horsemen ?—
how many ? " we inquired. " Five," was the
answer, " but there are more behind ; and then these
are the *Ajjem!* " "And if they *are* the Ajjem,
and only five of them, are you not forty of you
here and able to fight ? " " No, no ! " they
screamed, " you do not understand. These horsemen are Persians—Persians ; every one of them
capable of killing five of us." I did not think men
could be so craven-hearted. A few of the least
cowardly now crept up to the hill-top and one by
one came back to report ; the number of horsemen
seen rose rapidly from five to fifteen and even-

tually to fifty. When the last number was reached, the coward Ghafil, who had kept well in the middle of the mob, so as to be in the least possible danger, came to us with his softest and most cringing manner, forgetful of all his bullying, and begged us to be sure and do our best in the battle which was imminent. "You should stand in front of the others," he said, "and shoot as fast as you can, and straight, so as to kill these Ajjem—dead you understand—it is better to shoot them dead. You, khatún, know how to shoot, I am sure—and you will not be afraid." We could not help laughing at him, which shocked him dreadfully. Presently a man came rushing up to say the enemy was coming, and again there was unutterable confusion. The boy in green had begged some percussion caps of Wilfrid for his gun, and had been given fifty, and this now led to a wrangle, as he refused to share his prize with the rest. Everybody was trying to borrow everybody else's gun or spear or bludgeon, for they were very rudely armed, and nobody would stand in front, but everybody behind. The women alone seemed to have got their heads, while Ghafil, white in the face, walked nervously up and down. We and the cavass stood a little apart from the rest, holding our horses, ready to fire and mount, and Wilfrid occupied the interval of expectation with giving me instructions what to do if we got separated in the fray. I was too well mounted to be overtaken, and was to make for the Kerkha

river, which we knew could not be far away to the
east, and put myself under the protection of the
first Persian khan I should meet there; if possible,
Kerim Khan, to whom I had a letter in my pocket,
and who is a vakil of the Persian Government.
We hoped, however, that we might be able to keep
together, and beat off the enemy. Wilfrid called
out to Ghafil, "You must tell me when to fire,"
but Ghafil was too frightened to reply. Several of
the men, however, called out, "Shoot at anybody
you see—everybody here is an enemy." The camels
had been made to kneel down, and the cattle had
been huddled together; only a few of all the
mob looked as if they really meant to fight. They
were silent enough now, talking only in whispers.
So we remained perhaps for half-an-hour; then
somebody ran up the hill again to look, and
Wilfrid, tired of waiting, proposed that we should
eat our dinner, as we had had nothing all day. I
got some bread and a pomegranate out of the delúl
bag, and we were soon at work, much to the
disgust of the rest, who were shocked at our levity
in such a moment. Presently there was another
alarm and the people called to me to come inside
their square, meaning kindly I think, but of course
we would do no such thing, being really much safer
where we were with our mares. Still no enemy
came, and when we had finished our meal we tied
our horses' halters to our arms and lay down in our
cloaks; we were very tired and soon were sound

asleep. Nothing more was heard of the enemy that night.

But our troubles were not to end here. We were hardly comfortably asleep, before a tremendous crash of thunder roused us and a downpour of rain. On putting our heads out of our cloaks we saw our valiant escort rigging up our servants' tent for themselves. They were terribly afraid of getting washed in the rain, and were shrieking to us to come inside too, indignant at Wilfrid's " ma yukhalif " (" never mind "), with which he had already treated their remonstrances on other occasions. Indeed, " ma yukhalif " had now become a sort of nickname with them, and no dishonourable one, I think, for the person concerned. We neither of us could think of joining them in the tent, but having managed to get a couple of horse-rugs from the delúl bag, we covered ourselves over again and went to sleep ; Sayad and Shiekha creeping in under them to keep us company. All of a sudden the rain stopped, and before we were well aware, the mob was again on the march. It was pitch dark, and we were within an ace of being left behind, a circumstance which perhaps we should have hardly regretted. Still, now we felt that our position with the robbers was such, that we ran less danger in their company than alone ; and we all hurried on together. Ghafil was polite again ; and the rest, feeling, I suppose, that the journey was nearly over, and their power over us vanishing, even made us offers of assistance. A long, weary night march we had, and at dawn found ourselves descending rapidly into a broad plain, knee deep in pasture. This was the valley of the Kerkha ; and as it grew light we became aware of a long line of mounds, with two kubbrs or shrines in front of us, which Ghafil told us were the ruins of Eywan. At seven o'clock we saw tents within the circuit of the ancient city, and some shepherds in conical felt caps, and sheepskin dresses, the costume of the Bactiari and other tribes of Kurdish origin. We were in Persia.

Ghafil now went forward to announce our arrival to Sirdal Khan, the chieftain at whose tents we now are. But I must leave further details for to-morrow.

CANORA.

CHAPTER III.

"Henceforth in safe assurance may ye rest,
 Having both found a new friend you to aid,
 And lost an old foe that did you molest,
 Better new friend than an old foe is said."

FAERY QUEEN.

A prince in exile—Tea money—Rafts on the Kerkha—Last words
with the Beni Laam—Kerim Khan—Beautiful Persia—We
arrive at Dizful.

SIRDAL KHAN is a Shahzade, or member of the
Royal family of Persia, many of whom are to be found
living in official, and even private capacities in
different parts of the kingdom. He himself had
fallen into disgrace with the Court many years ago,
and had been exiled from Persia proper, a misfortune which led to his taking up his residence
with a section of the semi-dependent Seguand tribe
of Lurs, where he became Khan or Chieftain.
Both in looks and in manner, he stands in striking
contrast with the people round him, having the
handsome, regular features, long nose and melancholy, almond-shaped eyes of the family of the
Shah, which, I believe, is not of Persian origin, and
a certain dignity of bearing very different from the
rude want of manners of the Lurs. These would
seem to be of Tartar origin, coarse-featured, short-
faced men, honest in their way and brave, but

quite ignorant of those graces of address which
even the worst Arabs are not wholly without.
Sirdal, when he arrived among the Lurs, was
possessed of considerable wealth, which he invested
in flocks and herds, and until a short time before
our visit he was living in Bedouin magnificence.
But his enemies it would seem still pursued him,
and not satisfied with his disgrace, molested him
even in his exile. By some means, the rights of
which we did not learn, they managed to instigate
against him a rival chief, one Kerim Khan, who,
under Government sanction, made a successful raid
upon his flocks, stripping the unfortunate prince of
everything, and driving him and his tribe across
the Kerkha river into the No Man's Land, which
lies between Persia and Turkey, and which we had
just crossed. In this position he has been obliged
to maintain himself as he could, making terms with
Mizban and the Beni Laam, who are his nearest
neighbours westwards. The river Kerkha is considered the boundary of Persia, and as it is a large
and rapid river, nearly half a mile across, he is in
comparative safety from the east. Ghafil, therefore,
as a Beni Laam, was on friendly terms with him,
though it was easy to see that he despised and had
no kind of sympathy with him or the ruffians of
his band. By Hajji Mohammed's advice, and to
secure ourselves against further risks at their hands,
we accordingly placed ourselves at once under the
Khan's protection. Hajji Mohammed fortunately

knows both Persian and Kurdish, and soon explained to Sirdal the circumstances of our position, and he, delighted to meet once more with respectable people, readily assented. He received us with great kindness, made us comfortable in his tent, which, in spite of his poverty, was still more luxurious than any found among the Arabs ; having partitions of matting worked in worsted with birds and beasts, carpets, and a fire, and gave us what we were much in want of, an excellent breakfast of well served rice and lamb. Then, when we had pitched our own tent just outside, he provided us with an efficient guard of Lurs, who soon sent our robber acquaintance of the last few days about their business. There is no love lost between them and the Arabs. Presently I received a visit from the Khan's wife, whom he has lately married, and his mother, a well-bred person with perfect manners, and a refined, pleasing face. She was in black, in mourning she explained for a son ; she has five sons, including the Khan, whose brothers live with him. A crowd of Seguand ladies came in her company, and an Arab woman who had been nurse to one of the Khan's children, and who served me as interpreter. Ghafil's wife, too, one of the poor women who had travelled with us, came in and joined the conversation. She is loud in her complaints of Ghafil, who treats her ill. He is now very polite and presented himself during the after-

noon at our tent as if nothing had happened, with a
little girl named Norah in his arms whom he told
us was his niece, he having a sister here married to
one of Sirdal's men. I had a carpet spread for the
ladies outside our tent, for it could not have held
them all, and they sat round me for an hour or
more, curious and enquiring, but exceedingly polite.
They admired especially my boots and gloves,
which I pulled off to show them. One of them,
turning up my sleeve, exclaimed at the whiteness of
my wrist. At the end of an hour the elder lady
rose, and wishing me affectionately good morning,
took her leave, the rest following.

We then had a pleasant day of peace and a
sound night's rest, hardly disturbed by the ferocious
shouting and singing of our guard, which, under
other circumstances, might have been frightening.
Anything more wild and barbarous than their
chaunting I never listened to, but to us it was
sweet as music, for we knew that it was raised to
scare our jackals, the Beni Laam.

April 2.—Next day we crossed the Kerkha.
When we saw the size of the river, swollen with
melted snow and running eight miles an hour, and
as wide as the Thames at Greenwich, we felt
thankful indeed for having met Sirdal Khan.
Here there would have been no fording possible,
and we, or at least our goods, would have been at
the mercy of our robber escort. The Khan, however, agreed for a sum of money, 100 krans

(nothing in Persia is done for nothing, either by
prince or peasant), to have us ferried over with our
baggage to the Persian shore, and our camels and
horses swum after us. Hospitality is not a virtue
real or pretended with the Persians, and the Khan,
prince as he was and a really charming man,
explained to Hajji Mohammed without affectation,
that sixty of the one hundred krans he would count
as "tea money," or as the Spaniards would say,
"ruido de casa," payment for board and lodging.
To this, however, we were indifferent, and appre-
ciate none the less his kindness and good manners.
He rode with us himself to the river on a well-bred
Arabian mare he told us was "asil," as it well
might be, and saw that all things in the matter of
the rafts were done as they should be. At first we
rode through the mounds of Eywan, which are
disposed in a quadrangle fronting the river, and where
we found plentiful remains of pottery; then past
the kubbr of I forget what Mohammedan saint,
facing a similar kubbr on the eastern bank; then
across some fordable branches of the river and
islands clothed with guttub and canora trees, to
the main body of the Kerkha, where we found a
raft preparing. The canora bushes had fruit on
them, which the Khan politely picked, and gave me
to eat, little yellow fruits, pleasantly acid, like
medlars, and with stones inside.

The passage of the river was a tedious, not to say
difficult, process, the single raft being composed of

twenty skins only, and very crank. We found besides, to our disgust, and also waiting to take advantage of our passage, our late disagreeable companions, Ghafil, the one-eyed Kurd, and all the rest, who presently began a loud argument with the Lurs as to who should pilot our camels through the water, a ticklish duty, which required both knowledge of the animals and skill in swimming, to perform successfully. At first we were naturally in favour of the Lurs, and unwilling to trust any part of our property with the mongrel Arabs; but when it came to the point of testing their capabilities, the Lurs broke lamentably down, being hardly able to manage the camels even on dry land, so by the Khan's advice we let the Bedouins manage the business, which I must say they performed with no little courage and skill. It takes two men to swim a camel safely. First of all the beast must be unloaded to the skin. Then a cord is tied to the tail for one man to hold by, and another mounts on his back. Thus he is driven into the water, and pushed on gradually till he loses his legs. The man on his back then floats off down stream of him, and holding with one hand by the hump, splashes water in the camel's face to keep his head straight, while the other urges him from behind. The camel seems heavier than most animals in the water, showing nothing but the tip of his nose above the surface, and he is a slow swimmer. It was an anxious quarter of an hour for us while they were crossing, and great was the speculation among the bystanders as to the result. " Yetla," "ma yetla," " he does it," " he doesn't," were the cries as they were carried down the river. The strongest pushed fairly straight across, but those in the worst condition seemed borne helplessly along till camel and men and all disappeared out of our sight,—and we had already given them up as lost, when we saw them emerging quite a mile down upon the bank. Then we ourselves and the luggage were put across, the mares swimming with us, though they got across much quicker than we did. The raft was hardly eight feet square, a rough framework of tamarisk poles lashed together on twenty goat skins. Our luggage went first, with Hajji Mohammed perched on the top of it, booted and cloaked, and loaded with gun and cartridge bag, sublimely indifferent, though an accident would have sent him like lead to the bottom. We ourselves were more prudent, and divested our-selves of every superfluous garment before taking our seats, which we did in the company of our dogs and bird, and of Ghafil's wife, who nearly upset us at starting by jumping in from the shore upon us. Our feet were in the water all the way, and our hearts in our mouths, but by the mercy of Provi-dence, we finally reached land amid a chorus of such "betting on the event" as had accompanied the camels. The last creature of our party was the little hamra mare, which Sirdal's servant had been holding, and which, slipping her halter, came bravely across alone.

Just across the river lives Kerim Khan, Sirdal's enemy, a Kurdish chief in government pay. To him we had letters, and nothing more remained but to go to his camp, and ask his help to forward us to Dizful.

Our former enemies now came round us like a swarm of gnats, begging and praying us to let them be of some use. They wanted to tack themselves on to our party, and so go to Dizful in safety, under cover of our companionship; for it appears that they dare not go further than this without protection. The Persian authorities here are apt to imprison any of the Beni Laam who enter their district, and these people therefore seldom venture beyond the Kerkha, or just this side of it. Even so, they are sometimes caught: we saw a Beni Laam last night who had just arrived at the Seguand camp on his way home after three or four months' imprisonment at Dizful, besides having to pay a fine of one hundred and fifty krans. He was accused, no doubt justly, of sheep stealing, and he told us that several others of Mizban's people are at this moment in jail at Dizful.

The elder Ghafil finding that nothing could be got from us by persuasion, tried a little of his old blustering and threats, but several of Kerim Khan's people were standing by, and he was powerless here, so we had the pleasure of giving him a piece of our mind before he retired. His younger name-

sake, the man in green, could not contain his rage
at our escape, and openly expressed his regret that
we had not been killed in the wilderness as had
been intended. After this little scene we saw no
more of either of them, for though we afterwards
heard of them in Kerim Khan's camp, they never
dared come back into our presence.

There now came forward to welcome us a funny
little boy with half-shut eyes, riding a good-looking
chestnut mare. He dismounted, introduced himself
as the Khan's son, and invited us to his father's
tents. These he said lay close by, but we were not
yet at the end of this day's difficulties. A network
of irrigation, and a deep muddy canal had to be
passed, and the camels which had so successfully
escaped the dangers of the river, were again nearly
perishing, and more ignobly, in the mud. The
Kurds on this side the river were useless to assist
us, as in their ignorance of camels they only made
matters worse, and but for the sudden reappearance
of the one-eyed giant, who had been once our
greatest enemy, I think we should have all stuck
fast. But now he made amends for part of his
misdeeds and ill-designs by lending a powerful
hand. He and Wilfrid between them unloaded the
camels, and carried the luggage over on their heads
up to their waists in holding mud, and then
dragged through the camels. The boy, meanwhile,
had gone to fetch help from his father ; and we
were hardly across, when he reappeared, still on his

chestnut mare, a Kehîleh Harkan, he told us, from the Beni Laam, for all the tribes here get their horses from the Arabs. And then we saw a cavalcade approaching, and in the midst a portly figure on an old grey mare, whom the boy introduced to us as the Khan.

Kerim Khan is, after Husseyn Koli Khan of the Bactiari, the most powerful chief of Luristan. His tribe occupies most of the district formerly known as Susiana, and from his camp on the Kerkha the ruins of Susa, now merely mounds, were visible. The land east of the river is very fertile, and being moreover well irrigated, is mostly under cultivation. Though living in tents, these Lurs can hardly be called nomadic, for their camps are permanent ones, at least for many months together. The one where we now found ourselves was in appearance quite as much a village as it was a camp, the tents being pitched close together in rows, and from their pent house shape looking exceedingly like houses. In the centre of the camp is a large open space, within which the sheep and cattle of this section of the tribe are driven at night. These, however, are not numerous, for Kerim Khan's people are cultivators of the soil, rather than shepherds. We noticed many good-looking horses about, procured, they told us, mostly from the Beni Laam.

The tent in which we were lodged was a most elaborate construction. Its roof was of the same material as that used by the Arabs, goat's hair

cloth, but the side walls were of carpet stuff, with
intervals of open grass matting, through which the
air circulated pleasantly. It had, besides, a regular
door, while inside were some handsome Persian
carpets spread near a lighted fire, which we soon
made use of to dry our clothes, for we were wet
through, with the rivers and canals we had crossed.
The Lurs themselves differ even more from the
Arabs, than their habitations from Bedouin tents.
They have none of the Bedouin dignity of manner,
and their dress is a mean one, a square coat of
felt, and a little felt skull-cap, from under which
their black hair curls up in a single greasy wave.
Their voices, too, to one coming from among the
Arabs, sounded exceedingly absurd, as they have a
sort of sing-song intonation, and are pitched so
high as to be almost in falsetto.   This with the
drawl, which we had noticed before in Ali Koli
Khan, made us at first inclined to laugh.   Kerim
Khan keeps his people in excellent order, and no
crowding round us or importunate questioning was
permitted. The great man himself, though far from
dignified in appearance, was well-mannered, and
when he came, after having first sent us breakfast,
to see us in our new tent, conversed politely, first a
few words of Arabic, and afterwards in Kurdish,
which Hajji Mohammed interpreted. We told him
of our adventures, and of our intended visit to
the Bactiari chieftain, with whom he was well
acquainted, and of our journey from Haïl with Ali

Koli Khan, his son. I am not sure that he
altogether believed us, when Hajji Mohammed
added, that we were persons of distinction travelling for amusement. In Persia, it is the custom
to judge strangers entirely by the appearance they
make, and we, travelling in our poor Arab clothes,
and accompanied by a single servant, gained less
credit in his eyes than we should have found with
Arabs, who care nothing for externals. He promised, however, to send us on with two horsemen on the following day to Dizful, and thence,
if we would, to the Bactiari. In a private conference, however, later with the cavass, he imposed
his conditions. We were to pay him ten tomams
(four pounds sterling), as " tea-money," an exorbi-
tant demand, which we were nevertheless obliged to
accede to. Hospitality here is never given gratis,
nor has anyone much shame of begging, for even our
little friend and first acquaintance here, the boy on the
chestnut mare, though his father is evidently a very
rich man, spares no occasion of asking money, " for
his bride," he says. Gold is what he likes best.

April 3.—The Khan and his son rode with us for
half a mile this morning, to see us started on our
way to Dizful. He has given us two horsemen as
he promised, so at least we have something for our
money, and they seem respectable people. We had
hardly ten miles to go, and the road, for there was
a road, was in tolerable order, and the men helped
us drive our camels according to such lights in

camel driving as they possessed. At first, we made
a circuit, so as to cross the canal at a place where
there was an old stone bridge, and in so doing we
passed not two miles from Shush, the ancient Susa.
Wilfrid would have liked to visit the mound, but I
was impatient to get on, and in fact there is nothing
above-ground by all accounts to see. Then we
travelled through a beautiful plain, bounded by the
splendid line of the Bactiari mountains, still covered
almost to their base with snow, a refreshing sight,
for the sun was now very hot. At their foot, we
could make out the town of Dizful, indistinctly at
first, and then clearly, while all around us lay well-
cultivated fields of waving corn just turning yellow.
Here and there grew shady canora trees, and there
were many rills of water. Now and then, too, a
village shaped like a fortress, with a surrounding
wall of sun-dried bricks, on the roofs of which storks
had built their nests, and were clattering with their
bills. In the fields, we heard francolins calling and
quails; and the roadside was gay with flowers, red,
blue, and yellow. Several times we stopped in the
shade of a tree, and let the horses and camels graze
on the crops, for so our horsemen insisted we should
do, and there was no hurry. Travellers here are
probably too scarce for grazing rules to be enforced
against them. Nor did the peasants we met seem
to mind. We were in Persia at last, and the
country seemed very delightful.

At eleven o'clock, we came to a large village by

the side of a broad shallow stream of transparent water, flowing over a bed of pebbles, and overhung by shady trees. A group of women were washing their clothes, and the road was full of country people on foot and donkey-back, crossing the ford. A pretty picture, such as we had hardly seen since we left Syria. This, and a second river which we passed presently, are called the Bellarú, and cover with their various branches nearly a mile of country. The water in them was cold enough to make a pleasant coolness in the air, coming like the Kerkha water from the snows. Then at two o'clock, we found ourselves close to Dizful, set picturesquely on the great river Diz, which is spanned by a fine old bridge of squared masonry, the work of ancient times. The town itself occupies some high ground beyond the river, that is to say on its left bank, but on this side, there is not a single house. The bridge is the main feature. It has twenty-one arches, some pointed, some round, with buttresses to break the stream. It is very much out of repair, there being one hole in it big enough for a camel to fall through. It would seem to belong in part to the age of the Persian monarchy, in part to that of the Caliphs, but I have not sufficient knowledge of architecture to feel sure about this.

In any case, here we are at Dizful, and once more under a settled government, with police and soldiers, and all the other blessings of civilisation at our call. We may be thankful that it is so.

CHAPTER IV.

"In Kanadu did Kubla Khan
A stately pleasure-house decree,
Where Alph the sacred river ran,
Through caverns measureless by man,
Down to a sunless sea."
COLERIDGE.

Pleasures of town life—The Khani's court—Bactiari shepherds—
Shustar—Its palace, its river, and its garden—A telegraph
clerk.

April 4.—Dizful, though still alive with a
population of 30,000 persons, and a certain amount
of traffic, for it is the corn market of the tribes
westwards on the Ottoman frontier, and eastwards
on the Bactiari, now possesses but the shadow of
its past prosperity, if we may judge from the
neglected condition of its magnificent bridge and
the ruined walls which remain to mark its former
circumference. Between these and the limit within
which the present inhabited town has shrunk, lies
a widish strip of unoccupied land. Here we have
our camp in a hollow out of sight from the road,
and here we had hoped to remain unnoticed and
undisturbed. But alas, it was Friday, and the whole
population turned out at daybreak, and there was
no chance of escaping discovery. All the inhabitants of Dizful, men, women, and children, have
been idling about, holiday-making in their best

clothes all day long, with apparently nothing to
do but stare at us. I am sure they consider the
arrival of a party of strangers as a God-send, for
from early dawn until an hour ago, at the *asr*
when the governor sent three soldiers to disperse
them, they have literally swarmed round our tent
like their own flies. Not content, as Arabs are, with
looking on from a reasonable distance, these
Persians persist in trying to thrust their way inside
the tent, and not succeeding, they sit down in rows
so close to it that we cannot stir without pushing
somebody away. Besides, they cannot look with
their eyes; they must touch everything with their
fingers, and they must laugh and talk, and have
answers to all their foolish questions. They mean
no harm, but it is very tiresome, and has hindered
us not a little in our repairs and preparations.
The camel saddles and bags wanted mending, the
camels had to be doctored for mange, with an
ointment which had first to be mixed, the horses
to be shod, the stores looked through, purchases to
be made of rope and provisions, and all this with
several hundred persons at one's elbow ; each ready
with advice and interference.

Our appearance, I have no doubt, is a great
temptation to them, for there can be few things
more unutterably dull than one of their festivities.
Pigeon-flying is here as much the fashion as it is
at Aleppo, and there is the same element of
gambling in the performance. The birds are let

loose from their separate dovecots, and allure each
other home ; such at least is the explanation given
us of the excitement shown in watching them.
Whoever gets most birds from his neighbour wins.
Then there are dervishes and seyyids in green
clothes who go about selling sugar-plums and
collecting alms ; and a few of the richest have
horses on which they gallop about. We, however, in our Arab dresses, are a perplexity and
an endless source of inquiry to all ; and our dogs,
and our falcon, and our camels, excite almost
as much interest as they might in Hyde Park or
the Champs Elysées. We should have done far
better to stay the other side of the river, where
there is an honest bit of desert much more in keeping with our establishment, and where nobody
comes. Rasham, too, to add to our troubles, got
loose and flew wildly about over the crowd, and
could not be caught till Wilfrid climbed to the top
of a tower there was in the city wall, and lured
him down. We were almost at our wits' end with
the mob when the governor's guard arrived, and
restored order. I profit by the quiet thus secured,
and by the last hour of daylight, to write my
journal.

Besides the vulgar populace, several polite and
well-to-do inhabitants have called on us ; the most
agreeable of them, a party of four, came in the
morning, and afterwards spent the day sitting
under the shade of the ruined wall close by, where

Wilfrid returned their visit. In the afternoon they came again. They were Ardeshir Khan, a very dignified and very fat man; Pasha Khan, next in dignity and fat; Yusef Khan, thin and very dark; and lastly, Aga Shukr Allah, red-haired and speaking a little Arabic, and thus able to converse with us and interpret for his friends.

The wife of one of these gentlemen sent to propose to come and see me, and on my accepting, arrived immediately with a score of attendants. We sat together on my carpet, which I ordered to be spread near the tent; but with the best will in the world, our conversation was but halting; Hadji Mohammed is not a fluent dragoman, and he grows deafer every day. A seyyid also called on us and brought his little girl, named Khatún, a funny little thing of five, to whom I gave a silver kran; then some rather ill-mannered persons calling themselves Sabæans.*

Two or three people have been riding about on horseback; one on a very handsome little bay horse, said to be of Nejd origin, brought back by a pilgrim, as it is the fashion for pilgrims who can afford to do so, to bring back a colt from Nejd.

This year's pilgrims they tell us have not yet returned, and we are the first to announce their arrival at Meshhed Ali. We hoped to have heard something here of our friend Ali Koli Khan, but are disappointed. He intended to go by water

---

* Christians of St. John, see "Bedouin Tribes."

from Bagdad to Mohammra or Ahwas, and so to
Shustar and home—the usual route, in fact—for
ours is not a road travelled by respectable people.
Dizful communicates with the outer world only by
Shustar. It is of no use, however, waiting for
Ali Koli. We cannot spare the time, and must pay
our visit to Huseyn Koli Khan now or not at
all. No one can tell us exactly where to find the
Bactiari chief, some saying he is at Shustar, some
at Teheran, while all agree that some of his people
are encamped between this and Shustar, and to
Shustar we consequently mean to go.

Our last visit was from the governor or deputy-
governor, who being, we suspect, not quite sober,
(for the Persians drink wine) behaved so oddly that
Wilfrid had to beg him to take himself off there
and then. On the whole, our day's rest at Dizful
has been hardly a pleasant one.

April 5.—Shaking the dust of this very tiresome
city from our feet, we resumed our march to-day.
We are depressed at the poor reception we have
received after all in Persia, the country we have
heard of so long as famed for its politeness, but
perhaps we ourselves are to blame. Hajji Mohammed tells us we should have travelled in a
different way, and he is probably right. The
Persians, he says, judge only from what they see,
and have no idea that people travelling without
servants can be respectable. We should have come
with a retinue, an escort of fifty men and half as

many servants. Then we should have been *fêted*
everywhere. But it is too late now, and we must
travel on as we can.

We took the Shustar road this morning, a well-
travelled track, passing at first through corn-fields
and villages, and then across a fine plain of grass.
The soil here looks richer than any I have ever
seen in any part of the world, and it is well-watered
and wooded with canora trees. We are marching
parallel with the mountains, a lovely range crowned
with snow, and quite 8000 to 10,000 feet above the
sea. Immediately to our right, a wonderful square-
topped hill stands out in front of the main range ;
a *diz*, or fortress, the people call it. We have
passed several encampments of Bactiari ; wild-
looking people, who when you ride up to their
tents, run at once to their guns as though they
expected constantly to be attacked. They are
guarded by some of the most ferocious dogs I
ever saw, which were with difficulty prevented
from attacking Shiekha and Sayad. Their masters,
however, are not inhospitable when things are
explained, and we had several basins of milk offered
us on the way. From them we have learned
that the Khani, as they call their chief, is somewhere on the road, and the prospect has cheered
us not a little. To-night we are encamped all
alone, except for the company of an old Arab and
his wife, who joined us on the road—Chaab Arabs
they call themselves—who have been useful, help-

ing us with the camels. There are many Bedouin
Arabs, it appears, in this part of Persia. We have
got a sheep to-night, and are to have a feast.

April 6.—The Bactiari tents are like those of the
Arabs, but the men are dressed as I have described
the Seguand, and Kerim Khan's people. They keep
horses, and carry lances or guns, but I saw no horses
which seemed well-bred. Early in the morning a man
came from one of their tents, and told us that the
Khani had passed the night not ten miles from where
we were, at a place called Obeyd, which our two
guides from Kerim Khan knew well. It lay off the
high-road to the left, just under the square-topped
hill we noticed yesterday. Though anxious now to get
on to Shustar, where alone we can procure servants
(and they are a necessity we feel more and more
every day), we could not of course forego our
visit to Ali Koli's father, and taking a line in the
direction pointed out, struck out to the north somewhat back from our yesterday's line of march. It
was a rough bit of travelling over broken rocky
ground, cut up here and there with streams. Very
beautiful, however, for in every hollow there grew
real turf brilliantly green, and sprinkled over with
borage flowers and anemones ; and wherever there
was a pool of water, frogs were croaking among the
weeds. Our progress was slow, for Assad, one of
our men, had bought a donkey at the camp, with a
new born foal, and as the foal could not walk, he
carried it before him on his horse. He was

continually letting it slip off, and stopping to hoist
it up again. Towards nine o'clock, we came to a
ridge of limestone, overlooking a wide valley
out of which the square crag we had been following
rose like a wall of masonry, five hundred feet or
more ; beyond which again, lay the snow range of the
Bactiari. While we were looking and admiring, we
heard shots fired, and knew that there must be a
camp in the valley, the Khani's, we hoped, and
so it proved. But before descending, the two
Persians insisted upon going through an elaborate
furbishing of themselves and their clothes. There
was a little pool close by, and there they washed
and combed themselves, and then washed their
clothes, spreading them afterwards on the rocks to
dry. We in the meanwhile found a bit of shade
under a rock and slept. It was about noon when
we woke and went down to the valley, where we
presently saw a large building, the fort of Obeyd,
with half-a-dozen white canvas tents grouped round
it. This was Huseyn Koli Khan's travelling
camp, and the fort was also his. It is modern and
in good repair, a square building flanked with
towers, surrounding a courtyard.

In the middle of the camp stood the Khani's reception tent like a great umbrella, for the side walls
were taken down for the heat. There Huseyn
Koli sat in state surrounded by a kind of court.

Huseyn Koli Khan is the greatest chieftain of
all Western Persia. He is said to be able to put

20,000 horsemen into the field, and this may very well be true, as the whole of the south-western slopes of the mountains are occupied by his tribe. In person he is imposing without being particularly good-looking ; he is a thick-set rather heavy man, with a broad face, brown beard and hair, and I think grey eyes. He reminds me of a picture I have seen somewhere of Ghenghis Khan, or another Mongul prince, from whom it is not altogether impossible he may be descended. His manner is very straightforward and plain, and he gives one the impression of being altogether an honest man. He received us very cordially, made us sit down by him in the middle of his courtiers who were standing obsequiously round him, and gave us some cups of excellent tea.

The manner of tea-making in Persia deserves notice, inasmuch as the tea is there put into the boiling water, while with us the boiling water is poured on the tea ; and tea made in the Persian fashion is without the bitter taste too often the result of our method.

We spent an hour or two thus with the Khan, giving him the latest news of his son, who it appears is expected daily now from Ahwas, and learning much about the road which still lies between us and Bushire. The Khan is on his way to Teheran, where he has rank under the Shah as a general in the army, so is unable to invite us to visit him in the mountains where his home is,

and where he keeps the stud of Arab mares for
which his name is famous. This would be more
unfortunate if we did not now recognise the necessity of getting without further delay to the coast.
The weather in the last two days has become
suddenly hot, and it would be folly to allow ourselves to be caught by the summer with so long a
march before us. Besides, we are hardly in such
travelling order as to allow of great experiments.
In spite of all our exertions, and all our offers of
high wages, we cannot get any one to drive our
camels. The fact is, the camel is almost as strange
a beast here as he would be in England, and camel-
drivers about as scarce. So we are to go to Shustar
to-morrow accompanied by a confidential man of the
Khani's, who will put us into good hands.

We had a grand debate on returning to our tent
whether or not to send presents to our host; but on
Hajji Mohammed's advice, and rather against our
own judgment, at last did so. But our host would
receive nothing, saying that it was for him to do
honour to his guests, and that he wanted nothing.
He has sent us a most excellent dinner now,
consisting of half-a-dozen really well-cooked dishes,
things we had not tasted since we left Bagdad.
There is also a live lamb to take with us to-
morrow, and two large boxes of sweetmeats made of
fruits and flowers.

April 7.—Our visit to Huseyn Koli Khan,
though a disappointment in some ways, for it was

but a morning call, has been none the less a good
fortune to us. The confidential man whom the
Khan sent with us brought us early into Shustar,
and through his intervention we are now comfortably established in a really delightful place,
the deserted palace of the Shahzade, or Prince
Governor of the province, which is to us as a haven
of repose, fortress and palace and garden in one.
But all this requires description.

Shustar from the river is extraordinarily like
Dizful. The Karkería, on which it stands, is the
Diz over again, but I think a larger river; and
there is a stone bridge apparently of the same date.
The bridge of Shustar is a fine work. It is the
broadest I have ever seen out of Europe, for one
might drive a coach across it but for the holes ;
and it is quite fifty feet high above the water. The
most singular feature of it is that it is built in a
zigzag, and that it has immense piers to the buttresses, some of which seem to have held water-
wheels. The parapet is very low, and the whole
thing so much out of repair, that crossing it as we
did, in a hurricane of wind, we were rather nervous
about the camels. Below it is an immense weir,
over which the river falls with a deafening roar.
A fine arched gateway shuts it off from the city,
and just above stands the castle, where we are.

Shustar seems a larger town than Dizful, but it
is said to be less flourishing. They both have great
empty spaces within the walls, and plenty of ruins.

The kalat is an immense rambling place, enclosing a number of different buildings. First, there are rows of vaulted buildings, intended probably for barracks, with a large outer court, full just now of green pasture, a sort of mallow, on which we have turned our camels out to graze. These outbuildings are two storeys high, with loop-holes to shoot out of. From the outer court a paved causeway leads up to a narrow gate, the entrance of an inner castle, built round a large square court, with trees and flower-beds in the middle. From this again a flight of fifteen steps leads up to a terrace, garden, and pavilion three storeys high. This last is the hammam, and is the building specially placed at our disposal. The Shahzade is absent, and the only inhabitants of his kalat are a garrison of about a dozen soldiers, but they live in the outer circle of buildings, and will not disturb us. The prince-governor's absence is a disadvantage to us, although we profit by it to inhabit his house, for our letters are to him, and we do not know what sort of wakil he has left here. To-day, however, we have seen nobody, and have been very happy and content in the coolness and peace of all around. Only the river makes a distant roar, far below, for from the terrace one looks sheer down at least eighty feet to the water.

April 8.—This spot is like a thing in a fairy tale. Our pavilion contains several rooms on the ground-floor, grouped round a central piece where

there is a fountain ; and above this is a gallery with
more empty rooms round it. We live on the
ground-floor, and our windows open on to a narrow
terrace with a low stone parapet, from which one
can throw a stone down into the river. The
Karkaría makes a sharp bend just above Shustar,
round what looks like the most beautiful park, a
level greensward with immense dark green shady
trees, standing as if planted for ornament. Here
we sit, and late in the evening and early in the
morning I see a pair of pelicans swimming or flying
below. The terrace communicates with the garden,
which is gay with poppies, pink and lilac and
white, in full bloom. There is a little tank, and a
row of stunted palm-trees, where rollers, green and
blue birds like jays, sit, while swifts dart about
catching musquitoes and flies, only a few hundred,
alas, out of the millions that torment us. For there
is no rose without a thorn, nor is this lovely kiosk
and garden full of blooming poppies without its
plague. The flies and musquitoes are maddening,
and to-day the heat of summer has burst upon us.
After a hot night, the day dawned hotter still, and
a sultry wind blew up dark clouds, till now the sky
is black all round.

Towards evening we had thunder and lightning,
but hardly a drop of rain ; and to-night the air is
heavy as lead. I am getting anxious now about
the heat. I wish we could get away, either to the
hills or the sea; but I fear we shall be detained

some days. The storm has prevented the Shah-zade's wakil from paying us the visit he announced this morning, and we cannot even prepare to go on without seeing him; we are, in fact, dependent on his assistance. We sent him our letter for the Shahzade early this morning, and Hajji Mohammed brought back word that he was coming immediately; but we have been waiting all day, and he has not come. What is still more tiresome is the unfortunate circumstance that no letter has come for us from the British Consul at Bussora. This puts us into an awkward position; we had given out that we expected the letter, and it is worse to say that one expects such a letter and not to get it, than never to have mentioned it.

Several visitors have been to see us, two or three merchants, a doctor, and others; they all, on hearing we had not received the countenance we had expected, looked on us somewhat doubtfully, in spite of our talking about our letter of recommendation to the Shahzade. However, we shall see what the wakil says to-morrow.

April 10.—This is the evening of our fourth day at Shustar, and we are not absolutely sure of starting, though we hope to get away to-morrow morning. . . . Yesterday was a wretched day. The night before last Wilfrid was suddenly taken ill, and though the attack has now passed off, it has left him weak. A serious indisposition makes all minor difficulties seem trifles; but these become important when they cause delay, and we have been in much trouble about getting servants.

This town life is certainly not healthy in the great heat (and summer has come upon us in earnest) ; and every day wasted will make travelling more difficult, and the heat greater. We hope, however, that we have settled all with the governor, but until we are actually off I shall not be at ease.

The wakil has reluctantly promised us an escort for Bebahan, protesting that the country between it and Shustar is so unsafe, that he cannot guarantee our safety, but he may at the last moment recall his promise. And we are still without a servant, except a little man who takes the camels out to graze in the morning, and brings them home at night. This little man says he will go with us, but I doubt his doing so when the moment comes ; so many people have offered their services and then backed out, amongst them the so-called "Sheykh" Mohammed, our acquaintance of the mill and not a sheykh at all, only a zellem of Chaab extraction, and a householder of Shustar. But we do not like him, nor any of the candidates, except two soldiers, and these we cannot have, as they belong to the small garrison of the kalat, and the governor refuses to give them leave.

The governor has been very suspicious of us, and thrown all the obstacles he could in our way. He came yesterday, fortunately not till Wilfrid was better and able to receive him, and was evidently indisposed to further our wishes. His manner, though extremely polite, showed that he was determined we should go to Ahwas, not Bebahan. He strongly urged us to give up all notion of taking the Bebahan road ; the country was unsafe ; no escort short of a thousand men would suffice to get us through, and that number he had not at his disposal ; and besides, we should be wanting in respect to the Shahzade if we did not go aud present our letter to him ; we were really bound to go to Ahwas, where we should find him. As to a letter from the English balioz (consul) at Bussora, no such communication had been received ; and he the wakil, knew nothing about us. He could only repeat that he would do nothing for us except forward us to Ahwas. He positively refused an escort for any other object.

Things were in this position when the wakil left, and we were at our wits' end, when fortunately, a young gentleman called who belongs to the telegraph office, Mirza Ali Mohammed, of Shiraz, " captain of telegraphs," who talks a little Arabic, and a little French. It then occurred to Wilfrid to telegraph to the Legation at Teheran, requesting that the government there should be asked to order the wakil of Shustar to give us an escort to Bebahan. The captain of telegraphs carried off this message, which he had written and translated into Persian for us, and the money for its transmission ; but this morning he returned the money, with news that the telegram could not be sent. The fact is he dared not send it without informing his superior, who declined to let it go. But it has had its effect. The governor has no pretext now for doubting our respectability, for suspicious characters would not want to communicate with the central government at Teheran. So instead of a thousand, we are to have an escort of six men and a sergeant to accompany us to Bebahan. It has been unwillingly granted, and I shall not be surprised if it should even yet be withdrawn.

Later.—There seems to have been a storm somewhere; the air is clear, and we hope for less oppressive weather. But the foretaste of heat we have had, is a warning. We have talked over our plans, and agreed to give up all idea of pushing on to Bender Abbas, and to be satisfied with reaching Bushire. There can be no difficulty in finding Captain Cameron, for he will be obliged to pass between Bebahan and the sea, but we must make haste or he will have crossed our line before we can get to the coast. His intention was to keep as near to the coast as possible, so that we ought to meet him near or at Bender Dilam.

Three or four respectable merchants of Shustar have waited upon us this evening, and given us much friendly advice about the dangers of travel in which we do not much believe. They shook their heads when Wilfrid remarked, that surely under the administration of the Shahzade and his excellent

wakil, the country must be safe, and assured us
that the wakil was perfectly justified in dissuading
us from our undertaking. It would be much safer
to go to Ahwas. Another, Hajji Abdallah, had with
him a letter in English from an English firm at
Bushire, which he begged us to translate. It was
far from complimentary, and we had some difficulty
in disguising it under a form of Arabic politeness.
He, too, was loud in his dissuasion of our journey.

Our visitors shewed no sign of going away, and I
believe they would have sat on all through the
night talking, had we not dismissed them. Hajji
Abdallah's last words were an entreaty to recon-
sider our decision, and abandon the foolish plan of
going to Bebahan. He has once been that way he
says, and would not for the world go again; there
are not only dangerous wild tribes, but mountain
passes and impassable rocks. We listened un-
moved, and in fact we had no choice.

SHAGRAN.

CHAPTER V.

" Solitudinem faciunt, pacem appellant."
TACITUS.

Illness and misery—A Persian escort—The Shah's Arab subjects—
Ram Hormuz and its nightingales—Night marching—Deserted villages—How they collect taxes in Persia—Bebahan.

Friday, April 11.—It would be easy to quote
unlucky starts on Fridays, and I am afraid this is
one. Wilfrid is ill again, a passing fatigue we hope,
from loading the camels this morning in the hot
sun, and riding all day long in it. He is lying
down now in the tent and trying to rest, but the
flies are intolerable.

Our plan in leaving Shustar was to go with our
escort, seven soldiers on foot, armed six with
matchlocks and one with a narghileh, to Ram
Hormuz, a small town eighty miles on the road to
Bebahan, and there get a reinforcement from the
Ferraz-bashi or deputy governor of the place for
the other eighty miles. This sounded well enough,
but already our escort has deserted us, and we are
alone.

After delays of all sorts, for till the moment of
starting we were still without servants, we got our
camels loaded, and about ten o'clock rode out of the

palace gate and through the streets of Shustar, and
over a stone bridge, which spans the second of the
two branches of the river on which the town stands,
and into the open country beyond. It was terribly
hot, and the whole country is a plague of flies, which
buzz about one all day long, and settle on one's
head at night.

Our camels have profited by the mallows in the
court of the palace to such an extent that they are
all fat and frisky, and we had some trouble in
loading them. But, at the last moment, we had an
unexpected offer of assistance. A young Arab,
dressed in a green calico jíbbeh, suddenly appeared
upon the scene, and volunteered his services. He
had a pleasant face, so that we were taken with
him at once. He told us that he was a native of
some village on the Tigris near Bagdad, and that
he had been impressed by the Turks for their navy,
in which he had served three years, that he had
then managed to desert while in port at Bussorah,
and had fled across the border to Mohamrah. He
had since earned his bread by working as horse-
keeper for one of the Bawiyeh sheykhs, and later,
tiring of that, in service with different Persians at
Shustar. His idea now, was to get down to the sea
once more, and he begged us to take him with us
to Bushire. By accident Hajji Mohammed knew
something of some of his relations at Bagdad, and as
such a person was exactly what we most wanted, we
accepted him at once, on his own terms. This young

fellow's coming has been an advantage to us in more ways than one, for it had the immediate effect of inducing another of the crowd who were witnessing our departure to volunteer, and a little red-haired Persian in blue frock and trowsers, came forward to enlist in our service. Thus we are no longer wholly dependent on our old cavass and on ourselves.

As soon as we were outside the town, our sergeant and the six soldiers began to give themselves airs of military importance, advancing in front of us in skirmishing order, and enjoining us to keep close together, although the country had a quite peaceable appearance, the road much frequented by country people on donkeys, unarmed and peaceable folks. The track led through undulating ground chiefly barren, here and there a patch of cultivation, often between high banks. Our brave defenders here shewed their zeal by running up to the tops of the steepest and highest of these banks, firing off their guns at random, generally in the air, but one of the shots hit a lizard sitting in its hole. Their energy, however, cooled as the heat increased ; and towards noon, they were satisfied to trudge along with only an occasional diversion to look out for enemies. By a quarter to one o'clock, they all seemed tired, and we too were glad to halt for three quarters of an hour, under a large shady canora tree, in the midst of a field of oats. Here we ate our luncheon, while the animals fed on the oats. Wil-

frid complained a little of the sun, but it was not
till we had gone on again for a couple of hours that
he acknowledged he felt really ill. We were just
turning off the track to the north, to go to the tents
of a certain Hassan Khan, known to the soldiers,
when he said he could have gone no further. The
tents were not a mile from the road, but getting
there was almost too much for him. We found
them set in a circular enclosure, fenced in by a
hedge of branches, like a new made Sussex fence,
and evidently intended to last longer than a true
Bedouin camp ever does. Here there are about a
dozen small tents, half hair, half matting. Outside
the enclosure, a few mares and foals grazing, among
them one rather nice filly, Wadneh Hursan they say,
and animals of all sorts, cows, sheep, and goats
have been brought inside the hedge for the night.

Wilfrid is extremely tired. The rest seems to
have done him no good. He complains of his head
and of pains all over. I hope fatigue and the heat
are sufficient to account for his feeling ill. I dread
a return of the attack he had at Shustar. I wish
we had not left the town. This is a forlorn spot to
be ill in, and though at Shustar we should be no
better off, as far as concerns getting out of the
country, there would be a few more comforts, and a
chance of sending for help to Bussora. If he gets
worse we shall be in an almost hopeless position.
Every place seems frightfully far off the moment
there is a difficulty about moving ; to get back to

Shustar would be almost as impracticable as to go on to Ram Hormuz. Seven hours' travelling seems now an impassable gulf. I have arranged a sort of mosquito net for Wilfrid against the flies, but it only keeps them out for a time, and then a few manage to get inside it, and it has all to be re-arranged. But now it is nearly sundown, and the flies will go to sleep at dark ; and if the night is cool he may get some sleep.

Everybody here is fortunately kind. Hassan Khan, the chief, is away at Shustar, but his brother Kambar Aga received us well. He has good manners, speaks Arabic pretty fairly, and has been telling me about his tribe, a section of the Bawiyeh of Ajjem, as distinguished from the Bawiyeh of the Ottoman dominions. The people and their chief seem to be very poor. Kambar professes himself ready to accompany us to-morrow to another camp not far off, and on our line of march, that of Hajji Salman, an Arabic-speaking tribe ; this is fortunate, as our escort has deserted. They probably never meant to come further than this, but however that may be, they have in fact abandoned us and gone home to Shustar. In the middle of the day, while we were sitting under the canora tree, they demanded money, and Hajji Mohammed foolishly, without asking us, gave them as much as they ought to have had for the whole journey to Ram Hormuz, and as a consequence, having secured their pay, and with no further motive for taking trouble they departed. Their

company is no loss, they were disagreeable and tiresome, but they were of value as a mark of government protection, and in that respect it is unfortunate
that they have left us.

Escort or no escort I care not, if only Wilfrid
would get better, and he seems no better.

Saturday evening, April 12.—Wilfrid alarmingly
ill all night. He got rapidly worse, and then
seemed unconscious of all around; it seemed hopeless, but now he has rallied, and I think the worst
is over. Still I have made up my mind not to look
beyond the necessity of the moment, and indeed
these twenty-four hours blot out past and future.
I don't know why I write a journal. He cannot sit
up yet, though he says he shall be able to travel
to-night. I don't know what to think, but the
wish to move is something gained; a short time
ago he could hardly speak, and if he really has
turned the corner, a few hours may make a great
difference. He now says that by travelling at night
only, he shall be able to go on.

Ghada, our new Arab, has behaved very well. I
hardly know what I should have done without
him to keep the fire up all night, and help to
make medicines and beef-tea. In the evening and
night I tried everything I could think of out of our
small stock of medicines, and in vain. The sun rose
and blazed fiercely, and the flies swarmed as before.
But in the afternoon the illness took another turn,
and now, at any rate, the danger seems to be past

To please Wilfrid, though I doubt his being able to travel, I have packed up everything and got the tents down, and each separate load put ready ; for to carry out the plan of night-travelling, we must load after dark, that is, by the light of a very small moon, when it rises about one o'clock. We are then to be off, Wilfrid to ride his delúl, and we are to get as far as we can ; I have got cold tea and beef-tea in bottles, to be accessible at any moment. He has remained lying down on his rugs and pillow, the only things not yet packed, which, when the time comes, will be put on his delúl.

Kambar Aga and his tribe are good people. Nothing could be kinder than they have been. Hassan Khan has sent a third brother from Shustar, Aga Ibrahim, who is to accompany us with six of his men to Hajji Salman's camp.

April 13.—Wilfrid was able to travel for four hours, and though much exhausted seems really none the worse. We reached the Salamat camp about six this morning. We hope to set out presently—about sunset.

The moon rose last night towards one o'clock, but owing to the slowness of everybody the loading took more than an hour. They all wanted to wait till the moon should be high in the sky before starting. We first struck across the plain of pasture and scrub to get back to the track, and then pursued our way along it eastwards. At half-past

five we saw some tents to the south, but these our
guides said were the wrong ones. An hour later
met two zellems, who told us the contrary, but too
late for us to return ; and they added that they
came from a camp of Salamat Arabs an hour or so
further east. It was already hot, but we pushed
on, the road good and level, splendid pasture, hills
to the left, an interminable plain in front and to
the right, extending to the Karkaría and beyond it.
Some tents were pointed out to us, said to be on
the opposite bank of the river. We reached the
Salamat camp, Sheykh Abeyeh, at eight o'clock.

A few fairly good-looking but very small mares
are to be seen. The camp has been evidently on
the spot for weeks, and is accordingly unsavoury,
more like a village than a camp.

We have, or rather had, for I write while waiting
to start, our tent on a small tell separated by a dip
in the ground from the Salamat encampment.
The ground here is covered with a horrid little
spiked grass, like miniature barley to look at,
which pricks through everything. Its barbed thorns
are like fish-hooks, very difficult to extract, and all
our clothes and bedding are full of them.

Wilfrid spent the day lying down in the tent,
able to talk though tired. The people here are not
ill-bred, and they have even been kind to us.
Their Sheykh, Abeyeh, with several of his friends,
and relations, came to see us soon after our arrival.
Abeyeh told us that his tribe belongs to the Ahl es-

Shimal, and he knows all about the tribes of the Hamád and their horses. His brother Rashid showed us a very beautiful grey colt, which he offered to exchange for our hamra mare, who is suffering from a sore back. The colt is too young, or might have been worth taking ; the owner says he would not part with it but that the Shahzade has intimated an intention of buying it. The Shahzade is, it seems, in the habit of purchasing all the good-looking horses he hears of, and does not pay for them, but he does not take mares ; this, at least, is the tale told to us. Our mare, though thoroughbred, is in such wretched condition that the Shahzade would hardly care to seize her.

Abeyeh readily agreed to escort us to Ram Hormuz with six khayal, Rashid proposed to accompany us on foot as camel driver, and Aga Ibrahim (from Hassan Khan's), also offers to go on. It is five o'clock, time to pack. * * * Eight o'clock. Wilfrid felt so ill an hour ago that all these arrangements seemed to be vain. But he is better, and now we are off.

April 14.—Our new plan of travelling by night seems to answer well. Wilfrid was able to go on from nine till five o'clock. He is recovering, though reduced to the extreme of thinness. The heat during the day is insufferable, and even if there had been no cause of anxiety, we could hardly have continued marching by day. The flies are intolerable, they follow us, and are found every-

where; at night when we are riding they are sitting
in swarms upon our heads, and if driven off, perch
again in spite of darkness. However, in the dark
they are quiet unless disturbed, which is some small
relief. Last night our track went a good deal up
and down, crossing small ravines and watercourses,
and pools and ditches full of water. Sometimes we
waded through tall grass, splendid stuff, growing
quite wild and uncared for. The moon serves
us hardly at all, but we could see dimly by starlight.
The constellation of the Scorpion is now our guide,
rising as it does in the south-east. I have slept little
lately, and once last night I fell fast asleep on
horseback, and woke with a start at a sound of
munching. It was my mare grazing eagerly
knee-deep in wild oats. Where the camels were I
could not see, but heard them soon afterwards some
way off ahead. Wilfrid bore up as long as he could,
till at five o'clock he said he could not go a yard
further, and we camped for the day, pitching the
tent on a tell commanding all surrounding tells. Our
escort objected to this halt. "The Shirazi will
come down from those hills and rob us," said
Abeyeh, "and the town of Ram Hormuz is only
three or four hours further. Let us go on." His
objection was natural; this is very exposed ground,
and close to us on the north rises a range of crags,
from which the Shirazi robbers may be watching us.
But perched on the tell we get a little air, and this
is worth some risk. Besides, they have not come

yet, and we shall be gone presently. Abeyeh argued in vain ; if there had been legions of robbers in sight, I don't think Wilfrid would have moved. He was indeed unfit to stir, and has been lying on the ground under the shade of the tent ever since. A halt like this is not much of a rest ; the heat is too overpowering, the flies too troublesome. Beyond the rocky range we see high snow peaks, very tantalising in this furnace, and looking the other way, there is just below us a fine piece of meadow land on the banks of a running stream. In all the hollows there is rich pasture. Abeyeh and his men have kept a good look-out, some posted about on heights, and the rest watching the mares hobbled, and turned loose to graze.

It is four o'clock ; the heat lessening, and Wilfrid says he is ready to go on. We must pack. * *

April 15.—We have at last reached Ram Hormuz, or as it is pronounced " Ramuz." We left our bivouac on the tell at five o'clock yesterday afternoon. Wilfrid tried riding on horseback, but found the effort too great, and had to give it up and mount his delúl. Our way lay through more long grass, and ditches, and water. I, as sleepy as the night before, was constantly dozing off and waking suddenly in the middle of some long dream, unable to remember where I was. There is nothing so painful as this struggle with sleep, and it lasted all night long. At last we came suddenly in sight of some camp fires about half a mile away to our right,

and Abeyeh, fearing to advance further, ordered
a halt. There was danger, he said, in coming on an
encampment unawares, lest we should be taken for
enemies. We did not stop to argue, but with
delight obeyed, and in a few minutes were sound
asleep upon the ground—nor did we wake till day
was already breaking.

A discussion now arose what further was to
be done. The tents, we were informed, belonged to
the Khamîs, an Arab tribe, half Bedouin, half
fellah, and Abeyeh was for spending the day
with them. But the sound sleep had done Wilfrid
good, and as it grew light we could see the palm
groves of Ram Hormuz, apparently ten miles off, and
we knew that there we should get refuge from the
sun. So leaving the rest to follow or not as they
would—we got on our horses and started at a gallop,
Shiekha and Sayad bounding on in front of us
delighted at this unexpected run. At first there
was no road, and we got entangled in a series
of watercourses, but scrambling through these we
reached a footpath where the going was good, and
presently overtook a party of Arabs, men and women,
riding in on donkeys to market at the town. They
all expressed themselves much pleased to see us, taking
us to be Arabs like themselves, and here in Persia
they always seem delighted to meet their countrymen. They pointed us out the town, for there was
more than one grove of palms, and in the mirage
which hid everything as the sun rose, we had lost

sight of it. At half-past six we stopped at the ferraz-bashi's door, and in another minute were sitting in a cool court-yard under the shade of a wall, waiting till the respectable functionary, our host, had finished his devotions.

On the sight of our letters from the governor of Shustar he made us very welcome—conversing through the medium of his secretary, who knows Arabic. Carpets were brought, and tea made—the most delicious draught we ever tasted in our lives —flavoured with orange and some acid fruit. The gallop has cured Wilfrid, and he says he shall not be ill again.

Our caravan having arrived, we have moved outside the town, for the ferraz-bashi's house is not big enough to hold us all, and are encamped on a little mound overlooking the gardens which skirt Ram Hormuz. I wish I could describe the beauty of this place. Round us lie a few acres of green wheat, in which quails and francolins are calling, and through which a little stream of running water winds. Close by, on another mound, stands a beautiful little kubbr, the tomb of some saint, and on either side gardens half run wild, a delicious tangle of pomegranate, fig, and vine, with here and there lemon and peach, and groups of palm. The pomegranates now are in full flower, and so are the roses, and every thicket is alive with nightingales. It is nearly sunset, and groups of blue-gowned Persians are coming across the fields from the town,

to wash and say their prayers at the stream and the
kubbr.   The town itself is half hidden in the
gardens, but shows picturesquely through, backed
by a range of crimson hills, scored and lined with
blue shadows.   We have been following the edge of
these hills all the way from Shustar.   They are the
same which are supposed to hold the Shirazi robbers
our Arab escort feared so much.

The position of the Arabs here is a miserable
one.   At war with these Shirazi, and pillaged by
the Government which does nothing to protect
them, they still cling to their little bits of cultivation wherever there is water near the hills.   They
are half the year nomadic, going south and west
with the flocks, but in the spring return to the
hills, plough up a few acres, and gather in a crop if
possible before the tax-gatherer has found them
out.   The Persian Government is weak, and the
garrison of Ram Hormuz is generally only sufficient
for its duty of holding the town, but every now
and then a reinforcement arrives from Ahwas or
Fellahieh and then a raid is made under pretext
of a collection of arrears, and horses and cattle are
driven off in payment.   This seems to be the plan
throughout the province.   We asked Abeyeh and
the Khamîs Sheykh who came with him to-day to
our camp, why they put themselves into this
government trap by coming to the hills, when they
might remain unmolested in the plain, or go where
they would.   " It is the soil," they exclaimed,

"the soil which is so rich. Where should we find another like it?" Indeed, the whole of this side of Persia seems meant to be a garden. Unlike the plains of Bagdad, which never can have been cultivated except with irrigation, the land here grows crops as in Europe, watered by the rain from heaven. The range of Bactiari hills by attracting clouds gives it this rare advantage.

Ram Hormuz itself must have been a great city once. Its position at a point where several rivers meet, and at the foot of a gorge, leading through the mountains to Shiraz, makes it naturally a place of importance, but it is little more now than a market for the Bedouin tribes and a military station.

The ferraz-bashi has been very amiable to us, though, like everyone else, averse to our further progress in the direction of Bebahan. The road, he says, is most unsafe, every village at war with its neighbour, and he dares not send troops with us even if he had them. There is, however, in the town, a certain potentate of the district first to be traversed, one Mohammed Jafar, Khan of the village of Sultanabad, who can protect us if any one can. To him we are to be recommended, and perhaps he will go on with us to-morrow. Abeyeh and his men, alas, can go no further. They are Arabs, and honest men, and camel drivers, and we have bid them good-bye with regret. But the people further on are Persian, and Persian and

Arabian are everywhere at odds. The idea is not agreeable of plunging into a hornet's nest, such as the country beyond us is described to be, but there is no help for it ; to return is impossible. Every day becomes more and more fearfully hot, and our only hope now is the sea.

April 16.—We are refreshed by a good night's rest, such as we have not had since leaving Shustar. The ferraz-bashi called again this morning, walking out in the cool of sunrise, with a rose in his hand, to pay us his compliment. It seems to be the fashion among the Persians to go about with flowers, which they present to each other as polite offerings, and just now it is the season of roses. His Excellency informed us that Kaïd Mohammed Jafar would be ready to start for Sultanabad at the asr (about half past three), so we have made all our preparations for departure. Although the heat has been great, 96° at coolest, I have managed to make a sketch of Ram Hormuz, but nothing can do justice to its beauty. We have been more pleasantly received here, than anywhere else in Persia, and I feel sure we might make friends with the people if only we could speak their language. Travelling without knowing the language, is like walking with one's eyes shut.

April 17.—Mohammed Jafar arrived soon after four, and immediately we started. It was of importance that no time should be lost, for we had a river to cross, the Jerrahi which comes down here from the mountains, and runs into the Persian Gulf, at Fellahieh. The country, till we came to it, was a difficult one for camels, being a very network of irrigation, with the channels crossed by treacherous little bridges. But the camels managed it all without accident. The river, of which we crossed two branches, flows over a bed of gravel, and was nowhere over our horses' girths. The water very cold, with melted snow, so that a delicious breeze of iced air followed the current. It was now past sundown, and we were anxious to be clear of the inclosed ground, before it should be absolutely night; but the Kaïd, tiresome man, had made an arrangement with some friends at a little village beyond the river to dine with them, and then go on in the night, a plan which did not at all suit us. Indeed it was impossible for us, with our camels, to halt in such a spot, where we could not have prevented them trampling the standing corn, and where we should have been helpless after dark. So declining, as politely as we could, the hospitality offered, we left the Kaïd to take his meal with his four horsemen, and pushed on alone. A villager was sent to show us the way, for we were not a mile from open ground, and night was falling and every minute precious, and we were resolved to reach it if we could. Road, however, it soon appeared there was none, for to reach the village, the Kaïd had taken us away from the main path, and as it grew darker we got more and more

entangled, in dykes and ditches. At one moment
things seemed almost hopeless with us, a deep canal
barring all further progress, and the villager who
had brought us to this pass, profiting by the
confusion, having run away. Fortunately Wilfrid
perceived this flight in time, and riding after him
fired his pistol in the air, and brought him back,
when, under the compulsion of fear, he showed us
where to cross. It was a poor ford, and some of
the loads got wet, but beyond it we were. on hard
ground, and able now to wait in patience till the
Kaïd and his men should come. Our shot seemed
to have disturbed their feast, and we had not long
to wait. Then we marched on in silence and utter
darkness, but over a good road, till half-past one in
this morning, when a loud barking of dogs
announced our arrival at Sultanabad.

Here the Kaïd has a house to which he at once
retired, leaving us to lie down in our cloaks, with
our camels and horses, till daylight. He would
willingly have invited us in, but we dare not leave
our beasts and property, and now we have pitched
our tent for the day, looping it up as usual, like an
umbrella, to get every breath of air. When day
dawned, we saw the Kaïd's house on one side of us,
with three big canora trees overshadowing its
entrance, and a walled garden at the back of it ; on
the other side the village with its barley fields and
splendid grass crops. The houses of the village,
built of sun-dried brick, are in a cluster together.

about two hundred yards from our mound ; in front of them two or three black tents. The Kaïd's house is of considerable size, and appears to contain several court-yards. Sultanabad is itself a poor, mean-looking place, but if Hajji Mohammed is to be believed, a very nest of brigands, any one of whom for one single kran would kill a man, a real stronghold of robbers, and as such keeping the neighbouring country in terror. But I don't know what to think, for Hajji Mohammed believes every tale he hears, and the horsemen have been cramming him all the way along with stories of Mohammed Jafar's exploits, to enhance their chief's importance. How he does what he likes in the teeth of the government, who dare not punish him for having killed several of the Shahzade's people only a couple of years ago, how only he and his Sultanabadis can travel safely on the Bebahan road; and one can hardly blame poor Hajji Mohammed for expecting us to lead him into mischief, for we have before done so, and he thinks us reckless of danger. He is always lecturing us on prudence, though he himself is an odd combination of caution and rashness ; he once at a critical moment wanted to stuff his revolver into an inaccessible bag, merely because the strap of the belt belonging to it was broken ; another time he would have given his gun to a stranger to carry, had we not prevented his doing so. We spent this morning drinking tea and eating eggs and butter and a kid, and spreading wet things to dry. Fortunately no serious damage has been done, and the fierce sun soon dried everything. A breeze sprang up, too, which helped the drying, and drove away the flies.

Hajji Mohammed was commissioned in the course of the morning to negociate terms with the Kaïd, who had been already sounding the cavass as to how much money could be got from us. He has really done it very well, and arranged that at Bebahan we are to pay the Kaïd one hundred krans. The great man at first asked for an abba or a cashmere shawl, but here Hajji Mohammed seems to have spoken with proper firmness.

We want to start at half-past four, and ought to pack now, but the servants are dawdling over the remains of the kid; they will not move till they have devoured the last morsel. Besides, they have got several girths to mend before we can load.

April 18.—We had a great deal of trouble to start at all yesterday afternoon, and after a difficult march we have got no farther than the village of Jazûn, about fifteen miles, which was reached at five A.M. this morning. At this rate we shall be a month getting to Bebahan, especially if the pass over the range of rocky hills we must cross, is as rugged as report says.

It turned out that the Kaïd himself did not intend to start with us, but to send his nephew with four people on foot, and follow himself with the four horsemen. He stood by as we loaded, and

then wished us good evening. When all was ready
he asked us the favour to take with us a bundle of
brown wool for Bebahan, and as it was not heavy
we agreed. While Wilfrid turned to look at this
package, a villager took the rifle off his delúl, but
hastily put it back on Wilfrid's shouting "Stop
thief," and ran off accompanied by the little crowd
which had gathered round us, no doubt equally
guilty at heart, and expecting blows. Then we
started—it was about half-past five, a fine evening
with a breeze, which, alas, died away at sunset,
after which for two hours the air was extremely
sultry. The Sultanabad field crops had to be
crossed, but they were on dry land, with only a few
easy ditches. Then we came to ground like a
park, formerly cultivated, but now abandoned to
nature; canora trees dotted about like handsome
hawthorn trees, as if planted for ornament, the
grass all crops run wild, splendid oats and barley
now in the ear. Here and there an abandoned
village, the walls gleaming red in the setting sun.
Some of these were inhabited not very long since,
and we were told various tales regarding them;
from one place the inhabitants had gone away of
their own accord quite lately to escape the tax-
gatherer's next visit, leaving their corn standing;
from another they had been driven by fire and
sword, the soldiers burning the village after
sacking it.

After about two hours we crossed the river Abn'l

Faris; it is not many yards wide nor is it deep, but the banks are steep and overgrown with trees and thick bushes. A narrow and nearly perpendicular path leads down to the ford. The camels have become skilful, and managed the scramble admirably; Shakran now carries our personal baggage, he has completely recovered, and is the cleverest of them all. Hajji Mohammed sat imperturbable on Wilfrid's delúl, and nearly got his head caught in the tangle of branches. After this we had another water or two to cross in the dark, the approaches to which were always announced by the croaking of frogs; then the chirping of grasshoppers replaced the croaking, and we were again on hard ground, the country a good deal up and down and broken up into ravines and fissures caused by rains. At ten o'clock, as far as we could make out by starlight, we were on good flat pasture land, real pasture not crops, and trees growing in groups as in a park, with a low ridge on the left. Here we halted for an hour to eat, and thought to have a nap; but Mohammed Jafar, who after all joined us some time before, would not hear of this. It would be dangerous; the Shirazi would swoop down from those hills to the north. He altogether declined remaining longer than necessary, and there was an earnestness in his manner that brought conviction with it; he really believed in the danger he talked of. The night was fine, and it would have been a pity not to make use of it; we pushed on over good

ground for an hour, and after that through mud,
ditches, and frogs; about one o'clock a wide ditch
completely barred further progress. We had for a
good while been again among crops, so rank that
wading through them was hard work, and on
reaching this ditch, we all groped about, trying to
find a passage for the camels. There was no sort of
track; the horsemen had, in fact, got off the road
and could not find it again, but there was no
difficulty as to general direction, the Scorpion being
our guide. Here, however, we were stuck fast by
irrigation works, for at this particular spot the ditch
was impracticable for camels, and all efforts in the
dark to hit upon a ford were vain. The horsemen
had already got across, and were shouting to us to
follow; indeed, they had for the last hour guided us
in a hap-hazard way by shouts and singing. One of
them sang remarkably well, and kept up a sort of
refrain:

But now they screamed, shouted, and sang to no
purpose. We refused to waste any more time
in a useless search, and sat down to wait for
daylight. One of the khayal then returned and sat
with us till four A.M. talking all the while to Hajji
Mohammed about the Shirazi. We lay down and
went to sleep. By half-past four we had found a

passage through the mud and water of the canal,
and beyond it got on to desert ground, on which
we passed several small detached oasis-like palm
gardens.   Half an hour's march further took us to
Jazûn.

Jazûn is the only village left of many which once
existed between Sultanabad and Bebahan, and whose
ruins we have passed.   They were deserted only a few
years ago; the governors of the province, who found
it impossible to collect taxes from them, having
solved the difficulty by destroying them.   This
village is now a collection of little mud houses on
the left bank of a natural stream of running water.
It is surrounded by fields and groups of palm trees.
Our horses are tethered out by long ropes fastened
to palm trees, to feed on green barley; the camels
are further off with Shafi.   Shafi is an excellent
worker, but he does not speak a word of Arabic,
or I should tell him how well satisfied we are with
him.   We ourselves have encamped on the high
bank backed by the stream, so that the villagers,
who are a tiresome set of people, can only
approach us on one side.

Jazûn as well as Sultanabad, belongs to the family
of Mohammed Jafar.   He has been sitting here
talking to us through Hajji Mohammed.   He tells
us that his family, although they now no longer
talk Arabic, are of the Safeyeh tribe, and came
originally from Nejd, bringing their horses with
them ; and that a beautiful little white mare his

nephew rides, and which we admired yesterday
evening, is a Hamdanyeh Simri.   This mare is very
small, 13.2 at most, but almost perfect; the head
very fine with black nose, black round the eyes as
if painted, *jebha* prominent, and *mitbakh* extremely fine; tail properly set on and carried, a good
style of going, bones rather small, but legs apparently wiry and strong.   One of the men rides a
chestnut mare said to be Kehileh Sheykhah, about
14 hands, with four white feet, handsome head, and
mitbakh.   Mohammed Jafar mentioned that the
particular breeds now possessed by his tribe are
Hamdani Simri, Abeyan, Hadban, Wadnan, Me-
leyhan, Seglawi and Kehîlan.   His own grey mare
does not look thoroughbred, and he did not say
anything about her.   Mohammed Jafar now informed us that his nephew would proceed to Bebahan with us while he himself must go home, and he
wished to have the whole sum of one hundred
krans paid to him at once.   After some talk he
agreed to take seventy krans as his share, the rest
to be given to his nephew at the end of the
journey.   He certainly gets the lion's share, but
beggars cannot be choosers, and we are dependent
on his goodwill to pass us through this part of the
country, so that on the whole we ought to be glad
that he has not asked more.   We are altogether in
a false position, too weak to insist upon our own
terms, and our best plan is to march as fast as we
can to Bebahan.   Unfortunately there are not only

crags to cross, but the Kurdistan river has to be forded.

April 19.—A disagreeable twenty-four hours has passed, and we have scaled the crags, and escaped from the Jazûn people, who, it seems, had some evil design. But there is still the Kurdistan river between us and Bebahan.

We managed to set out from Jazûn soon after two o'clock in the afternoon, getting at once off the plain on to broken ground, which became more and more broken till at seven o'clock, when we halted, we were involved in a confused mass of hills apparently tossed together at random. We had crossed several small streams in deep ravines, and one narrow ledge of rock at the head of a ravine, which would have been unpleasant in the dark. Saw three or four gazelles, luckily not perceived by the greyhounds, for we cannot stop for sport. Sand-grouse, beebirds, plovers, and doves abounded. By seven o'clock we had done about ten miles and ascended over 600 feet, and Wilfrid proposed to halt for some hours. I was pleased, not liking passes and steeps in the dark, and we still had the pass itself before us, but Abdallah Khan, the Kaid's nephew, remonstrated and protested danger. Wilfrid, however, gave a peremptory order to unload the camels and we sat down to drink tea and make a frugal meal, and proposed afterwards to make aliek for the camels, as they have had a tiring march and cannot feed now in the night,

Before we had done eating Hajji Mohammed came to announce that forty Jazunis were following to attack and plunder us. Shafi, he said, had found this out, and told him, and he added that the welled Abdallah Khan had also been told of the plot and warned by the villagers not to stay with us. He called the youth, who confirmed the tale, as did all the others, the four men on foot who had come all the way with Abdallah. It seems probable that an attack really was contemplated, for Shafi could gain nothing by inventing such a story. But, as Wilfrid suggested, it may have been only a way of " expressing the polite feelings of the inhabitants of Jazûn." He however agreed that we ought to be on the watch and start as soon as possible—at this moment it was really impossible. Guns and revolvers were placed ready and sentinels posted, and Abdallah earnestly assured us he would stand by us. I think he would, he had been a much better guide than his uncle and was besides always ready to help and to wait for the camels at difficult places. After all this agitation, nothing happened except one or two false alarms, and I don't think I ever slept a sweeter sleep than between nine and two o'clock this night—no musquitoes and no flies.

It took us more than an hour to load in the dark, and we were not off till past three o'clock ; at first feeling our way in single file, led by Abdallah, along a very broken and steep road. For part of the way

we had a little assistance from a red crescent moon.
At a quarter to six, we had gained the highest point
of the ridge, between 1600 and 1700 feet above the
sea, making about 900 feet ascent from Jazun. Here
there was at last an open view, down towards the
Kurdistan river, with the palm village of Kaïkus
plainly visible, and other palm villages beyond the
river, and still further something vague, said to be
Bebahan.

A gradual descent brought us on to a strip of
plain, swarming with cuckoos, beebirds, doves, francolins, and sandgrouse, and dotted with canora
trees, singly or in clumps, here and there fields
of corn.

The sight of a mound commanding air, if air there
should be, decided us to halt, and here we now are,
waiting for the decline of day to set out again and
ford the river. This plain by the river is hardly
more than three hundred feet below the top of the
pass we came over this morning.

Sunday, April 20.—Bebahan has been reached
at last. Our final march, though not a long one,
took us till towards midnight to accomplish, for we
had the Kurdistan river to cross. This was the
deepest of any we had forded, and there was a long
delay in choosing a safe place; and then the water
was up to our saddle bows, and running almost like
a mill race. But the camels are now so used to
water in every form from mud to torrents, that all
marched bravely through, a portion only of the

luggage getting wet. Unfitted though the country
has been in many ways for camels, we may nevertheless congratulate ourselves with the thought that
with no other beasts of burden could we have got
our luggage across the rivers at all. Loaded mules
must have been swept away.

The Kurdistan forms the boundary on this side of
the cultivated plain of Bebahan. Beyond it, we
found ourselves travelling entirely between corn-
fields, and along a broad highway towards the
capital of Khusistan. When two hours from the
town we sent on Hajji Mohammed to announce us
to the governor, but the governor was already
asleep, and it was with some difficulty that we were
admitted by the guard within the gate ; nor was it
possible in the utter darkness of the night to choose
our ground within for camping. In the first open
place we stopped, and as we were, lay down and
slept (we care little now, how or where it is we lie,
the ground is always soft as a feather-bed). Then,
with the first light, we went on through the town
and stopped again in front of the Seraï. Here I
have been writing my journal and sketching the
picturesque old palace, with its tottering minarets
covered with storks' nests. " The Shahzade is still
sleeping," say the sentries, " and will not be
awakened."

CHAPTER VI.

"Last scene of all . . . . . .
A mere oblivion."—SHAKESPEARE.

A last rush through the sun—We arrive at Dilam on the Persian
Gulf—Politics of the Gulf—A journey "in extremis"—Bushire
—The End.

THE rest of our journey was little better than a
feverish dream of heat and flies. After a day spent
at Bebahan, where we were hospitably entertained
by the Shahzade, Ahtesham ed-Daulah, a Persian
nobleman of real good breeding, we recommenced
our weary march, thinking only now to get down
to Bushire alive.

The kind invitations of our host could not detain
us, nor the polite attentions of his wives, nor the
amiable visits of merchants, calendars, and other
idle persons, who thronged our lodgings from dawn
to dusk. The truth is Bebahan was like a furnace,
and we felt that it was more than our strength
would stand, to prolong our sufferings over another
week. The lowlands of Persia, bordering on the
Persian Gulf, are one of the most oven-like regions
of the world, and though Bebahan lies nearly 1400
feet above the sea, it shares the climate of the Gulf.

We had now, besides, nothing further to fear in the way of robbers or marauders, and prepared ourselves for a last desperate rush through the sun to Bushire. The distance was hardly more than a hundred and twenty miles, but between Bebahan and Dilam there lay a region of hills, worse, according to report, than any we had yet passed, and absolutely impassable for camels. Still we had good reason to feel confident in the climbing powers of our beasts, and could not think of leaving them behind. Accordingly the next day we started, our courage well screwed to the sticking point of endurance, and under escort of three of the Shah-zade's horsemen.

We set off at six in the afternoon, making the best of what daylight yet remained to get well started on our road. The difficulties are almost always greater close to the town, and once fairly on the beaten track, our camels would have no temptation to wander. From Bebahan to Dilam there are two considerable lines of ridges or hills—steps, as it were, and extremely precipitous ones, down to the sea coast. At first it was easy going for the camels, but presently, about an hour after dark, we found ourselves in broken ground, where, after stumbling on till half-past nine, we were brought to a dead halt by finding ourselves at the brink of a deep gulf, in which the road seemed to disappear. This made it necessary we should wait till daylight, and we lay down with our camels on the road, and slept soundly till the first streak of dawn at half-past four. Then we discovered we had left the road, though only a few yards, and that the fissure before us was a sufficient reason for the halt we had made. The chief formation of these hills is not rock but clay, which being entirely without vegetation except in favoured spots, is furrowed into ravines and fissures by the action of the rain, making the district impassable except along the beaten track. We had risen some hundred feet from Bebahan, and so had nearly reached the summit of the first pass, where to our joy we saw something far away which we knew by instinct must be the sea. This raised our spirits, and we began our descent at once.

The path was very precipitous, and looking down from the edge it looked impossible that a camel should get down the thousand feet of zigzag which one could see plainly to the bottom. In some places rocks jutted out of the soil, making awkward narrow passes, and in others there were drops of three feet and more. Our horses of course made no difficulty, but watching the camels was nervous work, knowing as we did how little could be done to help them. Still we did what we could, going in front and calling them "Hao-hao," according to Bedouin fashion, which they understand so well. They know us now and trust in us, and so came bravely on. Even the Mecca delúl and the Safra, the young and giddy ones, have learned sobriety.

Three hours exactly it took to get down, and without accident. Another hour brought us to Zeytun, a pretty village on the river Zorah, with palm gardens and a good patch of cultivated land. At the river we stopped, exhausted already by the sun and overcome by the sight of the cool running water. Here we lay frizzling till the afternoon.

At four we crossed the river, as broad but a little less deep than the Kurdistan (both have gravelly bottoms), and resumed our march. A last cup of the ice-cold water was indulged in, but it could not slake my thirst, which nothing now can cure, though as a rule we drink nothing till the evening. Our march was a repetition of last night's, a long stumble half asleep along a break-neck road ending as before in an "impasse," and the rest of the night spent on the ground. We are plagued now, especially in these night halts, where we cannot see to choose a bed, with the horrible little spiked grass. Every bit of clothing we have is full of these points. These and the flies make it impossible to sleep by day, and we are both very weary, Wilfrid almost a skeleton.

April 23.—At a quarter past three, we again went on, by the light of a false dawn, the Scorpion, still in front of us. We know exactly now the rising of these stars in the south-eastern sky. The ascent this time was longer and more gradual, and the descent shorter than the former one, but quite as difficult. This second ridge is considerably lower

than the first, and at the foot of it our path followed a sort of valley in which we found a few
pools of water. Then suddenly the gorge opened
and we found ourselves at eight o'clock in the
plain, with a village near us, and about eight miles
away Dilam and the sea, simmering like melted lead
to the horizon.

Eight miles, it sounds an easy march; but the
heat, which now on the sea coast is more insufferable than ever, stopped us half way, and again we
rigged up our tent on the plain, and lay under it
till evening. Then we rode into Dilam. Our first
question was for Captain Cameron, whose road
should here have joined our own; but no Frank or
stranger of any kind had passed that way.*

Dilam, like most maritime villages on the north-
eastern shore of the Persian Gulf, is inhabited by
people of Arab race, who have carried on a mixed
trade of commerce and piracy there from time immemorial. Of the two, the piracy seems to have been
the more profitable trade, for since its suppression
by the English or rather Indian navy, the villages
have languished. The Arab idea of piracy by
sea, is exactly the same as that of ghazús by land.
Any stranger not in alliance with the tribe, or
under its protection, is held to be an enemy, and

---

* Captain Cameron never started at all from Bagdad on the
expedition planned between us. Letters received, after we had left,
recalled him to India, and he went there by steamer down the
Tigris and Persian gulf.

his goods to be lawful prize. The greater part, however, of the armed expeditions, formerly made in the Gulf were directed by one tribe or village against another tribe or village, and were called in Arabic ghazús no less than if they had been made by land. The British Government, however, naturally found these ideas antiquated and the practice inconvenient, and in the interests of its commerce undertook, thirty or forty years ago, to keep the police of the Gulf. It compelled the Sheykhs of the various towns and villages to enter into what is called the Truce of the Gulf, and piracy has disappeared. Expeditions henceforth, if made at all, were to be made by land, and armed vessels, if met by an English cruiser, were confiscated. This sealed the fate of the coast villages, for the commerce of the Gulf alone being insufficient to support them, their inhabitants took up new quarters further inland, and from sailors became cultivators of the soil. The sea-port villages, where ports there are, still live on but poorly, and where there are no ports, the coast is abandoned. Dilam possesses no regular port, except for small boats, but the anchorage is good, and I believe the roadstead is considered one of the best in the Gulf. It has been talked of as the terminus of an Indo-Mediterranean railway.

Dilam now is a poor place of perhaps two hundred houses, but there are a few well-to-do people in it who presently came out to pay us their respects. The English name is well known on the coast, and there was no danger now of any lack of courtesy. We were besieged at once with hospitable offers of entertainment for man and beast, but as usual preferred our camp outside the town. This we placed on a strip of sand dunes fronting the sea, and dividing it from the level plain which runs inland ten miles to the foot of the hills. This strip was scattered over with thorn bushes, in one of which a pair of cormorants were sitting. Our visitors remonstrated with us on choosing such a spot, assuring us that it was full of poisonous snakes, but this no doubt was nonsense. Among the rest came a wild-looking man with a gun, who told us he was a Beluch, and sent by the governor of Dilam as a guard, to protect us during the night. He had been in Turkish service, and was now in the Persian. This was our first meeting with anything Indian. We liked the man. In the evening, when it was dark and all were gone, Wilfrid gave himself the luxury of bathing in salt water.

We had now done what few if any Europeans had done before,—come all the way by land from the Mediterranean to the Persian Gulf: our journey had been over two thousand miles.

April 24.—There was now a great debate whether we should go on still by land for the other hundred miles which remained to us before we could reach Bushire, or whether, selling our camels here at Dilam, we should hire a sefineh, or native boat, to convey us with our things by sea. Wilfrid

was much taken with this last idea, thinking that the
arrangement would save us from another week's
toil in the overwhelming heat; but to me the
sight of the rickety boats in which we should have
had to trust ourselves and our horses to the mercy
of the winds and waves, was sufficient to make me
rejoice that the negociation about a sea journey
failed. Then it was decided to march on as before.
There seemed something sad, too, in abandoning our
camels here, and taking to the ships of the sea
where they could not follow us; and though we
knew our parting from them was anyhow at hand,
it was a respite to take them on. We had got,
from our long care of them, to take great pride in
their condition, and they were now fat and free
from mange, a triumph of management which only
those who have travelled far and loved their camels
will understand.

On the afternoon of the 24th, having spent just
twenty-four hours at Dilam, we struck our tents,
and began our last march.

The country bordering the Persian Gulf is here
a dead flat, little, if anything, raised above the
level of the sea. It is very barren, and impreg-
nated for the most part with saltpetre, while here
and there broad tidal creeks intersect it, wherever
a stream runs into it from the hills. These formed
the only obstacle to our march, and we travelled
more easily now by night, for there began to be a
moon.

I hurry over these last days, indeed the heat and the march absorbed all our faculties and thought. Our plan was to start about three o'clock in the afternoon, when usually a light breeze sprang up from the south-east, and travel on till the moon set, or till some creek barred passage for the night; then sleep upon the ground till dawn, and on again till eight. By that hour the sun had become a fierce and importunate thing, beating as if with a weight upon our heads; and, choosing a place where there was some show of pasture, we unloaded and turned out our beasts to graze, and then rigged up the tent and lay gasping under it in the breathless air, supporting life with tea. Hajji Mohammed now was only capable of tea-making. In all things else he had become idiotic, sitting half back on his beast, or in the tent, ejaculating: " Allah kerim," God is generous. Our tempers all were severely tried, and we could do little now to help each other. Ghada and Rahim, Arab and Persian, were at daggers drawn. The horses' backs for the first time were getting sore, and the dogs were run nearly off the soles of their feet. Shiekha and Sayad in a course in which they killed a gazelle were injured, the former having cut her feet badly on the glazed edges of some dry cracked mud she had galloped over. Lastly, and this was a terrible grief, one of the camels being badly loaded had slipped its pack, and in the fall Rasham had been crushed. The falcon's leg was broken, and for the last three days of our journey, it seemed impossible he should live, clinging as he was obliged to do by one leg to the saddle. It was all like a night-mare, with no redeeming feature but that we knew now the end was close at hand.

On the 25th we reached Gunawa, on the 26th Bender Rik and on the 27th, Rohalla, where we crossed the river, and then marching on without halting through the night, we forded a shallow arm of the sea, and found ourselves the next morning about dawn upon the edge of the Khor, or salt lake of Bushire. As the sun rose Bushire itself was before us, and our long march was at an end.

It was now necessary to abandon our nomadic life, and shipping all our goods in a "baggara," and leaving the unloaded camels to be driven round at low tide to the neck of the Bushire peninsula, we put ourselves and our dogs and bird on board, and with a fresh breeze ran in two hours to the customhouse landing. There, taken for Arabs, we had long to wait, but in the end procuring porters, walked in procession through the streets to the Residency. When we arrived at the door of the Residency, the well-dressed Sepoys in their smart European uniforms, barred us the door with their muskets. They refused to believe that such vagabonds, blackened with the sun, and grimed with long sleeping on the ground, were English gentlefolks or honest people of any sort.

APPENDIX.

APPENDIX.

NOTES ON THE PHYSICAL GEOGRAPHY OF NORTHERN ARABIA.

ARABIA between latitude 34° and latitude 29°, may be described in general terms as a plain of sand-stone grit, or gravel, unbroken by any considerable range of hills, or by any continuous watercourse, if we except the Wady Hauran, which traverses it in the extreme north and in rainy seasons forms a succession of pools from the Harra, east of Jebel Hauran, to the Euphrates. This stony plain is known to the Bedouins as the Hamád or "Plain" *par excellence;* and though for the most part destitute of perennial pasture, or of water above ground, there are certain districts in it better provided which form their winter quarters. Such are the above mentioned Wady Hauran, the resort of the Bisshr Anazeh, and the Wady-er-Rothy, of the Daffir, and Shammar. A few wells would seem to exist on the line of certain ancient routes, traversing the Hamád from various points on the Euphrates, and these form centres of attraction to the tribes. But their immediate neighbourhood is invariably barren, having been pitilessly browsed down for centuries. Routes of this sort connect Káf with Shedadi, Meskakeh with Suk-esh-Shiôkh, and Jôf with Maan. But the best frequented of them and that best supplied with water is the great Haj road from Meshhed Ali to Jebel Shammar, called the road of Zobeydeh. On this wells and reservoirs were constructed in the 9th century, by the widow of Harun-el-Rashid, and khâns, for the convenience of pilgrims, the ruins of which still exist.

The *Hamád*, starting from the level of the Euphrates, rises rapidly for a few miles through a district much intersected by ravines, to an upper plateau, which thenceforward has a fairly regular slope upwards towards the west and south of 8 to 10 feet per mile. The drainage of the plain would not, however, seem to be continuous towards the river ; but to terminate in certain sandy hollows, known by the name *Buttn Jôf* or *Bekka*, all signifying belly or receptacle, which may in former times have been lakes or small inland seas. These do not now at any time of the year hold water above ground, but at the depth of a few feet below the surface it may be found in wells. Such are the Buttn on the Haj road, in which the Wady-er-Rothy terminates, the oases of Taïbetism and Jobba in the south, and I believe that of Teyma in the west ; but the most remarkable of them all is without comparison the so-called Wady and Jôf of Sirhan.

The *Wady Sirhan* bisects northern Arabia in a line parallel with the Euphrates and with the coast lines of the Peninsula, that is to say, nearly from N.W. to S.E. Immediately east and north of it the Hamád reaches its highest level, 2,500 feet above the sea; and the cliffs bounding it on this side are rather abrupt, corresponding, as I am inclined to think, with the general formation of the plain. This consists of a series of shelves set one above the other, with their edges opposed to the general slope ; a formation very evident on the Haj road, where the traveller from Nejd, though in reality descending at a general rate of more than eight feet to the mile, is tempted

to fancy himself on an ascending road, owing to the frequent *Akabas* or steep cliffs he has to climb. I am
inclined, therefore, to believe that the Wady Sirhan and the
Jôf receive their drainage principally from the west, and
that there is a second great watershed to the plain in the
volcanic region, which, according to Guarmani, continues the
Hauran ridge southwards to Tabuk. East of the Wady
Sirhan I was struck by the absence of large tributary wadys
such as one would expect if the area drained was a wide
one. The Wady Sirhan, however, in the days when it was
an inland sea, must have received contributions from all
sides. It lies as a trough between two watersheds in the
plain, and may have been supplied from Jebel Aja in the
south, as it is still supplied from Jebel Hauran in the
north. Its general level below that of the adjacent plain
eastwards, is about 500 feet, and the plain may rise again
still higher to the west.

Be this as it may, one thing is clear, namely, that the
Wady was and is the great central receptacle of the plain,
and corresponds pretty closely with its neighbour, the
still existing Dead Sea, while the Wady-er-Rajel entering
it from the north, holds towards it the position of the
Jordan. Water in the Wady Sirhan is found at a nearly
uniform level of 1850 feet ; and this rule applies to that
part of it which is known as the Jôf as well as to the rest.
The abundance of water obtainable from its wells along a
line extending 300 miles from the frontier of Syria, to
within 200 of the frontier of Nejd, points out Wady
Sirhan as the natural high road of Northern Arabia, and
such it must from the earliest times have been. It is
probable that in the days when Arabia was more populous
than now, villages existed in it at intervals from Ezrak to
Jôf. At present, the wells of these only remain, if we
except the twin oases of Kâf and Ithery, still preserved
in life by the salt lakes which supply them with an article

of trade. These are but poor places, and their population can hardly exceed two hundred souls.

Jôf and Meskakeh are still flourishing towns, but I have reason to think their population has been over estimated by Mr. Palgrave. I cannot put the total number of houses in Jôf at more than 500, nor in Meskakeh at more than 600, while 100 houses are an ample allowance for Kara and the other hamlets of the Jôf oasis. This would give us a census of hardly 8,000 souls, whereas Mr. Palgrave puts it at 40,000. I do not, however, pretend to accuracy on this point.

With regard to the geology of the Hamád and the adjacent districts north of the Nefûd, I believe that sandstone is throughout the principal element. In the extreme north, indeed, limestone takes its place or conglomerate ; but, with the exception of a single district about 100 miles south of Meshhed Ali on the Haj road, I do not think our route crossed any true calcareous rock. The cliffs which form the eastern boundary of the Wady Sirhan are, I think, all of sandstone, south at any rate of Jebel Mizmeh, as are certainly the hills of Jôf and Meskakeh, the rocks of Aalem and Jobba, and all the outlying peaks and ridges north-west of Haïl. These have been described as basaltic or of dark granite, the mistake arising from their colour which, though very varied, is in many instances black. The particular form of sandstone in which iron occurs, seems indeed to acquire a dark weathering with exposure, and unless closely examined, has a volcanic look. I do not, however, believe that south of latitude 31° the volcanic stones of the Haura are really met with ; unless indeed it be west of the Wady Sirhan. Jebel Mizmeh, the highest point east of it, is alone perhaps basaltic. The whole of the Jôf district reminded me geologically of the sandstone formation of Sinai, both in the excentric outline of its rocks, which are often mushroom shaped, and in

their colour, where purple, violet, dark red, orange, white
and even blue and green are found, the harder rock assum-
ing generally an upper weathering of black. I can state
positively that nothing basaltic occurs on the road between
Jôf and Jebel Aja. Of Jebel Mizmeh I am less certain, as
I did not actually touch the stone, but, if volcanic it be, it
is the extreme limit of the Harra southwards. The tells
of Kâf I certainly took to be of basalt when I passed
them. But I did not then consider how easily I might be
mistaken. On the whole I am inclined to place latitude
31° as the boundary of the volcanic district east of the
Wady.

The bed of the Wady Sirhan is principally of sand,
though in some places there is a clayey deposit sufficient
to form subbkhas, or salt lakes, notably at Kâf and Ithery.
About three days' journey E.S.E. of Ithery, I heard of
quicksands, but did not myself cross any ground holding
water. The sand of the Wady Sirhan, like that of all the
hollows both of the Hamád and of northern Nejd, is nearly
white, and has little to distinguish it from the ordinary
sand of the sea shore, or of the Isthmus of Suez. It is
far less fertile than the red sand of the Nefûd, and is more
easily affected by the wind. The ghada is found growing
wherever the sand is pure, and I noticed it as far north as
Kâf. In some parts of the Wady which appear to hold
water in rainy seasons, there is much saltpetre on the
surface, and there the vegetation is rank, but of little value
as pasture. In the pure white sand, little else but the
ghada grows. Wady Sirhan is the summer quarters of the
Sherarat.

The *Harra* is a high region of black volcanic boulders
too well known to need description. It begins as far north
as the latitude of Damascus, and stretches from the foot of
the Hauran hills eastward for some fifty miles, when it
gives place to the Hamád. Southwards it extends to Kâf,

and forms the water shed of the plain east of the Wady Sirhan. According to Guarmani, it is found again west of the Wady, as far south as Tebuk. The eastern watershed of the Harra would seem with the Jebel Hauran to feed the Wady-er-Rajel, a bed sometimes containing running water, and on its opposite slope the Wady Hauran which reaches the Euphrates. The Harra is more plentifully supplied with water than the Hamád, and has a reputation of fertility wherever the soil is uncovered by the boulders.

The Nefûd.—A little north of latitude 29°, the Hamád, which has to this point been a bare plain of gravel broken only by occasional hollows, the beds of ancient seas, suddenly becomes heaped over with high ridges of pure red sand. The transition from the smooth hard plain to the broken dunes of the Nefûd is very startling. The sand rises abruptly from the plain without any transition whatever; and it is easy to see that the plain is not really changed but only hidden from the eye by a super-incumbent mass. Its edge is so well defined that it is hardly an exaggeration to say that with one foot a man may stand upon the Hamád, and with the other on the Nefûd; nor is there much irregularity in its outline. The limit of the sand for several hundred miles runs almost evenly from east to west, and it is only at these extremities that it becomes broken and irregular. Such, at least, I believe to be the case; and if, as seems probable, the whole drift of sand has been shaped by prevailing easterly winds, the phenomenon is less strange than might be thought.

The great Nefûd of Northern Arabia extends from the wells of Lina in the east to Teyma in the west, and from the edge of the Jôf basin in the north to the foot of Jebel Aja in the south. In its greatest breadth it is 150 miles, and in its greatest length 400 miles, but the whole of this is not continuous sand. The extreme eastern portion (and perhaps also the extreme western) is but a series of long strips, from half a mile to five miles in breadth, running parallel to each other, and separated by intervening strips of solid plain. Nor is the sand everywhere of equal depth ; the intermittent Nefûds are comparatively shallow, and would seem to bear a certain proportion in depth to the breadth of the strips. Thus the highest sand ridge crossed by the Haj road is barely eighty feet, while others are but fifty and twenty feet. The continuous Nefûd on the other hand, between Jôf and Haïl, has a depth of at least two hundred feet. The intermittent ridges may possibly suggest an explanation of the original formation of the mass. It would seem as if the wind acting upon the sand drove it at first into lines, and that, as these grew broader and deeper, they at last filled up the intervening space, and formed themselves into a continuous mass at their lee end. If this be the case, the intermittent ridges show the direction in which the solid mass of sand is advancing, the direction, that is, contrary to that of the wind. I leave this deduction, however, to more competent persons than myself to draw, contenting myself with recording the fact.

The red sand of the Nefûd is of a different texture from the ordinary white sand of the desert, and seems to obey mechanical laws of its own. It is coarser in texture and far less volatile, and I am inclined to think that the ordinary light winds which vary sandy surfaces elsewhere leave it very little affected. A strong wind alone, amounting to a gale, could raise it high in the air. It is remarkable that whereas the light white sand is generally found in low hollows, or on the lee side of hills, the red sand of the Nefûd has been heaped up into a lofty mass high above the highest part of the plain. The Hamád where the Nefûd begins is 2,200 feet above the sea. No traveller can see this desert of red sand for the first time without acknowledging its individuality. It is as little like the ordinary sand dunes of the desert, as a glacier is like an ordinary snow field in the Alps. It seems, like the glacier, to have a law of being peculiar to itself, a law of increase, of motion, almost of life. One is struck with these in traversing it, and one seems to recognise an organism.

The most remarkable phenomenon of the Nefûd are the long lines of horse-hoof shaped hollows, called *fuljes*, with which its surface is pitted; these are only observable

W · E

where the sand has attained a depth of from 80 to 100 feet, and are consequently seldom found in the intermittent portion of the Nefûd; while it is remarkable that in the very centre of all, where it might be supposed the sand was deepest, the fuljes are less deep than towards the northern and southern edges, while the lines in which they run become more regular. Indeed, for some miles on either side of Aalem, which marks the centre of the Nefûd, there are no large fuljes; but their strings are so regular as to form, with the intervening spaces, a kind of shallow ridge and furrow running nearly east and west, and not altogether unlike, on a gigantic scale, those ridges in which meadows are sometimes laid down in England. From the top of Aalem this formation was very distinct.

The fuljes themselves are singularly uniform in shape, though varying in size. They represent very closely horse tracks on an enormous scale, that is to say a half-circle, deep at the curved end or toe, and shelving up to the level of the plain at the square end or heel. The sides of the

former are as precipitous as it is in the nature of sand to
be, and they terminate abruptly where they meet the floor
of the fulj. This floor, sloping downwards towards the toe
at an angle of about 70°, and scored with water-courses
converging to a centre, roughly represents the frog, so that
in plan the whole hollow would appear as in the woodcut
A; while in section it would appear as in woodcut B. It
is necessary, therefore, in entering
a fulj on horseback, or with camels,
to approach it from the east; but
on foot one can slip down the sand
at any point. I noticed that just
west of the deep fuljes there is
generally a high mound of sand,

A

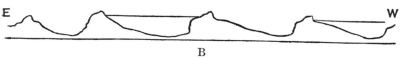

B

which adds considerably to their apparent depth and to the
delusion of their being artificial in their origin, as though
the sand scooped out has been thrown up by a digger.

The size and depth of the fuljes varies greatly; some
are, as it were, rudimentary only, while others attain a
depth of 200 feet and more. The deepest of those I
measured proved to be 280 feet, including the sand hill,
which may have been 60 feet above the general level of the
plain; its width seemed about a quarter of a mile. At
the bottom of these deep fuljes, solid ground is reached,
and there is generally a stony deposit there, such as I have
often noticed in sandy places where water has stood. This
bare space is seldom more than a few paces in diameter.
I heard of, but did not see, one which contained a
well. The wells of Shagik do not stand in a fulj, but
in a valley clear of sand, and those of Jobba in a broad

circular basin 400 feet below the level of the Nefûd. The fuljes, I have said, run in strings irregularly from east to west, corresponding in this with their individual direction.* They are most regularly placed in the neighbourhood of the rocks of Aalem, but their size there is less than either north or south of it. The shape of the fuljes seems unaffected by the solid ground beneath, for at the rocks of Ghota there is a large fulj pierced by the rocks, but which otherwise retains its semicircular form.

The physical features of the Nefûd, whether they be ridges or mounds or fuljes, appear to be permanent in their character. The red sand of which they are composed is less volatile than the common sand of the desert and, except on the summits of the mounds and ridges, seems little affected by the wind. It is everywhere, except in such positions, sprinkled over with brushwood ghada trees and tufts of grass. The sides of the fuljes especially are well clothed, and this could hardly be the case if they were liable to change with a change of wind. In the Nefûd between Jobba and Igneh I noticed well defined sheep tracks ascending the steep slopes of the fuljes spirally, and these I was assured were by no means recent. Moreover, the levelled track made according to tradition by Abu Zeyd is still discernible in places where cuttings were originally made. Sticks and stones left in the Nefûd by travellers, the bones of camels and even their droppings, remain for years uncovered, and those who cross do so by the knowledge of landmarks constantly the same. I am inclined to think, then, that the Nefûds represent a state of comparative repose in Nature. Either the prevailing winds which heaped them up formerly are less violent now than then, or the fuljes are due to exceptional causes which have not occurred for

---

* The exact direction of these strings it is difficult to determine accurately; but perhaps E. by S. and W. by N. may be accepted as nearest the truth.

many years. That wind in some form, and at some time, has been their cause I do not doubt, but the exact method of its action I will not affect to determine. Mr. Blandford, an authority on these subjects, suggests that the fuljes are spaces still unfilled with sand; and if this be so, the strings of fuljes may in reality mark the site of such bare strips as one finds in the intermittent Nefûds. It is conceivable that as the spaces between the sand ridges grew narrower, the wind blocked between them acquired such a rotatory motion as to have thrown bridges of sand across, and so, little by little, filled up all spaces but these. But to me no theory that has been suggested is quite satisfactory. What cause is it that keeps the floors of the deeper fuljes bare; floors so narrow that it would seem a single gale should obliterate them, or even the gradual slipping of the sand slopes above them? There must be some continuous cause to keep these bare. Yet where is the cause now in action sufficient to have heaped up such walls or dug out such pits?

Another strange phenomenon is that of such places as Jobba. There, in the middle of the Nefûd, without apparent reason, the sand is pushed high back on all sides from a low central plain of bare ground three or four miles across. North, south, east, and west the sand rises round it in mountains 400 and 500 feet high, but the plain itself is bare as a threshing-floor. It would seem as if this red sand could not rest in a hollow place, and that the fact of Jobba's low level alone kept it free. Jobba, if cleared of sand all round, would, I have no doubt, present the same feature as Jôf or Taïbetism. It would appear as a basin sunk in the plain, an ancient receptacle of the drainage from Mount Aja. Has it only in recent times been surrounded thus with sand? There is a tradition still extant there of running water.

Jebel Shammar.—A little north of latitude 29°, the

Nefûd ceases as suddenly as it began. The stony plain reappears unchanged geologically, but more broken by the proximity of a lofty range of hills, the Jebel Aja. Between these, however, and the sand, there is an interval of at least five miles where the soil is of sandstone, mostly red, the material out of which the Nefûd sand was made, but mixed with a still coarser sand washed down from the granite range. This rises rapidly to the foot of the hills. There, with little preliminary warning, we come upon unmistakeable red granite cropping in huge rounded masses out of the plain, and rising to a height of 1000 and 1500 feet. The shape of these rocks is very fantastic, boulder being set on boulder in enormous pinnacles ; and I noticed that many of them were pierced with those round holes one finds in granite. The texture of the rock is coarse, and precisely similar to that of Jebel Musa in the Sinaï peninsula, as is the scanty vegetation with which the wadys are clothed. There are the same thorny acacia, and the wild palm, and the caper plant as there, and I heard of the same animals inhabiting the hills.

The *Jebel Aja* range has a main direction of E. by N. and W. by S. Of this I am convinced by the observations I was able to take when approaching it from the N.W. The weather was clear and I was able to see its peaks running for many miles in the direction mentioned. With regard to its length I should put it, by the accounts I heard, at something like 100 miles, and its average breadth may possibly be 10 or 15. In this I differ from the German geographers, who give Jebel Aja a direction of N.E. by S.W., on the authority I believe of Wallin. But as they also place Haïl on the southern slope of the hills, a gross error, I do not consider the discrepancy as of any importance.

Of *Jebel Selman* I can only speak according to the distant view I had of it. But I should be much surprised to learn that any portion of it passed west of the latitude of Haïl. That portion of it visible from Haïl certainly lies to the S.E., and at an apparent distance of 30 miles, with no indication of its being continued westwards. It is by all accounts of the same rock (red granite) as Jebel Aja.

Between Jebel Selman and the Nefûd lie several isolated hills rising from broken ground. All these are of the sandstone formation of the Hamád, and have no geological connection with Aja or Selman. Such are Jebels Jildiyeh, Yatubb, and Jilfeh, Jildiyeh the tallest having a height of perhaps 3800 feet above the sea, or 300 above Haïl.

Haïl lies due east of the extreme eastern buttress of Jebel Aja, and not south of it as has been supposed. Both it and Kefar, as indeed all the towns and villages of the district, lie in a single broad wady, draining the south-eastern rocks of Aja, and sweeping round them northwards to the Nefûd. The height of Haïl is 3,500 feet above the sea, and the plain rises southwards behind it, almost imperceptibly. The small isolated hills close to the town, belong, I think, geologically to the granite range. The main drainage of the plain south of Haïl would seem to be received by the Wady Hannasy, whose course is north, so that the highest part of the plain is probably between Aja and Selman, and may be as much as 4,000 feet above the sea. This, I take it, is the highest plateau of Arabia— as Aja is its highest mountain, 5000 to 5600 feet,—an all sufficient reason for including Jebel Shammar in the term Nejd or Highland.

I feel that I am taking a very serious liberty with geographers in placing Haïl 60 miles farther south than where it is found in our modern maps. I consider, however, that until its position has been scientifically determined, I am justified in doing this by the fact, that my dead reckoning gave it this position, not only according to the out journey, but by the return one, measured from Meshhed

Ali. I am so much in the habit of measuring distances by a rough computation of pace and time, that I doubt if I am much out in the present instance. On this, however, I forbear to dogmatise.

I had hoped to conclude this sketch with a list of plants found in the Nefûd. But our small collection has proved to be so pulverised by its journey, that Sir Joseph Hooker, who kindly undertook to look over it, has been able to identify hardly half-a-dozen specimens.

Of wild animals, I have ascertained the existence of the ostrich, the leopard, the wolf, the fox, the hyæna, the hare, the jerboa, the white antelope, and the gazelle in the Nefûd; and of the ibex and the marmot in Jebel Aja. Of these it may be remarked that the ostrich is the most valuable and perhaps the most rare; I had not the luck to see a single wild specimen, though once a fresh egg was brought me. Neither did I see, except in confinement, the white antelope (Oryx beatrix), which is the most important quadruped of the Nefûd. This antelope frequents every part of the red sand desert, and I found its track quite one hundred miles from any spring, so that the Arabs may be pardoned for affirming that it never drinks. The hare too is found and plentifully throughout; but the gazelle haunts only the outskirts within reach of the hills or of wells where the Arabs are accustomed to water their flocks. The same may be said of the wolf, the fox, and the hyæna, which seem fairly abundant. The tracks of these grew frequent as we approached Jebel Aja, and it may be assumed that it is there they have their lairs, making use of the Nefûd as a hunting ground. The Jebel Aja, a granite range not less than 5,500 feet above the sea, furnishes the water required by these animals, not indeed in streams, for none such are found in the range, but in springs and natural tanks where rain water is stored. These seem by all accounts to be fairly numerous; and if so, the ancient tradition of a wild horse having also been found in the Nefûd, may not be so improbable as at first sight it seems. There is certainly pasture and good pasture for the horse in every part of it. The sheep of the Nefûd requires water but once in a month, and the Nefûd horse may have required no more.

Of reptiles the Nefûd boasts by all accounts the horned viper and the cobra, besides the harmless grey snake called Suliman, which is common everywhere. There are also immense numbers of lizards.

Birds are less numerous, but I noticed the frilled bustard Houbara, and one or two hawks and buzzards. A large black buzzard was especially plentiful. The Bedouins of Nejd train the Lanner falcon, the only noble hawk they possess, to take hares and bustards. In the Nefûd, most of the common desert birds are found, the desert lark, the wheatear, and a kind of wren which inhabits the ghada and yerta bushes.

Of insects I noticed the dragon-fly, several beetles, the common house-fly, and ants, whose nests, made of some glutinous substance mixed with sand, may be seen under these bushes. I was also interested at finding, sunning itself on the rocks of Aalem, a specimen of the painted lady butterfly, so well known for its adventurous flights. This insect could not well have been bred at any nearer point than Syria or the Euphrates, respectively 400 and 300 miles distant. Fleas do not exist beyond the Nefûd, and our dogs became free of them as soon as we reached Haïl. Locusts were incredibly numerous everywhere, and formed the chief article of food for man, beast, and bird. They are of two colours, red and green, the latter being I believe the male, while the former is the female. They both are excellent eating, but the red locust is preferred.

Sand-storms are probably less common in the Nefûd than in deserts where the sand is white, for reasons already

named ; nor do the Bedouins seem much to dread them.
They are only dangerous where they last long enough to
delay travellers far from home beyond the time calculated
on for their supplies. No tales are told of caravans overwhelmed or even single persons. Those who perish in the
Nefûd perish of thirst. I made particular inquiries as to
the simoom or poisonous wind mentioned by Mr. Palgrave,
but could gain no information respecting it.

In the Jebel Aja an ibex is found, specimens of which I
saw at Haïl, and a mountain gazelle, and I heard of a
leopard, probably the same as that found in Sinaï. The
only animal there, which may be new, is one described to
me as the Webber, an animal of the size of the hare, which
climbs the wild palms and eats the dates. It is described
as sitting on its legs and whistling, and from the description
I judged it to be a marmot or a coney (hierax). But Lord
Lilford, whom I spoke to on the subject, assures me it is
in all probability the Lophiomys Imhausii.

W. S. B.

LOPHIOMYS IMHAUSII.

HISTORICAL SKETCH OF THE RISE AND DECLINE OF WAHHABISM IN ARABIA.

COMPILED PRINCIPALLY FROM MATERIALS SUPPLIED BY LT.-COLONEL E. C. ROSS, H.M.'s RESIDENT AT BUSHIRE.

———◆———

AT the beginning of last century, Nejd, and Arabia generally, with the exception of Oman, Yemen, and Hejaz, was divided into a number of independent districts or townships, each ruled by a tribal chief on the principle already explained of self-government under Bedouin protection. Religion, except in its primitive Arabian form, was almost forgotten by the townspeople, and little if any connection was kept up between them and the rest of the Mahometan world.

In 1691, however, Mohammed Ibn Abd-el-Wahhab, founder of the Wahhabi sect, was born at Eiyanah in Aared, his father being of the Ibn Temim tribe, the same which till lately held power in Jebel Shammar. In his youth he went to Bussorah, and perhaps to Damascus, to study religious law, and after making the pilgrimage to Mecca and Medina returned to his native country, and soon after married in the village of Horeylama near Deriyeh. There and at Eyaneh he began his preaching, and about the year 1742 succeeded in converting Mohammed Ibn Saoud, Emir of Deriyeh, the principal town of Aared.

The chief features of his teaching were :—

1st. The re-establishment of Mahometan beliefs as taught

by the Koran, and the rejection of those other beliefs accepted by the Sunis on tradition.

2nd. A denial of all spiritual authority to the Ottoman or any other Caliph, and of all special respect due to sherifs, saints, dervishes, or other persons.

3rd. The restoration of discipline in the matter of prayer, fasting, and pilgrimage.

4th. A strict prohibition of wine, tobacco, games of chance, magic, silk and gold in dress, and of tombstones for the dead.

Ibn Abd-el-Wahhab lived to an advanced age at Deriyeh, and died in 1787.

Mohammed Ibn Saoud, the first Wahhabi Emir, belonged to the Mesalikh tribe of Anazeh, itself an offshoot of the Welled Ali of western Nejd (deriving, according to the account of the Ibn Saouds themselves, from the Beni Bekr Wail, through Maane Ibn Rabiia, king of Nejd, Hasa, and Oman in the 15th century). He embraced the tenets of Abd-el-Wahhab, as has been said, in the year 1742, and was followed in his conversion by many of the inhabitants of Deriyeh and the neighbouring districts, who at last so swelled the number of Ibn Saoud's adherents, that he became the head of the reformed religion, and according to the Wahhabi pretensions the head of all Islam. Guided by the counsels of Ibn Abd-el-Wahhab, and carried forward on the wave of the new teaching, he gradually established his authority over all Aared and eventually over the greater part of Nejd. His hardest contests there were with the people of Riad, who, under their Sheykh, Mohammed Ibn Daus, long held out, and with the Ibn Ghureyr (Areyr or Aruk), Sheykhs of the Beni Khaled. These latter, who owned the districts of Hasa and Katif, though forced to tribute, have always been hostile to the Ibn Saouds, and are so at the present day. Another opponent, bitterly hostile to the new religion, was the Emir's brother, Theniyan, whose descendants still belong to the anti-Wahhabi faction in Aared. Mohammed Ibn Saoud died in 1765 and was succeeded by his son Abdel Aziz.

Abd-el-Aziz Ibn Saoud, a man of energy and ambition, completed the subjugation of Nejd and Hasa, and carried the Wahhabi arms as far northwards as Bussorah, and even it would seem to Mesopotamia and the Sinjar Hills. These latter raids so greatly alarmed the government of the Sultan, that in 1798 a Turkish expeditionary force was sent by land from Bagdad into Hasa, under the command of one Ali Pasha, secretary to Suliman Pasha the Turkish Valy. It consisted of 4000 or 5000 regular infantry, with artillery, and a large contingent of Bedouin Arabs collected from the Montefik, Daffir, and other tribes hostile to the Wahhabi power. These marched down the coast and took possession of the greater part of Hasa, but having failed to reduce Hofhuf, a fortified town, were returning northwards when their retreat was intercepted by Saoud, the Emir's son, who took up a position under the walls of Taj. A battle was then imminent, but it was averted by the mediation of the Arab Sheykhs, and Ali Pasha was allowed to continue his retreat to Bussorah, while Saoud retook possession of Hasa and punished those who had submitted to the Turks. This affair contributed much to the extension and renown of the Wahhabi power; and offers of submission came in from all sides. The Emir, nevertheless, thought it prudent to endeavour to conciliate the Turkish Valy, and despatched horses and other valuable presents to Bagdad.

The Wahhabi State was now become a regular Government, with a centralised administration, a system of tax instead of tribute, and a standing army which marched under the command of Saoud Ibn Saoud, the Emir's eldest son. The Emir, Abd-el-Aziz himself, appears to have been a man of peace, simple in his dress and habits, and extremely devout. Saoud, however, was a warrior, and it was through him that the Wahhabis pushed their fortunes. There seems, nevertheless, to have been always a strong party of opposition in the desert, where the Bedouins clung to the traditions of their independence and chafed under the religious discipline imposed on them. Kasim and Jebel Shammar, both of them centres of Bedouin life, never accepted the Wahhabi tenets with any enthusiasm, and the people of Hasa, an industrious race standing in close commercial relations with Persia, accepted the rule of the Ibn Saouds only on compulsion. Southern Nejd alone seems to have been fanatically Wahhabi, but their fanaticism was their strength and long carried all before it.

In 1799, Saoud made his first pilgrimage to Mecca, at the head of 4000 armed followers, and in the following year he repeated the act of piety. Passage through Nejd, however, seems to have been forbidden to the Shiah pilgrims whom the Wahhabis regarded as infidels, and a violent feeling was roused against the Wahhabis in Persia and in the Pashalik of Bagdad, where most of the inhabitants are Shiahs. It ended in the assassination of the Emir Abd-el-Aziz by a Persian seyyid from Kerbela in 1800, at the age of 82 years. (Colonel Ross gives 1803 as the date of this event, but, according to members of the Ibn Saoud family themselves, it happened three years earlier ; a date which accords better with other events.)

In 1801, a first expedition was despatched against Oman under Selim-el-Hark, one of Saoud's lieutenants; and in the same year Saoud himself, to avenge his father's murder, marched northwards with 20,000 men to the Euphrates, and on the 20th of April sacked Kerbela, whence, having put all the male inhabitants to the sword and razed the tomb of Husseyn, he retired the same afternoon with an immense booty. The success of this attack, made in the name of a reformed Islam upon the stronghold of the Shiah heretics and within the nominal dominions of the

Sultan, spread consternation throughout the Mussulman world.

In 1802 the island of Bahreyn was reduced to tribute, and the Wahhabi power extended down the Eastern coast as far as Batinah on the Sea of Oman, and several of the Oman tribes embraced the Wahhabi faith, and became tributary to Ibn Saoud.

In 1803, a quarrel having occurred between the Wahhabi Emir and Ghalib the Sherif of Mecca, Saoud marched into Hejaz with a large army, reduced Taif, and on the 1st of May entered Mecca, where he deposed the Sherif and appointed a Governor of his own. He did not, however, appear there as an enemy but as a pilgrim, and his troops were restrained from plunder, the only act of violence permitted being the destruction of the large tombs in the city, so that, as they themselves said, " there did not remain an idol in all that pure city." Then they abolished the taxes and customs; destroyed all instruments for the use of tobacco and the dwellings of those who sold hashish or who lived in open wickedness. Saoud returned to Nejd, having received the submission of all Central Arabia, including the holy city of Medina. This may be considered as the zenith of the Wahhabi power. Law and order prevailed under a central government, and the Emir on his return to Deriyeh issued a proclamation promising strict protection of life, property, and commerce throughout his dominions. This fortunate state of things continued for several years.

In 1807 Saoud once more marched to the Euphrates and laid siege to Meshhed Ali, but failed to capture that walled town and was forced to retreat.

In 1809 he collected an army of 30,000 men with the intention of attacking Bagdad, but disturbances having broken out in Nejd he abandoned his intention and marched instead with his army on pilgrimage to Mecca, whence he returned home by Medina, now annexed to his empire.

In Oman the Wahhabi arms continued to gain ground, and their name seems first to have become known in India in connexion with piratical raids committed on the Indian Sea. This led to an expedition undertaken in 1809 by the English against Ras-el-Kheymah on the Persian Gulf. But in spite of this, the Wahhabis advanced next year to Mattrah, a few miles only from Muscat, and to Bahreyn, which was occupied by them and received a Wahhabi governor.

In 1810 Saoud invaded Irak, and in 1811 his son Abdallah arrived close to Bagdad on a plundering raid, while another Wahhabi army, under Abu Nocta, a slave of the Emir's, invaded Syria and held Damascus to ransom. In Syria, indeed, for some years tribute had been paid by the desert towns of the Hauran and the districts east of Jordan to Nejd ; and it seemed probable that the new Arabian Empire would extend itself to the Mediterranean, and Abd-el-Wahhabi's reformation to all the Arab race. A coalition of the Northern Bedouins, however, under Eddrehi Ibn Shaalan, Sheykh of the Roala, saved Damascus from Abu Nocta, and after sustaining a defeat from them on the Orontes the Wahhabi army returned to Nejd.

The danger, however, to orthodox Islam was now recognized, and in the same year, 1811, the Ottoman Sultan, urged by his Suni subjects to recover the holy places of Arabia to orthodox keeping, resolved on serious measures against Nejd. Matters had been brought to a crisis the year before by an act of fanaticism on the part of Saoud which had roused the indignation of all sects in Islam against him. On the occasion of a fourth pilgrimage which he had then made, he had caused the tomb of the prophet to be opened at Medina and the rich jewels and precious relics it contained to be sold or distributed among his soldiers, an act of sacrilege which it was impossible to tolerate. The Sultan was reminded that one of the claims on which his ancestors of the House of Ottoman rested their tenure to the Caliphate was that they possessed the Holy Places, and he was called upon to assert his protectorate of Mecca and Medina by force. It is probable, indeed, that only the great interests at stake in Europe during the previous years of the century had delayed vigorous action. The invasion of Egypt by Napoleon, and the disorganisation of the Turkish Empire resulting from it, had contributed not a little to the Wahhabi successes. Now, however, Egypt was under the rule of Mehemet Ali, and to his vigorous hands the Sultan entrusted the duty of punishing the Ibn Saouds. The absence of the Emir's armies in the north gave a favourable opportunity to the Egyptian arms, a force of 8000 men was despatched to Hejaz, and Mecca was occupied by Tusun Pasha without resistance. On advancing inland, however, beyond Taif, Tusun was met by Abdullah ibn Saoud, and defeated in the desert with the loss of half his army; nor was he able to do more than hold his own in Mecca until relieved from Egypt.

In 1813, Mehemet Ali, impatient of his son's failure, went in person to Arabia, and seized Ghalib the Sherif, whom he suspected of Wahhabism, at Mecca and sent him prisoner to Cairo. Tusun was again entrusted with the command of an expedition destined for Nejd, but was again met and defeated beyond Taif in the spring of 1814.

In April 1814, while preparations were being pressed for a renewal of the campaign, Saoud Ibn Saoud the Wahhabi Emir, died, and Abdallah, his son and recognized successor, was acknowledged without opposition, chief of the Wahhabis.

In January 1815, Mehemet Ali inflicted a first serious defeat on the Wahhabi army, and Tusun having occupied Medina advanced into Kasim, in northern Nejd, where he took possession of Ras, at that time capital of the district.

Negotiations were opened from that point with the Emir Abdallah who had retired with his army to Aneyzeh ; and these resulted to the astonishment of every one (for Abdallah still had a powerful army) in the Emir's submission.

It is probable that in thus yielding, Abdallah felt his position in Nejd insecure. The Bedouins though subdued had never accepted the Wahhabi rule but on compulsion, and many of them were openly siding with the Turks, while his late defeat had destroyed much of his soldier's prestige. Be that as it may, the Emir agreed to the follow-ing stringent terms at Aneyzeh.

1st. He acknowledged as suzerain the Sultan of Turkey.

2nd. He agreed to give hostages for future condúct, and even, if required, to present himself in person at Constantinople.

3rd. He would deliver over Deriyeh, his capital, to a governor appointed by the Sultan ; and

4th. He would restore the jewels plundered from Medina on the occasion of his father's visit in 1810.

On these conditions peace was concluded between the Emir and Tusun, and Abdallah gave the hostages required. He did not, however, give over Deriyeh, but proceeded on the contrary to prepare it for a siege. Neither did Mehemet Ali, when he learned that Abdallah refused to come to Egypt in person, nullify the peace. Tusun was recalled, and Ibrahim, his second son, appointed commander of the army in Arabia in his stead.

In September 1816 Ibrahim Pasha left Egypt at the head of a considerable force and proceeded to the scene of action.

The first encounter seems to have taken place at Ma' Wiyah, where Abdallah ibn Saoud attacked the Egyptian

army and suffered a signal defeat. On this occasion
Ibrahim Pasha put to death all prisoners taken. The
pasha then advanced with 4000 infantry and 1200 cavalry,
besides contingents of the friendly Arab tribes, Beni-
Kháled, Muteyr, 'Oteybah, Harb, and Suhool against Ras,
which was held by a Wahhabi garrison. Before this town
Ibrahim Pasha suffered a serious check, and after besieging
it for three and a half months, and losing 3000 men, he
was obliged to agree to an armistice and abandon the siege.
The Egyptian general, however, masking Ras, continued to
advance eastwards on 'Aneyzah and the Emir retired
south to Bereydah. After six days' bombardments, the forts
of 'Aneyzah surrendered, and the entire district of Kasim
then submitted to the Egyptian commander. Abdallah
retired on Shakrah, a town in the district of Woshem, and
Ibrahim Pasha took Bereydah, where he halted two months
for reinforcements. During this time the pasha succeeded
in detaching from the Wahhabi cause many of those
Bedouins who still remained faithful to Ibn Saoud.
Among the first to join the Egyptians had been Feysul-el-
Dawish, Sheikh of the Muteyr, who, animated by an
ancient feud with the Ibn Saouds, was readily persuaded
by Ibrahim with the promise of being installed Governor
of Nejd, a promise which the pasha had no intention of
fulfilling.

Having received at Bereydah a reinforcement of 800
men, and two guns, as well as supplies of provisions and
ammunition, Ibrahim Pasha was able to continue his
advance on Shakrah at the head of 4500 Turkish,
Albanian, and Moorish troops in addition to Arab contingents. About 10,000 camels accompanied the force, and
the infantry soldiers were usually mounted two and two on
camels. The Emir Abdallah meantime retired on his
capital, wasting the country before the enemy, and sending
the surplus cattle and flocks to Hasa. This was in the latter

part of December, 1817. In the following month the Turkish army appeared before Shakrah, which was regularly approached under the direction of a French engineer, M. Vaissière, and capitulated on the 22nd of January, 1818. The lives of the garrison were spared, but they were deprived of their arms, and had to engage not to serve again under the Wahhabi Emir. Some time after, when Deriyeh had fallen, Ibrahim Pasha caused the fortifications of Shakrah to be demolished.

Abdallah ibn Saoud had now retreated to Deriyeh and before following him up to the capital Ibrahim Pasha judged it advisable to turn aside from the direct route to take the town of Dhoramah. At that place he encountered a spirited resistance, several of his men being killed. In revenge for this, the male inhabitants were put to the sword, the town pillaged and destroyed, and the women given up to the brutality of the Turkish soldiery. Only the governor and his guard, who had shut themselves in a citadel, were suffered to escape with their lives.

Detained by rains, it was March before Ibrahim Pasha advanced on Deriyeh which town he invested in April with a force of 5500 horse and foot and twelve pieces of artillery, including two mortars and two howitzers. Shortly after, reinforcements and convoys of supplies reached the Turkish camp from Medina and Busrah. The siege operations were for some time conducted without any success to the Turkish arms, and in the latter part of the month of May an explosion having occurred by which the pasha lost all his spare ammunition, his position became extremely critical. Indeed, the indomitable personal courage and good example of Ibrahim alone saved the army from disaster. The troops suffered much from dysentery and ophthalmia, and the Wahhabis thought to overwhelm the besiegers by a sortie in force. The attack was however repulsed and the opportunity lost

to the besieged ; for soon after the engagement caravans
with fresh supplies of ammunition and provisions reached
the Egyptian camp, and then reinforcements of infantry
and cavalry. News was also received of the approach
of Khalil Pasha from Egypt with 3000 fresh troops.
Early in September the Emir sent a flag of truce to
request an audience of the pasha. This was accorded, and
the Wahhabi chief was kindly received, but was informed
that the first and indispensable condition of peace was the
attendance of Abdallah in person at Cairo. The Emir asked
twenty four hours for reflection, which delay was granted,
and at the expiration of the time he returned to the pasha's
camp and intimated his willingness to fulfil the condition
imposed, provided Ibrahim would guarantee that his life
would be spared. Ibrahim Pasha replied that he had no
authority himself to bind the Sultan and the Viceroy on
that point, but that he thought both were too generous to
put him to death. Abdallah then pleaded for his family
and prayed that Deriyeh and his adherents there should be
spared. These terms were conceded and a peace concluded.
The ill-starred Emir at once set out on his journey under
a strong escort, and on reaching Cairo, was courteously
received by Mehemet Ali, who forwarded him to Constantinople with a strong appeal for his pardon. The
government of the Porte was, however, implacable : Abdallah ibn Saoud was paraded ignominiously through the
streets of the capital for three days, and then, with his
companions in captivity, was publicly beheaded.

Thus ends the first epoch of the Wahhabi rule in
Nejd. During the twenty-three years which followed the
destruction of Deriyeh, Nejd continued to be a province of
Egypt; sometimes occupied by Egyptian troops, sometimes tributary only. When Ibrahim Pasha first appeared
in Nejd, he commanded the sympathies of a great part of
the population, and especially in Jebel Shammar, Kasim,

and Hasa, where he was received rather as a deliverer from the Wahhabi yoke, than as a foreign conqueror. No Turkish army had previously been seen in Central Arabia; and the Arabs of the interior, when not fanatically biassed, had no special hatred of them. But the Turkish and Albanian troops left in garrison by Ibrahim soon excited by their cruelties the enmity of the people ; and as early as 1822 a first massacre of a Turkish garrison occurred at Riad, the new capital of Nejd (for Deriyeh was never rebuilt). This was followed in 1823 and 1824 by a successful rising of the Arabs under Turki ibn Saoud (see pedigree), and the re-establishment of his family as sovereign in Aared. Turki seized Riad, drove out the Egyptian troops still remaining in Nejd, and as leader of a popular movement against the foreigner, was recognized Emir by most of the tribes of Central Arabia.

For ten years—1824 to 1834—Turki consolidated his power in Nejd, Hasa, and even Oman, the whole coast of the Persian Gulf to Ras-el-Had acknowledging him and paying tribute. He, however, himself paid tribute to the Government of Egypt, which accorded countenance to his action in Arabia.

In 1834, Turki ibn Saoud was assassinated by a relative, Meshari, who was in turn put to death by Turki's son, Feysul, now recognised Emir in his father's stead.

In 1838, Feysul, having neglected or refused to pay tribute to Egypt, Mehemet Ali sent a force under Jomail Bey to depose him, and to establish Khalid, a rival claimant of the Ibn Saoud family, as Emir at Riad. Feysul then fled to Hasa, and Khalid, supported by a portion of the people of Aared and by reinforcements from Egypt under Khurshid Pasha, usurped the throne, but was shortly set aside by the Egyptian commanders, who established Egyptian government throughout Nejd. Feysul meanwhile had surrendered to them, and been sent prisoner to Cairo. The second Egyptian occupation of Nejd lasted for two years. Then the greater part of the troops were recalled, and Khalid left as Valy for the Turkish government.

In 1842, Abdallah ibn Theneyan ibn Saoud headed a revolt against Khalid, who with his few remaining Egyptian troops was ejected from Riad; and Feysul, having escaped from his prison in Cairo, reappeared in Aared, and was everywhere acknowledged as Emir. From this time neither the Egyptian nor the Turkish government have exercised any authority in Nejd.

Under Feysul, whose reign lasted after his restoration for twenty-three years, nearly all the former territories of the Wahhabi empire were re-conquered. Oman in 1845 was reduced to tribute; Hasa was forced to accept Wahhabi governors, and in Feysul's last years Kasim also was conquered. Jebel Shammar, which on the overthrow of the first Nejd empire by Ibrahim Pasha had reverted to independence under the Ibn Ali family of the Beni Temim, was now also annexed nominally to the Wahhabi state. With Feysul's help, Abdallah ibn Rashid, Sheykh of the Shammar, established himself at Haïl, and paying tribute to the Emir acknowledged his sovereignty. Only in Bahreyn were his arms unsuccessful, and that owing to the support given to the Bahreyn sheykhs by England.

In the later years of his life Feysul became blind, and the management of affairs fell to his son Abdallah, who by his fanaticism and his cruelty alienated the Bedouin population from his standard, and prepared matters for a third intervention on the part of the Turks.

Before narrating, however, the last episode of Arabian misfortune and Turkish annexation, it will be necessary to explain briefly the views and pretensions of the Ottoman Sultans with respect to Arabia.

The first appearance of the Turks in the peninsula dates from 1524, when Selim I., having conquered Egypt and usurped the Caliphate, till then held by members of the Abbaside family, took military possession of the holy places, Mecca and Medina, and annexed Yemen to his dominions. Beyond the districts immediately bordering on the Red Sea, however, no part of Arabia proper was at that time claimed by the Sultans; and in the following century a national insurrection drove them even from these, so that with the exception of the pilgrim roads from Cairo and Damascus, the Turks made no pretension of being masters in the Peninsula.

Ibrahim Pasha's expedition had been made not in assertion of a sovereign right, but as an act of chastisement and retaliation on a hostile sect; and once the Wahhabi government crushed, little care had been taken in retaining Nejd as a possession. The sultans were at that time far too anxiously occupied with their position in Europe to indulge in dreams of conquest in Asia, and were, from a military point of view, too weak for unprofitable enterprises not absolutely necessary. But at the close of the Crimean war the Turkish army was thoroughly reorganised, thanks to the English loan, which made its equipment with arms of precision possible; and the Sultan, finding himself in the possession of unaccustomed power, used it for the reduction first of the outlying districts of the Empire which had shaken off his yoke, and next of those tribes on its borders which appeared easiest of conquest. The frontier lands of Syria and Kurdistan were thus brought back into subjection, the Euphrates and Tigris valleys, independent since the days of Tamerlane, were occupied in force, and Irak was once more placed under the Imperial system of tax and conscription. The Suez Canal was opened, and Arabia, accessible hitherto by land only, was now for the first time within easy reach of Constantinople. With the sense of increased power, born of full coffers and an army ready and equipped for action, new dreams of conquest came to the Imperial government. The Sultan remembered what he seemed to have forgotten, that he was heir to the Arabian caliphate, and his Ministers of the day based on this fact a claim to all Arabia. The garrisons of Mecca and the Hejaz were increased, an expedition was despatched against Yemen, and Midhat Pasha, a man of a restless, unquiet temper, was appointed Governor of Bagdad, with orders to watch his time for extending the Sultan's influence in any direction that might seem to him advisable. The opportunity soon came.

In 1865 Feysul ibn Saoud died, and the Wahhabi State which under him had regained so much of its former power, was once more weakened by internal dissension. Feysul left two sons, Abdallah and Saoud, the former a strict Wahhabi, but the latter holding liberal opinions, national rather than religious. Each put himself at the head of a party ; Abdallah of the townsmen in Aared who were still fanatically attached to the reformed doctrine, and Saoud of the Bedouins. For a while they divided Feysul's inheritance between them, but coming to blows the younger brother forced the elder to fly from Aared, and Saoud established himself there as sole Emir. Jebel Shammar meanwhile and Kasim became completely independent, and Hasa and the rest of the maritime districts refused any longer to pay tribute.

In 1871 Abdallah, turned out of Aared, made his way with a few followers to Jebel Shammar, where Metaab Ibn Rashid was then Emir, and from that asylum (for he was treated there as a guest) put himself into communication with Midhat at Bagdad. Midhat, who saw in this circumstance an opportunity such as he had been instructed to seek, readily responded ; and at once issued a proclamation in which the sovereign power of the Sultan over Nejd was assumed, and Abdallah referred to as Caimakam or Deputy Governor of that province. It was notified, moreover, that a Turkish force would be despatched from Bagdad " to restore order, and to maintain the said Caimakam against his rebellious brother."

After some opposition on the part of the Indian Government, which for many years had insisted upon absolute peace being maintained in the Persian gulf, a rule which had been agreed to by all the chiefs of the Arabian coast, including the people of Hasa and the Wahhabi government, and which had been attended with excellent results, a military expedition was despatched by sea to Hasa. It consisted of 4000 to 5000 Turkish regulars, under Nazfi Pasha, and disembarked at Katif in the month of June. Abdallah in the meantime had returned to Nejd, and having collected a body of adherents, in union with the Beni Kahtan tribe, attacked Saoud from the west; but was defeated and took refuge in the Turkish camp.

Dissensions nevertheless broke out in Riad and forced Saoud to take the field against a third rival, Abdallah ibn Turki, at whose hands he sustained a defeat, and he was in his turn forced to retire to Katr. The Turks had now occupied all the seaboard of Hasa, and the inland fort and town of Hofhuf, whence they entered into communication with this Abdallah ibn Turki, whom they named Mudir of Riad, " pending the arrival there of Abdallah ibn Feysul; " but before the end of the year, Midhat announced that in consequence of a petition received by the Sultan from the principal inhabitants of Nejd* the Ibn Saoud family had ceased to reign, and that the country should henceforth be administered by a Turkish Governor. Nafiz Pasha was appointed in the same announcement Muteserrif or Governor of Nejd, and Abdallah was entirely put aside. The Emir Abdallah thereupon fled from the Turkish camp in Hasa to Riad.

---

* This seems to have been a forgery.

In 1872 Raouf Pasha, who had succeeded Midhat at Bagdad, opened negotiations with Saoud, and induced him to send his brother Abderrahman to Bagdad, where he was retained a prisoner till 1874.

In the same year Saoud returned to Riad, and once more ejected his brother Abdallah, who retired to Queyt, leaving Saoud in undisturbed possession till his death in 1874.

In 1873, the Turkish regular troops were withdrawn, and Bizi ibn Aréar, Sheykh of the Beni Kháled and hereditary enemy of the Ibn Saouds, was left in Hasa as Ottoman Governor, with a garrison of zaptiehs.

In 1874, Abderrahman, brother of the Emir Saoud, having been released from Bagdad, raised a revolt in Hasa, and was joined by the Al Mowak, Ajman and other Bedouin tribes, with whom he marched on Hofhuf and besieged Bizi there with his garrison, many of whom were slain. Whereupon Nassr Pasha was sent from Bussora with a battalion of regulars, by sea to Hasa, at the news of whose approach Abderrahman retired to Riad. Nassr then marched on Hofhuf and relieved the garrison, which were shut up in the fort; but gave the town to pillage. For several days the Turkish soldiers and their auxiliaries indulged in indiscriminate massacre and plunder of the inhabitants; men, women and children were shot down, and women were openly treated with the brutality peculiar to such occasions. It is said in extenuation that the Turkish officers remonstrated with the Pasha, but that he replied that it was necessary to make an example.

Shortly after this the Emir Saoud died at Riad, it has been said of poison; and in 1875 Abdallah returned to Nejd, where he found Abderrahman, his half brother, established. The brothers, after some disputing, came to an amicable arrangement with respect to the chief power, Abdallah holding the title of Emir, and Abderrahman of chief minister. Such is now the state of things at Riad. Overtures from the Turkish Government have been lately opened with the Emir, on the basis of his becoming Governor of Nejd as Turkish nominee, but have met with no response. Abdallah, it would seem, exercises little authority out of Riad, and none whatever out of Aared. He represents the party of Wahhabi fanaticism there, which is rapidly declining, and there are schemes on foot among the Bedouins and certain members of the Ibn Saoud family, for starting a new pretender in the person of one of the sons of Saoud, and claiming the protection of England. The power of the Ibn Saoud family in Arabia may, however, be considered at an end.

Hasa and the seaboard from Katr to Queyt is now held by the Turks, under whose system of stirring up tribal feuds among the Arabs, the commercial prosperity of the coast is rapidly disappearing. Piracy, under the protection of the Ottoman flag, has once more become the mode of life with the coast villagers, and intrigues have been opened with the Sheykhs of the districts eastwards, to induce them to accept similar protection on the promise of similar license.

Meanwhile all that is truly national in thought and respectable in feeling in central Arabia, is grouping itself around Mohammed Ibn Rashid, the Emir of Jebel Shammar, and it is to Haïl that we must look for a restoration, if such be possible, of the ancient glories and prosperity of the Nejd Empire.

W. S. B.

PEDIGREE OF THE IBN SAOUDS, EMIRS OF NEJD.

SAOUD IBN MOHAMMED,

Descended from Rabiia ibn Maane, Emir of Deriyeh in the 15th century, himself of the Mesalik tribe of Anazeh, deriving through Aduan from Ishmael, the son of Abraham.

Pedigree chart of the Ibn Saouds, Emirs of Nejd, with the following entries:

- MOHAMMED, 1st Emir of Nejd, 1745; embraced the Wahhabi faith, 1742; died 1765.
- MESHARI.
- FERHAN.
- THENEYAN.
- IBRAHIM.
- ABD EL AZIZ, 2nd Emir of Nejd, 1765; assassinated by a Persian fanatic, 1801.
- SAOUD, died *vit. pat.*
- ABDALLAH.
- SAOUD, 3rd Emir of Nejd, 1801; died 1814.
- TURKI, 6th Emir of Nejd, 1824; murdered by Meshari ibn Khaled 1834.
- IBRAHIM.
- MOHAMMED.
- THENEYAN.
- JALWI.
- ABDALLAH.
- ABDALLAH, 9th Emir, 1842; resigned in favour of Feysul, 1843.
- ABDALLAH, 4th Emir of Nejd, 1814; beheaded at Constantinople, 1818.
- FAHAD.
- MESHARI, 5th Emir of Nejd, 1818; nominally only, under Egyptian rule.
- KHALED, 8th Emir of Nejd, an usurper and nominee of the Sultan's, deposed by Abdallah 1842.
- FEYSUL, 7th Emir, 1834; deposed by Mehemet Ali, 1838; restored as 10th Emir, 1843; died 1865.
- ABDERRAHMAN.
- Three Sons, who died *s.p.*
- ABDALLAH, 11th Emir, 1865; deposed by his brother Saoud, 1871; restored, on his brother Saoud's death, as 13th Emir, 1874. The reigning Emir.
- SAOUD, 12th Emir, 1871; died 1874.
- MOHAMMED.
- MOHAMMED and others, Pretenders to the Throne.
- MOHAMMED.
- THENEYAN.
- ABDALLAH.

PEDIGREE OF THE IBN RASHIDS, EMIRS OF JEBEL SHAMMAR.

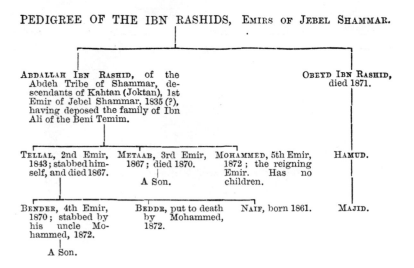

ABDALLAH IBN RASHID, of the Abdeh Tribe of Shammar, descendants of Kahtan (Joktan), 1st Emir of Jebel Shammar, 1835 (?), having deposed the family of Ibn Ali of the Beni Temim.

OBEYD IBN RASHID, died 1871.

TELLAL, 2nd Emir, 1843; stabbed himself, and died 1867.

METAAB, 3rd Emir, 1867; died 1870.

A Son.

MOHAMMED, 5th Emir, 1872; the reigning Emir. Has no children.

HAMUD.

BENDER, 4th Emir, 1870; stabbed by his uncle Mohammed, 1872.

A Son.

BEDDR, put to death by Mohammed, 1872.

NAIF, born 1861.

MAJID.

MEMORANDUM ON THE EUPHRATES VALLEY RAILWAY,

And its Kindred Schemes of Railway Communication between The Mediterranean and The Persian Gulf.

————•————

HAVING now completed the whole journey by land between Alexandretta and Bushire, the extreme points
usually mentioned as terminuses for a Perso-Mediterranean
Railway, and being, in so far, capable of estimating the real
resources of the countries such a railway would serve, I
make no apology for the few remarks I here offer on the
subject. I do so with the more confidence because I
perceive that of the many advocates these railway
schemes have had, not one has taken the trouble of thus
travelling over the whole distance, and that nearly all
calculations made regarding them, are based on a survey of
a part only of the road. It is seldom indeed that those
who write or speak about a Euphrates valley railway,
have done more than cross that river at Bir, or that they
carry their arguments much beyond a choice of the most
suitable Mediterranean port for a terminus, a kind of
reasoning sufficient, no doubt, for the purpose before them,
but in reality misleading. I believe, that one and all of
these schemes are based upon a deficient knowledge of the
facts.

A railway of this sort, to Englishmen, is naturally
attractive, and presents itself to them in a double aspect,
political and commercial. Politically it has been repre-

sented as an alternative route for troops to India, more expeditious than that by Suez ; commercially as a scheme that will open up a rich but neglected country to the operations of trade.

With regard to the first I would remark first that, having gone through the calculation carefully, I find that four days is the total saving between London and Calcutta which a line of railway from Scanderun or Tripoli to Bushire would effect, an advantage quite inadequate to the risk of transhipment, and the fatigue of a long desert journey ; secondly that the Persian Gulf is both hotter and less healthy than the Red Sea, and that the Syrian ports of the Mediterranean are peculiarly liable to fever ; and thirdly that such a line could be used for the conveyance of English troops, by permission only of whatever power might be in possession of Asia Minor.

When I was in India last summer I made acquaintance with a great number of British officials, and I was at some pains to learn from them their views on this "alternative route." I will not say that their answers to my questions were invariably the same, but I think I am making no mistake in affirming, that the consensus of intelligent opinion among them is wholly adverse to the notion. " The Euphrates route," say they, "would be of exceedingly little use to us. The mails, to be sure, would go that way, and we should get our letters from England three or four days sooner ; but, politically speaking, the mails are a matter of less consequence than they were. Nowadays all official work of real importance is transacted by telegraph, and when the mails come in afterwards, their interest has been forestalled. It would matter little at Simla or Calcutta whether they had taken three weeks or a fortnight on the road. Trade would certainly benefit somewhat in this way, but Government very little. As regards the sending of troops overland, there could be no question of it, as long

as the Suez route was open ; and if England cannot keep
the Suez route open, she had better give up India at once.
No Secretary at War would be so ill-advised as to send
troops, with the risk of cholera and over-fatigue, by the
land journey as long as they could be marched on board at
Plymouth, and landed fresh at Bombay." "Not even in
case of a new mutiny?" I asked. "Not even in a mutiny.
People in England have no idea of the meaning of a thou-
sand-mile railway journey in desert countries. For six
months in the year no passengers would go that way, except,
maybe, an occasional officer on a three months' furlough.
We should not take our wives and children there at any time.
The extra trouble and expense have prevented most of us
from making use of the Brindisi line, which really saves us
a week and avoids the Bay of Biscay; so we certainly should
not face the Persian Gulf for the sake of four days. The
Persian Gulf is hotter than the Red Sea." Lastly, as to
the strategical importance of the Euphrates and Tigris
districts to India, I found that these were considered, even
by the extremest advocates of conquest, quite out of our
line of march for many years to come. The veriest
Russophobe could not be made to believe, that a modern
army would attempt a march through any passes in Asia
Minor, or down any Euphrates valley, on India.

It may therefore be dismissed from our calculations that
India stands in need of a railway from the Mediterranean to
the Persian Gulf. The political advantage, if advantage there
be, would lie solely with Turkey, or with whatever power
may eventually become master of Armenia and Kurdistan.

As a commercial speculation, the Euphrates railway
scheme is, I believe, equally delusive. The additional cost
and risk of transhipment would be an effectual bar to
through traffic ; while local traffic alone, would be insufficient to secure the financial success of the line. The
Euphrates and Tigris valleys are often represented as rich

agricultural districts, waiting only the hand of the immigrant to become again what they were in classic and even mediæval times. It is argued that if, in the twelfth century, the Euphrates valley boasted such towns as Rakka, Karkesia, and Balis, such towns may exist again, and that a railway carried by that route to Bagdad, would surely revive the ancient wealth of a naturally wealthy district. But such an argument speedily vanishes on an examination of the facts.

1st. The Euphrates and Tigris valleys neither are nor ever were rich agriculturally. As corn-growing districts they cannot compare with the hill country immediately north of them, with northern Syria, the Taurus, or Kurdistan. They lie out of the reach of the regular winter rains, which cling to the hills, and for this reason are almost entirely dependent on irrigation for their fertility. At best, the Euphrates and Tigris valleys, through which a railway would pass, are inconsiderable strips of good land, hemmed in closely by a barren desert, and incapable of lateral extension or development. They are isolated, and have long ceased to lie on the track of commerce. At the present day they contain no place of importance, with the exception of the pilgrim shrines of Kerbela and Meshhed Ali, and the decayed city of Bagdad, nor along the greater part of their extent, more than a few villages, depending for their subsistence on the date-palm. They are, moreover, subject to the caprices of their great unmanageable rivers, which at flood time wreck half the valleys. The Euphrates for 150 miles, passes without alluvial belt of any kind, through a quite inhospitable desert, while lower down it loses itself in marshes at least as valueless. The Tigris, from Mosul to Bagdad, boasts but three inconsiderable villages, and from Bagdad to Bussorah, a poor half dozen. The Montefik country on the lower Euphrates, and the island enclosed within the Hindiyeh Canal, are the only important corn-growing districts now existing.

2nd. The great plain of Irak, the ancient Babylonia, is not only uncultivated now, but for the most part is uncultivable. A vast portion of it has been overflowed by the rivers, and converted into a swamp, while the rest is more absolutely barren than even the desert itself. It would seem that the water of the Tigris contains saltpetre in solution, and the plain below Bagdad, in the neighbourhood of the river, is in many places covered with a saltpetrous deposit, the result of over-irrigation in ancient days. The soil would seem to have been in some sort worked out. I believe, moreover, that from the denudation since ancient times of Armenia, from which the two rivers flow, their floods have become more sudden, and the water supply less calculable, and that the vast irrigation works from the Euphrates, which would be necessary before the fertility of Irak could be restored to what it then was, would still be liable to excessive flood and drought.

The ancient agricultural wealth of Babylonia was a purely artificial thing, depending upon a gigantic system of irrigation which has no parallel in anything now found in the world. When these vast works were begun is not known ; but it must have been in an age of mankind when Asia was densely peopled and human labour cheap. Indeed, we may feel sure that only compulsory labour could have carried them out at all, for they would have ruined any treasury at any rate of wages. This can hardly be done again. There are no captive nations now to be impressed ; no treasury capable of providing the funds. We see India, with its really great population, and its comparatively great wealth, sinking under the burden of irrigation works; and the miserable Arabs of Irak cannot be called on to square their shoulders and carry this far greater load. With all our knowledge, too, of engineering, there would still be some risk of failure ; for the Euphrates and the Tigris are not rivers to be trifled with, as Midhat Pasha found to his cost. I think it more than probable that in the day of Babylonian greatness, the flooding of both rivers was more regular and less subject to disasters of drought and excess than now. As I have said, the denudation of Armenia accounts, perhaps, for the destruction of Irak. In any case it is certain, that at the present moment the full energies of the existing population are required to preserve their footing, not to make new conquests on the river. Now, as I am writing, Lower Mesopotamia is expecting famine from the failure of the Tigris, for not an acre of wheat can be sown without its flooding. Last year all hands were at work damming out the Euphrates. These matters are worth considering.

3rd. In treating this question of Euphrates Valley communication, it seems to be forgotten that not only the circumstances of the Valley itself are changed, but those of all the world of Asia adjoining it.

To understand the present position of Mesopotamia and its adjacent lands, we must consider the history of their ruin. In the days of ancient Rome, not only the shores of the Mediterranean, African as well as European, but also all Western Asia, were a densely peopled empire. Even the lands beyond Roman jurisdiction were full of great cities, from Armenia, through the central plateau of Asia, to the edge of China. Land was everywhere taken up and everywhere of value, while a great surplus population was constantly being pushed out into poorer and still poorer districts by the struggle of life, until hardly a habitable corner of the old world remained unoccupied.

It is not surprising, then, that, with such a necessity for elbow room, the Euphrates and Tigris Valleys were early seized upon, and that at a later date, even poorer regions of the desert were conquered from sterility, and forced into the work of producing food. As long as Babylonia, and the kingdoms which succeeded it, maintained their fertility,

these valleys lay on the highway between them and Asia
Minor. Even so lately as the twelfth century, Benjamin of
Tudela, a Spanish Jew, found numerous large towns still
flourishing in Upper Mesopotamia. Palmyra, at that day,
was still a commercial city, containing with other inhabitants a population of two thousand Jews. On the
Upper Euphrates he mentions five towns, and on the Tigris
two or three. It must not, however, for a moment be supposed that these cities owed their wealth in any but a very
small measure to agriculture. Palmyra and El Haddr, the
two most important, never could have had more than a few
cultivated acres attached to them, while the towns on the
rivers, though making full use of the alluvial valleys, were
essentially commercial. The high road between Aleppo
and Bagdad then passed down the Euphrates as far as
Kerkesia (Deyr ?), whence striking across Mesopotamia to
El Haddr, it joined the Tigris at Tekrit. Along this line
cities were found at intervals, much as the posting-houses
used to be found upon our own highways, and with the
same reason for their existence. They gradually died, as
these died, with the diversion of traffic from their route.
Palmyra and El Haddr, which (to continue the posting-
house metaphor) had no paddocks attached to them, were
the first to disappear; and then one by one the river towns,
which for a time had still struggled on with the aid of
their fields, died too. In the thirteenth, and again in the
sixteenth centuries, the terrible scourges of Mongul and
Ottoman conquests passed over Asia, and swept the regions
surrounding Mesopotamia clear of inhabitants. All
Western Asia was at this time ruined ; and the first result
was the abandonment of outlying settlements, which only
the stress of over-population elsewhere had ever brought
into existence. The Tigris and Euphrates were gradually
abandoned, and only the richest districts of Armenia,
Kurdistan, and Syria retained. The Ottoman system of

misgovernment has done the rest ; and now at the present day there is no surplus population eastwards nearer than China, which could supply the deficiency. Until Persia and Armenia are fully occupied, it is idle to expect the comparatively waste lands of Mesopotamia and the river banks to invite immigration. Russia may some day assimilate Asia Minor, and Asia Minor may some day again become populous, but until that is done Mesopotamia must wait.

On the other hand, Europe is as little likely to send emigrants to the banks of the Euphrates. With such large tracts of good land on the southern shores of the Mediterranean and in Syria, unoccupied, there is nothing to tempt agriculturists to poorer lands so far away. Mesopotamia has hardly a climate suited to northern Europeans, while Italians and Maltese (the only southern nations with a surplus population) find openings nearer home. It is equally idle to talk of coolies from India, or coolies from China. These only emigrate, on the prospect of immediate high wages, to countries where labour commands its full price, and capital is there to employ it. As mere emigrants in search of land they will not come.

4th. Although South-western Persia, through which the last 400 miles of a railroad to Bushire might be made to pass, has not suffered from the same physical causes which have ruined Babylonia, its present condition as regards population, production, and existing wealth, are hardly less unfortunate. The government of Persia, which burlesques all that we most complain of in Turkey, has succeeded in reducing the production of a district, one of the wealthiest in natural advantages of all Asia, practically to nothing. With the single exception of a tract of cultivated land lying between Dizful and Shustar, and another between Dilam and Bushire, the railway would pass through a country at present uninhabited even by wandering tribes possessed of pastoral wealth. The policy of the Persian government in its dealings with Arabistan has been to depopulate, as the shortest and easiest mode of governing it, and the policy has been successful.

Still I consider, that a railway run along the edge of the Bactiari hills, would have a far better chance of attracting population towards it, than one in the Euphrates or Tigris valleys. The soil is naturally a very rich one, and the winter rainfall sufficient for agricultural purposes. Whereever cultivation exists it is remunerative, and the soil has not been worked out, as is the case in the plains. The line would doubtless serve the better peopled districts of Shirazd and Luristan; and Bebaban, Shustar and Dizful, would become once more important *entrepôts* for the wealth of the interior. With the security a railway would give, immigrants might even gradually arrive, and it is conceivable that the district might in the course of years be reclaimed, for it is well worth reclaiming, but the prospect is a distant one.

On the whole I would suggest that all calculations as to traffic should be based strictly on existing circumstances. It may be, that the present population and production are sufficient for the support of a railway, (I myself considerably doubt it), but investors should trust to these only. The future has only delusions in store for them. It is idle to quote the precedent of those American railways, carried through waste places, which have speedily attracted population, and through population, wealth. In Asia there is no surplus population anywhere to attract. Moreover there are existing circumstances of misgovernment, which no system of railways can cure, and till these are changed, it is idle to hope for other changes. Railways in Europe or in America, serve the interests of the people. In Turkey or in Persia they would serve the interests of their rulers only.

That readers may judge what the actual condition is, of the lands lying between the Mediterranean and the Persian

Gulf, I have put in tabular form the amount of cultivated and uncultivated land, of pasture and desert, afforded by the various lines of route which have been suggested for a railway. These are :

1.—*The Palmyra Route*, 555 miles.   Miles.

Tripoli to Homs, partial cultivation . . .	70
Homs to Palmyra, a pastoral desert	120
Palmyra to Hitt, uninhabited desert . . .	250
Hitt to Seglawieh, partial cultivation	65
Seglawieh to Bagdad, alluvial plain, uncultivated, } for the most part uninhabited . . . }	50
Total under partial cultivation . .	135
,, desert or pastoral	420
Total	555

This route has nothing to recommend it except its shortness. It would pass through but one considerable town, Homs ; it would serve no important agricultural district, and could count upon no local traffic. The greater part of its course is without water, fuel, inhabitants, or possibility of development. It would require considerable cutting and bridging (for ravines), and would have little strategical value.

2.—*The Euphrates Valley Route*, 625 miles.   Miles.

Lattakia or Alexandretta to Aleppo, cultivation .	100
Aleppo to Deyr, pastoral	210
Deyr to Abu Camal, pastoral, partly cultivated .	70
Abu Camal to Hitt, desert, with palm oases . .	130
Hitt to Seglawieh, partial cultivation . . .	65
Seglawieh to Bagdad, alluvial plain, uncultivated, } and mostly uninhabited . . . . }	50
Total cultivated and partly cultivated .	235
,, desert or pastoral	390
Total	625

This line passes through one town of eighty thousand inhabitants, Aleppo, and two small towns, Deyr and Ana, besides a few villages. It could count on very little local traffic; Deyr might export a little corn, Ana a few dates. Except in the northern portion it is not a sheep district. It has the advantages of water and fuel, but these would be to a certain extent neutralised if, as is probable, the line should have to pass along the desert above, instead of in the valley. In either case the construction would not be without expense, the river with its inundations causing constant obstruction below; while the desert above, is much broken with ravines. It could hardly pay the whole of its working expenses. Its principal advantage is, that in case of its being continued from Seglawieh to Bussorah, some miles would be saved, or a branch line might be made to Kerbela. The Euphrates line is strategically of advantage to Turkey, mainly as a check on the Bedouin tribes.

3.—*The Mesopotamian or Tigris Valley Route*, 700 miles.

	Miles.
Alexandretta or Lattakia to Aleppo, cultivation	100
Aleppo to Orfa, cultivation	120
Orfa to Mosul, by Mardin, partial cultivation	250
Mosul to Bagdad by the right bank of the Tigris, pastoral	230
Total cultivated and partly cultivated	470
,, pastoral	230
Total	700

This line has the advantage of passing through no absolutely desert district. It would be well watered throughout, and in the Tigris Valley would have a supply of fuel. It would, as far as Mosul, serve four large towns with an aggregate population of two hundred thousand inhabitants, besides numerous villages, and a nearly continuous agricultural population. Its stations would serve as dépôts for the produce of Upper Syria, Armenia, and Kurdistan from the north, and of a fairly prosperous pastoral district from the south. Below Mosul, however, there would be but two small towns, Samara, and Tekrit, and hardly a village. The engineering difficulties of this route, in spite of several small rivers besides the Euphrates (which all three lines would have to cross), would probably be less than in the others. Upper Mesopotamia is a more even plain than the Syrian Desert, and southwards is but little intersected with ravines. This route is strategically of immense importance to Turkey, and is perhaps the best. I would, however, suggest, that commercially, a better line would be from Mosul by Kerkuk to Bagdad. This would continue through cultivated lands, and is the route recommended by the very intelligent Polish engineer, who surveyed it some years ago.

Beyond Bagdad the routes to the Persian Gulf would be—

Miles.

1. Bagdad to Queyt by right bank of Euphrates,
serving Kerbela, Meshhed Ali, and the district
of Suk-esh-Shiokh 460
Or to Bussorah 400

This could be continued from Seglawieh, thereby saving fifty miles. It would serve two fairly flourishing agricultural districts, and should pass along the edge of the desert where the ground is nearly level. Queyt is a good port as to anchorage, but has no commercial importance. Bussorah is a river port much circumscribed by marshes.

Miles.
2. Bagdad to Mohamra by the left bank of the Tigris 320

This would be a difficult line to make, on account of the marshes, and would pass through a nearly uninhabited country. It has no advantage but its shortness.

Miles.

3. Bagdad to Bushire, along the edge of the Hamrin
   Hills to Dizful, then by Shustar, Ram Hormuz,
   and Dilam   570

This line would be an expensive one, on account of the six
large rivers it would have to cross, but it presents no other
engineering difficulties. It should keep close under the
Hamrin Hills to avoid marshy ground near the river. It
is uninhabited as far as Dizful, though the soil is good
and well watered. Dizful and Shustar are important commercial towns, being the principal markets of South
Western Persia ; the district between them is well cultivated. Beyond Shustar to Dilam there is but one inhabited place, Ram Hormuz (or Ramuz). There are a few
villages along the shore of the Persian Gulf to Bushire, but
very little cultivation. This route might be shortened by
taking a direct line from Ali Ghurbi on the Tigris to
Dilam, but it would then pass wholly through uninhabited
country, swampy in places. On the whole I prefer the
Dizful-Shustar route, as having better commercial prospects. These towns would supply no little traffic.
Bushire is an important place, and would make the best
terminus for a railway on the Gulf. I cannot, however,
recommend any of these lines south of Bagdad as commercially promising for a railway.

W. S. B.